The Politics of Governing

The Politics of Governing
A Comparative Introduction

Lawrence S. Graham
University of Texas at Austin

Richard P. Farkas
DePaul University

Robert C. Grady
Eastern Michigan University

George Joffé
University of Cambridge and
Kings College, London University

Donley T. Studlar
West Virginia University

Alan M. Wachman
The Fletcher School of Law and Diplomacy,
Tufts University

CQ PRESS

A Division of Congressional Quarterly Inc.
Washington, D.C.

CQ Press
1255 22nd Street, NW, Suite 400
Washington, DC 20037

Phone: 202-729-1900; toll-free, 1-866-427-7737 (1-866-4CQ-PRESS)

Web: www.cqpress.com

Cover and text design: Auburn Associates, Inc.

♾ The paper used in this publication exceeds the requirements of the American National Standard for Information Sciences—Permanence of Paper for Printed Library Materials, ANSI Z39.48-1992.

Printed and bound in the United States of America

10 09   08   07   06   1 2   3   4   5

Library of Congress Cataloging-in-Publication Data

The politics of governing : a comparative introduction / Lawrence S. Graham [et al.].
    p. cm.
  Includes bibliographical references and index.
  ISBN 1-933116-66-8 (pbk. : alk. paper)
  1. Comparative government—Textbooks. 2. Political science—Textbooks.
3. World politics—1989--Textbooks. I. Graham, Lawrence S. II. Title.

  JF51.P628 2007
  320.3—dc22
                                                                2006009892

Contents

Preface xi
About the Authors xv

1   **Introduction: A Compass for Studying
the Politics of Governing** **1**

2   **The United States: The World's
Oldest Constitutional Democracy** **7**

    The Constitution 8
    Social Dynamics 14
    Interest Groups 17
    Political Parties 21
    Elections 26
    The Presidency 32
    Congress 39
    The Federal Bureaucracy 45
    The Judiciary 49
    Conclusion: Inventing and Reinventing a Nation 55
    Suggestions for Additional Reading 57

3   **The Constitutions and Institutions
of Western Europe** **61**

    The British Constitution 67
        The Monarchy 69
        The Political Executive 70
        The Bureaucracy 71
        The Legislature 71
        The Judiciary 74
        Devolution and Local Government 75
    The French Constitution 77
        The Political Executive 78
        The Bureaucracy 80
        The Legislature 80
        The Judiciary 81
        Decentralization 82

The German Constitution 82
    The Political Executive 83
    The Bureaucracy 84
    The Legislature 85
    The Judiciary 86
    Federalism 86
Development of the Constitution of the European Union 87
    Institutions of the European Union 90
    Constitutional Prospects for the European Union 94
Conclusion 95
Suggestions for Additional Reading 96

4   The Dynamics of European Political Systems: The United Kingdom, France, Germany, and the European Union **99**

The Socioeconomic Setting 99
Political Culture 105
Civil Society and Social Movements 107
Interest Groups 109
The Media 113
Political Parties and Party Systems 115
    The British Party System and Political Parties 116
    The French Party System and Political Parties 119
    The German Party System and Political Parties 121
    The Party System of the European Union 124
Electoral Systems and Elections 125
Political Recruitment 132
Policy Processes 137
Theories of EU Development and Governance 139
Political Views of the European Union 140
Conclusion: Britain, France, Germany, and the European Union 141
Suggestions for Additional Reading 143

5   Transitional Politics in Central Europe: From Communism to Western-Style Democracy **147**

The Old System in a Nutshell 150
Comparisons 151
Framework Applied 152
Value Consensus 152
    Principal Agents 152
    How Refined? 153
    What Values? 153
Political Architecture of the State 155
    Basic Constitutional Framework 155
    More Political Architecture 158
    Economic Architecture 162

Political and Social Dynamics 166
   Forward- versus Backward-Facing 167
   Resource Needs. 168
   Legitimacy 169
   Elite Accountability. 170
   Elections as Political Art. 171
   Doors and Windows. 173
   Civil Society. 173
Leadership Cadre: "Driving Skills" 175
   Generational Change 176
   Confidence. 176
Prognosis 178
Suggestions for Additional Reading 179

**6 Transitional Politics in East and Southeastern
Europe: Russia, Ukraine, and the Balkans 181**
Russia 182
   Value Consensus 182
   Political Architecture of the State: The Constitution as an Issue. 186
   Economic Architecture. 186
   Political and Social Dynamics 189
   Leadership 193
   Prognosis 194
Ukraine 194
   Value Consensus 195
   Political Architecture of the State 196
   Economic Architecture. 197
   Political and Social Dynamics: Elections 199
   Leadership 200
   Prognosis 201
Bosnia and Southeastern Europe 201
   Value Consensus 202
   Political Architecture of the State 204
   Economic Architecture. 205
   Political and Social Dynamics 206
   Leadership 208
   Prognosis 210
Comparing Revisited 210
Suggestions for Additional Reading 211

**7 Political Systems in East Asia:
From a Great Unity (*da tong*)
to a Greater Diversity. 213**
Diversity in East Asian Politics 214
China's Ineluctable Influence 218
Confucian at the Core 219

The Political System of the PRC 222
    Political Party Structure..225
    The State 227
    The Constitution of the PRC.....................................228
    The Limits of Party-State Control 229
The Political System on Taiwan 231
The Political System of Japan 233
Suggestions for Additional Reading 235

8 Politics in the Muslim World:
**   Morocco, Iran, and Indonesia**........................ **237**
Traditional Principles of Governance 238
    Traditional Institutions and Political Culture 238
    The Colonial Experience 241
Examples of Governance 243
Morocco 244
    The Sultanate...244
    Colonial Legacy: From Ruling to Reigning 245
    Reform and Institutionalization 246
    Political Stability..248
Iran..250
    Dual Governmental System and the Power of the Jurisconsult..........250
    The Supreme Leader: Military, Judicial, and Security Power............253
    Hizbollahi Counters Reform 255
Indonesia 257
    Nationalism and Islam...258
    "Guided Democracy"..260
Suggestions for Additional Reading 261

9 Politics in Latin America:
**   The Mexican and Brazilian Political Systems**...... **263**
Mexico 264
    Constitutional Development......................................267
    Social Forces 270
    Interest Groups 273
    Political Parties 276
    Governmental Institutions.......................................278
    The System in Action 285
Brazil 285
    Constitutional Development......................................286
    Social Forces 287
    Interest Groups 288
    Political Parties 289
    Governmental Institutions.......................................290
    The System in Action 291
Suggestions for Additional Reading 291

10 **Regional Convergence in a Diverse World** **293**

The New Regionalism 293
Great Variety—Common Economic Problems 300
Common Third World Political Problems 305
Political Institutions and Processes 310
Futures in the Developing World 318
Suggestions for Additional Reading 320

Notes 321
Index 325

Preface

This brief book is different from other introductory texts. Why? The premise behind our collaborative endeavor is that now, more than at any previous time in the history of the American republic, U.S. citizens and others outside the United States need to understand the dynamics of this country's particular form of government as it has evolved over time and within the context of world governments.

Although the U.S. presidential, federal system, with constitutionally prescribed checks and balances, has served as a model for other presidential regimes, today it stands in distinct contrast to the far more numerous parliamentary regimes, unitary and federal, in which power is vested in corporate bodies that determine executive authority. Thus our initial challenge as a group of authors has been to bridge the gulf between those of us who focus on other regimes and those who focus their attention primarily on the dynamics of the American republic, in a world in which the issues of how to govern a particular body of people can no longer be separated from events and actions outside the country's borders. In today's world, issues of governance are embedded in a web of relationships that transcends the frontiers that governments fix but cannot control. The question of how to analyze this problem and cross well-established academic boundaries has led us to an approach that is strongly thematic, in which all the authors seek to answer the same set of questions. However, each author has had the freedom to deal with the questions in a way that matches his perception of the key issues in the regions and societies being examined. The regional focus, which gives this book comprehensive but not universal coverage, has led us to select country case studies that present students, and others attempting to understand today's world, with concrete examples that demonstrate how the book's themes play out.

This book's brevity also sets it apart from most texts on comparative politics or the discipline of political science. Rather than attempt to be all-inclusive, we have designed this text as an introduction to the study of politics. As such, it can be used as an introduction either to comparative politics or to political science in general, to which other materials can be added. Not only students but also citizens in today's world need concise books that can help them understand political dynamics in a broad context. We hope that this book's format will open new vistas for readers who would like to understand their own political world better and at the same time acquire a foundation in the government and politics of countries other than their own. Ultimately they will be the ones to judge whether we have succeeded.

THE BOOK'S ORGANIZATION

Lawrence S. Graham's chapter 1 is designed as a compass to point to the way we propose to go, the objectives we hope to reach, and some of the problems or difficulties we have encountered as comparativists dealing with a changing world. For example, how are we to approach the world's major regions, each made up of a number of independent states, and sample the enormous variation in political systems, cultures, and political experience without abandoning the criterion of brevity? Robert C. Grady has prepared chapter 2, which presents the United States as the leading example of a presidential system, with all its strengths and weaknesses. Texts of this sort rarely include the U.S. case in a single chapter, but we intentionally begin there, and from that base we move on to look at other countries and world areas.

Donley T. Studlar has written chapters 3 and 4, on European parliamentary systems, emphasizing the layering of national and supranational institutions that has changed the dynamics of European politics fundamentally. In chapters 5 and 6 Richard P. Farkas discusses first the Central European states, the countries to the east of the original core of the European Union (EU), which are the EU's newest members. From that basis he proceeds to outlying European areas: Russia and the Ukraine, directly to the east, and then to Southeastern Europe.

In chapter 7 Alan M. Wachman looks at the Asian world in terms of the very different kinds of states we encounter there before analyzing the People's Republic of China in some detail. Chapter 8, by George Joffé, uses religion and culture to illuminate the Muslim world—where there has been so much conflict and difficulty in accommodating traditional beliefs and ways of thinking to the modern world—with all its economic and political complexities. Rather than restrict his discussion to country cases in the Middle East, Joffé begins with Morocco in North Africa, before proceeding to Iran, and then moving to South Asia to look at political dynamics in Indonesia, the world's most populous Muslim nation.

In chapter 9 Graham takes the reader back to the Western Hemisphere, where he explores Latin America through two cases in which presidential regimes have become embedded in a people's national experience—Mexico in North America and Brazil in South America. In chapter 10 he goes on to discuss regional convergence, first in North America under NAFTA, then briefly in South America through Mercosur. The latter trade initiative is one that, although patterned in theory after the customs union that has evolved into the EU, in practice replicates the complexities encountered by the United States in broadening its trade agreements in North America to embrace a whole continent. From that base this last chapter surveys the way those developments tie in with the complexities of the developing world and the search for better ways to resolve the historic problems of underdevelopment.

THE BOOK'S HISTORY

This collective work constitutes a major revision of three earlier editions, and consequently it has a new title. It is both a new book and one with ties to previous editions originally published by Chatham House under the title *Government and Politics*. Although this new edition retains its analysis of the U.S. system, it now does so with a single chapter. There is also new comparative material on China. The most significant departure from earlier editions is George Joffé's discussion of politics in the Muslim world. That chapter has been added not only because of the pressing need for us all to understand politics in the Middle East, but also because this particular writer emphasizes the importance of first broadening our vistas to include North Africa and South Asia.

Nevertheless, this book remains an introduction to government and politics. Thus it does not attempt to cover all the important areas in today's world. Instead it intentionally leaves sufficient space for those using it as a text to add other materials of their own choosing, whether by following the suggested readings at the ends of chapters or by adding world areas and countries not covered here, for example, sub-Saharan Africa and the Indian subcontinent, where a major world region and a single state coincide.

ACKNOWLEDGMENTS

This book has benefited from earlier iterations and important contributions from past authors. The legacy of those authors carries on in this edition even though major updates and restructuring have taken place. In chapters 3 and 4, for example, Donley T. Studlar has abandoned the country focus in Jorgen Rasmussen's earlier editions to call attention to the intermingling of institutions and political dynamics in a unified Europe. In chapters 5 and 6 Richard P. Farkas, a contributor to the third edition, has completely reworked his East European materials in light of the collapse of the Soviet Union, first to focus on the Central European states that entered the EU in 2004 and then to discuss outlying areas to the east and southeast. In chapter 7, new author Alan M. Wachman discusses Asian politics by centering attention on the Chinese case and the larger Asian setting, rather than continue Taketsugu Tsurutani's original concern just with Japan. In chapter 9 Lawrence S. Graham adds new material on Brazil to a chapter previously confined to Mexico. Chapter 10 draws more heavily on previous editions than any other, by continuing to work from material first prepared by John T. Dorsey Jr. Yet for all these changes, there is continuity in these four editions, which can best be seen in the introduction. It draws on the original conceptualization and writing of Alex Dragnich, now tightened up and refined to give neophytes a somewhat structured way to approach the diversity of our contemporary world without imposing too-rigorous models and concepts.

All of us who participated in the earlier editions owe a huge debt to Edward Artinian, now deceased, the publisher and editor of Chatham House, who always emphasized the importance of preparing an introductory study to politics incorporating both the United States and comparative material that would remain "a brief introduction." In my own case, my two sojourns to northern Italy at the Rockefeller Foundation's Bellagio Study and Conference Center on Lake Como have had a lasting impact. I was there first as a scholar in residence in late fall 1993 and subsequently as a team leader of a six-person working group drawn from Latin America, Iberia, and Central and Southeastern Europe. That experience was important at the time for continuing my work in a large graduate research institution with a huge undergraduate enrollment. Yet its legacy has been more important in reshaping my life to focus on involvement in today's world in a variety of settings, not just as an academic specialist but as a university administrator and a consultant involved in international contracts. In more ways than one, the intellectual underpinnings of this particular book project, as reshaped here, are derived from those experiences. Hence I would like to express my gratitude to the Bellagio Committee for the creative environment in which I was nurtured and pampered intellectually for two all-too-brief stays in a marvelous study and residential center.

Appreciation is also very much in order for the support we have received from CQ Press, which acquired the Chatham House list of books. Shortly before I boarded a plane in early February 2004 for Lisbon, Portugal, I received an e-mail from Charisse Kiino, chief acquisitions editor of the College Division at CQ Press, asking if I would be interested in preparing a new edition. Thus began a productive relationship between the two of us, while I divided my time between Sintra (Portugal), Austin (Texas), and Daytona Beach Shores (Florida). I owe a great deal to Charisse, who has devoted countless hours to shepherding this project through the review process over the past two years. My coauthors and I also owe many thanks to the reviewers, who include Robert Behrman, at Marshall University; Ron Francisco, at the University of Kansas; Alfre Montero, at Carleton College; and John Robertson, at Texas A&M University. It was not a given that we would be able to rework this book fundamentally, respond satisfactorily to the independent critiques of the reviewers, and meet CQ Press standards. Once this project reached final form, with the fall 2005 submissions by the various authors, some old, most of them new, others at CQ Press became important. Nancy Geltman, our copy editor, has done a superb job in working with our materials. Likewise, Gwenda Larsen, our production editor, warrants acknowledgment and our thanks for overseeing the final formatting and editing.

Lawrence S. Graham

About the Authors

Lawrence S. Graham is emeritus professor of government at the University of Texas at Austin. A specialist in public policy and comparative politics, he has had a faculty appointment at UT since 1965. Throughout his career he has combined teaching and research with hands-on experience as a consultant for a variety of national and international organizations. This work has taken him throughout Latin America, Eastern and Southern Europe, and Africa. His publications—fourteen books and more than one hundred articles—have focused on development policy and administration in Latin America, principally in Brazil and Mexico, and in Southern Europe, especially in Portugal and Romania.

Richard P. Farkas is professor of political science at DePaul University. He has taught for more than three decades about Central and East European politics. He holds an honorary degree from Budapest University of Economic Sciences and Public Administration (now Corvinus University) and has lectured in Russia, Poland, Hungary, Croatia, Montenegro, Greece, and Kosovo. His research compares strategies for political and economic development in postcommunist countries and focuses especially on the future trajectory of these political systems.

Robert C. Grady is emeritus professor of political science at Eastern Michigan University. He received degrees from Centre College and Vanderbilt University. His research and teaching interests are seventeenth- through nineteenth-century British and American political theory, contemporary democratic theory, and American politics and government. He has published articles in several journals and a book on problems of representation in American politics.

George Joffé teaches the contemporary history, geopolitics, and international relations of the Middle East and North Africa at the University of Cambridge and at Kings College, London University. He was previously the deputy-director of the Royal Institute of International Affairs in London. He specializes in Palestinian issues and political developments in Algeria and Morocco.

Donley T. Studlar is Eberly Family Distinguished Professor of Political Science at West Virginia University, where he teaches courses in comparative politics and public policy. Past Executive Secretary of the British Politics Group, he has been a visiting scholar at the Australian National University; the Universities of Waterloo, Victoria, Toronto, and Regina (Canada); Strathclyde and Warwick (United Kingdom); Bergen (Norway); and Aarhus (Denmark). Studlar is the author of over one hundred published articles and four books, including *Tobacco Control: Comparative Politics in the United States and Canada*. His widely read "A Constitutional Revolution in Britain?" appears in Christian Soe, ed., *Annual Editions: Comparative Politics*.

Alan M. Wachman is an associate professor of international politics at The Fletcher School of Law and Diplomacy at Tufts University, where he teaches about the foreign relations of China. He served as president of China Institute in America (1995–1997) and was the American codirector of The Johns Hopkins University–Nanjing University Center for Chinese and American Studies (1993–1995). Chief among Wachman's publications are two books: *Why Taiwan? A Geo-strategic Perspective on the PRC's Quest for Territorial Integrity* and *Taiwan: National Identity and Democratization*.

The Politics of Governing

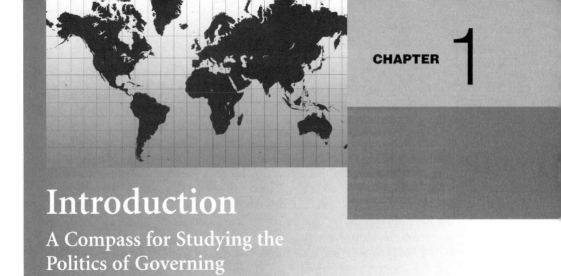

CHAPTER 1

Introduction
A Compass for Studying the Politics of Governing

The aim of this book is to provide useful and substantive knowledge about the political world to students and interested individuals who know very little about that world or how to proceed with learning about it. It is not a first course in professional training for prospective academic political scientists but an "eye-opening" work for all readers, whatever their disciplinary specialization, career plans, or interests. It is, in short, a book about government and politics in different world areas and selected countries that have contrasting political systems. Some chapters are concerned largely with the problems of establishing viable political systems in the former communist countries of East Europe and in the less-developed countries. Others deal with well-established and institutionalized democratic systems. Rather than introduce the study of politics in today's world as the analysis of political systems outside the United States, we begin with the U.S. case and, once it has been analyzed in detail, we proceed from that basis to examine other countries through comparison and contrast.

The number of political entities—variously called countries, nations, or states—existing today approximates 150. They vary considerably in geographic size, population, natural resources, and technological and economic development. Each is held together by a number of factors, among them race, language, attachment (a sense of belonging) to a particular piece of territory, and some common stock of shared beliefs (ideology), all of which contribute to people's rendering habitual obedience to a common political authority.

There are some notable exceptions to what has just been said, particularly in the breakup of the Soviet Union and Yugoslavia into a series of highly diverse successor states, as well as in the fragility of some of the less-developed nations. In these cases major changes in political demarcation are under way because significant segments of the population fail to render habitual obedience to a central government simply because they do not recognize a common authority. The problems facing Iraq today illustrate this point. But such situations are not new; history abounds with examples. The best known to American students are the Revolution of 1776 and the American Civil War. Divisive situations also exist in a number of well-established nations—for example, Northern Ireland in the United Kingdom, Quebec in Canada, and the Flemish in Belgium. Consequently, some of our generalizations in the preceding paragraph are just that—generalizations—to which there are exceptions. And political scientists are far from agreement as to the mix of ingredients necessary for a binding political agreement that is essential to sustain a national government.

Nevertheless, the modern nation-state, which really came into being only in the seventeenth century, is still the political unit that commands most people's highest allegiance. Despite all the discussion of a global economy or society, we still live in a world of nation-states. People have been willing to fight and die for such entities; no city, province, or other geographic unit has commanded comparable allegiance. On first inspection, it might well appear that these observations do not apply to the exceptions just referred to, where local or regional loyalties (for whatever reason) are in effect unrealized aspirations to nationhood. Yet, if we look more closely at current conflicts in a number of the successor states to the former Soviet Union—for example, Armenia, Georgia, or Azerbaijan—or at the former Yugoslavia or Czechoslovakia, we find national communities whose self-determination has long been repressed, which see in the fluidity of current events the opportunity to form their own nation-states, no matter how small they might be.

Political scientists are interested in the form of government a given country has. In their analyses they ask at least three broad questions: What are the purposes of government (the ends of politics)? What do governments do (the functions of politics)? Who exercises political power (the processes of politics)? Each of the systems discussed in this book seeks to answer the first question by its very nature: Generally speaking, democratic systems view the end of politics to be the provision, protection, or preservation of an atmosphere or social climate in which individuals may freely seek to realize their personal or collective aspirations, and they use constitutions to establish basic principles and laws for governance. In contrast, many authoritarian regimes, notably the communist ones in power before 1989, have viewed the purposes of government to be the realization of certain goals that their leaders envisage as necessary and correct. In such societies constitutions are largely irrelevant, as readers will find in examining the People's Republic of China. Accordingly, once we have finished with the U.S. case, the discussions in the following chapters deal with the last two questions in much more detail. While such questions are related and difficult to disentangle, they do lead to the concept of political systems, the comparative analysis of which is the oldest and most honorable tradition in political science, going back to Aristotle more than two thousand years ago.

Political systems have come into being and have evolved as a result of a complex of circumstances—basic beliefs and attitudes concerning human beings and their Creator, the influence of natural resources and other historical conditions or accidents, and the political ingenuity of those who have risen to positions of leadership. Although we cannot ignore the question of how political systems came to be what they are, our emphasis in this book is on understanding how they function today.

Political systems are somewhat like living organisms in that they change over time. More accurately, political systems are what political actors (government leaders and those who choose to influence them) make them, but political actors cannot always do as they wish. In large measure they are constrained and conditioned by the acts of those who preceded them and the traditions and usages passed on by previous generations generally. Hence changes in political systems are, in large part at least, controlled and guided by forces beyond the sole powers of any generation of political actors.

In a sense, it can be said that every political system changes or evolves (unless it is destroyed) according to shifting interactions between the forces of tradition and the imperatives of the changing environment, and between the creative-innovative impulse of political forces (leaders and parties) and cultural inertia (i.e., society's resistance to change).

One could argue that each political system is a creature of unpredictable combinations of circumstances, in some cases fortuitous and in others not, or less so, such as the influence of tradition, the cultural predilections of the majority in a given society, the perception of urgency and the capacity of the people to respond, the ideology and skill of the political elite, and the material endowment and the technological development of the society. To a degree, the uniqueness of the combination at a crucial moment in the development of a given nation-state renders its system distinct in the nature of political authority, in the quality of popular support, in the extent of its institutional integrity, in the manner of its functioning, and in the range and kinds of tangible and intangible benefits it confers on the people.

One consequence is that combinations of circumstances have produced some political systems that are quite similar and others that are very different from one another. This can be seen in the way the following chapters line up. Our discussions of politics and government in institutionalized systems—the United States, Great Britain, France, Germany—all follow substantially the some format in the subtitles and categories of analysis we have used. In contrast, when we enter that portion of the political world in which major transitions and upheavals are under way, we reframe the three basic questions identified above to focus on the value systems that the political actors and their publics share; the political machinery they have developed, through which leaders seek to articulate and implement their goals; and the leadership that takes control of the apparatus of government and attempts to rule by using the structures to make conscious policy choices.

In comparing and contrasting political systems, it is important to remember that in most states political boundaries are rarely congruent with cultural, technological, or economic bases of cohesion. National boundaries have often resulted from military conquest, without much consideration for ethnic, economic, or communal factors. Moreover, structures of political authority are likely to be based on a combination of force and fear, habit and convention, identification and consent. Additionally, functional arrangements for securing government services vary among industrialized countries, as well as between more- and less-modernized countries. Finally, differences between political systems are real, as one could observe if he or she were to live for a time in a religious theocracy and then move to a military oligarchy, or live first in a constitutional republic and then move to an institutionalized authoritarian regime, whether of the left or right. At the same time, in a certain sense all political systems have similar functions: protection from the forces of lawlessness; economic services, such as provision of a stable currency system, postal service, and sanitation; and institutions for resolving disputes.

In selecting political systems to write about we have been somewhat arbitrary, but our choices have not been random. In chapters 2 through 4 we focus on the leading examples of Western democracy. These are all societies with relatively homogeneous political cultures (attitudes toward, and values concerning, politics, political leaders, and governmental processes) but somewhat differing systems of democratic government. In each there has been acceptance of the political system for a relatively long period of time. The first, the United States, is described as a presidential system based on the concept of separation of powers. The other three are all parliamentary systems; however they differ considerably in the homogeneity of their political cultures. When contrasted with the politics of the successor states to the former Soviet Union or that of many developing countries, they appear to share relatively homogeneous political cultures in terms of commitment to their democratic regimes, as opposed to alternatives. But this does not mean an absence of internal differentiation. For example, scholars confining their attention to Western political systems often contrast what they call the "homogeneous" political cultures of the United States and Great Britain with the "fragmented political cultures" of France and Germany. In so doing, they are calling attention to the fact that for relatively long periods, sharp disagreements as to the acceptance of their respective political systems—especially before World War II—contributed to a lack of stability. At the same time, as a close reading of the chapter on the United States shows, one can also question the extent to which the image of the United States as having a homogenous political culture really fits the twenty-first century.

In chapters 5 and 6 we examine the political systems of Central and Eastern Europe, a number of which have embarked on new experiments in democracy after years of domination by the Soviet Union. Like Western Germany after World War II and prior to reunification with German territory to the east under

Soviet control, the political systems of Central Europe have replaced sharp differences over the desirability of democratic government with a strong commitment to political democracy. The rapid incorporation of East-Central European states, such as Poland, the Czech Republic, Hungary, and Slovenia, into the new European Union of the twenty-five stands in marked contrast to the difficulties of democratic governance farther east in Russia and the Ukraine, and to the southeast in Romania, Bulgaria, and the successor states of the former Yugoslavia.

In chapters 7 and 8 we encounter politics in Asia and the Middle East. The former surveys the political, economic, and cultural diversity of Asia, ranging from a brief discussion of Japan and South Korea, as countries with competitive political parties and regularly scheduled elections, to a more thorough analysis of China, the world's most populous country, well embarked on its economic transformation into the dominant economy in that region but embedded in the authoritarian practices of a party state, linked to its Maoist past. In chapter 8 we consider yet another dimension of the political complexity of today's world by surveying politics in Morocco, Iran, and Indonesia as a way to gain insight into the enormous range of human experience embraced in areas of the world where Islam is dominant, extending from North Africa, through the Middle East, to South Asia.

In chapter 9 we return to the westward expansion of the European world into the Americas, to a major region very different from the United States and Canada that is often neglected in the global concerns of U.S. foreign policy. We survey politics in Mexico and in Brazil—a South American country larger than the continental United States. The former, despite economic and cultural disparities with its neighbors to the north, is today thoroughly embedded in a new North America in the making. The United States, Mexico, and Canada are increasingly joined in a complex transnational economy, continental in nature, and characterized by enormous dislocations in human terms as large numbers of people move across the region despite political borders separating the three countries on the map.

Chapter 10 calls attention to the need for U.S. students in particular to gain a broader understanding of the world of which they are a part, at home and abroad, and to rethink not only the increased diversity within their own society but also the breadth of experience encountered in politics and the options pursued in a global setting.

Although there are some notable omissions in this brief introduction to government and politics, namely India and sub-Saharan Africa, we have endeavored to merge the study of U.S. politics into a global context that will introduce students to a more comprehensive perspective on their political world while limiting the size of the volume. By linking domestic and foreign concerns, yet keeping the text within the parameters of a brief introduction, we intend to make it possible for instructors to introduce other readings that will transcend these limits, especially additional comparative material that will sensitize students and other readers to the dynamics of India as the world's largest democracy and the complex political, economic, and cultural world of sub-Saharan Africa.

In each of the chapters, or pairs of chapters, dealing with institutionalized political systems, we discuss constitutions, their history and evolution, and the substance of their provisions, as well as present practice. We also examine the social forces that are contending for influence if not predominance. We identify major interest groups, their aims, their organizations, and how they seek to attain their goals. Next we consider political party systems, the nature and number of parties, how they are organized, how they seek support, and how they accept responsibility for governing. Finally, we deal with the governmental institutions—their nature, their powers or functions, and their relations to one another and to the public. In the end we make some observations on the systems in action, their performance in the task of governing, their difficulties and failings, and their future promise.

Complementing these three broad categories—the basic constitutional framework, social and political dynamics, and governmental institutions—are five analytical concepts: the state, the nation, elite accountability, representativeness, and the organization of civil society. Because of the diversity of the material each of the authors has had to confront and the need to provide comprehensive overviews of politics at home and abroad, we agreed not to impose these categories and concepts uniformly and sequentially throughout this brief introduction to government and politics. Instead each author was asked to use them as a checklist of items that must be covered. We leave it to the reader to decide how best to compare and contrast this material in discussing it with others and to debate whether or not operational definitions are required to specify these terms.

Each chapter is followed by a list of works selected as suggestions for additional reading. We have attempted to choose comprehensive books, as well as materials that offer discussions of various aspects of a political system in greater depth. Included are some works that are more historical in nature and others that are more contemporary. They can be used as guides to further reading in a course context or substituted or expanded according to an instructor's own preferences. Whatever the direction pursued, it is our hope that this book will offer an effective way for all readers to think globally while acting locally.

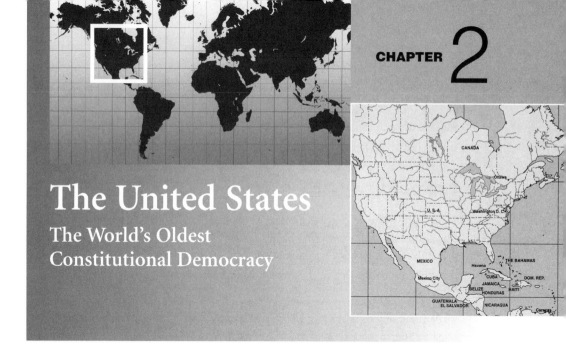

CHAPTER 2

The United States
The World's Oldest Constitutional Democracy

The United States is the world's oldest constitutional democracy, or "republic," as constitutional democracies frequently are termed. The Constitution provides for separation of powers among legislative, executive, and judicial institutions at the national level and establishes federalism for the allocation of powers between the national government and the states, which are equivalent to the regional jurisdictions or provinces of other nations. The institutions should "check and balance" one another, thus reducing the likelihood that a faction of political elites can rule or exercise power tyrannically.

Checks and balances are necessary to limit power, but they are not sufficient to ensure political accountability. For that the Constitution's authors relied on principles of republicanism. Republican government requires that governmental institutions be based on the consent of the people. In the original Constitution, only the House of Representatives was to be elected by the citizens themselves, but the people would elect their state legislatures (which would select senators) and indirectly elect the college of electors for presidential selection.

In the two-plus centuries since its ratification, there have been numerous changes to the Constitution and to political practices. The Senate and president, not solely the House, are subject to popular election. Today, the U.S. system is known as *presidential government,* suggesting that the presidency is the dominant institution. Unlike parliamentary governments, however, the power of the president does not derive from maintaining a legislative majority, and it does not require a system of strong political parties. In fact, voters frequently choose divided government, that is, choose to have the executive branch controlled by one party and the legislative branch controlled by the other party. Far from being a smoothly running system, the separation of powers invites inefficiency and seeming indecision in government by encouraging conflict rather than cooperation between the president and Congress.

THE CONSTITUTION

The U.S. Constitution was written at the Philadelphia convention of 1787. The convention delegates drew on a combination of historical studies and political principles and their own experiments in self-government. In the end, they made pragmatic compromises that reflected their different political, economic, and social interests.

The study of history showed that the people's liberties could be secured in small republics only temporarily until lost to internal conflict or conquest. Large territories had to be governed by centralized, autocratic governments that would provide security and defense but that would not permit republican liberty—as in the Roman and Ottoman empires, for example. The writings of political thinkers, however, provided insights for the creation of republican government in a large territory. Locke's notions of property rights and limited government and Montesquieu's and Harrington's prescriptions for balancing property, classes, and power were prominent influences, as were the writings of ancient Roman thinkers and of Machiavelli about civic responsibilities and patriotism. Adapting these ideas to the extensive territory of the former thirteen colonies, the convention delegates proposed a constitution in which the various societal interests would check and balance one another through their representatives within the government and throughout the nation. The advancement of self-interest and commerce, the delegates hoped, would affirm citizens' stake in the political system and promote civic responsibility and patriotism.

The colonists' experiments in self-government also helped shape the framing of the new Constitution. Prior to the Revolutionary War, the American colonies had grown increasingly independent of Britain and of one another. After the Declaration of Independence was proclaimed in 1776, the first attempt to create a national government, the Articles of Confederation, was proposed to the states but not finally ratified until 1781. The Articles provided for a congress and an executive committee but no strong executive and no judiciary. Members of the congress were appointed (and recalled) by their state governments. States had equal voting power in the congress. Constitutional amendments required unanimity among the states. The congress could not pass laws applying directly to individual citizens, and it could not compel states to maintain agreements with other states or with the congress. Finally, it lacked powers to tax and to regulate domestic and foreign commerce. With such restrictions on the government, economic and political chaos increased, and disenchantment with the Articles grew. Experience under the Articles helped to change people's expectations about government and made many receptive to the Federalist case for a new constitution with a stronger central government.

Basic Constitutional Principles The constitutional convention convened in Philadelphia in May 1787. Leading delegates who favored a strong national government proposed, with their Virginia Plan, that "a national government ought to be established consisting of a supreme legislative, executive, and judiciary." This plan favored large states by basing each state's congressional representation on population. Delegates from small states and some who preferred to amend the Articles countered with the New Jersey Plan. It lessened the influence of large states by giving each state equal representation, as under the Articles of Confederation, which the plan merely revised.

The Connecticut or "Great Compromise" reconciled these two proposals. It provided for a bicameral (two-chamber) legislature with a lower house, the House of Representatives, based on population and an upper house, the Senate, in which each state would have two votes or senators.

Another major compromise is known as the "three-fifths compromise." The populations of Maryland, Virginia, the Carolinas, and Georgia averaged 30 percent slave. Those states, where 90 percent of the slaves in America lived, wanted to count slaves in the census enumeration that would be the basis for representation in the House of Representatives (and for the number of each state's electoral votes). But they did not want slaves counted for purposes of apportioning direct taxes. Under the compromise, three-fifths of a state's slave population would count for purposes of representation and apportioning direct taxes. This helped achieve ratification of the Constitution, but it provided a framework to sustain slavery until it ended with the Civil War.

Other compromises underlie the provisions for constitutional ratification and constitutional amendment, which reflect elements of both popular sovereignty and state sovereignty. The provision for constitutional ratification required that it be done by representatives of the people in their states, but at specially elected conventions, not by the state legislatures (many of which had an interest in retaining the Articles). The provision for amending the Constitution requires that amendments be proposed through congressional action or a convention called by Congress and that they be ratified by the states. Both provisions reflect compromises between the Federalists and the Antifederalists. (During the ratification process, proponents of the new Constitution were called "Federalists." Opponents, who preferred a greater role for the states than the proposed new Constitution provided, were called "Antifederalists." The two sides disputed over what "real" or "true" federalism really meant, each claiming to be correct.)

Ratification of the Constitution was no easy task, and the ratification process involved a further significant compromise on the part of constitutional advocates. Massachusetts ratified the Constitution only after Antifederalists extracted a promise from the Federalists to create a constitutional bill of rights through the amendment process.

The convention's deliberations produced a Constitution grounded on six basic principles. The first principle clearly encapsulates the chief purposes or ends of government. The remaining principles provide the foundations for governance—for the scope of government and its functions, for the exercise of governmental power, and ultimately for the accountability of political elites.

1. **Limited Government, or Constitutionalism.** Government is created to preserve and enhance basic rights and liberties. It must, therefore, govern under the rule of law, not the rule of personal interest or individual will, and it must be limited so as not to violate individual rights and liberties. Only a few basic liberties are found in the body of the Constitution: Article I, section 9 requires *habeas corpus* (a person must be charged with a crime, not simply locked up on suspicion) and prohibits bills of attainder and *ex post facto* laws (respectively, laws that single out individuals for punishment and laws that make an action a crime after the fact). Article IV, section 2, guarantees that citizens in any state are entitled to the same rights (privileges and immunities) as citizens in the other states. The Bill of Rights (discussed at the end of this section) spells out additional liberties that government may not infringe.

2. **Republican Government.** What is republican government, or a republican form of government? Basically, it is what today we call *representative democracy* or *constitutional democracy*, characterized by popularly elected legislatures in either a separation-of-powers system or a parliamentary system. The Federalists opposed direct democracy, or rule by the people in person, because of the turmoil it had produced in ancient city states. They believed that the rule of law required slow deliberation and the opportunity to negotiate and compromise among conflicting interests. They preferred deliberation by representatives to rule by the people's interests and passions that demagogues might incite in direct democracy. The elective status of members of Congress and the president are spelled out in Articles I and II of the Constitution, modified by subsequent amendments. Also, the Constitution guarantees each state a "republican form of government" (Article IV, section 4).

3. **Federalism.** Federalism divides sovereignty between two levels of government—national and state—so that representation and accountability are divided across these levels. Neither level acting alone can change the Constitution (see Article I, sections 8–10; Article IV; and Amendments Nine and Ten). Federalism initially implied "dual sovereignty" (sometimes called "dual federalism"). Constitutional supremacy (the fifth constitutional principle) is a basis for resolving conflicts between these federal units. Technically, the term "federal government" refers to the whole system of federalism, national and state governments inclusively, but in common usage, "federal government" and such terms as "federal courts," "federal administrators," and so on, are used to refer to the central or national government.

4. **Separation of Powers (and Its Corollary, Checks and Balances).** Separation of powers is a functional division of power between the executive, legislative, and judicial branches of the national government (see Articles I, II, and III). It is operational thanks to the corollary principle of checks and balances, a principle that also pervades national and state relations under federalism. Congress is checked by the existence of two houses, by presidential veto, and by judicial review. The president is checked by the requirement for Senate approval of treaties and certain appointments, by congressional policymaking and appropriation of revenues (or refusal to appropriate) for programs, and by judicial review. The judiciary is checked by presidential appointment of judges and by the powers of Congress to impeach and try judges, determine federal court jurisdiction, and fund the courts. Theoretically, the result is a balance of contending claims to power, with no one branch gaining excessive power.

   The different institutions have shared and overlapping functions and responsibilities. The president has significant legislative powers and the ability to be engaged in the legislative process, and the Congress can intervene in executive functions, review executive policy implementation, and withhold approval of executive branch appointments. Such shared and overlapping activities provide both the means and the incentives for balancing power.

5. **Constitutional Supremacy.** The principle of constitutional supremacy is the ultimate grounding for the rule of law. It provides a basis for resolving disputes of a federal nature or among the separated branches of government (see Article VI). Significant constitutional and governmental powers that were necessary but ineffectual under the Articles of Confederation are sanctioned by this principle—the power to regulate commerce, to tax, to coin money and provide for a common currency, and so on.

6. **The Independent Judiciary.** An independent judiciary is a corollary of constitutionalism and the rule of law. Although the Constitution is the supreme law of the land, that statement is not sufficient to prevent Congress and the president from enacting federal laws that violate the Constitution or to prevent states from enacting their own laws that violate the Constitution. Consequently, the Supreme Court exercises its "judicial power" (granted in Article III) to determine whether such acts are constitutional or unconstitutional.

The six constitutional principles are foundational, but they are not unchangeable. The purposes of the U.S. government today are broader than in the Founders' era. The functions of government have expanded. The exercise of governmental power and the ways in which governing elites are held accountable have evolved. The next section illustrates how constitutional changes occur. The nature of the changes is seen in subsequent discussions of the Bill of Rights, of political parties and elections, and of the branches of the federal government.

How the Constitution Changes The amendment process is the formal method for constitutional change. The process begins when an amendment is proposed either by two-thirds votes of both houses of Congress or by a convention called by Congress (the latter has never been used). Since the country's beginnings, only twenty-nine amendments have been proposed and only twenty-seven have been ratified. To be approved, amendments must be ratified on a state-by-state basis, by legislatures or by specially elected conventions, in three-fourths of the states. The latter option has been used only once, to repeal the prohibition amendment (the Twenty-first, repealing the Eighteenth), at a time when elected conventions would represent state urban populations more adequately than state legislatures.

The amendment process is but one way, and the slowest, for the Constitution to change. The language of the Constitution itself is sufficiently general to permit significant change within the constitutional framework. For example, what is the "judicial power" (Article III)? As we saw above, the Constitution does not say. What is the "executive power" (Article II)? What does it mean for the president to "faithfully execute" the law? Again, the Constitution does not say. The outstanding example of constitutional change enabled by the Constitution's language is found in Article I, section 8, where the powers of Congress are specifically enumerated. The section ends with the innocuous-sounding general conclusion that the Congress also has the power to "make all Laws which shall be necessary and proper for carrying into Execution the foregoing Powers, and all other Powers." This "necessary and proper" clause is also known as the "implied powers" clause, or the "elastic clause," because it gives great leeway for Congress, and thereby the president, to act, and great leeway for judicial interpretation.

Judicial interpretations and precedents also effectively amend the Constitution in terms of its operation and functions. The Supreme Court's power to overturn acts of Congress or of state governments through constitutional judicial review is not enunciated in the Constitution's provision for the judicial power (Article III). But from that provision, coupled with the constitutional supremacy clause (Article VI), the Court was able to infer that it had authority to invalidate congressional, presidential, or state actions that violate the Constitution. The Supreme Court has based this authority on precedents established in two early Court rulings: first *Marbury v. Madison* (1803), which overturned a congressional enactment, then *McCulloch v. Maryland* (1819), which overturned a state act, both on grounds that they were unconstitutional. As Chief Justice John Marshall said in the Marbury case, where a law conflicts with the Constitution "the Court must either decide that case conformable to the law, disregarding the Constitution, or conformable to the Constitution, disregarding the law."

The president's power to dismiss executive branch officers is not found in the Constitution, but the requirement that his appointments receive the "advice and consent" of the Senate is there, and it implies senatorial concurrence with dismissals. Nevertheless, presidents early on established the precedent that they could dismiss on their executive authority alone. The important roles that political parties play in elections and representation, the organizational structures in Congress that control its work activities (the committee system, for example), and the expectation that elected representatives live in the district they represent are further examples of customs and traditions that have changed the Constitution without formal amendment.

The Bill of Rights The Bill of Rights illustrates how constitutional principles can be amended both formally and through judicial interpretation and precedents. It was proposed during the first Congress and promptly ratified by the state legislatures as the Constitution's first ten amendments. The Bill of Rights embodies a set of civil liberties, placing limits on government and thereby permitting individual freedom in the areas designated (speech, religion, and so on). In its original usage, the Bill of Rights limits the national government only, not the state governments. Bill of Rights protections were slowly "nationalized" in the twentieth century and applied to the states through judicial interpretation that incorporated them into the Fourteenth Amendment's due process clause—for example, First Amendment freedoms and criminal procedures under the Fourth, Fifth, Sixth, and Eighth Amendments.

The Bill of Rights does not directly protect civil rights, which are introduced into the Constitution through the Thirteenth, Fourteenth, and Fifteenth Amendments—the so-called Civil Rights Amendments—which were ratified after the Civil War. However, it took a mass movement—the civil rights movement of the 1950s and 1960s—and significant change on the Supreme Court before civil rights were widely acknowledged and protected by the state governments.

The last decade of the twentieth century and the first decade of the twenty-first have seen some classes of rights or responsibilities challenged by others. For example, the welfare and commerce clause grounds for environmental regulation (in Article I, section 8) have been challenged by the takings clause, which says that Congress cannot legislate the taking of "private property . . . for public use, without just compensation" (Fifth Amendment). The period has also seen the emergence of controversies over religion and cultural values and the assertion of "traditional" rights against "new" ones (or vice versa) regarding abortion, sexual orientation, the definition of marriage, the relationship between science and faith in education, and more. Demands to ensure civil rights protections for the nation's influx of ethnically and religiously diverse immigrants have exacerbated these latter kinds of controversies. Whether certain classes of rights will be restricted and others expanded cannot be foreseen. The impetus for many of these controversies is underscored in the next section, in which we discuss the dynamic makeup of society.

SOCIAL DYNAMICS

The United States is a large nation of significant geographical variety. From an initial population of less than four million shortly after the Constitution was ratified, the nation grew to approximately 282 million people at the time of the 2000 Census, with Census Bureau estimates of 300 million by mid-decade.

Demographic changes have had far-reaching consequences. Population shifts change the type and quantity of demands on governments for services. Urban areas, with their promise of employment, better schools and public services, and the like, once grew at the expense of rural areas. Subsequently, suburbia grew at the expense of central urban areas, promising better schools and services, lower taxes, and less racial heterogeneity. Suburban growth has generated its own suburbs and "fringe" cities—areas of commercial activity that grew to service the suburbs—that often produce the same kinds of problems that initially inspired population flight to the suburbs.

Among the numerous side effects of such demographic change are increased energy use and reliance on foreign sources for oil, as well as increased environmental degradation, such as air pollution from energy use and loss of habitat and wetlands that affects wildlife and water resources. Moreover, the U.S. population has noticeably aged, and continues to do so, as the baby boom generation born after World War II approaches retirement in the early twenty-first century. That has brought crises in government retirement and health care programs (Social Security and Medicare), particularly because more older people vote than younger working adults, and their concentration in key electoral vote states reinforces the prominence of such programs in national elections.

Immigration, Ethnicity, Culture The nation's regional differences are magnified by its wide array of population groups with their diverse ethnic, cultural, racial, and religious backgrounds. With the exception of Native Americans, the U.S. population reflects its immigrant origins. By the 2000 Census, Hispanics, at slightly over 35 million (12.5 percent of the nation's population), had surpassed African Americans (slightly under 35 million, or 12.3 percent of the population) as the largest minority. Early in the twentieth century it was fashionable to refer to America as a "melting pot" in which immigrants were assimilated to the American national ethos or creed. That image is no longer fashionable, or accurate. The U.S. population is likened instead to a tossed salad, a patchwork quilt, or a mosaic. The populace is a complicated mixture of nationalities and racial and religious groups that maintain in varying degrees the cultural and social traditions of their ancestries.

The status of legal immigrants (permanent resident aliens) and illegal aliens raises thorny constitutional and civil rights–civil liberties issues. Federal courts and some state constitutions require that states cannot exclude or discriminate against noncitizen immigrants when providing social services—for example, public education—regardless of whether the immigrants are in the country legally. Movements to require English as the official language in some states are balanced by bilingual education programs in other states. The federal government has tightened requirements for the granting of political asylum (created only as recently as 1980), excluding some potential émigrés on grounds that they seek to immigrate for economic rather than political reasons. Thus recent immigrants find many conflicting responses to their presence, as have previous generations of immigrants.

Race The term "race" may include many different minorities, but in the United States it is used most frequently in relation to African Americans. The respected social observer Studs Terkel calls race the American "obsession."[1] Politicians and media personalities play upon racial (and cultural) prejudices and fears and link them with particular government programs as suits their purposes—for example, associating welfare "dependency" with specific minorities before their electoral constituents and their audiences. Such controversies and racially charged tactics seem to intensify as the populations of minorities increase at greater rates than the overall population.

The original African American immigrants did not come to the country freely but as slaves. Although slavery was abolished and former slaves were proclaimed citizens by constitutional amendment at the end of the Civil War, *de facto* slavery persisted in many parts of the southern states. One result was northward migration. In 1910, 90 percent of the country's ten million African Americans lived in the southern states; by 2000, approximately one-half of almost 35 million lived outside the South. In the 1950s and 1960s, most efforts to improve race relations centered on the civil rights movement and hopes for political justice and economic opportunity. Advocates of improved race relations believed their goals would be realized through social integration.

Expanded welfare programs and efforts to engage in affirmative action to place minorities (and women) in jobs and educational opportunities faced a backlash in the 1980s that has continued to the present. In 1996 Congress and the Clinton administration passed a major revision of welfare programs that required recipients to obtain jobs after receiving temporary assistance. As for affirmative action, several statewide initiatives to limit its use have succeeded (for example, the California Civil Rights Initiative in 1995). However, in 2003 the Supreme Court upheld the core of its 1978 ruling in *Regents of the University of California v. Bakke,* that had affirmed the use of race as a consideration in university admissions policy, but rejected use of quotas based on race in two related cases. The Court ruled that the University of Michigan used an unacceptable quota system for undergraduate admissions (*Gratz v. Bollinger*), but it affirmed the university's narrowly tailored use of race in law school admissions to obtain the educational benefit of a diverse student body (*Grutter v. Bollinger*).

Class, Status, and the American Dream A traditional distinction between American society and the societies of Europe and Latin America has been the supposed lack of a rigid class system in the United States. Nevertheless, in some ways American society has a kind of class system based on income level. People with comparable incomes, occupations, and social positions tend to associate with one another, to live in neighborhoods distinguished by similar property values and hence by similar wealth and status, and to share similar political and social outlooks. Also, upper-income groups in affluent suburbs tend to perpetuate themselves over generations. Although there are no class-based major political parties, there is a class difference in voting turnout, with those most likely to benefit from government programs voting at the lowest rates. Finally, when the distribution of national income is divided into quintiles from highest to lowest, it is clear that income inequalities have become greater: The top one-fifth of the population increased its share of national income from 43 percent in 1970 to 50 percent in 2000. The share of the middle one-fifth decreased from 17 percent in 1970 to 15 percent in 2000. The combined share of the lowest two-fifths decreased from 15 percent in 1970 to less than 13 percent in 2000.[2]

Notwithstanding the different kinds of evidence that point to class differentiation, public opinion surveys consistently reveal that the United States believes it is a "classless" society. Possibly the concept of class is inappropriate to a study of U.S. society. Instead, the concept of status may better explain how people perceive themselves and others. For example, in Europe corporate executives receive lower salaries and bonuses than their American counterparts, and their corporate boards commonly include union representation, which is exceedingly rare in the United States. American society seems to accept the privileged status of business leaders more easily than other societies, perhaps because of the American dream of success through individual effort.[3]

One of the enduring myths of American political culture is that anyone can succeed with initiative and hard work. This American dream ideal holds that each generation can improve its status over that of the preceding one, as a result of such effort. Public education has been a traditional venue for cultural and ethnic integration and for class mobility; aspiration to the American dream has been socialized through it and sought by means of it. For most Americans, improved economic and social status does depend on getting an education and exerting initiative and hard work. But for most Americans also, the American dream myth has been sustained through significant doses of public policy and economic subsidization by government. Publicly financed education, government-backed mortgages, government-stabilized interest rates, and government-provided college education and housing subsidies for World War II and Korean War veterans helped underwrite the expansion of the middle class.

Whether the United States can sustain rising expectations to fulfill the American dream is problematic. Regardless of the benefits that government policies provide them, many Americans oppose welfare and affirmative action; they believe that government assistance goes disproportionately to ethnic and racial minorities, thereby undercutting the work ethic and its role in securing the American dream.

Culture Wars: Morality, Intensity, and Politics Tensions and conflicts emerge in many ways, some in the public schools and colleges. Should public schools, as part of the elementary curriculum, teach birth control and the causes and preventatives for AIDS and explain homosexual and lesbian lifestyles? Should public schools and colleges move from a curricular canon dominated by "dead white males" to one emphasizing minorities and women? At times American society seems to be engaged in "culture wars" or a "clash of cultures," to use phrases popular since the early 1990s. Approximately one-half of the U.S. population—140 million people—profess membership in a religion. Christians make up the largest religious group in the United States, with evangelical Protestants constituting approximately one-third of all Americans claiming religious affiliation (white evangelicals constitute one-fourth), compared with approximately one-sixth for mainline Protestants. Catholics constitute slightly over one-fifth. With their more conservative social and moral values, evangelicals, complemented by Catholics on many issues (abortion for example), have made conflicts about morality and the role of religion in politics increasingly salient.[4]

Life in contemporary U.S. society involves conflicts over these and other values as ethnic, cultural, religious, gender, and "lifestyle" groups promote their interests. The United States is not balkanized, but clashes over these kinds of interests take on vehemence and intensity unmatched in conflicts that are played out through more traditional means of political influence and power, such as interest groups and political parties.

INTEREST GROUPS

In a constitutional democracy, citizens have a variety of ways to influence government. They may personally contact their elected representatives or government bureaucracies. They may write letters to newspapers or purchase advertisements in the news media to influence the public and government officials. They may litigate, that is, file suit in court, to force government action. They may even take to the streets in protest.

All of these activities can be undertaken by isolated individuals, but each requires communication and organization skills and resources that are distributed unequally among members of society. Therefore, most attempts to influence government are more effective when they are made in a group or through collective action, since more resources are available and more leverage can be exerted with accumulated resources and strength in numbers.

To undertake collective action individuals must join interest groups or work with political parties in election campaigns. Interest groups are organizations that engage in activity relative to government decisions; that is, they try to influence government officials (by lobbying and other forms of pressure) for some type of policy action, favor, or redress of grievances concerning a relatively narrow range of issues. Interest groups tend to be exclusionary, restricting membership and representing social or private sector (or functional) concerns. Political parties, on the other hand, nominate their own candidates for office and run their election campaigns around a broad array of issues or policy concerns in efforts not simply to influence government but to control it. Hence they tend to be inclusionary, sometimes representing interest group concerns but more often seeking broad-based membership or support and representing coalitions of interests.

Interest Groups and Democratic Government In *The Federalist Papers* James Madison argued that interest groups, or "factions," as he termed them, could dominate government for their own ends and ignore, even trample on, other people's rights and interests. One advantage of dividing government functions and jurisdictions through the separation of powers and federalism, Madison thought, is a reduction in the likelihood that any one interest group or faction, or political party, can gain complete control of the government. Creating government institutions with limited powers would limit the opportunities for interest groups or parties to control the government for their own objectives— or so the Founders hoped.

But if interest groups are prone to disregard, even harm, the rights and interests of other individuals and groups, why not simply declare them illegal or create mechanisms to regulate and control them? For Madison in 1787, and for most supporters of constitutional democracy today, that is not a plausible option: The liberty the government was created to guarantee includes the liberty of individuals to pursue their own aspirations and interests. To do so, they join with others and form interest groups, and the First Amendment guarantees that government will not interfere with this activity when groups "assemble" to "petition" for "redress of grievances."

Therefore, in a constitutional democracy, interest groups are recognized as normal means by which individuals and groups pursue their rights and interests, but they are also recognized as problematic and likely to ignore the rights and interests of others if given the opportunity.

Types of Interest Groups: Objectives and Incentives An individual's incentives to join or support a group depend on the group's objectives or goals, and together these help us understand the types of interest groups that attempt to influence politics and policy.

- **Tangible Objectives: Economic Interests.** Most interest groups have economic interests to promote, and they organize themselves around specific material and tangible objectives. Such groups include businesses and trade associations, labor unions, agricultural associations, and professional associations. Consulting firms, public relations firms, think tanks, and the fabled Washington law firms are interest groups that serve other interest groups. They are associated principally with economic interests, and as with those interests, material or tangible reward or gain is the glue that holds them together; for a fee, they also can work for other types of interests.

- **Intangible Objectives: Public Interest, Cause, and Single-Issue Groups.** Citizens groups and public interest groups often appeal to ideological values, justice, and other such causes and purpose-driven commitments in promoting civil rights, job safety, protections for the disabled, environmental quality, and so forth. The NAACP, the Urban League, the National Organization for Women, and Common Cause are examples of such groups. Single-issue groups frequently organize around members' commitments to a kind of ideological or moral crusade. The National Right to Life Committee, the National Abortion Rights Action League, and the Family Research Council are examples. They take stands on such things as abortion, sexual orientation, and family values, as well as prayer in schools, public religious displays, and the teaching of creationism or intelligent design in the schools.

  People have incentives to join these kinds of groups because their views and values are more important than tangible or monetary benefits or costs. Also, a sense of solidarity with others for a common cause can encourage people to join groups—local citizens groups tied together by a threatened factory shutdown, for example—and unite groups of people who are "outsiders" to the political process or who feel oppressed by the process—as in the early stages of the civil rights movement, for example.

- **Hybrid Groups.** Finally, many interest groups are hybrids. They have both intangible and tangible objectives. Veterans groups (the American Legion and Veterans of Foreign Wars), senior citizen organizations (American Association of Retired Persons), and civil rights organizations (the NAACP, the Urban League) tend to have solidarity and cause motivations and incentives for action. They also promote the economic well-being of their members, the veterans and seniors associations especially.

Interest Group Tactics Interest groups provide ways for individuals to participate in politics as they promote their interests. They represent people who may feel unrepresented by their elected representatives, and they help shape political agendas and policies. Means or methods of promotion tend to vary with the type of interest group and the incentives used to maintain membership.

- **Education, Public Relations, and Grassroots Pressure.** Information and publicity can be directed at the general public, at particular constituents of public officials, and at government officials. An interest group may work to maintain or develop a favorable climate of opinion for its goals or a favorable image of the group among the general public. Television spot commercials that portray caring teachers or health care professionals, for example, aim to reinforce public support for those professions. Public relations campaigns directed at public officials are often designed to educate them concerning their constituents' views, that is, to convince them that there is public support for the interest group's position.

- **Partisan Politics.** Interest groups, obviously, can engage in partisan politics. Partisan activity includes all forms of election campaign help—canvassing and making door-to-door contacts; providing office space, equipment, phone banks, fund-raising assistance, and public appearance venues; in short, virtually anything a campaign needs. Labor unions long used the promise of grassroots support during campaigns, as well as strong turnout among union members on election day, to help politicians (usually Democrats) who would promote union positions. More recently, conservative groups have published the voting records of liberal members of Congress and urged their supporters, frequently single-issue oriented in their voting, to work and vote against liberal incumbents and for conservatives (usually Republicans). Since passage of the Federal Election Campaign Act (FECA) in 1971, political action committees (PACs) have become the preferred form of campaign organization for interest groups, particularly for corporations. (PACs and the more recent 527 groups are discussed under Elections: Reforms of Campaign Financing on page 27.)

- **Lobbying.** The term "lobbying" derives from the nineteenth-century practice of meeting legislators in the lobby of the Capitol building to press claims on them. It is the traditional form of influence that interest groups bring to bear on legislators, members of the executive branch, and bureaucrats. Lobbying encompasses a broad spectrum of activities. They range from face-to-face contact in the public official's office or at social events, through testifying at committee hearings or conducting research and writing speeches for members of Congress and White House staff, to funding internships and reporting on agency activity. Lobbying also includes mobilizing grassroots pressure and organizing coalitions of constituent groups and interest groups that share similar positions. The intent of lobbying usually is not to convert opposition members of Congress (and its practitioners hope not to alienate allies with excessive pressure) but to reinforce commitments and draw greater attention to a policy.

- **Access.** An interest group with access does not need to exert the usual pressures associated with lobbying because it has the sympathetic ear of a public official. Access is predicated upon significant past political support, expertise and knowledge central to the public official's role, or an identity of interests with the official's constituents—or all of these. In other words, access is for "insiders," those interest group members who are part of the decision-making process. One of the most effective (and notorious) forms of access is the iron triangle or subgovernment. The "iron triangle" metaphor refers to a strong, persistent set of relationships among interest groups, administrative agencies and executive departments that deal with the interests on a regular basis, and the congressional standing committees that oversee the interactions between agency and interest group.

("Subgovernment" connotes processes beneath the surface or behind the scenes.) With such access an interest group may not simply influence an appointment process or the writing of administrative regulations; it may be part of the process, having its representatives appointed to executive departments or congressional staffs, where they can be directly involved in framing regulations.

- **Litigation.** Direct litigation by interest groups occurs when they file suit to challenge laws, as the NAACP did during the civil rights movement and as industrial groups and environmentalists have done recently to test or expand the protections of environmental regulations. An interest group may also file an *amicus curiae* ("friend of the court") brief in a suit. Interest groups file such briefs to help bring media attention to the litigant and to help the court understand the groups' positions regarding possible rulings. Often litigation is a tactic that emerges when an interest group lacks resources to exert influence in the legislative or administrative process or when an influential interest group has failed at those levels and the policy threatens its tangible interests.
- **Protest and Direct Action.** "Outsiders" are those who lack direct political and lobbying influence or resources, who are excluded from legislative and executive-administrative processes for political reasons, or who do not have the money to purchase public relations campaigns or undertake litigation. Almost of necessity, they must resort to more intense, direct measures such as protest activities if they are to influence policy. However, as interest groups have learned the value of the "media event"—of staging a rally or protest to garner television coverage—mainstream groups increasingly rely on pseudo-protest and pseudo–direct action techniques as means of obtaining cheap publicity and disseminating their views.

The Significance of Interest Groups Interest group activities are inevitable, essential, and effective in a constitutional democracy. As the role of government has expanded, greater numbers of interest groups, with broader scopes of activities, have emerged. But interest groups remain exclusionary, not inclusionary. They are more likely to reflect the interests of the upper economic strata and the politically well placed than of lower economic groups and the politically weak. People with resources—wealth, education, organizational skills—are more likely to join and lead interest groups than people lacking such resources. In principle, these kinds of inequalities and differences among citizens are equalized or canceled out in the voting booth, where elections are inclusive.

POLITICAL PARTIES

As we saw in the preceding section, various means are available to citizens if they want to influence government in a constitutional democracy. Most of them are exclusionary, open to some members of society but not to others. Elections offer citizens more than a means to influence government; they permit citizens to control government, at least indirectly. However, if citizens are to exercise effective control over government through elections, candidates must be selected and organized in slates with programs of action ("platforms"). Political parties fulfill these selection and organization functions.

Unlike the activities of interest groups, which attempt to influence public officials over matters that are comparatively narrow in scope, political parties attempt to attain a wide array of objectives by nominating candidates and seeking through elections to secure public office for them. When a party or a coalition of parties wins control of government and attempts to bring the various offices and processes of government under its control, it assumes general responsibility for the conduct of public affairs, and it attempts to govern based on proposals set out in the campaign platform. The party can claim legitimacy for its governing status since its officeholders are chosen through the constitutionally prescribed method of elections. Citizens can hold the governing party accountable for performance or nonperformance at the next election (at least theoretically).

Party Organization U.S. political parties have few formal members. Most party supporters are considered loyalists or people who identify more with one party than another. (Party identification is discussed at Elections: Voter Choice and Campaigning, below.) The size and diversity of the nation, compounded by the federal structure of national, state, and local intergovernmental relations, almost guarantee that political parties can be organized only as coalitions of volunteers, not as centrally governed organizations with formal mass membership. Moreover, the Constitution does not formally recognize political parties, and consequently there has been no legal or historical basis to legislate about national party organizations. The national parties are coalitions or confederations of state parties, whose organizations, in turn, are built around grassroots or local party organizations of volunteer participants. The national political parties have national committees, which are their year-round governing organizations. However, the Democratic and Republican National Committees (DNC and RNC) lack any effective means to control the parties in Congress, the presidential candidate's campaign, or the state and local parties.

A system of weak, coalition-type political parties that depend on volunteers has several consequences. Formal political participation, as measured by voting, is lower in the United States than in most other western democracies. Comparatively low voting rates are not caused by a system of weak parties. Election rules and a tradition of suspicion of things partisan encourage lower participation. Weak parties simply make higher voting participation difficult to attain. Also, compared with citizens in other democracies Americans tend to participate more through informal means such as interest group organizations and other venues.

The two major parties, when organized for their national election campaigns, are based on broad coalitions of diverse social forces and regional, socioeconomic, ideological, and political interests. Citizens and the various groups and interests they belong to or support cannot agree on clear-cut, united policy stances, and so parties cannot, either. Independents and weak partisan voters are discouraged from participation in elections or, occasionally, motivated by third-party protest. In recent elections, the United We Stand, America party in 1992 and its Reform Party successor in the 1994 and 1996 elections originated with Ross Perot's campaign to fix problems neglected by the Democratic and Republican Parties. Similarly the Ralph Nader–led Green Party in the 2000 and 2004 elections stressed the corporate ties of both parties and their shared failure to address issues of equity and the environment.

The appeal of third parties to certain voters is understandable, as is the long-term survival of the Democratic and Republican political parties. U.S. parties are not responsible or strong parties, but they are capable mechanisms for interest aggregation, that is, for combining diverse interests in a broad coalition before an election. Particularly in presidential elections (if not in House and Senate races), the candidates must develop broad-based coalitions of diverse interests to be successful. In these elections voters can have a sense of what the government will look like if their preferred party wins. In multiparty systems, by contrast, smaller, more-disciplined parties are often responsible, but they accomplish interest aggregation poorly, if at all. Coalitions within government frequently must be formed after the election results are in. Ironically, voters who support strong, responsible parties may find their partisan commitments compromised after the election, as the actual governing coalition is formed.

The Two-Party System: Origins and Characteristics Since near the end of the presidency of George Washington, the United States has had some form of two-party competition for offices in the federal government. Although the campaign to ratify the Constitution was waged by groups that could have evolved into political parties (for example, the Federalists and the Antifederalists), only remnants of the Federalists became organized as a political party in Washington's administration. The Jeffersonian Republicans emerged as the first opposition party. After Jefferson won the presidency over Adams in 1800, the party evolved into the Democratic Republicans and finally the Democratic Party, which today claims to be the world's oldest party in a democratic government.

In 1824, a four-way presidential race resulted in the House of Representatives selecting the president, John Quincy Adams, under constitutional provisions invoked when no candidate receives a majority of electoral votes. Andrew Jackson, who had garnered the greater popular vote among the candidates, pushed his faction of the Democratic Republican party to organize a national nominating convention for the election of 1828. Jackson was nominated for president, signaling the births of both the modern Democratic Party and the national election campaign. By 1834 a new opposition party, the Whig Party, provided a degree of two-party competition. Over the next two decades, each party split over slavery, sectional conflicts, and the power of the federal union.

In 1854, the Republican Party was formed, largely in opposition to slavery, and the Whigs failed to field a presidential candidate in 1856. After the Civil War, through the end of the nineteenth century, the Democratic and Republican Parties alternated in control of Congress, and the Republicans most frequently controlled the presidency. From the latter part of the nineteenth century until the 1930s, the Republican Party coalition of northern industrial and financial groups and midwestern farmers dominated national politics, while the Democrats labored under the onus of being the party of rebellion.

The economic distress of farmers and laborers in the 1920s and 1930s led more members of those groups into the Democratic coalition and provided the basis for an era of Democratic Party dominance of national politics beginning with the election of 1932, in the midst of the Great Depression. From 1932 until the 1994 off-year election, Democrats held a majority of seats in Congress, with the exceptions only of the early 1950s and early 1980s, when Republicans controlled the Senate. But since the consecutive terms of Presidents Franklin Roosevelt and Harry Truman, Democrats have won the presidency only in 1960, 1964, 1976, 1992, and 1996—five of fourteen presidential elections.

Policy and Ideological Characteristics of the Parties Although the parties have clearly differed on policy matters during particular periods in history, their differences have changed and evolved through the years. In general, compared with parties in other nations, the contemporary Republican Party can be construed as a right-of-center party; the Democratic Party as a centrist party. Each party, the Republican in particular, is hospitable to various elements of the ideological right, but neither party seems hospitable to elements of the ideological left. Within the parties, Democratic and Republican leaders and activists tend to be more clearly divided along ideological lines than their parties' supporters or loyalists, who tend to overlap in the middle of the ideological spectrum.

In congressional elections parties often display different characteristics than the presidential-election-year parties. In congressional districts that are safe for one party's incumbent (that is, that lack significant competition from the other party), more ideologically extreme representatives can be elected, as is evident in the radicalization of the Republican Party in the House of Representatives after the 1994 election. Traditionally safe seats have developed when representatives fulfill their constituency representation services and, through so-called pork barrel legislation, bring federal dollars, jobs, and other benefits to their home districts. These representatives are typically more pragmatic than ideological, and questions of the extent to which elected officials are ideologically aligned with voters are secondary to whether they "bring home the bacon."

Factors Sustaining a Two-Party System Why has a two-party system been the norm in the United States? Scholars and pundits have cited various factors to explain the persistence of the two-party system.

- **History of Two-Party Competition and Influence of Political Culture.** First, there are historical and cultural explanations for the persistence of a two-party system. The oldest explanation is that after a party formed in opposition to the governing cliques in the Washington and Adams administrations, state and local slates for office began to be organized around the national parties, to take advantage of the appeal of the national ticket, and loyalties first to the Jeffersonian (later Democratic) Party and later to the Whig and Republican Parties deepened. When partisan loyalties become ingrained among the electorate, a party defeated nationally still can remain viable at the state and local levels in the federal system. Furthermore, the American public tends to be moderate and to prefer moderate or middle-of-the-road parties and candidates. There is, therefore, little interest in radical party alternatives and no room in the middle for a third party.
- **Institutional Explanations: the Impact of Election Systems and Separation of Powers.** Second, there are institutional explanations. Most elections at every level in the United States are plurality-win elections in single-member districts. In other words, a candidate who gets the most votes (not necessarily a majority) wins the office. This winner-take-all electoral process tends to discourage third and other parties from entering the election campaign, and when they do, it tends to discourage voters from voting for them because they doubt the third party has much of a chance of victory. Also, although the United States does not have institutional incentives for congressional and presidential parties to work together, as legislators and cabinet must in parliamentary systems, the institutional separation of the president from Congress means that there is little likelihood that a third party could form a swing voting bloc or force the necessity for a governing coalition, as one may do in a parliamentary system.
- **Political Explanations: Restrictive Ballot. Access and Gerrymanders.** Third, there are political explanations for the persistence of a two-party system. In most state legislatures, Democratic and Republican representatives agree to impose or maintain restrictive requirements for ballot access by minor parties, allegedly to prevent "frivolous" candidacies from cluttering the ballot and confusing voters. This explanation is, of course, a truism. Democratic and Republican legislators do not like to encourage competition. This collusion between the two parties for their mutual benefit is reflected also in the decennial efforts to redistrict following the Census. Traditionally, redistricting has been used to protect incumbents and give advantages to the party that controls the redistricting. Such redistricting has usually been more pragmatic than ideological in focus and outcome, and it is never undertaken to open up the electoral process to third and minor parties.

ELECTIONS

When citizens vote in elections, they aim to gain representation in government and to hold their governing elites accountable for their actions. Rules that govern voter eligibility, direct voter initiatives such as recall and referendum, the nomination of candidates for elective office, and the financing of campaigns are discussed in this section. All of these affect the political parties and the party system.

Campaigns and elections operate under rules that establish the criteria for voter eligibility (the franchise), the scope of elections, and the conditions for candidate nominations and for the conduct of their election campaigns. Beginning with the controversial 2000 election, Americans have seen how seemingly minor matters can have significant consequences for citizen voting and, arguably, for election results—for example, the format of ballots, proof of registration, adequate staffing at polling places, and absentee ballots for Americans abroad (civilian and military).

The Franchise: Voter Eligibility and Voting Rights Today in the United States, virtually any citizen eighteen years old or older, who has resided in a community for thirty days, can vote, subject to certain state restrictions. Whereas early in the nation's history there were property qualifications, then taxpaying qualifications, these were all but eliminated by the mid-nineteenth century. After the Civil War, the Fifteenth Amendment gave African American citizens the right to vote, although southern states established numerous legal and informal restrictions on voting. Poll taxes, literacy tests, and white primaries were ways of excluding people from voting, and racial gerrymanders and at-large electoral districts were also used to dilute black voting strength. Gradually these were overturned, either by Supreme Court decisions invalidating state laws or by congressional enactment (chiefly the Voting Rights Act of 1965 and subsequent amendments to it). Women did not have the right to vote nationwide until the Twentieth Amendment was ratified in 1920; prior to that, women could vote in only twelve states after 1869.

Currently the major legal restrictions on voting are those on convicted felons. After completion of their prison terms, former felons are permanently or partially disenfranchised in fourteen states. No official nationwide statistics are available, but watchdog interest groups estimate that those fourteen states disenfranchise some 1.5 million citizens, of whom approximately one-half million are African American. In the other states, former felons regain voting rights upon release from prison on completion of their full sentences, including parole. (Only two states, Maine and Vermont, allow incarcerated felons to vote.) Since the United States has the highest rate of incarceration among the modern industrial democracies, and since those incarcerated are disproportionately African American and Hispanic, the rate of disenfranchisement can have a significant impact on election turnout in areas with concentrations of these minorities.[5]

Direct Democracy Reforms In the late nineteenth and early twentieth centuries, a movement of Progressives and other reformers successfully promoted a series of reforms of governmental and electoral processes. Such procedures as direct primary elections to replace party caucuses, use of office-bloc ballots instead of party-column ballots to discourage straight party voting, and the initiative and referendum are now institutions in many states. Direct democracy movements also took place in the 1960s and after. A 1970s antitax movement aimed at reducing property and other state taxes and fighting "fraud, waste, and abuse" of taxpayer dollars started in California and spread to other states. It had national repercussions in the Reagan administration and each subsequent presidential administration. The movement also inspired renewed use of initiatives, referendums, and recall elections nationwide.

Reforms of Candidate Nomination Rules Through the 1960s, the national party conventions in presidential election years convened delegates (selected in state caucuses and conventions) to choose the party's presidential and vice-presidential candidates and to write the party's campaign platform. Beginning in the late 1960s, reformers promoted changes in the presidential nomination process with two objectives: First, they wanted to expand public participation in the process of nominating the party's presidential candidate. The way to achieve that was by expanding the number of presidential primary elections. Public participation has increased, although voter turnout is very low: Before 1968, about 10 percent of the eligible electorate participated in primaries; now more than 20 percent participate. Second, reformers hoped to expand representation of key groups within the party, chiefly minorities and women (and early on, youth), so that the nomination process and convention would more adequately reflect the demographics of the party identifiers and the general electorate. This goal has been largely attained through a variety of affirmative action incentives and quotas applied to state delegations.

Unexpectedly, and counterproductively in the view of many party stalwarts, these reforms caused the parties to lose control over the nomination process. The staggered calendar of state presidential primaries produces a long campaign schedule for both parties that begins two years before the election. A successful candidacy requires early support from campaign contributors, the development of an organization of personal loyalists, and success in early primaries, so that the news media will respond positively to the candidate and additional contributors will join the candidate's cause. This process has enabled candidates who may not appeal to a broad national electorate to gain control over large blocs of delegate votes and sometimes win the nomination. Also, it gives the victorious candidate's personal loyalists and contributors disproportionate influence relative to other party loyalists in the general election campaign.

Reforms of Campaign Financing Campaign finance reforms have affected both presidential and congressional election campaigns. The Federal Election Campaign Act (FECA) of 1971 attempts to limit the influence of extremely wealthy contributors and special interest groups, requires public disclosure of campaign financing, and regulates expenditures. FECA was amended in 1974 to establish an enforcement arm, the Federal Election Commission (FEC), and to establish contribution limits for individuals and special interest organizations (in response to the Watergate scandal). It was amended again in 1976, after the Supreme Court rejected expenditure limits for candidates as unconstitutional violations of the First Amendment's freedom of speech guarantee (*Buckley v. Valeo*), and in 1979. FECA provides matching funds to certain presidential candidates, with cost-of-living increases in succeeding election years.

Loopholes in the FECA led to an exponential growth of political action committee (PAC) and "soft money" contributions and expenditures. The FECA's restrictions on special interest campaign contributions actually helped usher in the era of PAC influence in elections.[6] Major interest groups, particularly labor unions, had used PACs for years before FECA was passed. In 1974, before the first elections conducted under FECA rules, there were approximately 600 PACs. FECA provided incentives for other organizations, particularly corporations and cause groups, to use PACs as a way of channeling campaign support and bypassing the intent of FECA to limit the influence of special interest money in politics. By the 1980 election cycle, there were 2,500 PACs. Since the 1984 election, the number of PACs has ranged slightly on either side of 4,000. Over the past four presidential election cycles PAC contributions to all candidates for federal office have increased from $179.4 million in 1992, to $292.1 million in 2004.

In response to the soft money loopholes, in 2002 Congress passed the Bipartisan Campaign Reform Act (BCRA), popularly known as the McCain-Feingold Act after its sponsors, Arizona Republican senator John McCain and Wisconsin Democratic senator Russ Feingold. The act bans soft money contributions to political parties, and it prohibits PAC issue advertisements shortly before federal elections that support or oppose candidates' positions on issues, even if they do not explicitly urge citizens to vote for or against the candidates. Not surprisingly, McCain-Feingold has its own loopholes. It does not address spending incentives provided by the Internal Revenue Code, which gives tax-exempt status to nonprofit PACs under its Section 527. The 527 organizations, as they are called, can advocate issue and policy positions but must not coordinate their activities with, or contribute to, presidential and congressional election campaigns. The 527s report to the Internal Revenue Service, not the FEC, and they have much greater flexibility in their actions than do PACs created under the FECA. (The content of their media advertisements, however, falls under FEC regulation.) The 527 groups were not widely recognized by the public and mass media until the 2004 election, when they played highly visible roles on both sides.[7]

Reforms: Costs versus Benefits Changes in political party nomination procedures and in campaign finance rules have brought presidential candidates in closer contact with voters, but they have weakened the candidates' relationships with their political parties. Furthermore, when congressional candidates rely on PACs, independent of their party's presidential campaign, the members often owe their reelection to constituency interests at odds with party or presidential platforms, and the presidential candidates become increasingly independent of congressional party constraints. Even when the same party controls the executive and legislative branches, presidents have difficulty mobilizing their party's majority for their domestic legislative agenda. In the cases of health care reform, in the Clinton administration's first term, while there was still a Democratic majority in Congress, and social security reform, in the second President Bush's second term, after he claimed a mandate following the 2004 election both presidents learned that they did not control their parties, even on major initiatives like these. (Foreign and military policy and crises, such as 9/11, are another matter.)

Voter Choice and Campaigning In campaigning for office, candidates and their organizations are concerned with three principal factors that influence voters' decisions: party identification, issues or policy positions of candidates as they relate to policy preferences of voters, and the perceived character of the candidates.

Party identification is the most significant long-term influence on voting decisions, although the proportion of the electorate that claims a form of partisanship has declined since the mid-twentieth century. Partisan identification is elicited in public opinion polling and survey research with such questions as, "Do you usually think of yourself as a Democrat, a Republican, an independent, or something else?" In recent presidential elections, partisan identifiers have divided fairly evenly between the two parties—for example, 37 percent with each party in 2004, and 39 percent Democratic and 35 percent Republican in 2000. In a typical presidential election year, over 80 percent of each party's identifiers will vote for their party's candidates on election day.

Since the 1960s the level of Democratic partisan identification has declined relative to Republican, and identification with both parties has declined relative to independents. (The latter usually lean toward or prefer one party over another, notwithstanding their professions of independence.) The Democratic Party's original basis for voter loyalty to and identification with the party—the New Deal coalition—has weakened with generational change. The importance of partisan identification has waned also because political campaigns have become candidate centered and personalized, and such campaigns preempt programmatic campaigning and discount the role of parties.

Over the same period *issue voting,* or the apparent demand of voters for issue-oriented campaigning, has increased. However, the new campaign techniques and increased personalization of campaigning have made it more difficult for voters to undertake reliable issue analysis. Voters' evaluations of candidates' issue positions are often intertwined with their perceptions of the candidates' character. The *perceived character* of a candidate is especially important when voters lack information about the candidate's past behavior and policy stands. Relatively few voters choose candidates principally according to their positions on issues; frequently issue positions are viewed through the lenses of image or character: whether the candidate is sufficiently "tough" to make hard choices. In the 2000 election low expectations of George W. Bush's abilities seemed (counterintuitively) to neutralize his personal foibles as factors, whereas widely held views of Al Gore as a policy technician and intellectual seemed to harm his candidacy. In 2004, Bush's personal foibles gave way to an image of a resolute war president, and a video of John Kerry tacking against wind on a sailboard was used effectively by opponents to reinforce an image of him as one who "flip-flops" on issues.

The Electoral College and Its Reform The Constitution's Article II and subsequent amendments provide for two four-year terms of office for a president. Each state has a number of electoral votes equal to its congressional representation (seats in the House of Representatives plus its two Senate seats). To be elected president, a candidate must receive a majority of the electoral votes. All but two states allocate their total electoral votes to the popular-vote winner in the state. Consequently candidates attempt to win a plurality of the popular vote in a sufficient number of states to attain the necessary majority of electoral votes. If no candidate wins a majority of Electoral College votes, the House of Representatives chooses the president, with each state delegation casting one vote. This has occurred once, in the election of 1824 which, as we have seen, was the impetus for the emergence of national presidential campaigns and a national two-party system.

The Electoral College method of electing the president reinforces institutional incentives for conflict between executive and legislative branches. Many proponents of reform believe that an electoral process that more directly reflects popular majorities will reduce the incentives for conflict and deadlock between the president and Congress. One proposal—the direct election plan—would abolish the Electoral College and replace it with a national popular vote. Another—the proportional plan—would allocate each state's electoral votes to candidates in proportion to their share of the state's popular vote. And a third—the district plan, recently promoted as "the Electoral Fairness Project"—would allocate a state's electoral votes to candidates based on the number of House of Representatives districts that they win. The 1992 presidential election, with its unusually large third-party vote, would have tested some of these reform panaceas, as would the 2000 election, the first election since 1876 in which the victorious presidential candidate did not also win a plurality of the national popular vote.

In the three-way race of 1992, Ross Perot received a larger percentage of the popular vote than any third-party candidate since Theodore Roosevelt's Progressive Party challenge in 1912. Perot nonetheless received no electoral votes. Clinton held a popular-vote plurality (43 percent to Bush's 38 percent and Perot's 19 percent) and a decisive electoral vote majority (370, or 69 percent). Had the Electoral College been replaced before 1992 with the national popular vote system, Clinton's popular-vote plurality, and thus his governing mandate, would have been diminished. Had it been replaced with the proportional plan, no candidate would have secured a majority of electoral votes, and the election would have been decided by the House of Representatives.

Under the current system, popular pluralities fade in significance when compared with the magnitude of such electoral vote majorities as Clinton received in 1992—or so pundits and political scientists confidently observed until the election of 2000. In that election, Democratic candidate Al Gore became the first candidate since Samuel J. Tilden, in 1876, to win the national popular vote but lose the electoral vote. (Gore had a plurality of just over 48 percent; Tilden had a majority of 51 percent.) The election of 1876 became mired in controversy over disputed electoral votes in several former Confederate states. In the absence of constitutional guidance, Congress appointed a special commission to sort out the contested electoral votes, and the commission voted along party lines to allot them to the Republican candidate, Rutherford B. Hayes. Not to be outdone in controversy by its 1876 predecessor, the election of 2000 saw the Supreme Court respond to the Bush legal brief (*Bush v. Gore*), reject the Florida Supreme Court's order for selected vote recounting, and thereby effectively give the Florida electoral votes to Bush, ignoring the Electoral Count Act of 1887 that Congress passed in response to the 1876 controversy.

Had the Electoral College been replaced before 2000 with the national popular vote system, Gore would have been elected with a slim 48.4 percent plurality—one-half percent over Bush's vote, the narrowest popular-vote plurality since 1960. Had it been replaced with the proportional plan, the result, like that of 1992 under this plan, would have required the election to be decided by the House.

Some advocates of the national popular vote plan and the proportional plan recognize the potential problems with their proposals, as seen in the foregoing examples, and include provisions for a runoff election if no candidate attains a popular-vote majority. However, a runoff election might also erode the authority of the presidency. Voter turnout in runoff elections is frequently lower than in general elections (though there has never been such an event at the national level), and the runoff winner could achieve a lower vote total than he or she received in the general election. Also, a national popular vote with runoff provisions may elicit charges of political chicanery, deal making, and the like. It is likely that a third party would try to leverage its position vis-à-vis one of the major parties in exchange for postelection considerations, perhaps withdrawing its candidate or instructing its voters to vote for one of the other candidates.

Such speculation, of course, is used to derail Electoral College reform efforts. The proposed district plan, or Electoral Fairness Project, attempts to minimize such possibilities. It would not change a state's electoral vote total as provided in the Constitution (the sum of the state's House representation plus its two senators). Instead, it allocates one electoral vote to the plurality winner of the popular vote in each House district, and two electoral votes to the candidate who receives the statewide popular plurality. From the standpoint of the 2000 election controversy, the plan would tend to limit controversies over challenged ballots to the districts within which they were cast and not call into question the entire state's electoral votes. (Florida considered adopting this plan in 1992, but Republicans in the state senate were able to stop the bill. Had it been adopted, the outcome of the 2000 election might have been less contentious, with Bush winning 288 electoral votes, not the one-vote majority of 271 that he secured after the Supreme Court effectively decided the election in his favor.)

The 2000 election produced more calls for Electoral College reform and for ballot and voter registration reform. Substantial reform or amendment of the Electoral College seems unlikely for several reasons. The most salient is that numerous constituencies benefit under the status quo—small states and large metropolitan areas in key, battleground states, to give two examples with typically different demographic and geographic characteristics. There are also more subtle but nonetheless important factors that must be considered, such as whether popular-vote alternatives (direct national or proportional) might further intensify regional and ideological divisions, further weaken political parties and representative institutions, increase chances of political instability, and the like. Improvements in balloting, in the voting process, and in voter registration are under way. Under the American system of federalism in which election mechanisms traditionally are under state government jurisdiction, improvements have been slow, piecemeal, and inconsistent.

THE PRESIDENCY

Formal powers of the presidency are provided in Article II of the Constitution, which vests the government's "executive power" in the president. Presidential powers are broad: The president appoints certain executive branch officials, U.S. ambassadors, and federal judges—all with the "advice and consent" of the Senate. Foreign ambassadors present their portfolios to the president, and the president makes treaties, subject to Senate approval. The president is commander in chief of the armed forces and may use this power (through interpretation of Article IV and statutory powers) to protect states from invasion and (at a state's request) from "domestic violence." The president has legislative responsibilities to provide Congress with information about the state of the Union, to recommend bills for passage, to veto bills (granted in Article I), and to convene and adjourn Congress under certain circumstances, and he may require the advice of executive branch officials. The president is empowered to grant reprieves and pardons for federal offenses (excluding impeachment). The president is charged to "take care that the Laws be faithfully executed," a responsibility exercised not only through the powers of the presidential office but also by seeking and enforcing judicial rulings.

Sources of Presidential Government: Constitutional Vagueness and Historical Precedents The Constitution's longevity is frequently attributed to its brevity and adaptability to change. With respect to the presidency, the Constitution leaves it to presidents, to Congress, and to the courts to determine the scope of the president's executive power, whether constitutionally designated or implied. (Implied powers, in some instances, are said to be "inherent" to the office.) Nor is it obvious what the Constitution requires for laws to be "faithfully executed." Some presidents have vigorously enforced laws; others have simply made good faith efforts; still others have balked at enforcing certain laws on grounds that they violated the spirit of the Constitution or for politically expedient reasons.

In his classic study *Presidential Power and the Modern Presidents,* Richard Neustadt argued that presidential power is the power of persuasion. Power is not command; it is the ability to bargain and to convince others that what the president wants is in their interests also. From this perspective, formal constitutional powers are resources that must be marshaled effectively to exert power. The successful exercise of power therefore depends on the personal characteristics of presidents, as well as the circumstances in which they find themselves. Constitutional vagueness provides presidents with the leeway to claim and justify inherent powers and prerogatives.

The earliest presidents needed to develop an office that was ill defined by the Constitution; if not, they would lose in their conflicts with Congress. George Washington asserted presidential control over the cabinet, responsibility for suppressing domestic disorder (in the Whiskey Rebellion), a monopoly on communications with foreign governments, and presidential direction of foreign policy in his proclamation of neutrality in a war between the British and French. Washington's precedents implied the notions of inherent powers and prerogatives that subsequent presidents proclaimed overtly. In the Louisiana Purchase, Thomas Jefferson presented Congress with a *fait accompli* instead of first seeking Congress's policy guidance or assent. Andrew Jackson used the veto as a political tool to force policy changes on Congress rather than justify his vetoes on constitutional grounds as his predecessors had done.

Abraham Lincoln is an early model for crisis management presidents. In the midst of civil war he blockaded ports, summoned state militias, issued the Emancipation Proclamation, and suspended *habeas corpus* without congressional assent. He is said to have believed that there were two options: to save the Constitution or the Union, and he invoked presidential prerogative in proclaiming the emergency powers that suspended parts of the former to preserve the latter. The first twentieth-century president, Theodore Roosevelt, popularized the idea, implicit in the actions of these earlier presidents, particularly Lincoln, that the president should act as a "steward" for the country, taking the initiative in using powers and setting policy when Congress could not or would not do so.

Contemporary presidents thus have at their disposal an array of extraconstitutional powers established and refined by their nineteenth-century and early-twentieth-century predecessors. From the third decade of the twentieth century forward, presidents have acted as "chief legislators" who lead Congress and further the expansion of the presidency. They have exercised their roles of chief administrator and commander in chief to the limits of their abilities. The first presidency of the twenty-first century, that of George W. Bush, has continued the expansion of presidential powers.

Twentieth-Century Presidential Government Congress has delegated authority to the president and the executive branch bureaucracy (as well as independent regulatory agencies) to formulate and implement domestic policy. Such delegations are the hallmark of modern presidential government since the 1930s. Requirements of the national security state in the aftermath of World War II and the cold war between the United States-led "free world" and the Soviet-led communist bloc encouraged Congress to delegate virtually all foreign and military policy responsibility to the president—intelligence, strategic, and ultimately, warmaking powers.

Not that Congress had much control in this area in the first place. Even in the nineteenth century, presidents used the armed forces abroad without a declaration of war by Congress on forty-eight occasions. (The century began, in 1801, with President Thomas Jefferson sending naval and marine personnel to fight a "defensive" war in Tripoli.)

With or without congressional acquiescence, presidents have reinforced their authority over foreign and military policy, in some cases expanding constitutional interpretation and usage. For example, the use of executive agreements instead of Senate-approved treaties increased dramatically in the second half of the twentieth century—the era of U.S. superpower status, when Congress has been more acquiescent to the president. Presidents Eisenhower, Kennedy, and Johnson reaffirmed the domestic use of the military. They left little doubt that presidents can deploy troops to enforce civil rights and attempt to quell domestic violence. President Truman demonstrated formal presidential and civilian control over the military in sacking General MacArthur for exceeding his authority in the Korean War.

Since the 1970s, in the aftermath of the Watergate scandal and the unsatisfactory conclusion to the war in Vietnam, Congress has attempted to compensate for its loss of standing in the Constitution's separation of powers system. Principally, Congress has relied on extensive use of its oversight and investigation powers in both foreign and domestic policy. However, notwithstanding its War Powers Resolution of 1973, which sought to regain a degree of congressional control over war making, presidential ability to make war has not depended on congressional declaration of war. Instead, Congress passes resolutions (in almost all cases after the fact) that support the president's actions or appropriations bills that support the military missions. The two major exceptions were the congressional resolutions authorizing the two wars with Iraq—major endeavors that, the presidents believed, required mobilization of public support in advance.

Crisis Management and Popular Leadership After World War II, with the advent of the cold war, the superpower status of the United States propelled it on a course of "crisis management" or "crisis leadership" in foreign and military policy. Modern presidential government is the focal point for crisis management, and its role was reaffirmed with the end of the cold war, the decline of Soviet hegemony in Eastern Europe, the Middle East, and north-central Asia, and the increase of intense ethnic and nationalist conflicts. Although U.S. intervention in these conflicts in the former Soviet sphere of influence encouraged Congress to reassert its foreign and defense policy interests, the emergence of terrorism as an international presence, not merely an occasional problem, and after the 9/11 attacks, the U.S. war on terrorism have reaffirmed the primacy of the presidency.

The responses of presidents to international and national security crises complement and reinforce another aspect of presidential government: The presidency has come to be viewed as the only nationally elected office, notwithstanding the state-by-state campaigns that are effectively required by the Electoral College. Presidents have expanded their constituencies to include the entire nation. As we saw earlier, this phenomenon has been aided by changes in political party nomination procedures and campaign finance rules, which have brought presidential candidates in closer contact with voters and weakened their relationships with the political parties, particularly the congressional parties. Successful candidates, on becoming president, are encouraged thereby to increase their ties with, and reliance on, the electorate. More critically, in the years between elections, presidents rely on public opinion and appeal directly to the public in efforts to shape public opinion in the face of congressional resistance.

These tendencies have been reinforced by modern mass media and by scientific public opinion polling.

Mass media communications enable presidents to address the public directly. President Franklin Roosevelt brought his voice into the homes of Americans via radio, and President Kennedy used his interpersonal skills more effectively than his immediate predecessors to make television the main communications tool of the presidency. So well practiced was he at use of television that President Reagan was dubbed the "great communicator."

Presidents have learned to adjust their messages based on scientific public opinion polls. Opinion polling allows presidential administrations to assess popular reaction to their actions and to identify and address people's hopes and fears. President Clinton's ability to project empathy, mediated for the public by television, helped him garner sympathy during his impeachment. Public opinion polls registered an upsurge of approval of his performance and disapproval of Republican partisanship in seeking impeachment and reinforced the administration's strategy for weathering the impeachment crisis. As a presidential candidate in 2000, George W. Bush sharply criticized the Clinton-Gore administration for governing by public opinion poll, but the Bush administration has proved adept at emulating the Clinton administration. It claims not to craft policies to fit public opinion, but it clearly crafts the way it presents its positions based on polling data. Emphasizing his "one of us" image, the president appears in "town hall" settings with ordinary citizens (screened for their political views) and with thematic words emblazoned on the backdrop to reinforce his qualities and message for the television audience.

The Institutional Presidency With the growth of presidential government, the persons elected to the office of president have come increasingly to rely upon an expanded, "institutional presidency," a bureaucracy that presidents staff partly by using their patronage powers to bring in loyalists as aides, one that also comprises many career personnel, who serve as part of the permanent institutional presidency.

The extent of the institutional presidency would have been unimaginable two hundred years ago, or even seventy years ago. By the 1990s, the White House Office (WHO, or the White House Staff), the people performing the day-to-day tasks of the president, many of whom are close to him, had grown to almost 700, from about 150 during the Franklin Roosevelt administration. The chief of staff and the press secretary are the most visible appointees and serve to receive, and deflect, criticism aimed at the president.

The Executive Office of the President (EOP), created by Congress in 1939, is the formal management institution for the executive branch. The EOP is truly the embodiment of the institutional presidency. The EOP had thirty-seven staff in its first year; it now employs approximately 2,000, if those assigned from non-EOP agencies are included. Among the important EOP offices are the Office of Management and Budget and the National Security Council. The Office of Management and Budget (OMB) was created in 1970 in a reorganization in which it replaced the Bureau of the Budget. OMB is charged to determine the budgetary needs of all government agencies, and it is the president's policy clearinghouse for proposals from the agencies to Congress for budgetary appropriations. The National Security Council (NSC) was created in 1947 to help the president coordinate military and diplomatic policy.

The heads of major executive branch departments (the attorney general, the secretary of agriculture, the secretary of defense, and so on) form the president's cabinet. Some presidents choose strong leaders and loyalists to lead the cabinet departments. Others parcel out cabinet positions as a form of patronage, rewarding political allies and leaders of their party's coalitions. Most presidents develop their cabinets with a combination of these approaches, placing potentially strong leaders and loyalists in departments that the president anticipates will be central to the administration's mandate and policy objectives and making patronage appointments to the leadership of departments that are planned to have less visibility.

The latest cabinet addition is the Department of Homeland Security (DHS), established in 2002 by the Homeland Security Act. The creation of the department is the most significant reorganization of the federal government since creation of the Department of Defense (out of the original Department of War) and the National Security Council in 1947. Spurred by the 9/11 attacks and subsequent investigations of intelligence and strategic failures, the act merged more than twenty agencies (the Coast Guard, Customs, Immigration and Naturalization, and Secret Service, to name the more salient). It also provided for coordinating activities with other departments (mass transportation safety and security with the Transportation Department; nuclear security with the Energy Department). Creating the DHS necessitated a massive upgrade of computer hardware and software to enable the integrated and coordinated agencies and departments to communicate and share records. The department relies on the intelligence-gathering efforts of the Central Intelligence Agency and the Department of Defense's National Security Administration, as well as the Federal Bureau of Investigation.

When presidents rely on cabinet officers and their assistants, they rely on them individually as advisers, confidants, and friends, not collectively. Congressional committees often have greater control and influence over cabinet departments than do the department secretaries. Committee members frequently use department staff to provide constituency and clientele services, and the departments are among the chief mechanisms for distributing the benefits of pork barrel legislation.

Presidential-Congressional Relations and Impeachment The development of modern presidential government was not preordained by the Constitution. The authors of *The Federalist Papers* thought Congress would be the preeminent institution, and for most of the country's first century, it was. In 1888 Woodrow Wilson, the future president, criticized the central role of Congress and its committee system in his political science doctoral dissertation, titled *Congressional Government*. The Founders' framework and the future twenty-eighth president's lament to the side, the fact remains that the presidency is at the center of contemporary U.S. government.

From time to time Congress has attempted to assert its authority and re-balance the separation of powers. It sought to rein in an "imperial presidency" with the War Powers Resolution of 1973. It limited the president's power to impound funds appropriated by Congress with the Budget Impoundment and Control Act (1974); presidents must spend funds appropriated unless Congress agrees to cancel the expenditure. (The act also created the Congressional Budget Office as a check or counterweight to OMB.) It has used the legislative veto—a method of stipulating, in a statute, that the executive branch can act in the future to accomplish some objective (specified in the statute) unless Congress disapproves or "vetoes" the action. It has impeached (but not convicted or removed from office) a president.

Each of those actions relies on Congress's oversight and investigation powers, not its legislative authority. Each one (save impeachment) takes for granted a system of presidential government in which congressional delegation of its legislative authority is the norm for public policy. The effectiveness of Congress ultimately turns on whether the sitting president wants to play the game. There have been several instances in which presidents have simply ignored Congress. The War Powers Resolution of 1973 is perhaps the outstanding example. The heart of the resolution is a legislative veto (to force the withdrawal of troops from abroad), but its stipulation hinges upon acknowledging the president's power to commit military forces in the first place. Likewise, the Budget Impoundment and Control Act, a response to President Nixon's refusal to spend funds appropriated by Congress, requires presidents to spend appropriated funds unless Congress agrees to cancel the expenditure. This also is a form of legislative veto, and the expenditure requirement serves, among other things, to protect congressional pork barrel projects. (The Supreme Court ruled the one-house legislative veto unconstitutional in 1983 in *INS v. Chadha*. Congress has persisted in evading the Court's intent, using joint resolutions and joint legislative vetoes in efforts to limit the executive branch.)

Congress, in short, is more effective in conducting its oversight and investigation responsibilities than in exercising its legislative responsibilities. As we see in the next section, there are very good political reasons for members of Congress to behave this way: they get more credit from constituencies for investigating bureaucratic malfeasance and presidential misconduct than for legislating, even if some of the malfeasance is a product of the Congress's own imprecise delegations of authority.

Presidential impeachment represents the most extreme form of oversight. The Constitution stipulates grounds for a president's removal from office as impeachment and conviction of "Treason, Bribery, or other high Crimes and Misdemeanors" (Article II, section 4). Constitutional scholars dispute whether these are legal or political criteria, whether "crimes and misdemeanors" that may be unrelated to the responsibilities of office when committed (for example, civil infractions between private parties or litigants) are sufficient grounds, and so on. In the steps leading to a possible impeachment of President Nixon (who resigned from office before an impeachment vote was taken) and in the impeachment of President Clinton, the prevailing view was that the criteria are narrowly legal—that specific crimes and misdemeanors must be alleged and, in a Senate trial, proved. There is no consensus or prevailing view regarding the accuracy, or propriety, of the allegations against President Clinton or regarding the motivations of his antagonists, however.

Defenders of President Clinton—those who asserted that he should not be impeached (whether they excused or criticized his actions)—tended to argue that the legal charges against him were thinly veiled claims that covered a political vendetta. Yet in this defense, they implicitly acknowledged the view that James Madison is said to have held on the subject: that a "high misdemeanor" subject to impeachment and conviction is a president's "common fame," that is, a reputation that brings discredit on the office of presidency or on the constitutional system. In the absence of party discipline and linkages between the presidential and congressional parties, when temporary majorities in Congress face presidents of a different party and fail to secure legislative victories, the give-and-take of the separation of powers system may give way to increased reliance on impeachment.

CONGRESS

The U.S. Congress is a legislative body as well as a representative one. Congress is extremely jealous of its prerogatives vis-à-vis the president. This remains the case today even though, compared with the Congress that Woodrow Wilson observed in the 1880s, Congresses have delegated to the executive branch many of their legislative responsibilities. Congress seldom pays the political price for its actions that parliamentary representatives in other nations must pay when they assume collective or party responsibility for accepting or rejecting the government's policies. It is no minor matter to bring about the collapse of a government and new elections, in which parliamentary representatives may be voted out of office. Congressional majorities are seldom implicated in presidential transitions, partly because weak congressional parties absolve members from collective responsibility and partly because of the separation of congressional election campaigns from presidential campaigns and their separate campaign organizations, as discussed in the Parties and Elections sections.

Legislative Powers The statutory or legislative powers of Congress are expressly granted in Article I, section 8 of the Constitution and implied there and in precedents and judicial decisions. The principal express legislative powers concern revenues, expenditures, commerce, and defense (only two and one-half of the eighteen paragraphs deal with other subjects: naturalization, establishment of lower courts, and governance of the capital district). For a bill (a draft of proposed legislation) to become law, it must be passed by each house of Congress and approved by the president (Article I, section 7). If the House and Senate versions of a bill differ, they must be reconciled. To do this, a conference committee is convened, usually composed of members from the committees of each house where the bill was originally proposed. The conference committee reports its reconciliation, or compromise bill, to each house for floor approval. The bill then goes to the president, who can approve or veto it. A veto can be overridden, and the bill become law, if two-thirds of each house votes to override. Most vetoes are sustained.

The implied powers of Congress derive from a variety of sources. Precedents and tradition have secured a wide array of powers. For example, top-level executive appointments require senatorial approval. Legislative investigations and oversight are implied, inasmuch as Congress must determine if the laws are "faithfully executed" by the president or presidential appointees, particularly where Congress delegates its decision-making authority to the executive branch. These and judicial decisions have further extended congressional powers. The most explicit source of congressional implied powers is, of course, the necessary and proper clause in Article I, section 8 of the Constitution. Congress and the courts have interpreted it to give wide latitude to an array of express powers and some that were not expressly granted in the first place. This last source of congressional power has affected, most notably, the constitutional provision for federalism and the regulatory powers of the national government.

Congress also has other expressly granted powers. The Constitution grants it presidential electoral powers, to determine election dates, and provides for the House of Representatives to act if the Electoral College vote fails to produce a president. It grants Congress powers concerning both the proposal of constitutional amendments and the implementation of amendments. Also, in the case of the Senate, the Constitution grants the power to give advice and consent for certain executive appointments and treaties (including formal approval of treaties). Finally, the Constitution grants Congress power to establish its own internal rules and the eligibility of its members. In other respects, bicameralism, or the two-chamber Congress, works on a more-or-less coequal basis.

The Organization of Congress Congress is organized around political parties and the committee system. An increasingly important component of its organization is the staff system for committees and for individual members of Congress. There are also a number of informal caucuses, such as the Democratic Study Group, the Black Caucus, the Woman's Caucus, and other caucuses and alliances organized around regional or economic interests. Finally, seniority still has a role, although it is less significant than in the decades before the mid-1970s.

The presiding officer of the House of Representatives is the Speaker of the House. The Speaker is the acknowledged leader of the majority party, nominated by it and formally elected by all House members. The presiding officer of the Senate is the vice president, who has no real institutional role but who can cast a tie-breaking vote in floor votes. The vice president rarely attends, and the president *pro tempore,* a senior member of the majority party, presides. (The vice president presides when close votes are expected on bills in which the president has a stake, when a tie-breaking vote may be needed.)

At the beginning of each congressional session, in both the House and the Senate, each party meets as a caucus and elects floor leaders: the majority and minority leaders and the whips. When the congressional parties take positions on key legislation (frequently with or against the president), the floor leaders attempt to mobilize their respective partisans to support the leadership's position. The single best predictor of a vote by a member of Congress is the member's party affiliation, but compared with other parliamentary systems, collective party responsibility, or "party discipline," is low. Party leaders usually can succeed in getting support from their members on floor votes when the leadership is committed and active and the issues are procedural and have low visibility. But when substantive issues are at stake, when they have great visibility, and when there is mobilized constituency or interest group pressure, party responsibility weakens and party voting declines. Party leaders have few tangible incentives with which to ensure collective party discipline or responsibility. However, Congress has become more polarized on partisan and ideological lines since the mid-1990s, and when substantive issues or policies align with partisan ideology, the leaders can count on their members for support. Indeed, in some instances, leaders have found they need to attempt to rein in their members.

The committees do most of the substantive work of Congress. The House has twenty standing, or permanent, committees (which have approximately one hundred subcommittees), and the Senate sixteen (with approximately seventy subcommittees). Committee leadership is based chiefly on seniority, a long-standing tradition in both the House and the Senate. Membership on congressional committees is roughly in proportion to party membership in each house. The party leadership makes committee assignments based on seniority and membership preference, with final assignments ratified by the party caucus. Both senators and representatives seek particular committee assignments to further their reelection chances, to make good public policy, and to exert power in Congress—and in roughly that order of preference. Some House committees exercise significant power within the chamber—Appropriations, Budget, Rules, and Ways and Means—and senior members from safe seats tend to gravitate to them. Other committees in the House and Senate deal with broad policy matters and with constituency services and benefits, the latter significant for reelection.

For the most part, standing committees are functional units that correspond to executive branch bureaucracies and clientele interests. When bills are introduced in the respective chambers, they are assigned to a standing committee, usually based on the type of bill and function of the committee. Most bills do not survive committee scrutiny; typically, about 90 percent to 95 percent of approximately 8,000 bills introduced annually die in committee, and about 175 might be passed into law. Important bills are generally divided and assigned to the committee's subcommittees, where hearings are held and testimony is taken (from experts and lobbyists) and the bill sections are "marked up" (revised and rewritten). The bill or its sections are reported back to the full committee, which can also hold hearings, accept the subcommittee recommendation, reject it, or table the bill.

When a committee reports a bill to the floor, its leadership has usually determined that the bill has a reasonable chance of passage. Between committee and floor, the sponsors of significant bills try to have them considered by their political party's leadership (the steering and policy committees) for support. In the House, major bills go before the Rules Committee, where special floor debate, amendment, and voting rules are established. In the Senate, a "unanimous consent" agreement is necessary to limit debate. If one cannot be achieved, a form of unlimited debate, known as a "filibuster," can occur. Members opposed to a bill use it as a delaying tactic to extract concessions from the bill's sponsors. A filibuster can be curtailed by a vote to invoke "cloture," a move that requires a three-fifths majority of the members.

Throughout this process, members of Congress rely on staff support. Standing committees of the House average over sixty staff assistants; those of the Senate, about fifty-five. House and Senate members also have staff assigned to their offices (additional aspects of their roles are discussed later). The staff research issues; generate reports; organize and help run hearings; serve as liaison with constituents, interest groups, and executive branch committees; and so on. Staff support gives the committees and members greater independence from the executive branch (which otherwise could control information) and more ability to place issues on the national agenda independently of the president or the political parties.

Constituent Districts, Gerrymanders, and Safe Seats Article I, sections 2 and 3, of the Constitution (and the Fourteenth and Seventeenth Amendments) prescribe the selection process for representatives and senators, but the Constitution is silent on how the members of Congress are to carry out their powers of representation. *Whom* do members of Congress represent, and *how?* The two issues are interrelated. To "represent" is to stand for, or act on behalf of, constituents and their interests. Members of Congress may identify with the voters of their geographic district or with more specific groups within the district: the voters who count in reelection campaigns, loyalists, advisers, friends. The constituency can also be defined as an inclusive interest for the district, or even the nation, or as a "special" interest, one that may happen to be the predominant one in the electoral district.

Since the 1960s, following Supreme Court rulings, state legislatures have been required to make electoral districts for the House of Representatives as equal in population as practicable. (The Senate is excluded from this requirement, since the Constitution expressly designates senators as representatives of their states.) When redrawing the House districts, they frequently *gerrymander* them—a term coined after Governor Elbridge Gerry of Massachusetts oversaw the drawing of electoral districts in odd and uneven shapes to give advantage to his partisans. Political cartoonists of the day visualized these districts as the contorted bodies of salamanders. To gerrymander is to manipulate the boundaries of a district to give an advantage to some and a disadvantage to others. In the United States, the most common forms are racial gerrymanders and political gerrymanders.

A racial gerrymander is designed to give advantage to one racial group and disadvantage to another, usually by reducing its political power. In 1960, in the early stages of the civil rights movement, the Supreme Court ruled, in *Gomillion v. Lightfoot,* that a racial gerrymander is unconstitutional because it denies equal protection of the laws. Congress, in the Voting Rights Act of 1965, reinforced the Court's ruling. Racial gerrymandering took a different turn in the late 1980s, however. In its 1982 amendments to the Voting Rights Act, Congress stipulated that votes cast by members of groups historically discriminated against (principally African Americans and Hispanics) should not be "diluted." In plain language, districts could not be gerrymandered or apportioned so as to virtually eliminate opportunities for minorities to elect representatives of their choice. Ironically, the simplest way to meet this nondilution requirement is to develop a racial gerrymander that enhances or increases opportunities for minority voters to elect minority representatives. As a result, congressional districts that elected minorities to the House doubled to fifty-two after the 1990 Census, from twenty-six following the 1980 Census, and increased slightly following the 2000 Census,

to fifty-nine. One unexpected outcome of this process is that the newly delin-
eated districts not only increased the number of minority, mostly liberal representatives but also produced a larger number of white, conservative districts,
thereby weakening minority (and liberal) influence on legislation.

A political gerrymander—one designed to give advantage to one political
party and disadvantage to another—is more difficult to recognize since, among
other things, a voter's partisan leanings are presumably voluntary and changeable, whereas racial and other demographic categories are not. Nonetheless, in
principle a political gerrymander is as problematic as a racial one from a legal
standpoint. The Supreme Court, however, has qualified the extent to which a
political gerrymander may be unconstitutional. As long as a politically inspired
gerrymander, taken "as a whole," does not frustrate the "will of the majority" or
deny political minorities a "fair chance to influence the political process," it
passes constitutional scrutiny (*Davis v. Bandemer*, 1986). Thus with each decennial Census, state and local legislative bodies redraw electoral district boundaries in such ways as to maintain equal populations and to avoid discriminat-
ing based on race (save in cases where the nondilution standard must be met),
but also to give advantage to the majority political party in the legislature.

Representatives: Their Roles and Styles How members of Congress represent
their constituents varies partly as a function of whom they think they represent,
partly as a function of self-identified roles or styles, and chiefly as circumstances
shape their alternatives. In principle, a member of Congress can choose a role
or style of representation from among two classical models: the representative
as instructed "agent" (or delegate) or the representative as "trustee." In practice,
the representative's role is less a matter of choice than a matter of circumstances
and the context in which the member operates. The bicameral distinction
between House and Senate is one such factor: When the Constitution was
framed, *The Federalist Papers* authors expected the House of Representatives to
be the more radical or liberal of the two houses. Why? Representatives would be
directly elected by the people, who might not restrain themselves and might
support, for example, policies to redistribute wealth. Senators, by contrast,
would be selected by state legislatures and be more apt to deliberate as trustees
in representing the interests of their states. Those expectations have not been
realized. Since passage of the Seventeenth Amendment to the Constitution in
1913, senators have been elected by the voters of the states in statewide electoral
districts. They more easily identify with the voters than with the state as a corporate body, but in so doing they have tended to be less provincial than their
House counterparts. The six-year terms of senators give them autonomy to act,
or claim to act, as trustees, by representing interests with statewide or even
national scope. The two-year terms of House members keep them more closely
attuned to events within their districts and provide incentive to represent its
dominant interests.

Some members appear to play the role of either agent or trustee, as circumstances and personal orientation dictate. Particularly in the House, members

develop their own "home styles" according to the needs and interests that prevail in their districts. Also, the likelihood of regular electoral challenge keeps some more attuned to constituent needs as their agents, whereas relatively safe seats permit greater freedom to act as trustees. The number of marginal or competitive congressional seats has declined substantially over the past four decades (as noted in Policy and Ideological Characteristics of the Parties, above), giving members of Congress, collectively, greater job security and therefore greater autonomy to play the role of trustee. However, individually the representatives tend to constituent concerns as though constantly "running scared" of facing a costly campaign against a challenger in the next election.

The Institutionalization of Congress: Pork, Popularity, Perks, and PACs The public generally does not hold the Congress in high regard for its legislative activities. Regularly published polls register lower public approval of Congress than of virtually any other public or corporate institution. Notwithstanding the public's disdain for Congress as an institution, individual members of Congress seem to be held in high regard by their most important public—their voters. House incumbents regularly win reelection at a success rate of 90 percent and above, and Senate incumbents win reelection 75 percent to 80 percent of the time.

This phenomenon of low public regard for the institution juxtaposed to voter support for incumbents is not lost on members of Congress. They undertake their legislative responsibilities by promoting pork barrel legislation. They also perform constituent services, meeting with constituent groups in "public education" or information venues and undertaking casework and intervention with administrative agencies on their behalf. These activities serve to reinforce ties between incumbent members of Congress and their district constituents. Their cumulative benefits produce an "incumbency effect" of greater name recognition and positive associations among voting constituents than challengers have. The incumbency effect may be more significant than the advantages of political gerrymandering in explaining incumbents' high rate of reelection success.

Members of Congress enhance their constituency representation abilities by maintaining certain perquisites of office ("perks") that clearly give advantages to incumbents. The franking privilege allows members of Congress to mail news items, opinion surveys, and the like free of charge. The ostensible purpose of surveys is to solicit voter views to inform the representative, but their chief aim is to remind voters of the representative's activities. Congressional travel budgets, coupled with schedules that provide light legislative agendas on Mondays and Fridays, permit members to travel to their home districts and meet with constituents. Aside from the legislative support noted previously, funding for expanded congressional staffs enables House members in particular to assign personnel to handle constituency service and representation activities.

Finally, visible and successful incumbents breed increased financial support for their campaigns. Political action committees are a critical source of approximately 40 percent to 50 percent of the money spent in congressional election campaigns, and PACs prefer incumbents, at contribution rates seven to ten times greater than those for challengers. Typically, House incumbents outspend their challengers three and one-half times over; Senate incumbents, twice over.

Incumbency advantages—pork, popularity, perks, and PACs—are significant in explaining incumbents' reelection success but cannot always account for it by themselves. It is likely that most incumbents do a good job as representatives. Members of Congress typically do not take systematic, scientific opinion polls, but where polling data exist, the voting records of congressional representatives are consistent with district and national opinions approximately two-thirds of the time.

Representing constituents and interest groups is also more politically advantageous than undertaking the responsibilities (and risks) of legislating and governing. The former permits members of Congress to ask constituents what they want and how the member can help them. The latter requires members of Congress to take votes on matters that regulate and coerce, that say, in effect, "Do this; don't do that," rather than posing the representational question, "What can I do for you today?" Consequently, it is understandable that Congress finds delegating its authority to executive branch administrative bodies more politically palatable than exercising collective responsibility through its legislative enactments. Nevertheless, the public's generally negative evaluation of Congress the institution persists, largely because of Congress's legislative failings or its failure to exercise collective responsibility. This failure has been reinforced by the decline of political parties as vehicles for members' election to Congress.

THE FEDERAL BUREAUCRACY

Modern bureaucracy is characterized by a division of labor organized around functional specialization or the subject matter expertise of administrators, a hierarchical system of authority (a chain of command) designed to ensure accountability, and clear standards for policy to achieve efficiency and minimize the individual discretion of administrators. Max Weber, the famous German sociologist, provided the seminal study of bureaucracy and recognized the tensions it raises between expertise and efficiency, on one hand, and democratic governance and popular control, on the other.

Bureaucracies make and implement public policy, sometimes in conjunction with the other branches, sometimes autonomously. The development of the federal bureaucracy has coincided with the emergence of presidential government. To understand its activities and processes, think of the federal bureaucracy as a fourth branch of government, even though it is classified formally as part of the executive branch.

Bureaucratic Structure and Functions When Americans complain of big government, most have bureaucracy in mind. The national government employs about

2.8 million civilian personnel. Approximately 98 percent of this workforce—the "federal service"—is employed in the executive branch. The legislative branch employs 37,500 (1.4 percent); the judiciary, 21,500 (0.8 percent). The federal service, however, lags both private sector employment and employment in state and local governments, where so many federal functions are implemented and where those governments, as well as private business contractors, perform many former federal services. To put this in perspective, there are approximately 4.2 million state and 10.2 million local government employees, and approximately 8.0 million private employees contracted to perform governmental services.[8]

Some form of civil service merit system covers most federal service employees. The Office of Personnel Management administers the civil service system for most departments, although such specialized ones as the Public Health Service, the National Aeronautics and Space Administration, and others have their own civil service rules and procedures. The Senior Executive Service covers certain upper-level policymaking positions. Finally, there are the top political appointments—department heads and under secretaries and assistant secretaries. Thus it is a mistake, but a common one, to think that most federal employees in the executive branch are directly subordinate to the president in a hierarchical structure. Only a very small fraction of executive branch employees can be hired and terminated by the president—some of the Senior Executive Service and, of course, the top political appointees. Presidential patronage does not loom large as a source of control over the federal service bureaucracy.

The functions that departments, agencies, and commissions perform vary with the type of bureaucracy, its mission, and the interests affected by its activities. Functions often overlap, so that a bureaucracy may appear to have contradictory aims (for example, providing a public good while also promoting a particular interest's benefit at public expense).

- **Public Goods.** Some bureaucracies provide public goods—benefits or services available to the general citizenry and whose costs are borne (usually) by the general citizenry. Chief among these are the Departments of Homeland Security, Defense, State, Justice, and Treasury. Many of the administrative activities of these organizations also promote or regulate particular interests or redistribute benefits from one group to another, even when their existence may be proclaimed in public interest terms. (The defense iron triangle is one example.)
- **Promotion of Interests.** Other bureaucracies promote particular interests with benefits and services that are not available to the general citizenry. Promotional bureaucracies are chiefly cabinet departments and various executive agencies and government corporations created to "foster, promote, and develop" (in the words creating the original Department of Commerce and Labor) domestic economic and social programs. Promotional activities benefit a narrow segment of society, typically interest groups and businesses, while the costs are borne by a broader segment, typically consumers, who pay higher prices, or taxpayers in general.

Frequently program administrators develop clientele relationships with their constituent groups and with congressional oversight subcommittees in mutually supportive relationships. The long-term success of the tobacco industry (farmers and cigarette manufacturers) in sustaining subsidies in the face of mounting criticism of smoking is partly attributable to its representation in the Department of Agriculture and within congressional subcommittees. Likewise, weapons specification bidding and procurement by the Department of Defense, in conjunction with House and Senate Armed Services Committees, has promoted the economic vitality of key weapons contractors. (These are notable examples of the phenomena of subgovernments and iron triangles discussed earlier; see Interest Group Tactics: Access.)

- **Regulatory Activities.** Bureaucracies that undertake regulatory functions and policies benefit relatively broad segments of the population, while imposing costs on relatively narrow segments. For example, the Consumer Product Safety Commission enforces consumer protection and public safety regulations, and the Environmental Protection Agency enforces environmental and public health standards, at costs to the offending interests. Because the costs of compliance are usually borne by businesses (and some labor unions, indirectly), such regulations as these are often criticized as being antibusiness and adding to the costs of business.

Regulatory agencies often act to promote particular interests. Their promotional activities are not always publicized as such; they can be subtle and couched in the language of promoting the public interest. Moreover, not all regulations are perceived negatively by the regulated; some are requested and supported by them. For example, the Interstate Commerce Commission (ICC) was created (in 1887) partly because farmers wanted the benefits of regulated railroad rates. In short order, the ICC was protecting railroads from competition, and this function was transferred to the trucking industry as it emerged as an alternative to railroad shipping. Similarly, the Civil Aeronautics Board (CAB) set rates and routes for airlines. When the Carter administration proposed to deregulate the functions of the ICC and the CAB, the strongest opponents were truckers and airlines (the commissions were terminated in 1990 and 1984, respectively).

- **Redistributive Activities.** Finally, bureaucracies can engage in redistributive activities—activities that often must be regulatory or promotional as well. For example, the Treasury Department and the Federal Reserve Board engage in regulatory activities that are also redistributive. Fiscal policy (the tax side of which is carried out by Treasury) and monetary policy (decided and implemented by the Federal Reserve Board, or Fed) shift income from some groups to others in ways that can either be progressive or regressive but that are hardly ever neutral.

Progressive taxes shift income from wealthy to poor; regressive taxes shift income from poor to wealthy by taking a greater proportion of the poor's income than the wealthy's. When the Fed increases interest rates, it decreases economic activity, and it also affects lower-income people more adversely than wealthy ones by increasing the proportion of their incomes that goes to pay for auto loans, mortgages, and the like. Conversely, when it decreases interest rates, it increases economic activity, and lower-income people benefit.

Bureaucracy and Democracy? Implementation of public policy is no simple government activity. It is not merely a matter of ensuring that the laws are "faithfully executed." What if the law is vague? Or requires the implementing agency to write rules for compliance or enforcement? Or to make the policy? To what extent is enforcement to be implemented? To the strict letter of the law? To a reasonable extent, with the administrator's discretion to be exercised on a case-by-case basis?

Bureaucracies frequently receive vague or unclear missions or objectives when Congress passes their enabling or authorizing legislation. In some instances, the legislative charge to the agency amounts to a statement of good-will. What does it mean for the Federal Trade Commission to follow the "rule of reason," or for the Interstate Commerce Commission to set "reasonable rates," or for the National Labor Relations Board to enforce "fair standards" in labor negotiations—and for all these agencies to act "in the public interest"? When the mandate or mission is vague, an agency is fully capable of creating rules and regulations to cover every possible exigency and capable of fine-tuning regulations in a seemingly infinite number of ways. The mandate of Title IX of the Education Amendments of 1972 is a one-sentence prohibition against gender discrimination in schools. Without further guidance, it should not have been surprising that the Department of Education's forerunner would create a fourteen-page set of regulations.

Such regulatory excess appears to be driven by agency convenience and tunnel vision rather than by the impact of the rules and regulations on the larger society, let alone on the activities to be regulated. That is partially correct, but it is not the whole story. It also is a direct outgrowth of Congress's providing minimal substantive guidance to the bureaucracy. The example underscores the dilemma of attempting to follow congressional intent when the intent is found not in the one-sentence legislative mandate but in the voluminous record of debate—a record subject to "correction" by members of Congress after they have an opportunity to reconsider public or media reaction to their actual statements. Under this circumstance, an agency necessarily becomes subject to political pressures because every potentially affected interest group will want to avoid having its ox gored. This in turn lends support to critics of bureaucracy who claim that it is out of control, although such claims often are made by those who oppose an agency's mission.

Since the Carter administration, every presidency has signaled its intent to get bureaucracy under control through cost containment, administrative reform, rational budgeting, strict application of benefit-cost analysis to regulations, reduction of duplication and red tape, deregulation and privatization, and so on. The bureaucracy is a favorite target of politicians and the public. When the public is polled and its scorn for bureaucracy is elicited, however, the pollsters also find public support for the programs the bureaucracy provides. And when presidents and other politicians propose to cut bureaucratic waste and unnecessary, costly regulations, they are selective about their targets. Yet when the president and Congress agree, even agencies that promote and subsidize businesses can go the way of the dinosaur (such as the CAB under airline deregulation).

Underlying the particular political agendas of elected officials is the broader problem of how to reconcile bureaucracy with democracy.

The great reliance on bureaucracy in a democracy underscores the problem of the relationship between professional expertise and political accountability. Is it possible to keep politics out of policy (for example, to have experts overrule pork barrel projects), or is it desirable to keep democratic accountability out of policy? To the extent that personnel policies and procedures shield or insulate bureaucracies from political pressures, their range for discretion and judgment also increases. But if democratic accountability means doing what satisfies the test of the next reelection cycle, short-term planning and superficial but newsworthy events may supersede the judgment of those who look beyond the election cycle. Ironically, a bureaucracy's commitment to a long-range mission may be more representative of the public and may serve the public interest better than the actions of elected officials, particularly when the elected have little competition for office and benefit from gerrymandered electoral districts that reduce the likelihood of electoral competition.

THE JUDICIARY

The United States judicial system, like the British, is rooted in the common law tradition, which relies on judicial interpretation and precedent. But the U.S. judiciary can nullify legislation, something the British judiciary cannot do in the absence of a written constitution that is paramount to Parliament. This power is known as *judicial review*. The Supreme Court can exercise it to determine if state or national laws are constitutional, and it can void those laws, that is, declare them unconstitutional. The judiciary has taken upon itself the responsibility charged it by Chief Justice John Marshall in *Marbury v. Madison* (1803): "[I]t is emphatically the province and duty of the judicial department to say what the law is."

Organization and Functions The Constitution's provision for the "judicial Power," in Article III, is that it "shall be vested in one supreme Court, and in such inferior Courts as the Congress may from time to time ordain and establish." As with its stipulation of the executive power, the Constitution is vague about what the judicial power involves. Presumably it means judging, but judging what, with respect to what?

The U.S. judicial system is an adversary system. That is, an individual or government must claim harm or injury caused by another party to seek redress or justice through court action. The judiciary does not issue rulings about hypothetical or possible future situations, nor does it provide advisory opinions to the other branches of government (as Germany's highest court can do). Instead, judges (and juries) attempt to resolve or settle disputes, or cases, based on law and fact. The disputes may involve civil law issues between individuals or between individuals and government about such matters as equity, enforcement of contracts, or negligence. Or they may involve criminal law issues in instances when government charges individuals with violating the law. ("Individuals" includes groups and such organizations as corporations and unions.)

When U.S. courts act to resolve disputes, they do so in the form of rulings or opinions (the opinion of the court is not mere opinion but a ruling based on well-reasoned analysis of law and fact pertinent to the case). These rulings on the case also can change or modify public policy, or even establish policy; in effect courts can make law. That may result when a court finds that the law applicable to the case is insufficient or inconsistent with other laws or with the Constitution.

Authority for judicial decisions derives from four sources: case law, statutory authority, administrative law, and the Constitution.

Case law is judge-made law that, in most instances, is developed through application of the common law precept of *stare decisis* (essentially, adherence to judicial precedent). *Statutory law* is law made by legislatures. Judges rely on judicial precedents in interpreting and applying statutory law. *Administrative law* is similar to statutory law and has the same binding effect, but it is made by independent regulatory commissions and administrative law tribunals (delegated the authority to do so by Congress). These agencies can establish administrative law either by promulgating rules and regulations or by adjudicating disputes about rules.

Constitutional law is based on the language and structure of the Constitution and its amendments, and on court interpretations of the Constitution and constitutional law. Theoretically the Constitution is written by "the people," that is, it is the juridical embodiment of popular sovereignty. In practical terms, constitutional law is derived from judicial decisions, since ultimately the constitutional standing of administrative and statutory law depends on judicial interpretation. When we analyze U.S. government in this chapter and discuss how the Constitution has been changed by Supreme Court decisions, in virtually every instance the Court's rulings are about constitutional law—rulings that have changed civil liberties and civil rights, electoral processes, and relations between the presidency and Congress.

The United States has a dual court system. This is a product of the constitutional provision for federalism. The Judiciary Act of 1789, the first judicial enabling legislation passed by Congress pursuant to Article III of the Constitution, established the lower federal courts. The federal courts deal with national law, and the state courts deal with state laws. (Citizens have more contact with state courts, where about ninety-five million cases are filed each year, than with the federal courts, where almost 300,000 cases are filed annually.) State judiciaries are autonomous. In certain types of cases, however, state courts may be asked to rule on federal laws, and federal courts on state laws. How are such potential conflicts resolved? The Constitution is not clear. An implication of Article VI, which says the Constitution and its national laws "shall be the supreme Law of the Land" and "the Judges in every State shall be bound thereby," is that decisions of state judiciaries can be reviewed by the Supreme Court. The landmark case that affirmed both constitutional supremacy and the Court's authority to enforce it through its appellate jurisdiction over state acts was *McCulloch v. Maryland* (1819), which applied the principle of judicial review, previously established in the *Marbury* ruling, to state acts.

Supreme Court Jurisdiction and Criteria for Review Today the Supreme Court exercises appellate jurisdiction over cases from state courts of last resort (usually named state "supreme courts") and the thirteen U.S. Courts of Appeal. In a typical year, the Supreme Court receives from seven to eight thousand requests for appellate review from both the state supreme courts and federal appellate courts. Technically these requests come as "writs" of *certiorari*, appeal, and *habeas corpus*. These distinctions are important for lawyers and legal scholars. For students of government, the important distinctions involve the criteria the Court uses to decide whether to hear a case and on what terms.

The Supreme Court renders opinions on approximately seventy to eighty cases each year. It literally undertakes the administration of justice, since it must maintain its annual docket at a manageable level. If the Court is too free in granting review, its load becomes unmanageable; if too restrictive, significant constitutional issues may be decided by lower courts. Over the years, the Court has developed criteria to screen cases; judges in lower courts have learned to use these. Also, the Court appears to be responsive to certain external, not overtly political influences. We consider these under three headings: (1) criteria for litigants, (2) criteria for the case on appeal, and (3) enforcement criteria.

1. **Criteria for Litigants.** There are certain requirements that the litigants must meet. Because the U.S. judicial system is an adversary system, the case must be a real case or controversy. The issue raised must be concrete, not abstract or hypothetical. Also, the case must be "ripe," that is, all other remedies must have been exhausted by the litigants. And it must not be "moot," that is, the issue should not already have been resolved in another way. Finally, litigants must have "standing" and the Court must have "jurisdiction."

   An example illustrates how these criteria can be used and also that they tend to be interrelated. Since 1948 the Supreme Court has refused to enforce racially restrictive covenants (clauses in deeds prohibiting sale of land to someone of a particular race). The Court reasoned (in *Shelley v. Kraemer*) that the Fourteenth Amendment prohibits an agency of government from denying equal protection of the laws; therefore, courts lack jurisdiction over such covenants, and anyone seeking their enforcement has no standing to sue. Lack of jurisdiction can have great consequences. In fact, the Court's ability to engage in judicial review was established when it claimed it lacked jurisdiction in the landmark case *Marbury v. Madison.*

2. **Criteria for the Case on Appeal.** The case itself must be suitable for judicial deliberation and not subject to political decision making. The term the Court uses is "justiciability." A case must be "justiciable," that is, it must concern a legal issue appropriate for a judiciary to decide. A related criterion is the "doctrine of political questions." A case cannot be a "political question," that is, a matter of policy appropriate for the "political" branches or the state governments to determine.

   Several examples illustrate the application of these criteria. Until the 1960s, electoral district reapportionment cases were claimed to be political and reserved to state legislatures under the Tenth Amendment. The Court discovered the relevance for representation of the equal protection clause of the Fourteenth Amendment, and such cases became justiciable (*Baker v. Carr,* 1962), with the Court subsequently requiring, in a series of 1964 rulings, "one person, one vote" for both congressional and state legislative districts.

   Separation-of-powers questions are often political, but by no means always. In 1974, the Court ruled that the president cannot claim an absolute right of executive privilege, rooted in inherent powers, although there is a limited or conditional one (*United States v. Nixon*). And in 1983 the Court declared unconstitutional the congressional legislative veto (*INS v. Chadha*). With respect to presidential war powers, however, the Court has been disinclined to review cases, claiming they are political and to be resolved by the president and Congress. For example, when military conscription opponents challenged the constitutionality of the draft during the undeclared war in Vietnam (*Massachusetts v. Laird,* 1970), the Court deferred to the political branches. On the other hand, when foreign nationals and U.S. citizens challenged their incarceration as "enemy combatants" at the Guantanamo Bay, Cuba, military base, the Court, in 2004, ruled against the Bush administration in three of four cases (*al Odah v. United States, Rasul v. Bush, Hamdi v. Rumsfeld*).

3. **Enforcement Criteria.** The Supreme Court also appears to consider the likelihood of a case being so controversial that its ruling may be difficult to enforce. Congress has control over monies, and the president has control over enforcement agencies, but the Supreme Court has no tangible enforcement resources. It must rely on public acceptance and on the willingness of the other federal branches and of state policymakers to support its rulings. The Court's justices (the term for Supreme Court judges) appear to consider the extent to which lower courts, especially

state lower courts, have the ability to enforce decisions. The justices appear to take cues from litigants and others about the Court's likely rulings.

Interest groups, for example, recognize the Court's concern with public acceptability. Consequently, they may attempt to aid litigants and, in effect, help the Court consider other consequences than those articulated in the litigants' respective briefs by filing *amicus curiae* briefs. Although the friend of the court has no tangible interest in the case, its *amicus* brief informs the Court from the interest group's perspective about the level of public acceptance of a potential ruling.

Similarly, the U.S. solicitor general—the chief practicing lawyer in the Justice Department—may influence the Court. Approximately one-half of the cases on the Court's docket are under the supervision of the solicitor general whose approach to a case can provide a powerful cue to the Court as to the thinking of the executive branch and its enthusiasm for a particular outcome. The solicitor general can also enter a case with an *amicus curiae* brief to signal the Court as to the executive branch position on the issue.

Judicial Review and Statutory Interpretation If, under its power of judicial review, the Supreme Court can review acts of Congress, the president, and the states as to their constitutionality, then certainly it can engage also in statutory interpretation. "Statutory interpretation" means that the judiciary can alter or modify existing public policy by ruling about the meaning, scope, and applicability of existing policy and statutes without overturning them.

The Constitution is silent about judicial review and vague about the judicial power, as we have seen. Alexander Hamilton enunciated a provisional doctrine of judicial review in *The Federalist Papers.* And the Supreme Court itself ruled in 1796 (*Hylton v. United States*) that it had the authority to declare an act of Congress unconstitutional (although it found constitutional the one being litigated). The Court established its authority in *Marbury v. Madison,* when it invalidated section 13 of the Judiciary Act of 1789.

The exercise of judicial review has gone through three discernible periods in U.S. political history and currently may be in a fourth period:

First, for about its first seventy-five years, the Supreme Court acted chiefly in the areas of governmental structure and the scope of governmental power. Under Chief Justice John Marshall, the Court confirmed principles of national supremacy and then, under Chief Justice Roger B. Taney, adopted "dual federalism" (and reinvigorated states' rights). Second, from after the Civil War through approximately the middle of the New Deal, the Court became increasingly activist on behalf of business interests and invalidated federal and state regulations concerning business and labor relations. Third, from shortly after the end of World War II to the last decade of the twentieth century, the Supreme Court exercised judicial review in the areas of civil liberties and civil rights and held a discernible "presumption of constitutionality" toward federal economic regulation. Critics of the Court decried its "activism" and urged judicial "self-restraint." In that view, judges should be "strict constructionists" of the law and the Constitution, limiting themselves to legal interpretation and not legislating from the bench.

Such criticisms have been acknowledged by recent conservative presidents in their judicial appointments. Their impact may be producing a fourth, contemporary period in which judicial review takes on a different role than in the decades following World War II. In certain cases a narrow majority of the Supreme Court claims to be more attentive to literal legal interpretation than to expansive rulings. The most recent version of such judicial self-restraint is known as "originalism"—the Court is admonished by originalists to adhere to the original intent of the framers of the Constitution or, in the cases of statutory interpretation, to the intent of framers of legislation.

If the originalist doctrine of judicial self-restraint becomes the standard for Supreme Court decisions, it could reduce reliance on legislative histories and compel Congress to be more clear and direct in its enabling legislation that directs bureaucratic policymakers. (To the originalist, the final words of a statute, not legislative histories, are the source of legislative intent.) In some instances this has occurred in Court opinions from the mid-1990s. In several legislative redistricting and government contract affirmative action cases, the Court has used the "strict scrutiny" standard to rein in the use of race as the sole policy criterion to meet the objectives of, respectively, the Voting Rights Act 1982 nondilution standard and affirmative action policies (for example, *Shaw v. Reno,* 1993, and *Adarand Constructors v. Pena,* 1995).

Whether the Supreme Court should embrace judicial activism or the originalist version of judicial self-restraint is controversial. In juridical terms it may be semantic: It is difficult for a Court ruling not to be a policy statement or a law-making statement. Defenders of so-called judicial activism argue, for example, that the Constitution is a living document to be adjusted to contemporary norms. Originalists reject that, but as the Court's action in *Bush v. Gore* (2000) demonstrates, judicial self-restraint does not require the Court to adhere to legislation that governs disputed Electoral College votes. In that case, the Court intervened in a state problem and chose to ignore the 1887 Electoral Count Act, which would have placed the final decision in a situation such as Florida's in the halls of Congress, not the Supreme Court.

The Supreme Court's action in *Bush v. Gore* is revealing and supports the view that the activism-versus-restraint debate is more about politics than jurisprudence. In the end, judges, and justices of the Supreme Court, act on their judicial philosophies, which are intertwined with their political philosophies. The justices may not be as partisan as we ought to expect members of Congress or the president to be, but they are highly political people. This would be easily understandable in the context of Congress. Conservative Republicans long criticized liberal Democrats for expanding the scope and powers of government. Yet once in the majority in Congress, conservative Republicans have been hard pressed to reduce government; indeed, they have proved as adept at pork barrel projects as the Democrats had been.

Judicial Appointments A discussion of the judiciary's role in shaping or changing public policy and law invariably requires consideration of the politics of court appointments. In the United States the president nominates candidates for federal court appointments and asks the Senate for its advice and consent. In the process, each branch calculates the probabilities that the nominee will sustain or oppose its policy preferences.

Notwithstanding high-flown rhetoric, federal court appointments have always been political. The opportunities for presidents to make Supreme Court appointments are infrequent and the stakes are high. They are also highly visible, and senators are wont to appear as petty partisans. Appointments to the federal circuit and district courts, however, are not as visible, and partisan divisions have stood out. Republican senators blocked numerous Clinton administration appointments, and Democratic senators returned the favor with the second President Bush's nominees. Their partisan opponents have claimed that presidents have used "litmus tests" for nominees to the federal courts, screening them based on whether they are pro-choice or pro-life, devoted to original intent, and so on. To pass presidential muster is not to be assured that there will be no senatorial litmus tests based on political considerations. The Senate Judiciary Committee has been known to give overbearing "advice" and to refuse "consent," assuring that the president's nominee exits voluntarily or is defeated on the Senate floor.

Even if the process of presidential nomination and senatorial advice and consent could become a nonpartisan affair, the fact remains that judges are political actors themselves. They come to the bench with developed political, economic, social, and religious values. They are not ideologues in a fanatical or strident sense, but they tend to have well-developed ideologies in the sense of a philosophy of social and political life and an understanding of the consequences of public policy and judicial decisions.

CONCLUSION: INVENTING AND REINVENTING A NATION

The United States is considered the world's "first new nation"—one created by actions of its citizens in throwing off the yoke of colonial power and forming a popular or democratic government.[9] A few others followed in the late nineteenth and early twentieth centuries, but it was not until after World War II that the world experienced a proliferation of new states, with the end of European colonial rule in Asia and Africa. The past two decades have seen the reemergence of old nationalities in the form of new states with the end of communist hegemony in eastern and southern Europe and central Asia. The effects of globalization and the emergence of Islamicist fundamentalism, which is forcing change in the Islamic regions (and whose effects are felt globally), appear to threaten new states that have shallow-rooted constitutions. The first and even second constitutions of many of the new states have not survived. Some have been transmogrified from constitutional republics into effective dictatorships, and some of those have been overturned by popular movements. Global nation-building today stands in stark contrast to the experience of the United States which, after rapidly abandoning its first constitution, has lived with its second one for almost 220 years.

Or has it? The U.S. Constitution is sometimes referred to as a "living document" because it has proved adaptable to changing circumstances. There have been relatively few formal amendments. In some ways, the United States still has its original second constitution. But in many significant ways, the U.S. Constitution has become a different constitution than the one ratified in 1787–1788—not least in its transformation from a separation of powers system leaning toward congressional dominance, and a federal system with few national domestic policy arenas, to a presidential system responsible for the national economy and social welfare. The Civil Rights Amendments laid the basis for a more egalitarian government, one that began to take shape after World War II; the New Deal created a positive, interventionist regulatory and welfare state; the past three decades have witnessed reactions against each.

The United States was "invented." It was and remains the closest approximation to the social contract model of liberal democracy that was popular in the seventeenth and eighteenth centuries. If the United States lacks a viable socialist tradition because it had no *ancien regime* from which to emerge, it likewise has had no organic conservative tradition (although numerous movements have attempted to invent both traditions). A nation invented undergoes continual reinvention. Created and reinvented through choice and consent, the sense of being a nation is fragile and malleable, not rooted in race, religion, and the like, as in many older and some newer states. An aspect of this fragility was recognized half a century ago by Louis Hartz, who worried that the United States had defined itself by what it was against—communism—rather than what it was for. Hartz's concern seems relevant again in the aftermath of the September 11, 2001, terrorist attack, when "homeland security" became a politically useful rhetorical device.[10]

Prior to 9/11, references to the United States as "motherland," "fatherland," or "homeland"—terms applied to older nations whose identities preceded social contract thinking—were virtually unheard. After 9/11, debates about multiculturalism have intensified. Scholars now question whether an influx of diverse immigrants can be incorporated within the traditions of the nation's liberal constitution, or whether its liberal traditions must give way to corporatism or worse. If the past is prelude to the future, these debates, like the race and immigration debates of the nineteenth and early twentieth centuries, will result in further reinventions of the political system. If the past is prelude to the future, these reinventions will retain the core elements of the nation's first invention.

Suggestions for Additional Reading

The Constitution

Ellis, Joseph J. *Founding Brothers: The Revolutionary Generation.* New York: Knopf, 2000.

Hamilton, Alexander, James Madison, and John Jay. *The Federalist Papers.* Any edition.

Rossiter, Clinton. *Seedtime of the Republic: The Origin of the American Tradition of Political Liberty.* New York: Harcourt, Brace, 1953.

Wood, Gordon S. *The Creation of the American Republic, 1776–1787.* New York: Norton, 1972.

Social Dynamics

Finke, Roger, and Rodney Stark. *The Churching of America, 1776–2005: Winners and Losers in Our Religious Economy.* 2nd ed. New Brunswick, N.J.: Rutgers University Press, 2005.

Hacker, Andrew. *Money: Who Has How Much and Why.* New York: Scribner's, 1997.

Hochschild, Jennifer L. *Facing Up to the American Dream: Race, Class, and the Soul of the Nation.* Princeton: Princeton University Press, 1995.

McClosky, Herbert, and John Zaller. *The American Ethos.* Cambridge: Harvard University Press, 1981.

Walzer, Michael. *What It Means to Be an American.* New York: Marsilio, 1992.

Interest Groups

Berry, Jeffrey M. *The Interest Group Society.* New York: Longman, 1997.

Browne, William P. *Groups, Interests, and U.S. Public Policy.* Washington, D.C.: Georgetown University Press, 1998.

Cigler, Allan J., and Burdett A. Loomis, eds. *Interest Group Politics.* 6th ed. Washington, D.C.: CQ Press, 2002.

Parenti, Michael J. *Democracy for the Few.* 7th ed. New York: Wadsworth, 2002.

Walker, Jack L., Jr., et al. *Mobilizing Interest Groups in America: Patrons, Professions, and Social Movements.* Ann Arbor: University of Michigan Press, 1991.

Political Parties and Elections

Epstein, Leon D. *Political Parties in the American Mold.* Madison: University of Wisconsin Press, 1986.

Issacharoff, Samuel, Pamela S. Karlan, and Richard H. Pildes. *The Law of Democracy: Legal Structure of the Political Process.* Rev. ed. *2005 Supplement.* New York: Foundation Press, 2005.

Malbin, Michael J. *The Election after Reform: Money, Politics, and the Bipartisan Campaign Reform Act.* Lanham, Md.: Rowman and Littlefield, 2005.

Nelson, Michael, ed. *The Elections of 2004.* Washington, D.C.: CQ Press, 2005.

Patterson, Thomas E. *The Vanishing Voter: Public Involvement in an Age of Uncertainty.* New York: Knopf, 2002.

Polsby, Nelson W., and Aaron Wildavsky. *Presidential Elections: Strategies and Structures of American Politics.* 11th ed. Lanham, Md.: Rowman and Littlefield, 2004.

Wattenberg, Martin P. *The Rise of Candidate-Centered Politics.* Cambridge: Harvard University Press, 1991.

The Presidency

Barber, James David. *The Presidential Character: Predicting Performance in the White House.* 4th ed. Englewood Cliffs, N.J.: Prentice-Hall, 1992.

Gelderman, Carol. *All the Presidents' Words: The Bully Pulpit and the Creation of the Virtual Presidency.* New York: Walker and Co., 1997

Lowi, Theodore J. *The Personal President: Power Invested, Promise Unfulfilled.* Ithaca, N.Y.: Cornell University Press, 1985.

Milkis, Sidney M., and Michael Nelson. *The American Presidency: Origins and Development, 1776–2002.* 4th ed. Washington, D.C.: CQ Press, 2003.

Nelson, Michael, ed. *The Presidency and the Political System.* 8th ed. Washington, D.C.: CQ Press, 2005.

Neustadt, Richard E. *Presidential Power and the Modern Presidents: The Politics of Leadership from Roosevelt to Reagan.* Rev. ed. New York: Simon and Schuster, Free Press, 1991.

Congress

Dodd, Lawrence, and Bruce Oppenheimer, eds. *Congress Reconsidered.* 8th ed. Washington, D.C.: CQ Press, 2004.

Fiorina, Morris P. *Congress: Keystone of the Washington Establishment.* Rev. ed. New Haven: Yale University Press, 1989.

Hibbing, John R., and Elizabeth Theiss-Morse. *Congress as Public Enemy: Public Attitudes toward American Political Institutions.* Cambridge: Cambridge University Press, 1995

Lee, Frances E., and Bruce I. Oppenheimer. *Sizing Up the Senate: The Unequal Consequences of Equal Representation.* Chicago: University of Chicago Press, 1999.

Mayhew, David R. *Congress: The Electoral Connection.* New Haven: Yale University Press, 1986.

Schoenbrod, David. *Saving Our Environment from Washington: How Congress Grabs Power, Shirks Responsibility, and Shortchanges the People.* New Haven: Yale University Press, 2005.

The Federal Bureaucracy

Kettl, Donald F., and James W. Fesler. *The Politics of the Administrative Process.* 3rd ed. Washington, D.C.: CQ Press, 2005.

Kingdon, John W. *Agendas, Alternatives, and Public Policies.* 2nd ed. New York: Longman, 2002.

Quirk, Paul J. *Industry Influence in Federal Regulatory Agencies.* Princeton: Princeton University Press, 1981.

Ripley, Randall B., and Grace A. Franklin. *Congress, the Bureaucracy, and Public Policy.* 3rd ed. Homewood, Ill.: Dorsey, 1984.

Wilson, James Q. *Bureaucracy: What Government Agencies Do and Why They Do It.* New York: Basic Books, 1989.

The Judiciary

Abraham, Henry J. *The Judiciary: The Supreme Court in the Governmental Process.* 10th ed. New York: New York University Press, 1996.

_____. *Justices, Presidents and Senators: A History of the U.S. Supreme Court Appointments from Washington to Clinton.* 4th ed. Lanham, Md.: Rowman and Littlefield, 1999

Baum, Lawrence, *The Supreme Court.* 8th ed. Washington, D.C.: CQ Press, 2003.

O'Brien, David M. *Constitutional Law and Politics.* 6th ed. New York: Norton, 2005. (Author and publisher supply an annual update supplement, *Supreme Court Watch.*)

_____. *Storm Center: The Supreme Court in American Politics.* 7th ed. New York: Norton, 2005.

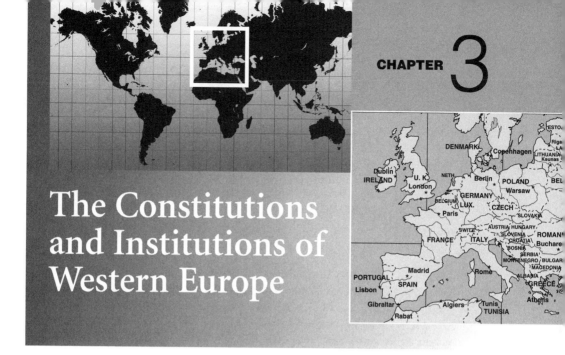

CHAPTER 3

The Constitutions and Institutions of Western Europe

The traditional definition of what constitutes "Europe"—geographically, if not politically—is that it extends west to east from the Atlantic Ocean to the Ural Mountains and the Black Sea in Russia, and north to south from the Arctic to the Mediterranean, with the Bosphorus linking the Black Sea and the Mediterranean in the southeast. With some 725 million people (third-largest in population among continents) on the second-smallest continent in land area, Europe is densely packed and has had a tumultuous history. The continent of Europe has long had primacy of place in the study of comparative politics, for at least three reasons: First, for much of the past few hundred years, all of the major powers in international relations were located there. Even in its reduced international status after World War II, several "middle powers" of Europe remained prominent in international relations.

Second, European culture, economic systems, and political institutions have had a worldwide impact, both through forced colonization and through imitation by other countries, such as Japan. At the zenith of imperialism in the late nineteenth and early twentieth centuries, Europe controlled much of the world's territory and population, either formally, through colonial rule, or informally, through its influence on supposedly independent states, such as Egypt. The two tiny islands of the United Kingdom (also called Britain) controlled about 25 percent of the world's population and land area by itself, and its rivals on the Continent, some of them quite small, such as the Netherlands and Portugal, had their own overseas empires. Russia's empire was contiguous rather than overseas. Even when not forced to do so, other countries wanted to learn from, and if possible imitate, the patterns that had led to European dominance over the world. The "Western values and influences" that people speak of were, until the twentieth century, almost exclusively European, and that part of the world continues to be influential elsewhere, even with the rise of the United States. Among its values are those based on the major religions of Europe, Christianity and Judaism, whose influence within Europe is discussed in chapter 4.

Third, Europe is the source of many modern political practices and ideologies, such as state sovereignty, liberalism, democracy, nationalism, fascism, and communism. Although these ideas have been transplanted elsewhere, sometimes by expatriates, and flourished to various degrees, their origins are distinctly European. "Liberal democracy," as it is usually termed today, has two dimensions: "Liberalism" refers to freedom of conscience and behavior for individuals, especially those who are citizens of a country, within the limits of that state's laws but with guaranteed freedoms that stem from the individual's human rights, rather than from a concession by an all-powerful ruling body. "Democracy" emphasizes the group, rather than the individual, and consists primarily of the capacity to participate in the selection of those who rule through regular, free, and fair elections. Especially now that liberal democracy is in its "third wave" of growth, the longest-enduring exemplars of such rule outside the United States have been in Europe, although sometimes democratic rule has been interrupted by forms of dictatorial rule for longer or shorter periods. The persistence of democracy in Europe, despite wars and other hardships, has made it a fertile source for lessons. This is especially true because more of the world's functioning democracies are based on the parliamentary form, common in Europe, than on the presidential form derived from the United States.

A fourth reason why Europe is an appropriate area to study comparative politics is the emergence of the European Union (EU), a unique international organization that has acquired authority over some areas of domestic policy within its twenty-five member countries, especially economic matters such as trade, agriculture, regional aid, and monetary policy, as well as having some coordinating capability in foreign policy and more restricted authority in other domestic policy areas. The specifics of these policy jurisdictions will be discussed later. The EU has its own flag (gold stars in a circle on a blue background), motto ("Unity in diversity"), currency (the euro), holiday (May 9), anthem (a variation on Beethoven's "Ode to Joy"), and passport for its citizens, along with its own diplomatic representatives around the globe. It also has twenty different languages rather than one or a few official ones. The EU is clearly a major force both in its member countries and more generally in the world.

With the fall of the Berlin Wall and communism in Central and Eastern Europe, starting in 1989, those areas have become more aligned with their "natural" partners in the West. The dissolution of Yugoslavia and the outbreak of violence there, however, were a reminder that all of Europe is not peaceful and democratic, even yet. Along the eastern and southeastern border with Asia, in particular, current European tendencies toward liberalism and democracy are not firmly established. Nevertheless, the countries newly liberated from communism were eager to join Europe, not only culturally, economically, and politically, but also through such prototypical European organizations as the EU and the North Atlantic Treaty Organization (NATO). Even some now-independent countries formerly contained within the Soviet Union desire these goals. Thus the power of favorable ideas associated with Europe continues to be a strong magnet.

"State sovereignty" refers to the political arrangements whereby constitutional authority is through a regime led by a government ruling over a population within defined boundaries. This right to rule is recognized by other states in the international system. This became the pervasive basis of authority in the West, and eventually the whole world, with the Treaty of Westphalia in 1648, which recognized the mutual legal existence of Protestant states as well as Catholic ones.

Politically, Europe consists of some forty sovereign states, including Turkey and Russia. With only 5 percent of the world's population, Europe has one-third of the world's economic output and one-half of the world's trade, including trade among the members of the EU. The twenty-five countries of the European Union together have a population of 464 million people and an economy of $11 trillion. Both the population and the size of the economy are the largest under one democratic authority in the world. The comparable U.S. figures are 293 million people and also $11 trillion. There are vast economic disparities, in general, between the fifteen western, older members of the EU and the ten, mainly central and eastern, newer ones. Purchasing power per capita varies from $10,200 in Poland and Latvia, to $50,600 in Luxembourg. The "EU-15" average is $23,400 per capita, compared with the "EU-10" average of $14,250 per capita.

For a country that has had such a large impact on the world, the United Kingdom of Great Britain and Northern Ireland is astonishingly small in land area, only about the size of the U.S. state of Illinois. Yet 60 million people reside there, giving it the highest population density among the three countries considered here. Located in the North Atlantic Ocean, it is just off the coast of France; the distance between the port cities of Dover, England, and Calais, France, is only eighteen miles. Although it is surrounded by water except for the border with Northern Ireland, Britain's other close neighbor is also a part of the British Isles, namely, the Republic of Ireland. Once a part of the United Kingdom, Ireland gained its independence in 1922 after an armed rebellion of the overwhelmingly Roman Catholic population against British rule. Other near neighbors are Norway (close to Scotland and sharing the North Sea oil fields) and the Benelux countries of Belgium, Netherlands, and Luxembourg across the English Channel. Even though the nautical distance from the continent of Europe is small, the separation loomed much larger in the days before modern transportation and communication. Britain became a maritime state,

Table 3-1 Basic Data on European and U.S. Regimes

	Capital	Total area (1,000 sq. km)	Population, 2004 (millions)	Population density, 2003 (per 1,000 sq. km)	$ per capita purchasing power parity, 2003
United Kingdom	London	245	60,271	245	27,100
France	Paris	549	60,424	107	26,900
Germany	Berlin	357	82,424	230	26,600
EU-25	Brussels	4,016	464,269	116	23,400 (EU-15)
United States	Washington	9,372	293,027	29	36,100

	Total government expenditure as % of GDP, 2001	Gini Index of Inequality,[a] 2004	% population 65+, 2004	% feeling "European" to some extent, 2004
United Kingdom	40	36	18	29
France	53	33	19	67
Germany	48	26	21	52
EU-25	44 avg. (1.0 EU budget)	28	N.A.	54 (EU-15)
United States	36	41	14	—

[a] The Gini Index of Inequality indicates how equally the population of a country shares in that country's wealth. If all people had the same income, the Gini Index of Inequality would be 0.0 (no inequality). Thus, the higher the index, the greater amount of inequality of wealth.

with an emphasis on oceanic trade protected by a strong navy. The British also conceived of themselves as separate from other European countries, and that conception has influenced British foreign policy from its nineteenth-century, "perfidious Albion" diplomacy of balancing continental powers against each other and staying aloof from wars on the Continent, to its present-day, "awkward partner" status within the European Union.

France, with its 60 million people, lies astride the western flank of the continent of Europe. France is a country decidedly of the North Atlantic area. It stretches from the English Channel in the north, to the Mediterranean Sea in the south, and to the Bay of Biscay in the west, with a land area about two-thirds the size of Texas. As with any large country, it has several neighbors, ranging from the Benelux countries and the United Kingdom in the northwest, to Germany and Switzerland in the east, to Italy in the southeast, and to Spain in the south. It is also not far across the Mediterranean to North Africa, and several countries in the northern, Arab- and Muslim-dominated part of that continent were once French colonies. With this location and extensive ports, France has been well placed to be influential not only in Europe but also more broadly in the world.

The Federal Republic of Germany has the largest population among EU members, almost 83 million. Even more than France, Germany lies at the heart of Europe geographically and, for the past century, also at its heart politically. A large land area, about the size of the U.S. state of Montana, it shares land borders with several countries, notably Benelux, France, Denmark, Poland, the Czech Republic, Austria, and Switzerland. Italy is not far away. Germany's North Sea maritime border is not far from Sweden and other Nordic countries, as well as Russia. Since its unification through force of arms when Prussia defeated France in 1871, Germany has maintained interests throughout Central and Eastern Europe, both because of its economic and political importance to those smaller countries and because several of them have sizable German-speaking populations.

Although there are some variations among the four jurisdictions, all three countries, as well as the European Union, and especially the EU-15, have relatively educated and wealthy populations. The industrial revolution, which occurred first in Europe, produced enormous wealth, and the agricultural population has continued to decline as mechanization has generated higher productivity on the land. Today the services sector, especially those parts based on electronic communication, is of increasing importance in the economy. These also are called the "primary" (agricultural and minerals), "secondary" (manufacturing), and "tertiary" (services) sectors. The small land area, dense population, and heavy industrialization of European states make them large energy importers, and that is a source of delicate relations with the United States, Russia, and countries in the Middle East. Other relevant social and economic dimensions of these states, especially as they affect politics, are discussed in the next chapter.

European countries are members, often key ones, of many international organizations, including the United Nations (where Britain and France sit on the Security Council), NATO, the World Bank, the International Monetary

Table 3-2   Basic Data on European Union Members

Members	Year joined	Seats in European Parliament	Qualified majority voting votes	Share of EU budget, 2003 (%)	Net gain/loss as % of EU budget, 2003	% agricultural workers
Austria	1995	18	10	2.3	−0.3	4.0
Belgium	1958	24	12	4.2	−2.0	1.3
Cyprus	2004	6	4	N.A.	N.A.	9.2
Czech Republic	2004	24	12	N.A.	N.A.	7.4
Denmark	1973	14	7	2.1	−0.3	4.0
Estonia	2004	6	4	N.A.	N.A.	7.4
Finland	1995	14	7	1.6	+0.1	8.0
France	1958	78	29	18.1	−1.3	4.1
Germany	1958	99	29	23.0	−9.5	2.8
Greece	1981	24	12	1.8	+4.4	12.0
Hungary	2004	24	12	N.A.	N.A.	4.8
Ireland	1973	13	7	1.3	+2.1	8.0
Italy	1958	78	29	14.1	−0.5	5.0
Latvia	2004	9	4	N.A.	N.A.	13.5
Lithuania	2004	13	7	N.A.	N.A.	19.6
Luxembourg	1958	6	4	0.2	−0.1	1.0
Malta	2004	5	3	N.A.	N.A.	1.9
Netherlands	1958	27	13	5.9	−3.4	4.0
Poland	2004	54	27	N.A.	N.A.	18.8
Portugal	1986	24	12	1.5	+4.6	10.0
Slovakia	2004	14	7	N.A.	N.A.	6.7
Slovenia	2004	7	4	N.A.	N.A.	9.9
Spain	1986	54	27	8.9	+11.5	5.3
Sweden	1995	19	10	3.0	−1.2	2.0
United Kingdom	1973	78	29	11.9	−4.1	1.5
EU–15		570	237	N.A.	N.A.	4.3
EU–10		162	84	N.A.	N.A.	13.8

Fund (whose presidency is reserved for a European), the World Trade Organization (WTO), and the "Group of 8," or G-8, representing the world's largest economies (the United Kingdom, France, Germany, and Italy are members). There are also many Europe-wide regional organizations for specialized purposes besides the EU. In summary, Europe as a whole, especially the three largest countries and the EU, continues to be a major political, economic, social, and cultural force in the world.

   A constitution is the structure of fundamental laws and customary practices that defines the authority of state institutions and regulates their interrelationships, including their relationships to citizens of the state. Although almost all states have formal, written constitutions, many of these are nominal only, rather than functional. The real constitution, the operative system of institutions and their interrelationships, may operate differently than what is formally stated.

We will consider the institutions of the four regimes here under the categories of the executive (political and bureaucratic), the legislature, the judiciary, and the degree of centralization of authority. The "political executive" refers to those few positions in the administration that are either elected or politically appointed. In other words, they are the part of the executive that is accountable, directly or indirectly, to the citizenry. This category consists of the head of government (the prime minister, premier, or chancellor), the cabinet, and other high executive officials appointed through patronage. In France the president also is part of the political executive. But the overwhelming majority of officials in the executive branch are in positions in the bureaucracy—advising on policy and implementing it subject to direction by their political superiors. The monarchy, the political executive before liberal democracy arose, is now largely symbolic although it has not become part of the bureaucracy. The equivalent office—head of state—is the presidency in both Germany and France. The duties of the head of state are formal and nonpartisan, although the French president also has partisan, policy powers.

While much policy is made in the executive branch, the legislature—or at least one chamber of it—is directly elected by the population and therefore can be held accountable by the electorate for policy. Although the legislature's role in formulating laws is secondary in Western democracies, it still must officially approve policy (legitimation) as well as hold the executive responsible to the broader population. The judiciary is responsible for adjudicating disputes about the law's applicability and interpretation. The degree of centralization of authority in a regime indicates how uniform the laws are and how much concentrated power the central government has. While these concepts are readily grasped in the case of a sovereign state, matters are more complicated with respect to the European Union, especially inasmuch as some bodies combine executive and legislative functions.

THE BRITISH CONSTITUTION

The United Kingdom, long recognized as an exemplar of limited government (sometimes called "constitutional" government), is the most prominent of the tiny number of states operating without a single, formal document called a "constitution" that functions as an authoritative reference point for disputes about the law. Sometime it is said that the United Kingdom has an "unwritten" constitution, but that is only partially true. Some of its practices are based on "custom and convention"—as indeed is the case in every country (for example, the convention that the U.S. Supreme Court possesses the power of judicial review). This means that they are widely accepted as valid in the political culture, based on the evolution of practices over time. But other British constitutional practices have a firm foundation in statute. In the United Kingdom, however, all statute laws are equal and can be changed through ordinary, majority-rule processes of Parliament. Therefore, the "constitutional" status of such laws depends on the subject matter. There are no laws that can be changed only through extraordinary majorities of the legislature, referendums, or judicial review.

As a state in international law, the United Kingdom is made up of four constituent parts—England, Scotland, Wales, and Northern Ireland—acquired historically through conquest (Wales and Northern Ireland) and peaceful union (Scotland) with England. These constituent parts technically are not provinces, since Britain formally is not a federal state, despite some decentralization. All are under the authority of the queen in Parliament, the central authority, in London. The four parts are very unbalanced in territory and population. England makes up 55 percent of the land area of the United Kingdom, but it contains 81 percent of the population. Scotland has 32 percent of the land area and 9 percent of the population; Wales has 9 percent of the land area and 6 percent of the population; and Northern Ireland has 4 percent of the land and 3 percent of the population.

There are also social, economic, and political differences among these units of the United Kingdom, which are especially pronounced in Scotland and Northern Ireland. Scotland, in particular, retains its own institutions in its official church (Presbyterian rather than Anglican), its own legal system, its own education system (four years of undergraduate training rather than three), and even its own currency notes (issued by the Bank of Scotland and sometimes not recognized south of the border). Politically, Northern Ireland is very different from "mainland" Britain (the other three parts across the Irish Sea).

Because of the unique nature of the British constitution, almost any alteration of the interrelationship of political institutions can be considered "constitutional." Although in principle it appears to be very flexible, in practice the British constitution is difficult to change. The socialization of political elites in a small country (see chapter 4) helps maintain a political culture in which custom and convention make participants reluctant to change practices that brought them to power and that are widely seen to have provided generally responsible and responsive government over a long period of time.

There is a tension in British constitutional practice between the rule of law and representative democracy. Even though Britain is under the rule of law, this is subject to change through "parliamentary sovereignty." Instead of a written constitution with a complicated amending process, a simple majority of the House of Commons can change any law, even over the objections of the House of Lords, if necessary. The same bill only has to pass the House of Commons in two consecutive sessions uninterrupted by a general election. Individual rights are protected by ordinary law and custom, not by an entrenched bill of rights.

The British electorate is asked once every four or five years to choose a team of politicians to rule the central authority through the election of members to the lower house of Parliament at Westminster, the House of Commons. The single-member district, simple-plurality electoral system, with the leading vote-getter winning the one legislative seat per district, usually has resulted in one party receiving a majority of the Members of Parliament (MPs) in the House Commons, even if that party lacks a majority of the vote (see chapter 4). That party is then rewarded by having its leaders form the executive government (the prime minister and cabinet), which is directly accountable to the House of Commons rather than to the electorate. This represents what Walter Bagehot, the famous nineteenth-century commentator, called a "fusion of power," rather than a separation of powers between the legislature and the executive. Thus a single-party government based on a majority of seats in the House of Commons has almost untrammeled formal power, what Lord Hailsham, a former Conservative cabinet minister, called an "elective dictatorship." There have been few referendums, and formally they are only advisory. Parliament has final authority.

The Monarchy

The monarch retains considerable formal authority but is now considered a "constitutional" monarch, not an absolute one, despite various titles such as Her Majesty's Government (as well as Her Majesty's Loyal Opposition), the Royal Mail, Her Majesty's Ships, and so forth. The conventional way of describing this arrangement is that the monarch "reigns but does not rule." The monarch's duties usually are limited to the nonpartisan, good-government duties of the head of state—sending and receiving ambassadors, giving out honors and awards, making formal tours, and making speeches, including notably the "Queen's Speech" that opens each parliamentary session by setting out the program of Her Majesty's Government. The speech is actually written by the prime minister and cabinet, who stand at the back of the room, invited guests to the House of Lords, while the queen delivers it from a throne in the front of the room. In times of extraordinary political crisis, such as when there is no majority party in the House of Commons, the monarch may exercise more discretionary authority.

Queen Elizabeth II has been the monarch since 1952. Although somewhat reduced in scope recently, the British monarchy continues to be the last large-scale, "pomp and circumstance" royalty in Europe. Although the queen is estimated to be the richest person in Europe, the government continues to provide money through the "civil list" for her public duties. She is assisted in performing those tasks by other members of the royal family.

The monarchy has come under increased scrutiny in recent years, although there is no popular demand for change. In fact, the monarchy appears to be more popular with the general public than with the political elite, especially those on the political left. The monarch remains the "Defender of the Faith," that is, temporal head of the established Anglican Church, and inheritance of the throne is governed by long-standing laws. They include laws that male children of the sitting monarch, starting with the eldest, receive preference and that the monarch must be an Anglican.

The Political Executive

Within the executive, the prime minister and cabinet wield the power that the monarch once possessed, with the democratic authority of their selection by, and accountability to, Parliament, principally the House of Commons. This political executive is the partisan, directing hand. It consists of the prime minister, the cabinet (approximately twenty-five heads of major executive departments), and other ministerial personnel responsible to Parliament, including dozens of junior ministers in the departments. Altogether the government payroll consists of about one hundred people, or about 25 percent to 33 percent of the members who constitute the government party's majority in the House of Commons under normal circumstances. The prime minister ascends to that position through being head of the majority party; the other members of the government are dependent on prime ministerial appointment and serve at the chief executive's pleasure. Although most have seats in the House of Commons, a few come from the House of Lords and present the government's program in that body.

The cabinet usually meets twice per week to take up important matters that need collective discussion and perhaps decision making. Although the traditional view is that the prime minister is "first among equals," increasingly it has been recognized that he or she is the directing force for most cabinet decisions. An argument has even emerged that, in terms of the authority it wields over the rest of the cabinet, the office has become "presidential." Most policy, however, is developed below full cabinet level, through cabinet committees of a few ministers and coordinated action among high-level civil servants in government departments.

Ministers are expected to maintain collective responsibility for government policy and individual responsibility for their departments. Collective responsibility means that members of the government publicly stand united behind policy that has been approved in cabinet. If a minister cannot support government policy in this manner, he or she is expected to resign from the government and go to the backbenches of the House of Commons, where the ordinary legislators of the governing party sit. Individual ministerial responsibility means that ministers are responsible politically for what transpires in their departments in terms of policy and administration. They receive the credit if things go well and the blame if there are difficulties. They are the ones answerable to Parliament, the news media, and the public for policy and administration in their department.

The power that ministers wield comes from Parliament in the form of specific laws and "statutory instruments" or delegated legislation allowing the executive to change laws to meet changing conditions. Some of it, however, comes through administrative orders in council, essentially the broad executive powers that once belonged to the monarch. Cabinet offices can be reorganized, for instance, at the prime minister's direction, without the consent of Parliament.

With the derogation of authority from the monarch, plus legislation such as the Official Secrets Act (1906), punishing unauthorized revelations of government documents and deliberations, British executive government has been highly secretive. It has become somewhat less so recently, with increasing leaks to the press and the passage of a freedom of information law allowing greater access to the communications of government agencies.

The Bureaucracy

The part of executive government in Britain that employs the most people is the bureaucracy, including the civil service and its military counterparts. These thousands of individuals are responsible for the administration of government services, often through a tradition of self-enforcement negotiated with those affected by government regulation. In Britain traditionally there has been a division between politics and administration, although that is now somewhat weakened. Under this doctrine, whereas ministers take the lead on policy and public accountability, civil servants are supposed to be politically neutral, and their individual roles and advice in official actions are largely unknown to the public.

On the other hand, some critics, especially on the left, suspected that civil servants really were generally conservative "lions under the throne," wielding considerable power through their knowledge of the labyrinths of power in Whitehall (the street in London where several government departments are located) as well as the expertise they had to offer to generalist, often short-term ministers. This view was the basis of the long-running and popular television series seen all over the world, *Yes, Minister* (later, *Yes, Prime Minister*), in which a clever, high-ranking permanent secretary (the highest-level civil servant in a department), Sir Humphrey Appleby, tries to thwart political initiatives by his minister.

But life has changed for the civil service. The government of Conservative prime minister Margaret Thatcher (1979–1990) was concerned about the political orientations of higher civil servants and how they might affect their official duties. Although the careers of politics and the civil service are still largely distinct, the power of the civil service in relation to political figures probably has been reduced. More temporary "special advisers," especially on political and media issues, were appointed to the civil service. Under the doctrine called "New Public Management" (NPM) the Next Steps initiative in Britain made the implementation of many government programs eligible for bidding by private firms, and that reduced the official number of full-time civil servants.

The Legislature

The United Kingdom has a bicameral legislature, but the powers of the two houses are unequal. The House of Commons is the only fully democratically elected body. Formerly the superior body, because it was composed of landed aristocrats, the House of Lords has lost authority as mass democracy was extended. That occurred particularly in the reforms of 1911 and 1949, which limited the chamber's capacity to oppose the wishes of the House of Commons. The House of Lords now normally acts as a house of revision and administrative detail rather than intense partisan controversy. While legislative procedures allow the lords enough time to consider bills, their powers of amendment and delay are limited. By passing an identical version of a bill twice in a one-year period, the Commons can overrule the House of Lords' objections, but this is rarely necessary.

Currently composed of 646 members, the House of Commons contains the only central-level legislators directly elected by the citizens of the country. As noted previously, a new general election can occur anytime within the five-year limit on the term of a Parliament, and it takes place in single-member districts with simple-plurality voting. Election procedures are discussed further in chapter 4.

Once it has been elected, the first business of Parliament is to choose the government. This is actually *pro forma* when a single party has a majority in the House of Commons. The party leader becomes prime minister and chooses the rest of the ministers within the constraints previously mentioned. If no party receives a majority of seats, however, then there may be negotiations among parties about forming a coalition government. More likely, a minority government, with less than an overall majority of seats, will be formed, with a view toward running the affairs of the country for only a relatively brief period before a new election is called in an attempt to bring about a majority government.

All governments, however, can only exist with the continuing support of the House of Commons. In effect, the House of Commons acts as an ongoing electoral college, which installs a government in office and can remove it for any reason. Periodically the opposition may call for a vote of confidence in the government. If a government fails to receive majority support from those voting, then the confidence of the House is considered withdrawn, and the government must resign *en masse*. Then there will be either negotiations for a new government and/or a general election to resolve the issue. Despite this potential, the only successful votes of no-confidence in a government since 1900 have occurred when there was a minority government, in 1924 and 1979. Usually a majority-party government has little to fear, even on issues that are controversial within the party, because party control of the executive is necessary for its MPs to obtain maximum benefit for their careers, policy goals, and constituents. An election would put that control at risk, especially if precipitated by a divided party.

The House of Commons is organized to give priority to two things: (1) the government's agenda and (2) organized public debate on the government's proposals. A Speaker is chosen from among veteran MPs as a nonpartisan umpire for procedures. Members of the government party sit on the benches to the right of the Speaker; members of the opposition parties to the left, starting with the members of Her Majesty's Loyal Opposition, the second-largest party in the Commons. On both sides, MPs are divided into what are called "frontbenchers" and "backbenchers." The frontbenchers, literally sitting in the front row next to the Speaker's Table, are the government ministers on the one side and the members of the "shadow cabinet" on the other.

The shadow cabinet is headed by the leader of Her Majesty's Loyal Opposition, in effect, the alternative prime minister. He receives a small salary from the government, emphasizing the role of organized debate in the Commons. The other members of the opposition frontbench serve, in effect, as an alternative cabinet and are organized to debate, and often oppose, government policy in particular departments. Other parties also have leaders and shadow spokespersons, but they do not have the privileged status in the Commons of Her Majesty's Loyal Opposition.

Backbenchers are the members of all parties who have no official position in the leadership. They have only limited opportunities to take part in most debates, usually following discussion across the floor of the House by frontbench members, especially those of the two leading parties. During "question time" (see below), however, backbenchers receive the majority of the time.

The government has priority for its proposed legislation through control of parliamentary time. The overwhelming majority of time is devoted to debate on government bills, and debate can be limited if necessary. Budget bills are high-priority items and are considered matters of confidence. Thus the budget in Britain is an executive budget, unaffected by legislative amendment. The opposition has some influence on the agenda through an allocation of time to raise issues that it wants to debate, although it cannot introduce its own legislation. The small remaining time is allotted to what are called "private members' bills," nonpartisan legislation, often on behalf of a small group of people or concerned with morality, that backbench MPs offer. Unless the private member's bill receives sympathy from the government, in the form of bill drafting and extra time to discuss it, it is unlikely to reach the statute book.

Both houses of the legislature also perform important oversight functions, that is, checking on executive performance. The most famous method of doing this is through question time, when government ministers, including the prime minister, are subjected to both written and oral questions from any member of the House on any topic within their duties. The prime minister's question time is noted more for partisan bickering than for enlightenment on major issues of the day.

Most important activity in the Commons occurs on the floor rather than in committees. Generalist rather than specialist committees consider legislation, and few amendments are successful, since the majority party backs the government. Since 1979, however, there have been specialist committees to hear testimony from ministers and even civil servants on oversight questions.

As noted earlier, the House of Lords no longer has coequal power with the House of Commons, and it mainly serves to raise issues, conduct oversight, and sometimes to delay bills. Near the end of a parliamentary term, however, those delays can lead to legislation's failing to pass or to the government's dropping a bill. Traditionally the House of Lords was composed of hereditary peers, those who received aristocratic titles from the monarch that they could pass on to their heirs. In 1958, life peers were added; these are people given titles and a seat in the House of Lords for superior service to the country, usually political service, upon recommendation by the prime minister. Thus many senior politicians served in the Lords after their retirement or defeat for the Commons. Until 1999 the hereditary peers were numerically dominant, even if the life peers carried much of the work burden. In that year the number of hereditary peers was reduced from 726 to 92. And the right of this rump group to sit in the House of Lords was due to expire once the "second stage of Lords reform" was agreed to. This was part of the Labour Party government's promise of democratic constitutional reform.

Reform of the House of Lords would appear to be relatively simple, inasmuch as a government majority in the House of Commons can eventually override any objections that the members of the upper house might raise. Nevertheless, lack of agreement about desirable new arrangements has delayed completion of Lords reform. The Labour government prefers a body entirely appointed by the prime minister, with an independent Appointments Commission to examine the credentials of all candidates. Critics would prefer a body with greater democratic legitimacy, one better able to act as an occasional check on the government majority in the House of Commons. The Labour government elected in 2005 promised a free vote (one not bound by party loyalty) on the second stage of Lords reform.

The Judiciary

The United Kingdom founded common law, which means that interpretation of the applicability of the law to particular cases lies in the hands of presiding judges, who use both statutory law and their own understanding of legal principles, rather than relying on a comprehensive, legislatively written code of laws. The common law system also incorporates the principle of *stare decisis* ("let the decision stand"), which relies heavily on previous decisions by judges in similar cases. Those cases are communicated through being written in "case books" of decisions to which jurists can refer. The process is adversarial; that is, the accused in a criminal case is presumed innocent in court until proven guilty, although that does not prevent indictment and preventive incarceration.

Despite the interpretive power in the hands of jurists, the British judiciary seldom makes politically important decisions. The reason is that it lacks the power of judicial review; it is not the guardian of the constitution. It can overturn executive (but not legislative) decisions, however, on the basis of *ultra vires,* that is, that the government acted without the consent of law. But even those decisions can be overridden by Parliament's simply passing a law to authorize the action, after the fact (*post facto*) if necessary. Although there is no entrenched bill of rights, Britain signed the European Convention on Human

Rights in 1951. Since 1966 it has allowed appeals to the European Court of Human Rights, at Strasbourg, where it has lost more cases than any other country. Through Labour government legislation, the Human Rights Act incorporated the European Convention on Human Rights into domestic law. British judges, rather than European judges, now make the decisions about whether Britain is conforming to the convention, which enhances the ability of British citizens to raise issues of human rights in domestic courts. Parliamentary sovereignty is maintained because Westminster retains final authority as to whether judicial decisions will be followed.

Recently the Labour Party government has moved toward greater separation of powers among the executive, legislative, and judicial branches of government. Previously the lord chancellor was considered a member of all three branches—a minister in the cabinet, head of the judiciary (with the authority to appoint judges), and also Speaker of the House of Lords. The highest appeals court has been the Appellate Committee of the House of Lords ("Law Lords"), consisting of the lord chancellor, twelve life peers specially appointed for this purpose, and other members of the Lords who have held high judicial office. Acting within his executive prerogative, Prime Minister Tony Blair replaced the lord chancellor's position in the cabinet with a new "secretary for constitutional affairs," mainly responsible for legal administration. The government also introduced legislation to abolish the office of lord chancellor entirely, to remove the judiciary from the House of Lords, and to designate as the highest appellate court the Supreme Court, with a reformed Judicial Appointments Commission to make recommendations for all judgeships.

Devolution and Local Government

Officially Britain remains a unitary state, with all constitutional authority belonging to the central government, rather than a federal state with a formal, even if vague, division of powers between the center and a designated lower level of government. Some argue that Britain would more properly be called a "union-state," since the relationships of the four parts to the central government are not all on the same terms. Even before devolution of authority to Scotland in 1998, central legislation often concerned England and Wales only, with separate bills necessary to change laws in Scotland and Northern Ireland. Although limited devolution has been implemented in the past, especially in Northern Ireland from 1922 to 1972, the central government retains the authority to intervene in lower-level affairs, including local government matters. Authority devolved to a lower level can be taken back by the central level through ordinary legislation, as was done with Northern Ireland in 1972. In other words, the lower level has no inherent right to exist. The British Parliament also has rearranged local government structure throughout the country several times in the past.

Upon gaining office in 1997, New Labour immediately instituted a program for devolution of power to Scotland and Wales. These plans had been developed to allow more local self-governance, to alleviate separatist sentiment, and to give the dominant Labour Party in each region a reward for its loyalty during the preceding eighteen years, during which the Conservative Party ruled in London. Referendums showed support for devolution to be stronger in Scotland than in Wales. The Scottish Parliament has more authority, covering nearly all of domestic policy, as well as limited power to tax, whereas the Welsh Assembly is responsible for implementing legislation after the primary bills have passed through the Westminster House of Commons and has no taxation powers. In its third term of office, Labour will seek expanded powers for the Welsh Assembly through the referendum procedure. Elections in each region in 1999 and 2003 were held under a mixed system of single-member district, simple-plurality and party list proportional representation; these yielded no clear majority in either legislature. Instead, Labour–Liberal Democrat coalition or minority governments have been formed. No devolved authority along similar lines has been implemented for parts of England.

Northern Ireland is a perennial problem, a remnant of the separation of Ireland from the United Kingdom in 1922. The six counties in the northern part of the island of Ireland, approximately two-thirds of whose population consisted of Protestants favoring continued union with Great Britain, remained in the United Kingdom. Many Catholics, north and south, remain convinced that there should be one, united country of Ireland on the island. This fundamental division of opinion over which country should have sovereignty over the territory led to organized violence by partisans of both sides, especially since the late 1960s. The Provisional Irish Republican Army (PIRA) was the principal organization fighting for a united Ireland.

The Good Friday Agreement of 1998, brokered by the U.S. Clinton administration, was a peace accord that promised a different future through new institutions. In 1999 devolution of power from the Westminster Parliament to the Belfast parliament ushered in a period of what the British call "power sharing," or what others would call "consensus democracy." It entails not only joint authority over internal matters by both Protestants (Unionists) and Catholics (Nationalists) through the requirement of supermajorities in the Northern Ireland Assembly and executive, but also regular consultation between the United Kingdom and Ireland. Both countries have pledged that Northern Ireland will remain part of the United Kingdom as long as a majority of the population in the province wishes. The latest census showed Protestants continuing to be in the majority, but only by 53 percent to 44 percent.

Referendums on the Good Friday Agreement passed overwhelmingly in both Northern Ireland and the Irish Republic; the latter also repealed its constitutional claim over the province. As expected, devolved government in Northern Ireland has been rocky. Groups representing formerly armed adversaries, including Sinn Fein, closely linked to the IRA, assumed ministerial positions in the power-sharing executive. Some dissident factions refused to pledge nonviolence. The major issues have been the needs to verify the decommissioning of weapons and the renunciation of violence by the IRA and to incorporate

Catholics into the overwhelmingly Protestant police service, as well as divisions among Protestants about how far to cooperate with the new government. These divisions have led to the suspension of the Northern Ireland Assembly and government several times, with direct rule from the central government in London replacing the power-sharing executive. Despite some progress, deep cleavages and a general lack of trust between the two sides will continue to hinder normal politics in the province.

"Mainland Britain," the rest of the United Kingdom, considers Northern Ireland a place apart, and much of the public would happily be rid of the whole expensive problem if the groups in Northern Ireland could only agree on a solution. The government of the United Kingdom has even agreed to cede Northern Ireland if majority opinion in the province ever chose that option.

Although local government has many important functions in Britain, especially in regard to delivery of such services as social welfare, policing, and education, it is dependent on the central government both for policy and for its finance in the form of grants and allowed taxation rates. Although there are locally elected officials, central government dominance makes local government its dependency rather than an important political actor in its own right.

THE FRENCH CONSTITUTION

In contrast to Britain's evolutionary constitutional change and vague but generally observed principles, France relies heavily on written rules and has had several abrupt changes of its constitution. The first violent upsurge was the French Revolution, commencing in 1789. It had worldwide, if ambivalent, influence in that it overthrew a domestic rather than an overseas regime in the name of the collective interests of the people. Not only did it follow the principles of the American Revolution in demanding a constitutional basis for limited government, thus restricting the executive's discretionary powers, but it also is considered the foundation of modern, ethnic-centered nationalism. The much-cited Article III of the Declaration of the Rights of Man and of the Citizens (1789) stated, "The principle of any sovereignty resides essentially in the Nation. No body, no individual can exert authority which does not emanate expressly from it." By this doctrine, the only legitimate basis for a state is the united, communal feeling (nationalism) of its citizens; hence the term "nation-state." It is a doctrine that has led to continuing conflict internationally, as distinct ethnic groups have become disaffected with the state of their residence and demanded secession or internal autonomy.

Until recently, however, the principles of the French Revolution have had only tenuous acceptance in their home country. Revolutionary violence led to counterrevolution, and subsequent political regimes were often short-lived. Since 1789 France has had sixteen regimes, in a period in which the United Kingdom has had, arguably, one. The problem lay in a conflict within French political culture, which has had two orientations difficult to reconcile: The first was a legislatively based, representative, limited-government tradition, as reflected in the French Revolution and the Third (1871–1940) and Fourth (1946–1958) Republics. Some conservative elements in France, however, were reluctant to accept the principles of the French Revolution, and that led to a second cultural orientation toward a strong executive, using his discretionary power with few restrictions from the legislature or the constitution and consulting with the population at large through referendums (votes on specific issues) and plebiscites (popular votes of confidence in the government). That tradition was reflected in the regimes of Napoleon Bonaparte, Napoleon III, and Vichy during World War II.

A new regime, the Fifth Republic, was created at the behest of Charles de Gaulle in 1958 to allow him to assume the presidency during a crisis over the revolt by the French army in Algeria. Initially the Fifth Republic appeared to be a return to the executive-centered tradition. De Gaulle once remarked that he wanted to represent the interests of France, not the opinions of Frenchmen, a clear statement of the first tradition. The president would have broad authority, especially in foreign policy; the legislature would have only limited authority and be chosen through a single-member district system to reduce party fragmentation in the assembly; and referendums were allowed. Even though the president officially chooses the premier, a limited form of parliamentary government also was established, inasmuch as the premier heads a government that is accountable to the lower house of the legislature, the National Assembly, and is subject to the possibility of a vote of no confidence. Surprisingly, not only has the Fifth Republic lasted almost a half-century (the second-longest regime since 1789), but it also has managed to alleviate some of the tensions between the two conflicting constitutional traditions.

The Political Executive

The 1958 constitution, written by de Gaulle's lieutenant Michel Debré, is considered the first of a new type, often called "semipresidential" government (also a "hybrid" or "dual executive"). A 1962 constitutional amendment, adopted through a referendum, further enhanced the authority of the president by providing that he or she be chosen through direct election. There is no term limitation. The president has an array of powers, including the role of commander in chief. The president appoints members of the Council of Ministers (the cabinet), presides over cabinet meetings, and may declare a constitutional emergency and then rule by general executive decree. Since presidential terms were for seven years and assembly terms for a maximum of five, however, there was potential for partisan conflict, or divided government, within the executive branch. That problem was partially relieved through the provision that the president can dissolve the assembly and call for new elections once per year.

The potential for a two-headed executive of divided partisan disposition was not realized for almost thirty years. As long as the president and the premier were of the same party, it was clear that the president was the chief executive of the country and the premier his lieutenant. But eventually the problem arose, specifically, once France had a Socialist president, François Mitterand, and his government lost its parliamentary majority, in 1986, midway through his presidential term. At that point a pragmatic solution was found, namely "cohabitation" of the two executives. Under cohabitation, the premier, as long as he or she holds the confidence of the majority of the National Assembly, effectively appoints the remainder of the cabinet and is the chief domestic policymaker. In foreign policy, the president has more constitutional authority and is more likely to be influential, both in appointments and in policy, but again the premier has a role. At summit meetings of the European Council or the G-8, both officials represented France.

Subsequently there have been two other periods of cohabitation. In all instances there was agreement that the deadlock would be resolved by the next presidential election. In all of those presidential elections, the sitting premier was a candidate for the presidency. Once a new president was elected, he dissolved the assembly and called for a new election. Since the president was in his postelection "honeymoon" period, in each instance this procedure has resulted in a victory for his party group (left or right). Thus, after President Jacques Chirac's reelection in 2002, he dissolved the legislature, was rewarded with a conservative majority, and appointed Jean-Pierre Raffarin as premier. After the defeat of the European Constitution in a referendum in 2005, Chirac replaced Raffarin with Dominique de Villepin.

Nevertheless, under cohabitation smooth functioning of the executive was hindered, especially through the potential for a weakened presidency partway through a term. It may also, however, have resulted in more moderation in policy. During the longest period of cohabitation, 1997–2002, a constitutional amendment was adopted, through popular referendum, that reduced the president's term of office from seven years to five, beginning in 2002. This change limits both the likelihood and the potential duration of cohabitation. The first election under the amendment will take place in 2007, the same year as the next scheduled election for the National Assembly. With the presidential election scheduled first, as in 2002, the Fifth Republic may revert to the more president-dominated system of its earlier years.

The Council of Ministers functions much as does the cabinet in Britain. The council's composition has varied between twenty-four and forty-nine members, including junior ministers, and included people with both political and administrative experience. The council operates on the basis of collective responsibility for government policy and individual ministerial responsibility for the conduct of the departments. The council meets about once a week, and the members also have to answer written, and occasionally oral, questions at a weekly question time in the legislature.

The Bureaucracy

The tradition of a strong, centralized state in France, which dates back to medieval times, has enhanced the prestige and effectiveness of the civil service. Among European countries, France is unusual in the large percentage of its population that are public employees at all levels of government. The French bureaucracy is famed for its effectiveness, its combination of political and civil service functions, and its recruitment processes (which we will discuss in chapter 4). Although the French civil service long has functioned on meritocratic principles, there is a place for the politically connected as well. First, every French minister has a *cabinet* (this is a French term, not to be confused with the cabinet) of at least ten patronage appointments, both from within and outside the civil service, to supervise policy in the department. Second, in contrast to the situation in Britain, there are not distinct career paths for bureaucrats and politicians.

The French bureaucracy is renowned for its prowess in carrying out official tasks with a large amount of administrative discretion as to how to proceed, as well as its close relationship with the private sector. The latter is due to state ownership of some firms, a process of indicative planning to aid government-business cooperation, and interchange of high-level personnel between the two sectors. For instance, public officials kept the state functioning, presiding over some of the most economically productive years in French history, during the tumultuous Fourth Republic, when there were twenty-two governments in thirteen years. Under the Fifth Republic, with more policy carried out by executive decree and only a limited role for legislation, the role of the bureaucracy has been strengthened, despite increased privatization. There is, however, a system of administrative law in France under which citizens can take their grievances with respect to how they have been treated by officials to special courts that hear such complaints. The Council of State, the highest administrative court, is independent of the executive and is recognized as a guardian of citizens' rights against abuse by the state.

The Legislature

France's legislature embodies a version of "weak bicameralism." In contrast to what was the case in the Fourth Republic, the executive has primacy in the legislative process. It is difficult for the legislature—even the lower house, the directly elected National Assembly of 577 members—to delay, amend, or defeat government proposals. Government bills have priority, and delays, especially on finance bills, are not allowed. The government controls parliamentary time even more tightly than in Britain, with no days set aside for the opposition to set the topics for debate. Not only is the questioning of government ministers more limited than in Britain, but the constitution restricts the areas in which the legislature may act. Policy on everything else is formulated through executive decrees. Only six committees, some of them huge, are allowed under the constitution. They are weak and cannot change the substance of government bills before they reach the floor of the assembly. While a vote of no confidence, or censure, by the assembly is still possible, strict rules minimize its likelihood. A confidence vote has occurred only once in the Fifth Republic. Party loyalty, especially on the government side, is the dominant operative principle in the Assembly.

The 321 members of the upper house, the Senate, are chosen by an electoral college, composed mainly of elected local and regional government officials, for terms of nine years each, with one-third selected every three years. The members of the Senate have only an indirect relationship to the populace and continue a long French tradition of overrepresentation of rural interests in this chamber. As does the House of Lords, they offer sober second thoughts on legislation and can delay it. That is especially likely to occur when a left-wing majority controls the Assembly.

In the case of differences between the two houses, the premier can convene a conference committee. If the two houses still disagree, the premier can ask the lower house to rule definitively. Thus the upper house cannot block the government if it is determined to have its way and is supported by a majority of the National Assembly.

The Judiciary

Although France does have a form of judicial review through the Constitutional Council, it is considered a relatively weak form. The president, the head of the National Assembly, and the head of the Senate each appoint one judge triennially to nonrenewable, nine-year terms, with seniority and partisan qualifications dominating legal ones. Only members of the elected political elite, not ordinary individuals, can refer to the Constitutional Council matters concerning draft laws before they go into effect. Although the Constitutional Council is empowered to decide jurisdictional disputes between the executive and the legislature, it has not acted as a brake on executive power. It has, however, acted to widen the civil liberties enjoyed by citizens, since the French constitution does not provide a bill of rights.

More generally, France operates under a code law, inquisitorial system, with emphasis on legislatures' and executives' writing detailed laws that leave little room for judicial interpretation. Judges are seen as civil servants applying the law, rather than as priestly legal interpreters in robes. The judicial system emphasizes the careful gathering of evidence before an indictment is brought and contains an assumption that if there is enough evidence for the case to be brought, then the accused is presumed to be guilty. Although it is not impossible for a defendant to be found not guilty, it is more difficult than in the Anglo-American system of adversarial and common law. The Napoleonic Code is the most famous set of laws developed in France, and many of them still stand.

Decentralization

With the strong conception of a single nationhood (a group of people united by their political belief system) inherited from the French Revolution, France traditionally has been one of the most centralized states in Europe, although that has changed somewhat in recent years. "France, one and indivisible," summarizes the French conception of equality before the law, which allows for little differentiation by locality. There was general fear of allowing provincial or regional governments to have substantial powers, and a centralized state, served by uniform, bureaucratic rules, has been the norm. Famously, a French education minister supposedly once looked at his watch and proclaimed that at this hour, classrooms for the same grade all over France were reciting the same verse of Virgil. Almost all domestic policies are made by the central government and enforced by a responsive civil service, accountable to the center, in *départements* (regional units) throughout France.

Despite being a centralized state, France does have several lower levels of government. There are 22 regions, 96 mainland and four overseas departments, and 36,700 communes. Regional governments and local mayors were intended to benefit from the decentralization reforms undertaken by the Mitterand government in 1982, but the local *préfet,* the agent of the central government, remains, even if his office is supposed to be more responsive to local concerns than previously. The conservative government enacted further decentralization in 2002. Local and regional governments now control almost one-half of public expenditures.

Not all parts of France have been uniformly loyal to the state. Notably, historically Alsace-Lorraine has been the subject of dispute with Germany, and separatist movements in Brittany and Corsica have been active, with the latter being more inclined toward violence. Even though France has a small Basque population along its southern border with Spain, that group has acted mostly as a haven for Basques pursued by Spain, rather than desiring union with them. Corsica has been the problem that has flared regularly in recent years, with the Corsicans thus far rejecting French offers of greater autonomy within the republic.

THE GERMAN CONSTITUTION

Both statehood and democracy came late to Germany. Previously composed of several independent, German-speaking principalities and city-states, it did not achieve unity as a sovereign state until 1871, under the leadership of the Prussian King Wilhelm I and his "Iron Chancellor," Otto von Bismarck. After Germany's defeat in World War I, an attempted communist revolution failed, and a fledgling parliamentary democracy, the Weimar Republic, was established in 1918. It ended with Hitler's rise to power in 1933. After World War II, the question arose of how to fashion democratic institutions in a Germany reduced in size through the loss of some of its territory to neighboring Poland. Because of the cold war, the problem focused on the British, French, and U.S.-controlled sections in West Germany, since the Soviet Union refused to countenance German reunification except on its own terms. The liberal democratic institutions adopted for West Germany were so successful that when the Berlin Wall collapsed in 1989, East Germany, which had lived under fascist or communist dictatorship since 1933, readily became part of the newly reunified Germany. Eastern Germany adopted almost all of the western institutions and policies *tout court*, with only a few transitional exceptions, notably the application of some parts of election law and abortion policy.

The Basic Law of the Federal Republic of Germany, established in 1949, was intended only as a temporary measure, pending reunification of the country. Nevertheless, West Germany became so successful politically and economically that the desire for a full-scale constitutional revision has dissipated, even after the incorporation of East Germany. The constitution embodied in the Basic Law was the result of compromises between traditional German views and those of the occupying powers, principally the United States and Britain. The occupying allies were concerned that the multiparty parliamentary democracy that operated in Germany during the Weimar Republic had not prevented the rise of Hitler and believed that additional safeguards were necessary.

The Political Executive

As in all contemporary democracies, the most powerful institution in Germany is the political executive, led by the head of government, the chancellor, who is the equivalent of a prime minister. There is a separate head of state, the president, but that person is chosen by an electoral college of central and state legislators for a five-year, renewable term (with a two-term limit) and is solely concerned with dignified duties such as formally proposing the installation of a new government, sending and receiving ambassadors, and giving nonpartisan "good government" speeches. The chancellor is the effective chief executive for a renewable term of up to four years before a new election. The dominance of the chancellor in politics and policy has led some observers to refer to Germany as having "chancellor democracy." As in most parliamentary systems, that person is chosen based on the shares of seats the parties hold in the lower house of the legislature, the Bundestag. Germany's particular electoral and party systems (described in chapter 4) make a single-party majority in the legislature unlikely; all of its post–World War II governments but one have been coalitions. The negotiation of an agreement among parties in the Bundestag concerning policy directions and the division of portfolio responsibilities is necessary to form a coalition government. The government normally consists of a chancellor from one of the two larger parties, Christian Democratic Union (CDU) or the Social Democratic Party (SPD), and a cabinet that includes at least one of the smaller parties, usually either the Free Democrats (FDP) or Greens. On one occasion in the late 1960s there was a "grand coalition" of the two largest parties, the CDU and SPD, leaving only the FDP in opposition at the time. After indecisive federal election results in 2005, another grand coalition was formed.

The government normally continues for its full four-year term, until the next election, although two procedures are available for a change of government ahead of that schedule. One is the unique practice of a "constructive vote of no confidence" by the Bundestag. The opposition cannot vote the government out of office unless there is an alternative "government-in-waiting," ready to take power with majority support in the Bundestag within forty-eight hours. No election will be called. The procedure has been invoked successfully only once, in 1982, when the SPD-FDP government led by Helmut Schmidt was replaced with a CDU-FDP government led by Helmut Kohl. This procedure is one of the safeguards against partisan extremism's leading to the fall of governments and their replacement with equally weak governments, considered one of the major problems undermining the stability of the Weimar Republic.

Under the second procedure the government can arrange, under narrow legal procedures, for its own defeat on a confidence motion and then petition the president for an early election. In 2005 Chancellor Gerhard Schröder used this second procedure to call for an election a year ahead of schedule. After negative results for his party, the SDP, in several *länder* (state) elections, and facing a large opposition majority in the upper house of the legislature, the Bundesrat, Schröder wanted the direct test of a renewed mandate for his government's controversial policies to strengthen economic performance by loosening some traditional welfare state guarantees.

Because most governments are coalitions with a dominant party, cabinet positions are divided up accordingly. The leader of any minor party involved usually gets a plum position, often that of foreign minister. Germany, like France, operates on a "specialized" recruitment basis, with ministers not having to come from the legislature, but there is no necessity for elected ministers to resign their seats in parliament. All of the approximately fifteen ministers, including the chancellor, are considered accountable to the Bundestag for their ministry's policies and administrative performance.

The Bureaucracy

The German bureaucracy is famed for its devotion to specialization and efficiency, principles enunciated by the noted early-twentieth-century scholar Max Weber, and to legalism, or statutory rules. Dating back to the days of the kaiser, public officials have been seen as representatives of the state, worthy of respect and obedience. The German bureaucracy also has been responsible for implementing many social welfare programs, such as social insurance for workers as early as 1883; that program has survived the various changes of regime that have occurred subsequently. Today, much of the bureaucracy is located in the states, which are responsible for carrying out many centrally passed programs under "administrative federalism." Like that of France, but unlike that of Britain, the German civil service is highly specialized, with career patterns normally relying on performance within one department. Top-level appointments in the civil service and oversight boards are subject to party influence at all levels of government. There is a system of administrative law to prevent abuse of citizens. Not only is the German bureaucracy relatively decentralized, but it also operates several semipublic agencies, such as those that administer the health insurance system.

The Legislature

Despite the limits on its power to remove a sitting government, the German bicameral legislature is stronger than most. Because of rules governing allocation of seats to minor parties (see next chapter), the Bundestag does not have a fixed number of seats but has instead a minimum, currently 598 seats. As long as the coalition partners in the executive can agree, party loyalty will ensure that there will be few serious challenges to the government on the floor of the house. Although questions may be posed to other ministers, the chancellor is not required to respond to questions. There is considerable cooperation across party lines, however, especially in the specialized committees that scrutinize legislation for its effectiveness, according to the tradition of German legalism, before it reaches the floor of the chamber. German parliamentarians also have more information resources at their disposal to assist them in their jobs than do their counterparts in France and Britain.

The upper house, which represents the *länder,* the Bundesrat, has nearly coequal power with the Bundestag, except on foreign policy. All government legislation has to go to the upper house first, for commentary, before it is introduced in the lower house. The German constitution assigns many powers to the states, as well as making them responsible for carrying out central-level policies. On those matters, some 60 percent of the total, the Bundesrat has equivalent power to the Bundestag; on the rest, including the budget, it has a qualified veto that can only be overridden by an equivalent majority (simple or two-thirds) in the lower house. In addition, the states now are guaranteed a consultative role concerning EU affairs because so many of those decisions have an impact on domestic politics. Differences between the two houses are discussed in a mediation committee. Allocation of seats in the Bundesrat is based on a narrow range of three to six per state, based on population size, for a total of sixty-nine seats. The seats are occupied by ministers from the *länder* or their designated civil service substitutes. State delegations vote as a bloc on instructions from their *länder* cabinets. They represent the political executive of that particular state; thus when the government of a state changes, as happens almost annually because of staggered elections, the partisan representation in the upper house changes as well. This has led to situations in which the upper house is controlled by a party or parties not in charge of the Bundestag, which in turn generates the need for compromise on some issues to pass legislation. Germany has one of the strongest bicameral legislatures outside the United States.

The Judiciary

Germany, like France, operates under a code law, inquisitorial system of justice, with a supreme court as the highest appellate court. Although Germany has long operated under the concept of the *rechtstaat,* or a state based on law, concern by the occupying powers about legal deference to Hitler's rise to power led to the incorporation of judicial review in the Basic Law. There is a separate constitutional court of sixteen members, divided into two benches, which specialize in different cases. One considers cases involving constitutional liberties, and the second is for all other cases. Half of the members are appointed by the Bundestag, and half by the Bundesrat, by a two-thirds vote in each case, for twelve-year, nonrenewable terms. Unlike the U.S. Supreme Court, the constitutional court has no regular or appellate authority. Its sole purpose is to adjudicate cases involving serious constitutional questions, whether raised by another institution (federal executive, state government, one-third of the Bundestag, or lower courts) or by individuals. Also unlike the U.S. Supreme Court, the court can be called on for advisory opinions on the constitutionality of legislation or executive actions before they come into force, as well as concrete judgments on particular cases.

Although judicial review was foreign to German conceptions of law before 1949, it has been successfully adapted. The constitutional court has made major decisions on a wide variety of issues, including control over broadcasting, civil liberties, electoral law, abortion, gay rights, political party funding, use of military forces abroad, religious symbols in classrooms, and German adherence to European Union treaties. Many of these issues have involved the resolution of disputes between the central government and states. In the Nazi era, Hitler used plebiscites and referendums to justify acceptance of his rule. In the postwar era, Germany has avoided these procedures and relied instead on the constitutional court as the final arbiter of controversial policies.

Federalism

Federalism is an old principle in Germany, as one might expect in a country that adheres strongly to local and regional governance. But the federal system established for Germany after World War II did not observe traditional boundaries for two reasons: First, it was originally drawn for West Germany only, since East Germany was in the Soviet communist orbit. Second, the occupying powers thought it desirable to break up some previous federal boundaries to encourage a more democratic political culture. Originally there were eleven states (*länder*), ranging widely in population and size. When East Germany joined the West in 1990, another five states became part of Germany, raising the total to sixteen. In addition to the implementation of federal legislation, the *länder* are particularly responsible for education, broadcasting, culture, policing, transport, and administration of justice functions. All of the *länder* except Bavaria have unicameral parliaments, with electoral systems similar to the central one and often coalition governments, but not necessarily of the same parties as the current central government. The chief executives in the *länder* are called "minister-presidents"; they may also have a seat in the Bundesrat as part of their state's delegation.

Land elections occur at different times during the term of office of a central government and are considered barometers of the current popularity of the central governing coalition. Thus, poor results in *länder* elections may lead to policy or personnel changes by the federal government. In 2005 an unusually long series of bad results even brought about an early federal election.

DEVELOPMENT OF THE CONSTITUTION OF THE EUROPEAN UNION

The European Union currently consists of twenty-five members in a unique international organization with major economic and political purposes. Other intergovernmental organizations rely on the consent of their members, especially the most powerful ones, before they can act. In contrast, the EU has mutually recognized authority over all of its members and can act without unanimous consent, or even without the approval of all of its most powerful members. Its authority is reinforced by the existence of the European Court of Justice, which wields the power of judicial review over EU-related matters. Thus the EU has authority over matters within its agreed competence that in non-EU countries would be viewed as internal, domestic matters. Most of these are economic in focus, but the reach of the EU has become ever-greater. Thus it is included here as a major element of domestic comparative politics within the European context, as well as a major international actor.

A basic problem of Europe has been that there have been multiple sovereign states, often very small ones, based on language, religion, culture, nationalism, conquest, treaties, and dynastic inheritance, within the relatively small land area of the continent. The result has been bitter economic and political rivalries, often leading to armed conflict. In the twentieth century, both World War I and World War II emanated largely from Europe, and the costs for all countries involved became horrific. The idea of a peaceful union of European states is an old one, embraced by various thinkers over the centuries. More often, however, European unity was attempted through the use of force, as the examples of Napoleon and Hitler illustrate. After World War II, however, practical idealists such as Jean Monnet and Robert Schuman seized the opportunity of rebuilding the infrastructure of the continent to push for greater economic and political integration of countries. The movement was aided by the requirement of the United States that European states act in concert to organize implementation of Marshall Plan aid.

What is today the European Union started with a small number of countries and a narrow focus, but it has grown over the past half-century in both dimensions. Its origins were in the European Coal and Steel Community (ECSC), which formed in 1951 and commenced operations in 1952, and which united those particular economic sectors of Germany, France, Italy, and the Benelux countries into a "high authority" for unified, rather than competitive, production. It worked so well that further discussions were held among interested countries about a larger organization, economically focused but also incorporating the ambition of alleviating European state rivalries under a common political authority. The United Kingdom still saw itself as a world power, with the Anglo-American "special relationship" and its worldwide Commonwealth of former colonies in addition to its European interests. Thus it chose not to join the newly formed European Economic Community (EEC) or Common Market. The original six members who signed the Treaty of Rome in 1957 were the same as in the ECSC; the EEC came into being on January 1, 1958.

Over the years both the competences and the membership of the EU have grown. Initially its focus was on lowering internal trade and tariff barriers, while imposing a common external tariff to encourage the common market for products, and developing the Common Agricultural Policy (CAP) to boost self-sufficiency in that sector. With increased economic growth in the six member countries, the EU became attractive to others. At first Charles de Gaulle used France's strong position as one of the two largest members in the new organization to veto new applications, especially the British one. Eventually, however, membership grew to nine, with the accession of the United Kingdom, Ireland, and Denmark in 1973, to ten with the addition of Greece in 1981, to twelve when Spain and Portugal joined in 1986, and to fifteen with the entrance of Sweden, Finland, and Austria in 1995.

The fall of communism in Central and Eastern Europe in 1989 brought requests from countries in those areas to join the European Union. And there were others with long-standing ambitions to join, such as Turkey, and smaller countries that saw the end of the cold war as an opportunity to claim the status of association with a successful organization encompassing almost all of Europe. Besides the economic incentives, some of those countries also sought EU membership as a buttress for developing democratic institutions. Their demands led to a dilemma for the EU. Although an economically underdeveloped East Germany was simply taken into the EU as part of a unified Germany in 1990, it was far more daunting to consider potential new members with average economic status far below that of current members, many of them early in their transition toward democracy.

The EU was founded primarily as an economic organization, and most of its achievements lie in that area, including raising the living standards of its citizens, making Europe more than self-sufficient in food production, lowering trade barriers, generating more trade among the member states, and developing economies of scale that allow European industries to compete with those in other advanced industrial countries, principally the United States. But with the admission of three economically poor southern European countries that had recently emerged from dictatorship—Greece, Spain, and Portugal—the EU had already accepted that reinforcing democracy where it might be shaky was one of its principles as well. This idea was formally promulgated in the Copenhagen criteria of 1993, which set down the democratic principles that applicant countries had to meet to join the EU, including free and fair elections, respect for the law, and ensuring civil liberties, including those of minority groups. Political as well as economic criteria were enforced through aid and scrutiny in the transition periods for new members. In 2004 ten new members were admitted—Poland, Hungary, the Czech Republic, Estonia, Latvia, Lithuania, Malta, Cyprus, Slovenia, and Slovakia. Two other poor, formerly communist countries, Romania, and Bulgaria, are due to join in 2007. Turkey remains an applicant and may be joined by some of the former Yugoslavian and Soviet Union republics, with Croatia being the first.

In addition to the formal members, there are also a few members of the European Economic Area (EEA)—Norway, Iceland, and Liechtenstein—that since 1994 have agreed to abide by EU rules on the single market (see below) to obtain access to the purchasing power of the EU population as well as to EU products. These associate members are not included in other EU policies, including those having to do with agriculture, regional aid, or monetary union. They do not have voting status in EU institutions, and thus they are subject to single-market rules but have no formal voice in deciding those rules. Switzerland has a separate treaty allowing similar access to the EU market.

The EU has operated not on the basis of a formal constitution but instead through a series of treaties among its members. These were considered to have the status of a constitution and were enforced by EU institutions. The treaties began with the founding document, the Treaty of Rome, which established the EU as an "ever-closer union" based on the "pooling of sovereignty" by the member states. The Single European Act of 1986 provided increased authority for the EU to lower trade barriers until there was free movement of goods, services, labor, and capital, with a target date of 1993. The Maastricht Treaty of 1992 changed the name of the organization to the European Union, authorized a common monetary system and currency, and provided standards for the admission of new members. The Amsterdam Treaty of 1997 (ratified in 1998) clarified the authority of various EU institutions. The Nice Treaty of 2000 (ratified in 2001) restructured the institutions of the EU in anticipation of the organization's enlargement and to allow for some variation in the adoption of common policies.

All of the treaties allowed countries to resolve immediate problems within the EU framework, but there was a growing perception that the EU needed an encompassing document. After two years of deliberation and drafting, agreement on an EU constitution was reached in June 2004. The proposed constitution provided for streamlining EU institutions to facilitate decision making in a larger group of twenty-five or more. There was to be more emphasis on "qualified majority voting" in the Council of Ministers, and coequal power of the European Parliament in making decisions for the EU would rise to approximately 95 percent of the relevant policies. By 2014 the number of seats on the European Commission would be reduced to two-thirds the number of EU members, and these would be rotated among the member countries. An individual

EU president would coordinate the European Council for a period of two-and-a-half-years, although one country would still be responsible for convening the Council of Ministers on a six-month, rotating basis. There also would be an EU foreign minister to speak for the organization. Aside from the European Charter of Human Rights, adopted by the Nice summit, becoming binding, there were few changes in EU policy competences. Neither EU "federalists"—those wanting greater centralization of authority in the EU over individual member states—nor their adversaries, the "intergovernmentalists"—those wanting a more decentralized organization with more power residing with the member states—were clear winners in the long process leading to the final document. In fact, one widely read international publication, *The Economist,* said that the outcome of their dispute would await decisions by the European Court of Justice interpreting what the powers of the EU were under the new constitution.

To come into force, the new constitution would have to be ratified by all twenty-five members of the EU by 2006, through methods that each country chose. For many members, joining the EU is a compromise with the historic doctrine of state sovereignty derived from the Treaty of Westphalia in 1648. Referendums to obtain the electorate's consent for such a fundamental constitutional change have become the norm for joining the EU and, in some countries, for ratifying other EU treaties. Ten countries, including France and the United Kingdom, indicated that they would ratify the EU constitution only if their citizens supported it in a referendum. After nine countries, including Germany, representing 49 percent of the population, had ratified the constitution, France and the Netherlands, two traditionally pro-integration countries, rejected it within a week in 2005, throwing the whole process into doubt. Nevertheless, many of the provisions in the constitution could be adopted piecemeal through mutual consent.

Institutions of the European Union

Currently there are six major institutions in the EU: (1) the Council of Ministers; (2) the European Commission; (3) the European Parliament; (4) the European Court of Justice; (5) the European Council; and (6) the European Central Bank. There are dozens of other institutions located across the EU member states. Perhaps the most important is the Committee of Permanent Representatives (COREPER), located in Brussels, which consists of the permanent civil service delegations representing the member states in the EU. A considerable amount of negotiation over possible EU initiatives takes place in COREPER. Nevertheless, the above-named six are usually considered the major institutions, where formal decision making and legitimation of EU policies take place.

These institutions are not as easily divided into executive, legislative, and judicial branches as are the regimes of states. Reflecting the fact that the EU has been an elite-dominated organization with relatively little popular input, there are more executive institutions than legislative or judicial ones. The Council of

Ministers, European Commission, European Council, and European Central Bank all have various executive functions. The Council of Ministers and the European Parliament can also be considered the legislative bodies of the EU. Judicial functions are lodged in only one institution, the European Court of Justice.

The Council of Ministers (also called the Council of Europe) was designed to be the highest organ of EU decision making. Increasingly, however, it has had to share its powers with other institutions, including the European Council, which was not originally envisioned in the Treaty of Rome, and the European Parliament. The latter procedure is termed "co-decision," requiring approval from both bodies. The Council of Ministers consists of political representatives from the government of each member state. Which government ministers appear at the meetings in Brussels, Belgium, the general headquarters of the European Union, depends on what topics are under consideration and where responsibility for those policies lies within the governmental structure of the home country. For instance, a minister from the devolved Scottish government or from a German *land* may represent their country on issues within their jurisdiction. The minister who appears is briefed on the issue at hand by domestic and COREPER civil servants to ensure that the positions they adopt in negotiations are consonant with the desires of the central government in the country they represent. Unlike most international organizations, decisions are not made on the basis of "one state, one vote" or some members' having an absolute veto. Instead, there is weighted voting, with more populous member states having more votes but smaller members being more powerful than their populations would warrant. Increasingly decisions are made through "qualified majority voting" (QMV), a procedure adopted for the first time in the Single European Act (SEA), which requires 232 of 321 (72.3 percent) of the total votes, from a majority of the member states, representing at least 62 percent of the population of the EU, to approve a decision. QMV is the standard decision-making method for most policies within the EU remit, including the core ones: single market, agriculture, cohesion, and monetary union. Unanimous decisions by the Council of Ministers are still required for other policies within the EU remit, such as accession, defense, immigration, foreign policy, and taxation, and that inevitably makes these more difficult, given diverse interests. Thus the Council of Ministers has both legislative and political executive functions.

The European Commission has only executive functions, but they are both political and bureaucratic. The commission, with offices in Brussels, consists of twenty-five commissioners—a president and twenty-four others who head the various departments (directorates-general) responsible for EU policy areas. They are responsible for directing their cabinets of political advisers and the 17,000 "European" civil servants who work in the agencies (the "eurocracy"). The term of a set of commissioners is five years. First, one person is designated by agreement among the member states to be the president of the commission. That person then chooses the remaining members, based on the principle of each member state having one commissioner, and assigns them to particular departments. The designation of the individual commissioners occurs in private, in negotiation with the states from which they come. Nevertheless the commission, from top to bottom, is supposed to represent the interests of the EU as a whole and not the interests of the individual states. The latter are represented through the Council of Ministers and COREPER. Once the nominated commission has been designated, it is presented to the European Parliament for approval. That usually presents little difficulty, but in 2004 the parliament held up approval of the commission. Jose Manuel Durao Barroso, formerly prime minister of Portugal, became president of the European Commission for 2004–2009. The commission is responsible both for agenda setting in the EU, that is, drawing up plans and policies for consideration by the Council of Ministers, the European Council, and the European Parliament, and for implementation of EU decisions. Direct implementation of EU decisions is the responsibility of the member states, through their legislatures changing domestic law as needed and their bureaucracies applying EU law. The European Commission coordinates with member states in implementation of EU policy, monitors their performance, and if necessary, takes cases to the EU Court of Justice to obtain judgments about disputes over compliance.

The third major institution of the EU, the European Council, did not achieve formal legal status until the Single European Act in 1986. It had already been found, however, that regular summit meetings among the chief executives of the member states were necessary to set the broad agenda for development of the EU and to resolve difficult problems. As the final political executive authorities in their respective states, they were able to stamp EU decisions with the highest member state authority, irrespective of the formal treaty provisions. As the institution has evolved, one of the countries assumes the six-month, rotating "presidency" of the EU (as distinguished from the presidency of the European Commission) and is responsible for organizing the agenda of discussion and, if possible, helping to resolve contentious issues. Although previously the meetings were held exclusively in the country holding the presidency, since 2004 they have also met in Brussels. A country's reputation within the EU depends somewhat on the perceived success of its presidency.

The fourth major executive institution of the EU, the European Central Bank, has its headquarters in Frankfurt, Germany, and only came into being shortly before the launch of the common currency, the euro. The Maastricht Treaty of 1992 provided for a European monetary union (EMU) to be established, based on a common currency. This was a big leap forward in terms of EU competence, inasmuch as monetary policy (currency, interest rates) constitutes one-half of macroeconomic policy, along with fiscal policy (raising and spending revenue through the budget). The latter remained within the jurisdiction of individual member states, although annually the Council of Ministers does set broad policy guidelines for the economic policies of its members, as well as for the EU as an organization. However, it was necessary for economic conditions in the then-fifteen countries to be sufficiently similar to justify a common interest rate, a key ingredient for a common currency to work. Thus a stringent "stability and growth" pact was adopted. Countries had to reach set goals with respect to annual budget deficits and total debt as a share of their economies to qualify for inclusion in the monetary system. The United Kingdom, Sweden, and Denmark declined on principle to join the EMU. All of the other members at the time, except Greece, qualified to join, and Greece later joined as well. New members pledge to join the system once transition arrangements are completed.

Although the euro was acceptable for bank financial transactions from 1999, it did not become a full-fledged currency until 2002, when it replaced the separate monetary units of the then-eleven members. Subsequently, the benefits of the euro through the stability and growth pact have come under strain because of resistance by some of the largest members, namely France, Germany, and Italy, to maintaining budgetary discipline during economic downturns. This is a key conflict in terms of the interaction between fiscal and monetary policy, as well as the respective roles of suprastate authority and state sovereignty within the EU.

The European Central Bank operates to set interest rates, with a principal goal of price stability within the EU. Its day-to-day operations are the responsibility of the executive board, composed of a president, a vice president, and four others. They are chosen through consensus of the member states and deliberate over monetary policy during their eight-year, nonrenewable terms. The executive board works within the guidelines of the governing council, which includes the governors of the member states' central banks.

The EU is said to suffer from a "democratic deficit," that is, its institutions lack direct accountability to citizens. The second legislative body, the European Parliament (EP), is the only organization within the EU that is chosen by citizens exclusively for EU purposes. It consists of 732 members of the European Parliament (MEPs), elected every five years (described in the next chapter). Although their number is not based strictly on population, larger states do have more legislators (see Table 3-2 on p. 66). To encourage "Europe-centered" thinking, MEPs do not sit in the chamber by country, but by "party family" or ideology. The parliament chooses a president of the EP to preside. Unlike other EU institutions, the EP does not function in a single location. MEPs have offices and hold committee meetings and some plenary sessions in Brussels, but most plenary sessions are in Strasbourg, France. The administrative offices of the EP are in Luxembourg, not far from Brussels.

EP powers of "co-decision" with the Council of Ministers have increased over the years, especially since the SEA and the Amsterdam Treaty. Currently the EP has the power to reject the European Commission as a body (but not individual commissioners), can dismiss the commission by a two-thirds vote, can reject the budget by a two-thirds vote (but has only limited power to rearrange spending categories within the budget), and must approve all matters regarding economic and trade policy, the core EU functions. It retains strong oversight authority, including questioning commissioners, and has consultative powers on most other matters, such as agriculture. Many EP activities take place through committees, which, along with the need to establish distinct EP influence over decisions, encourages consensus across party lines. Over the years the EP has become more willing to challenge other institutions. Its finding of malfeasance in the commission in 1999 led to the latter's early resignation, and its delay in approving a new commission because of doubts over the human rights views of the proposed justice commissioner in 2004 resulted in a reformulation of the proposed commission. Several times earlier it had rejected the budget. When the EP and the Council of Ministers disagree in the co-decision procedure, there is a conciliation committee to resolve differences. In summary, the EP has exercised its increased power mainly through forcing the European Commission and the Council of Ministers to rethink their positions, rather than creating policies of its own.

The final major, treaty-based institution of the EU, the Court of Justice, in Luxembourg, has wielded significant authority in EU affairs through its capacity to resolve disputed issues by interpreting EU law. Currently there are twenty-five judges, one from each member country, who sit on the court for six-year, renewable terms, staggered in three-year intervals; they are chosen by consensus of the member states. One judge serves as president for a three-year, renewable term. Since 1989 there also has existed a Court of First Instance to hear cases brought by individuals, competition policy cases, and others not considered of major constitutional significance.

Despite the various legal systems employed in the member countries, especially the distinction between common law and code law, it has been possible to develop a body of EU law based on treaties, laws, and regulations to provide jurisdiction over the areas of EU policy competence. Furthermore, despite a disinclination to accept the doctrine of judicial review in many domestic legal systems, EU members have agreed that the EU Court of Justice is the final authority for resolving disputes among member states over the implementation and interpretation of EU law. EU law is unique among international law regimes in that it allows individuals and groups (corporations, unions, nonprofit organizations) as well as states to have standing before the court. Thus member states do not have to give their consent before the European Commission, a citizen, or a group is allowed to bring a case to the court over a country's possible violation of EU law. Unlike most international organizations, the EU has the authority of law, as interpreted by a court of last resort with an accepted power of judicial review, to bind its members to uniform practices.

Constitutional Prospects for the European Union

Overall the EU has experienced remarkable growth of its constitutional status and institutions. That is especially true if one considers the history of Europe and the nature of the Westphalian system of state sovereignty, still the foundation of international politics. Remarkably, EU members, still jealous of their state sovereignty in various ways, have been willing to embark on common programs, especially in the areas of economic production, trade, and monetary matters, that involve a considerable degree of cooperation among often-diverging interests. Furthermore, the members have agreed that EU law supersedes that of the member states, even to the point of subjecting their policies to judicial review by the European Court of Justice. Agreed, specific goals requiring joint action have often been able to overcome reservations. The fact that the EU is constantly changing, with several projects on the agenda, has probably aided the spirit of cooperation in that states see benefits for themselves in some projects, even if they are hesitant about participation in others.

With or without the EU constitution, an organization of at least twenty-five members is a more difficult enterprise to manage than a smaller one. Nevertheless, the EU already accounts for nearly half of the legislation in the member countries, as they have to adapt their own laws to EU decisions. The EU has had a major constitutional impact in its member countries. It is a factor not only of international policy, but also of domestic policy in Europe.

CONCLUSION

There have been three trends in the development of institutions in these four regimes since World War II. First, there has been more "constitutionalization" of institutional principles in the form of written expressions of fundamental law, court cases, and a stronger power of judicial review. It has been uneven across countries, but even those that resist such movement, especially the United Kingdom, have been part of the process. Second, there has been a trend toward greater authority for international bodies, specifically the EU. For instance, some analysts argue that the most significant constitutional change in the United Kingdom has come through three measures—joining the European Community (1972), approving the Single European Act (1986), and signing the Maastricht Treaty (1992). Third, there has been a trend toward decentralization within the states. In Germany it occurred through the strong federal provisions in the Basic Law; in France through the decentralization reforms of the Socialist and Gaullist governments; and in the United Kingdom through the devolution policies of the Labour government. In all three countries there is now what one might call "de facto decentralization," with powers granted to regional and local governments, however uneven (United Kingdom) and limited (France). Even the EU has endorsed the principle of "subsidiarity"—that authority over policy should be wielded at the lowest possible level.

On the surface it might seem that authority flowing upward from sovereign states toward the EU and downward toward regional and local government would be contradictory, but in practice, the two tendencies have reinforced each other. The EU has adopted regional aid policies, based on states' willingness to match them and has recognized substate jurisdictions as legitimate participants within EU councils through a Committee of the Regions and other bodies. In response, substate actors have not only lobbied individually for their interests and those of their respective countries within the EU, but also developed transborder organizations and communications to advance their mutual concerns. In some policies, cooperation between the EU and substate jurisdictions has eroded the authority of the central governments of the states. In Europe, state sovereignty has been voluntarily compromised although not ended.

Despite different institutional configurations and interests, overall the institutions of Europe have become remarkably complementary over the past half-century, especially when one considers the turmoil that preceded this period. While retaining their cultural and institutional differences, the three major states of Germany, France, and even the United Kingdom have worked together for mutual benefit not only through the EU but also through other regional and international organizations. Although some may yearn for greater influence for individual states on the world stage, the overall verdict must be that for Europe as a whole, especially the citizens of these countries, the current arrangements largely have been beneficial. But domestic and international tensions remain and will determine what changes may occur. The political dynamics that influence these institutions in operation are the subject of the next chapter.

Suggestions for Additional Reading

Books

Bale, Tim. *European Politics: A Comparative Introduction.* New York: Palgrave, 2005.

Bulmer, Simon, and Christian Lequesne, eds. *The Member States of the European Union.* New York: Oxford University Press, 2005.

Cole, Alistair, Jonah Levy, and Patrick Le Gales, eds. *Developments in French Politics 3.* New York: Palgrave, 2005.

Conradt, David. *The German Polity.* 7th ed. New York: Longman, 2000.

Dinan, Desmond. *Ever Closer Union.* 3rd ed. New York: Palgrave, 2005.

Gallagher, Michael, Michael Laver, and Peter Mair. 2005. *Representative Government in Modern Europe.* 4th ed. New York: McGraw Hill, 2005.

Hix, Simon. *The Political System of the European Union.* 2nd ed. New York: Palgrave, 2005.

Hooghe, Lisbet, and Gary Marks. *Multilevel Governance and European Integration.* Lanham, Md.: Rowman and Littlefield, 2001.

Lijphart, Arend. *Patterns of Democracy: Government Forms and Performance in Thirty-Six Countries.* New Haven: Yale University Press, 1999.

Norton, Philip. *The British Polity.* 4th ed. New York: Longman, 2000.

Piper, J. Richard. *The Major Nation-States in the European Union.* New York: Pearson/Longman, 2005.

Rosamond, Ben. *Theories of European Integration.* New York: Palgrave, 2000.

Rose, Richard. *What Is Europe?* New York: Longman, 1997.

van Oudenaren, John. *Uniting Europe: European Integration and the Post-Cold War World.* 2nd ed. Lanham, Md.: Rowman and Littlefield, 2004.

Zeff, Eleanor E., and Ellen B. Pirro, eds. *The European Union and the Member States.* 2nd ed. Boulder: Lynne Rienner, 2006.

Web Sites

British Broadcasting Corporation, www.bbc.com
British Politics Group, www.uc.edu/bpg
CIA World Factbook, www.cia.gov/cia/publications/factbook
The Economist, www.economist.com
Election Process Information Collection, www.epicproject.org
European Union Studies Association, www.eustudies.org
Freedom House, www.freedomhouse.org
German Information Center, www.germany-info.org
German News, www.germnews.de/dn/about
Information on France, www.france.com
International Institute for Democracy and Electoral Assistance, www.idea.int
The Inter-Parliamentary Union, www.ipu.org
Richard Kimber's Political Science Resources, www.psr.keele.ac.uk
World Press Review, www.worldpress.org

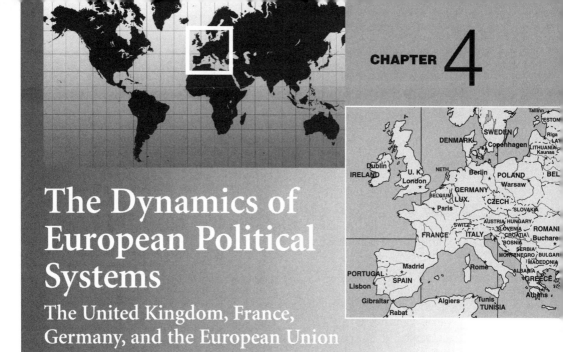

CHAPTER 4

The Dynamics of European Political Systems

The United Kingdom, France, Germany, and the European Union

onstitutions and government institutions provide the framework of a political system; other actors provide active elements by invigorating the legal blueprints. This chapter describes dynamic elements of the four political systems considered—the United Kingdom, France, Germany, and the European Union. We divide these elements as follows: the socioeconomic setting, political culture, civil society, interest groups, media, political parties and the party system, the electoral system and elections, political recruitment and leadership, and policy dynamics. These categories comprise the general relationships among institutions and actors that create policy in a particular regime. We will discuss broad, comparative politics themes, with applications to each of the four regimes.

THE SOCIOECONOMIC SETTING

The socioeconomic setting of countries presents both opportunities and constraints with respect to what they are able to achieve politically. Some of the opportunities and constraints are based on numbers of people and geography, as outlined in the previous chapter, including natural harbors, arable land, mineral deposits, the relative importance of protecting one's boundaries through a land force (army) and/or a maritime force (navy), and relative economic reliance on particular sectors, domestic consumption, and international trade. Although these attributes are still important, in the modern world a state's politics is also dependent on "human capital," including such qualities as gender stratification, ethnic composition, education, religion, and social class. These factors in turn influence the political culture, the set of values, attitudes, and beliefs about politics operating within a particular jurisdiction that conditions political behavior at both mass and elite levels. The socioeconomic environment of a jurisdiction also is the basis for civil society and for the formation of interest groups that pursue particular political goals. The image that a mass democratic society has of itself and its politics depends more than ever on the role of the media, including television, radio, the Internet, and periodical publications, especially newspapers.

The countries under discussion here share several similarities. They are all rich, highly industrialized, market-based economies, although the degree of government intervention in the economy differs, even in an age of global neoliberalism and the influence of the Single European Act of the EU. The individual countries have all experienced the movement from a more industrialized toward a more service-based economy, what some call "postindustrialism." Agriculture is efficient, constitutes only a small share of the economy, and occupies only a small share of the population in France, Germany, and the United Kingdom, but it remains politically important. The Common Agricultural Policy (CAP) of subsidies to farmers absorbs nearly half of the EU budget. When one adds aid to economically underdeveloped areas, called, "regional policy" (in whatever country they may be), the two together account for 75 percent of the EU budget. France, with the largest number of agricultural workers among the EU-15, is the major proponent of the CAP.

The economic situation is different for the newer members of the EU, as well as eastern Germany. As noted in chapter 3, the new members, including potentially Bulgaria and Romania, have substantially different economic profiles than the older members. In addition to the wide average differences in per capita GDP, 25 percent of the workforces of the new members are agricultural workers, versus 4 percent of the EU-15. To join the EU, some countries have had to eliminate remnants of large-scale government economic interventions left over from their time under communism. After the demise of that system, several suffered serious deindustrialization, as their subsidized sectors were unable to compete in the international marketplace. Thus the new members of the EU are looking to the organization to help them achieve better economic conditions as well as stabilize their democratic political institutions, even though they will only receive full CAP payments after a decade in the organization. Based on the experience of previous EU "laggards" such as Ireland, Greece, Spain, and Portugal, closing the economic gap may take considerable time and also may be uneven within the countries.

Europe as a whole, as well as the three countries we specifically examine, has a history of ethnic diversity. Until the past half-century, most of the diversity came from historical conquest and the settlement of boundary disputes. More recently it has developed through large-scale immigration from foreign countries, first from the former colonial empires abroad and subsequently from countries in Central and Eastern Europe and the Middle East suffering turmoil.

Traditionally European countries, including the United Kingdom, France, and Germany, were ruled by hereditary monarchies interrelated through marriage. Even as late as World War I, George V of Britain and Kaiser Wilhelm II of Germany were first cousins. The boundaries of European countries were decided through dynastic inheritance, military conflict, and diplomatic negotiation, with little reference to the social characteristics of the population. Often ruler and subjects spoke different languages, and there was not necessarily even a common tongue among the population. Initially after the Protestant Reformation, rulers on both sides of the divide forced religious unity on their populations; eventually greater tolerance became the norm. The outburst of the American and French revolutions not only began the end of absolutist monarchies but also ushered in the rise of modern nationalism and the concept of citizens with individual liberties who could hold their rulers responsible for governance. As industrialization and urbanization continued, a common language became prevalent in many countries, although the mismatch of boundaries and peoples (or states and nations) continued, leading to periodic political conflict.

There have been shifting socioeconomic diversities across Europe over the centuries. The major cleavages, or politically important social divisions within the population, endure in European countries today, even if in weakened form. They are (1) the center-periphery cleavage; (2) the state-church cleavage; (3) the agricultural-industrial cleavage; and (4) the owner-worker cleavage. At various times, these cleavages have become so divisive that they threatened the continuation of regimes and even states. Even in less-intense form, they provide the basis for much of political debate and partisan choice in these countries.

The "center-periphery cleavage" refers to the role of the central state apparatus in the capital versus the outlying areas. The latter were often less loyal to the center, spoke different languages, practiced different religions, and may have had more affinity for their ethnic kin across the formal boundaries of the state than toward the central government. What are called "nationalist," "separatist," or "irredentist" (border) problems continue in some of these areas today, such as Northern Ireland, Scotland, Wales, Brittany, Corsica, and the Basque country. Germany's boundaries have shifted more frequently than those of the other two states. There continue to be German speakers in other states in Central and Eastern Europe and that was a rationale for the Third Reich's incursions into the areas. Under the traditional German citizenship doctrine of *jus sanguinis*, which means citizenship through blood rather than territory of birth, the Federal Republic preferred to welcome German speakers back to the homeland, even going as far as paying ransoms to communist states. Thus far the EU has been able to avoid becoming entangled in nationalist disputes, although some of those groups look to the EU as a counterweight to their central governments.

The second cleavage refers to the respective roles of the state and church in society and politics. Germany was home to the Protestant Reformation, although not all German princes embraced it at the time and the country was not yet united. In England and Wales, Anglicanism became the state church through the decision of King Henry VIII to leave the Church of Rome. Scotland, then an independent kingdom, eventually became Presbyterian. Once the Protestant Reformation was successfully established, rulers simply wedded their choice of religion to their state. What room could be allowed for religious dissidents? How could the realms of state and church be separated, even when there was a church officially sponsored by the state? At times, as noted above, this division overlapped with the center-periphery one, making its resolution even more difficult. Religious wars were connected to the aspirations of certain individuals to the throne, especially in Britain. Nevertheless, over time there developed greater religious tolerance, in terms both of allowing religious dissidents to practice their beliefs and of allowing them civil rights within the state. With industrialization and urbanization, religion became less central to Europeans' lives, even if established churches were maintained, religious symbolism continued, and outposts of religious devotion persisted. The French Revolution established the principle of separation of church and state although, as noted below, even in that country there has been a continuing problem of the proper provinces of state and church in education. Even though Britain and Germany retained their state churches—Anglicanism in England and Lutheranism and Catholicism in Germany by province (until 1918)—which gives those religions various advantages, there is now state tolerance for other religious practices.

Today there are only a few remnants of religious conflict in Europe. They mainly involve Islam, a religion of recent immigrants, rather than the Christianity and Judaism long practiced in Europe. Anti-Semitism has not disappeared, however. The conflict in Northern Ireland, despite being identified as one between groups of Protestants and Catholics, is actually more an issue of nationalism (or center-periphery), an unresolved border issue.

The third cleavage is between a socioeconomic structure dominated by agriculture and one dependent on industrialization. As the latter took hold in the seventeenth and eighteenth centuries, the economic role of the hereditary aristocracy (large landowners) declined. The growth of factories led to a huge population shift to cities, different forms of social organization, and the extension of individual rights to social mobility. A host of political reforms followed. Although agrarian, including fishing, sectors of the economy and society are now small, they are well organized. As a critical resource component of society, their political power now often exceeds their numerical socioeconomic significance. Since the EU has taken over agricultural policy for all three countries here considered, debate has shifted to that forum. The CAP has proved to be one of the most difficult policies to change.

The fourth cleavage is the one that has dominated European politics through much of the past century, the owner-worker cleavage. As capitalist manufacturing came to be the dominant form of economic production in Europe, workers began to demand more social as well as political rights. Initially they were handicapped by having no voting (suffrage) rights and no social benefits from either the companies for which they worked or from the state. With long hours, child labor, and harmful working conditions the norm; with no sickness, injury, pension, or unemployment benefits; and subject to the whims of employers and supervisors, the lot of workers was a miserable one. In addition, men were often the sole breadwinners for their families, with women in a supportive role at home, in contrast to agrarian life, in which women were more directly engaged in economic production.

With economic and political power arrayed against them, many despaired of ever improving such conditions. The most systematic critique was delivered by the radical journalist and philosopher Karl Marx (1818–1883), who lived much of his life in the United Kingdom, the leading country of the industrial revolution in the nineteenth century. In such works as *The Communist Manifesto* (1848), Marx argued that capitalist industrialization was a necessary element in economic development because it released the abundance that existed in the world. No longer was life inevitably "poor, nasty, brutish, and short," in the classic words of Thomas Hobbes. Instead the problem was how to allocate the newly emerging wealth. Marx was a material determinist who saw economic power leading directly to political power. The capitalists, like other ruling groups before them, had no interest in sharing power or ameliorating the conditions of the workers.

According to Marx, change would only occur when the increasing misery of the workers (the proletariat) forced them to achieve sufficient class consciousness to organize an armed revolt against the now dominant, middle-class factory owners (the bourgeoisie). That uprising would result in a permanent, more equitable redistribution of economic, social, and political power.

The doctrine of Marxist communism had limited appeal until the early twentieth century, when Vladimir Lenin, in Russia, transformed it into an activist, elitist, power-seeking doctrine through his emphasis on the leadership of the workers by the Communist Party. Meanwhile, other groups and thinkers produced various proposals for social, economic, and political reform to improve the situation of the growing working class, whether by peaceful or violent means. Trade unions formed to advance and protect workers' rights. The question of the means by which change in the interest of workers and the broader population was to be achieved divided reform movements in Europe and eventually led to the formation of separate Communist (revolutionary) and Socialist (reformist through parliament) Parties. The issue of class had assumed predominant importance in the domestic politics of European countries. In Germany, Chancellor Bismarck tried to prevent insurrection by granting social benefits to the working class in 1883, but few other countries followed. By the turn of the twentieth century, some European countries started extending voting rights to the working class.

This process was interrupted by the dislocations of World War I. The first state based on Marxist-Leninist doctrine, the Soviet Union (formerly Russia) was established, and there were attempts to seize power in other European countries, notably Germany. Despite alarm over the rise of a Marxist regime in one of the major states of Europe, between the wars socialism made more political gains than communism, taking advantage of the newly enfranchised working class in several countries to become the major party on the left in most democracies. Fascism, which enshrined hypernationalism based on race rather than class as its organizing principle, also made greater political inroads than did communism and eventually precipitated World War II through its military aggression. After the war, communism became dominant in countries of Central and Eastern Europe through its imposition by the (Soviet) Red Army, and it remained so until 1989.

The economic and military successes of the Soviet Union, plus its ability to hide its problems, made the communist alternative attractive to certain groups in Western Europe as well, especially in France and a few other countries. Nevertheless, "gradualist socialism" became the major orientation of the left, although that evolution occurred more slowly in France than in Britain or Germany. More generally, what was called "social democracy," collective redistribution of economic proceeds through the state, sometimes through public ownership (nationalization) of major economic sectors and always through the growth of social welfare programs, became a generally shared ideology spanning the center-left to center-right in the postwar period. In most European countries, unlike the United States, collective social hierarchies and a strong governing power had always existed, even if that power acted only in a limited area. Few people considered a "state of nature," allowing rampant individualism, realistic. Under social democracy, instead of only a few elites' enjoying access to state power, the general population was to share in the material benefits of the state.

Postwar social democracy, especially in the form of the welfare state, grew until the Arab oil embargo of 1973 dealt Western countries their first major economic setback since World War II. That setback led to the questioning of the principles of Keynesian economics that were the underpinning of social democracy. Before World War II, British economist John Maynard Keynes had developed ideas that relied on countercyclical government fiscal policies to combat economic downturns. By putting money into the hands of the less-wealthy, the government could increase their purchasing power, and that would boost economic recovery. According to Keynesianism, however, the solutions to inflation and deflation involved opposite government policies: budget surpluses in the first instance and budget deficits in the second. During the oil crisis, however, symptoms of both inflation (high prices) and deflation (high unemployment) occurred simultaneously ("stagflation"). Thus the world market seemed immune to the country-specific interventions of Keynesians attempting to fine-tune domestic economies. This has led to the rise, however unevenly, of neoliberal principles of allowing more freedom and flexibility for world markets (globalization) without government fiscal interventions.

The extension of mass suffrage to the working class in Europe led to the rise of class politics, emphasizing redistribution of wealth and the role of the state as both an economic engine and a safety net for the poor. In all countries, one or more parties on the left claimed to represent the workers and challenged the previous dominance of middle-class parties. Leftist parties relied on support from the large class of manual workers and their families, while rightist parties tried to mobilize voters based on patriotic, nationalist themes and macroeconomic governance skills.

More recently it has been argued that increased prosperity has brought a decline of class politics, with those issues figuring less prominently in political debate. Working-class parties such as the German Social Democrats, the British Labour Party, and the French Socialists especially, have moderated their appeals to attract middle-class voters rather than relying solely on mobilization of their working-class base. There still are substantial class differences in voting behavior, however, to which we will return.

One influential theory about a possible new cleavage is "postmaterialism." According to that view, the unprecedented long-term economic growth of the post–World War II period, up until 1973, led to a more general sense of collective domestic security through the socialization of generations born in those years. They were less concerned about the material issues that were at the root of class politics and more concerned with ideals such as protection of the environment, civil liberties, and equality for minority groups (women, ethnic minorities, homosexuals). The first sign of those concerns was the "social movement" politics of the 1960s, in which mass demonstrations and other unconventional methods of political participation were organized in pursuit of these goals. In some instances this change eventually led to the rise of significant new parties, such as the Greens in Germany; in other countries the existing parties have managed to address the new concerns.

The postmaterialism thesis is controversial, since established parties and material concerns still dominate the policy agenda in most countries. There is, however, increasing attention to the environmental implications of the drive for continued economic growth through industrial means, as seen in concerns over nuclear power and support for the Kyoto Treaty. Some argue that the postmaterialist thesis insufficiently recognizes right-wing issues, such as concern over immigration, that have arisen in all three countries in recent years.

POLITICAL CULTURE

Each of these regimes has a political culture that has been characterized in various ways. "Political culture" means the dominant set of attitudes, beliefs, and values that obtain among the population. Citizens of a country learn a political culture through the process of political socialization, that is, the direct and indirect influence of those around them, including family, school, churches, media, government, political parties, and peer groups. Within one political culture there exist various subcultures that may not agree completely with all tenets of the overall political culture. Common divisions within the political cultures of these regimes have been discussed above. One can also divide political cultures into elite and mass components, which may differ to some degree. The belief systems of the population of a country undergird its constitution and political practices. No less an authority than James Madison, in *The Federalist Papers,* contended that constitutions are only parchment unless people believe in them. However, there are several different ways of characterizing the political cultures of individual countries, making comparisons difficult.

What elements constitute a democratic political culture? Except in Northern Ireland, the United Kingdom has been characterized as a pragmatic and civic political culture based on political compromises that developed slowly over time, with a balance of elite direction and mass participation. The lack of a single, written constitution, the reliance on custom and convention, and the evolutionary change of political institutions, including maintenance of some "feudal hangovers" such as the monarchy and the House of Lords, have been cited as examples of how this political culture has operated.

On the other hand, the political culture of France is often characterized as fragmented, with the two conflicting constitutional traditions outlined in the previous chapter. One is concerned with countrywide unity through a strong executive; the second emphasizes representation of the diverse interests of groups through the legislature. Those fundamentally different views of what constitutes a fully legitimate political order may help explain the problems France has had over the years in maintaining a stable regime. Nevertheless, the long tenure of the Fifth Republic suggests that the conflict between the two constitutional traditions now may have been successfully overcome.

After World War II German political culture needed to be remade into a democracy from its authoritarian, hierarchical roots, with only the unsuccessful period of the Weimar Republic, between the two world wars, as a previous democratic experience. For a long time the prospects for Germany were considered fragile as citizens seemed more attached to the new regime for its economic accomplishments than its democratic principles. Subsequently, however, German democracy has proved to be stable. Nevertheless, the long-term problems of incorporating East Germany into the country, after its long experience under fascism and communism, have demonstrated some serious regional rifts in the political culture. Much of the eastern population resents its treatment by "Wessies," and a substantial portion even long for a return to communist-era economic and social security.

The political culture of the European Union is difficult to characterize. It operates on multiple levels, with sovereign states as its members, and these countries themselves contain different political cultures, some only recently democratized. Many of the institutions and practices of the EU, especially those aimed at affecting citizens directly, constitute an attempt to build a political culture of the EU distinct from those of individual countries and not entirely dependent on them. Perhaps it might best be characterized as one of "consensus," in that it recognizes the many existing differences in its members but encourages following designated political leaders representing the interests of the various groups in negotiating binding decisions. Policies in the EU formally require supermajorities, or even unanimity, rather than simple majorities, another indicator of a political culture of consensus, similar to systems found within some member states, especially Belgium and the Netherlands.

Recently there has been concern about the decline of social and political participation in European countries, as evidenced by low voting turnout, among other things. The decline has helped to popularize "social capital" theories of political culture, which hold that a high degree of voluntary social trust is necessary for a democratic polity to function effectively. People who work in groups for a common cause develop interpersonal skills, tolerance for others' views, and trust, which helps not only the group but also the political culture. These are all important skills for the give-and-take of a democratic political system. One of the problems of modern society is that it is isolating and atomistic, with fewer people joining purposeful social groups such as churches, bowling leagues, scouts, and other organizations.

Loyalty to one's state—what most observers refer to as "nationalism," although it is more accurately called "patriotism"—continues to be an important element of political culture, even in those states that are members of the EU. Public opinion surveys show that people continue to be most loyal to their own country and secondarily loyal to the EU. But there is substantial loyalty, at least passively, to the EU as well, which suggests that the organization has made inroads in the popular mind as well as among the political elite. Younger, better-educated, more-informed, and higher-social-class groups demonstrate higher support levels for the EU. Although support for the EU is generally greater among the populations of the two "core" EU members, Germany and France, than in the United Kingdom, the differences are often not vast. More disturbing for advocates of greater European integration is that general support for the project has declined since the mid-1990s.

CIVIL SOCIETY AND SOCIAL MOVEMENTS

The politically interested but largely inactive part of a polity is called "civil society," based on private, voluntary collective arrangements among individuals and groups and not under the direct control of the state. While normally quiescent, at times this element becomes aroused, motivated, and mobilized to action. That is what is called a "social movement," a surge of mass opinion with a floating membership that pursues particular political issues, perhaps over an extended period, often through unconventional methods such as demonstrations. A social movement usually weakens over time through a combination of exhaustion, satisfaction of its demands, lack of stable organization, and conflicting interests. Social movement politics is often cited as being of increased importance since the 1960s in seeking peace, women's rights, and ethnic and racial minority rights and promoting environmentalism. However, such movements existed earlier in more sporadic form, as the movements for woman suffrage and temperance and against slavery indicate.

Civil society in Britain, France, and Germany includes a large population of identifiable ethnic minorities. Europeans live in densely populated areas, usually close to other countries and peoples with differing languages, cultures, ethnicities, and religions, and that has sometimes led to political problems, even among long-settled groups. Most notoriously, anti-Semitism became genocidal under Hitler during World War II. Gypsies (the Roma) also have suffered from discrimination. Some ethnonationalist groups desire a large amount of autonomy, or even complete separation, from the other occupants of the country in which they live. Even so, for the most part territorial groups have managed to live peacefully and settle their mutual grievances without violence in European democracies.

Recent immigrants to Europe from developing countries and from Eastern Europe, however, have faced hostility, which in some cases has increased rather than abated. Most of these people were poor, often of different religions and ethnicity, had few desired economic skills, and lacked the opportunity to gain citizenship readily in their new countries. Traditionally Britain, France, and Germany have been countries of emigration, not immigration: Their citizens went elsewhere in support of empire, trade, military security, and religious and humanitarian projects, and few people came from other countries to reside permanently.

That changed after World War II. With growing prosperity, Europe experienced a labor shortage. Each European country looked to nearby states and to its own colonies for unskilled labor to fill manual jobs, while the native population took the better-paying ones. In France that meant large-scale immigration from Africa, especially populous North Africa. In Germany it meant immigration from southern Italy, Yugoslavia, and Turkey. In the United Kingdom it meant immigration from India, Pakistan, and the West Indies. Only in Britain was it easy for immigrants to obtain citizenship; elsewhere they were "guest workers" (*gastarbeiter*), considered temporary migrants, who were expected to leave the country after their period of work ended. But immigrant repatriation policies were difficult to enforce, especially on a large scale. Even when economic growth became more erratic after 1973, many of these workers and their families, now including descendants born in Europe, remained. Thus large sections of major cities in all three countries became immigrant areas occupied by first-generation migrants and their descendants. Today the estimated share of the population that is foreign born is 8 percent in the United Kingdom, 10 percent in France, and probably slightly more in Germany.

Even though the relative proportion of immigrants and their descendants was small, residential segregation was common, and social conflicts with nearby white citizens ensued. Right-wing populist parties drew their support disproportionately from working-class whites living near immigrants. In France the National Front party, with anti-immigrant and anti-EU positions, has secured a continuous 15 percent of the vote in legislative elections over the past twenty years. The fall of communism in 1989 also led to a large influx of new immigrants; later there were political refugees from southern Europe and the Middle

East, which led Germany to change its liberal asylum laws (although it also lib-eralized somewhat its laws on citizenship acquisition). In Britain, an influx of political asylum seekers and illegal immigrants in recent years has generated continuing political controversy that resulted in the Labour government's enacting further restrictions.

The terrorist attacks of 9/11 exacerbated these problems in that they called attention to the differences between the Muslim immigrants in Europe and other citizens. Not only did several of the terrorists have German connections, but others captured by the United States in the war in Afghanistan were resi-dents, and sometimes citizens, of European countries. In France, a new law banned the wearing of religious symbols in schools. Although it also covered Christian crucifixes and Jewish skullcaps, the main target was headscarves worn by Muslim women. Suspicion has increased on both sides, and integration of immigrants into these countries remains difficult. This was demonstrated by the London subway bombings of July 2005, carried out by British-born Muslims, and the riots in immigrant areas of France in fall 2005. The native-born populations, overwhelmingly white and Christian influenced, want limits on the number of immigrants allowed, even as their own birthrates dwindle and the population ages. With longer life spans, maintaining welfare state pro-grams, especially health care and pensions, in an increasingly aged population will be an enormous challenge for future governments.

Women's groups are another major element of civil society. The struggle for woman suffrage was a long one, culminating in voting rights for women in Germany in 1918, in France in 1944, and in the United Kingdom in two stages, 1918 and 1928. Another movement for women's equality began in the 1950s, as more women entered the paid workforce. That movement became a significant force in the 1960s. Although the EU has enforced gender equality in the work-force, even to the extent of forcing Britain to change its pension laws because they were judged to be discriminatory, there are still variations in women's sta-tus from country to country. Women are less represented in the workforce in Germany than in France or the United Kingdom. On issues other than those that clearly are matters of economic equality, such as equal pay for equal work, pensions, and conditions of work, practices differ from country to country, for example, what constitutes unfair hiring practices or sexual harassment. Except in the choice of political candidates, affirmative action is not pursued as a gen-eral policy in any of the countries or in the EU. Increasing numbers of women have reached the top levels of the legislature and executive.

INTEREST GROUPS

Interest groups can be defined as sections of public opinion organized to pur-sue their few common interests, in contrast to political parties, which have to take stands on many issues for electoral purposes even if the party is small. Another distinction from parties is that interest groups normally do not run candidates under the group label, although in multiparty countries this difference may be less distinct. Interest groups can be divided into those pursuing material interests for the economic welfare of their individual members and those espousing ideal interests, values that the members want their government to embrace even if it would not make their members economically better off. Examples of the latter would be groups concerned about abortion, capital punishment, or in the United Kingdom, hunting foxes with hounds.

Interest groups sometimes work in concert with social movements but are more institutionalized in form, usually maintaining formal lobbying organizations in the capital of the country. Some interest groups develop out of social movements; others emerge to defend vested interests within a country. Major interest groups in these four jurisdictions include business and commercial groups, trade unions, agricultural organizations, religious groups, and other levels of government.

There are two major ways of characterizing the interest group configuration within a democracy. The first is called "pluralism," meaning that there are many (plural) groups competing for the attention of the authorities, with no group maintaining a consistent, structurally powerful, advantageous position across a range of issues, governments, and time.

The second is called "corporatism" (also "neocorporatism" or "democratic corporatism"), a more elitist view of interest group influence. Under corporatism a few privileged interest groups have major, continuing influence on the government. The issues are almost entirely socioeconomic and depend on the interest groups involved to speak for their section of society in singular, hierarchical fashion. In most European countries these groups are likely to consist of one organization representing business interests and one representing trade unions. This is also sometimes referred to as "social partnership" and "tripartism" in recognition of the three bargaining partners—government, business, and labor. In some countries agriculture may be a participant if it is an established actor that governments regularly consult on major decisions.

Corporatism is thought to be particularly characteristic of smaller regimes in which cooperation from each sector is critical to the economy and even the national security of the country. Pluralism is more likely to occur in larger countries, where there are more groups and even economic interests are difficult to organize in a united and hierarchical manner. In pluralist systems not only businesses but also unions compete for members, for recognition by government, and for their more narrowly defined interests. Nonetheless, Germany is often cited as a prime example of a corporatist interest group structure. France and the United Kingdom are more pluralist, with no long-term, privileged consultative status for any interest group with governments of all political stripes.

Within Europe all interest group structures have become oriented toward multiple levels of government. On some issues, groups may lobby their member-state governments as well as the EU, since countries, through the Council of Ministers, have major power within the EU. The existence of the EU has allowed the rise of "venue shopping" by interest groups among multiple points of access to governing institutions. That is certainly the case for agriculture, over which the EU has the major authority. Subsidies under the Common Agricultural Policy remain high because agrarian states, led by France, defend them. Demonstrations by farmers and their supporters in France are designed to show their government, as well as those of other EU members, that they care intensely about this issue.

It is difficult to characterize the interest group structure of the European Union. Because the political culture of the EU is largely consensual, one would expect the interest group structure to be more corporatist. But given the diversity of groups, across countries, that are engaged in lobbying EU institutions, through representatives in Brussels as well as venue shopping, it probably more closely resembles pluralism. As groups learn to cooperate across country boundaries for their sectional rather than country interests, the interest group structure could move toward corporatism, but for the present it remains relatively fragmented.

Businesses in these countries tend, in general, toward cooperation with, rather than resistance toward, the state. Although capitalist in orientation and often global in operation, they are usually not as aggressively "free market" as those in the United States, and the government often relies on them to help enforce legal regulations rather than using bureaucratic overseers and the courts. Also, the tradition of state intervention—not just through macroeconomic fiscal and monetary policy but also in particular sectors through subsidies—has made businesses amenable to working with the state, more so in corporatist systems but also somewhat in pluralist ones.

Trade unions are most powerful in Germany, have been reduced in power in the United Kingdom, and have had a fragmented history in France. The approximate percentages of unionized workers are as follows: Germany, 30 percent; United Kingdom, 29 percent; and France, 9 percent. In each country, major trade unions have had close links to leftist parties—the SPD in Germany, Labour in the United Kingdom, and the Communists in France. In Germany corporatist arrangements have led to labor peace, but the budget burdens of the social wage have increased in a slow-growth economy in recent years. Through the practice of codetermination, German workers even are entitled to seats on the governing boards of private businesses. In France, unions traditionally have not had strong inside connections to the government because of their ties to the Communist Party but instead have had to rely on "street politics"—strikes and demonstrations—as political expression. This is often a sign of weakness. Nevertheless, if enough public sympathy can be generated, as in the 1990s demonstrations against government budget cuts for social spending, it can be effective.

In the United Kingdom, trade unions long had a strong role in the internal politics of the Labour Party, although their increasing defiance of Labour governments in the 1960s and 1970s damaged the party's electoral prospects. Unlike those in Germany, trade unions in Britain were more fragmented in their organization and operation. One of the demonstrable policy impacts of the long Conservative rule in Britain, 1979–1997, was the passage of laws making it more difficult for unions to organize, achieve recognition, and take strike action through the decisions of their leaders alone. That, plus large-scale unemployment in the 1980s and the decline of some heavily unionized industrial sectors, such as coal mining and car manufacturing, reduced the trade union share of the workforce from about half to a third. Furthermore, in the interests of appealing to the middle class and avoiding internal party struggles, the Labour Party under Tony Blair's leadership also reduced the structural power of the trade unions within the party.

Religious organizations occupy a curious position in these countries. Only two of them have formal separation of church and state (France and Germany), but all three countries have become more secular and less Christian over time. A large majority of the population claim belief in a higher power, but religious practice is considerably less. Thus individual beliefs and practices do not correspond to the role of religion as recognized by the state. In Britain, 53 percent of the population are Protestants, 10 percent are Roman Catholics, 1 percent Jews, 3 percent Muslims, and 33 percent nonbelievers. In most of the United Kingdom, the Church of England (Anglican, Episcopalian) is the official church, but the Church of Scotland (Presbyterian) is the established church there. The queen is the temporal head of the Church of England and officially appoints high church officials, although the prime minister (regardless of religious persuasion) actually chooses them. Most members of these churches, especially of the Church of England, are only nominal members. They are baptized, married, and buried in the church but otherwise rarely frequent it. Overall weekly church attendance in Britain is around 10 percent, and that composed disproportionately of older people. Muslims attend weekly services in greater proportion than the rest of the population. Otherwise, only in Northern Ireland is religious affiliation taken seriously, by both Protestants and Roman Catholics, and weekly church attendance is almost 50 percent.

Although rules of religious affiliation still apply to the monarch, who must be a Protestant, in practice religion plays little role in most people's lives, and it does not affect politics anywhere nearly as much as it did as recently as a century ago. Religious instruction is still offered in state schools, but today it is more likely to be optional and conducted according to the family's religious belief, rather than the previously required instruction in Christianity. Many politicians view religious organizations mainly as "moral support" groups for social welfare causes. Although issues of morality sometimes occur in British politics, they rarely divide people consistently along lines of religious affiliation, except in Northern Ireland.

In Germany many churches also have a privileged position despite declining popular devotion. The religious affiliations of Germans are 37 percent Protestant (predominantly Lutheran), 35 percent Roman Catholic, 4 percent Muslim, less than 1 percent Jewish, and 24 percent nonbelievers. Weekly church attendance is about 9 percent. Churches registered as "public law corporations" have taxes from their members collected by the state. Although some have questioned whether the subsidy should continue, thus far it has been upheld. Occasionally religious issues have come to the fore, as with conflicting abortion rules after reunification and the controversy over crucifixes in public classrooms in heavily Catholic Bavaria. For the most part, however, religion-based morality issues do not play a large role in German politics.

In France, religion has been kept at arm's length from the state since the French Revolution, when the Catholic Church, a large landowner, was considered one of the forces of reaction supporting the monarchy. Religious affiliation is 82 percent Roman Catholic, 2 percent Protestant, 1 percent Jewish, 7 percent Muslim, and 8 percent nonbelievers. Only 8 percent attend weekly services. Although officially there is separation of church and state, education is an arena where devout and secular viewpoints collide, as they did over the issue of clothing and religious symbols in schools. State aid to private, religion-based schools has been the source of periodic, ferocious political debate. But like the other two countries, France today is largely a secular society, with a shrinking number of devout religious believers and only a few issues that mobilize religious sentiments.

The state of religion in modern Europe is exemplified by the fate of a reference to religion in the European Constitution. Religious groups, led by the Catholic Church, called for recognition of Europe's common Christian heritage in the new constitution. The final document did not include any reference to God or Europe's Christian roots but did indicate a willingness to engage in dialogue with religious organizations. Officially the EU is a secular organization that does not take any account of religion in its obligations. Altogether, only 21 percent of Europeans say religion is "very important" to them (the U.S. figure is about three times higher), and only 15 percent attend church services weekly. Yet among the concerns that Turkey's application for EU membership has raised, in addition to its poverty, largely agrarian economy, checkered democratic past, and treatment of minorities, is the fact that, if admitted, it would have the second-largest EU population, consisting of 70 million Muslims.

THE MEDIA

Another interest, but one with an ambiguous status in the political realm, is the media. Although traditionally "the media" refers mainly to newspapers, more recently the term encompasses radio, television, and new interactive technologies, primarily the Internet. The media have their own interests, sometimes conflicting, but also serve as the major communication channel between the government and the public. Literally, what the public knows about politics depends mainly on what the various media communicate. Most people rely on television as their major news source. The government wants to ensure that its messages are being communicated to the public, and the media desire independence from close government control.

The pattern of media-government connections varies across these jurisdictions. In all of them, newspapers are privately owned and compete with each other, although they often do so through market segmentation between what the British call "broadsheet," or serious, publications and "tabloids," which are smaller in size and are mostly mass-market entertainment vehicles. Some newspapers are distributed countrywide; others are more regional or local. Britain, with one of the highest newspaper readerships as a share of the population in Europe, has several national newspapers with a substantial daily readership all over the country even though their headquarters are in London. These include the *Times* (traditionally the newspaper of record), *Guardian, Daily Telegraph, Independent,* and *Financial Times,* among quality papers, as well as the *Sun, Daily Mail, Daily Mirror, Daily Express,* and *Daily Star* among the tabloids. The influential weekly the *Economist* calls itself a newspaper although most people would deem it a magazine.

Because Germany and especially France have larger territories and smaller shares of newspaper-reading citizens, the leading papers, at least in terms of readership, are regional rather than national ones. The most famous French newspapers, such as *Le Monde* (the paper of record), *Le Figaro,* and *Liberation,* are distributed mainly in Paris; the highest circulation newspaper is *Ouest-France,* published outside the capital. Weekly publications include *L'Express, Le Nouvel Observateur,* and *Le Canard Enchaîné.* On a politically neutral basis, the French press receives financial aid from the government, usually indirectly in the form of publication and distribution subsidies. Major German papers include *Die Welt* and *Bild* but also such regional leaders as the *Frankfurter Allgemeine Zeitung, Sueddeutsche Zeitung, Der Tagesspiegel, Frankfurter Rundschau,* and *Berliner Zeitung.* The leading weekly publications are *Die Zeit* and *Der Spiegel.*

Within the electronic media, there is a strong public ownership tradition in each of the three countries. Originally radio and subsequently television were considered public assets that, for reasons of objectivity, access to information, and avoidance of commercialism, should not be allowed in private hands. Thus public broadcasting networks were created first in each country and were supported by a license fee from users. Only gradually were private networks allowed to compete with them. Now there are private as well as public television and radio stations and also cable and satellite channels as well as private cross-media ownership by such journalistic titans as Rupert Murdoch. The government role in what is allowed to be broadcast is said to be arms-length in each country, although somewhat less so in France than in the other two. In Germany, media regulation is largely in the hands of the *länder.* In each case there is a delicate balance to be maintained between the public interest and the public's right to know.

As indicated by the mixed ownership patterns of major television and radio outlets, the electronic media market has faced a fragmented audience in recent years, even more so with the rise of interactive technologies. Almost half of European viewers subscribe to cable or satellite television. According to some, that has led to more "personality news," although serious coverage of political news is still a niche that is filled in all three countries. Various claims have been made about the influence of the media on election outcomes, but the most established finding is that people tend to select their media, especially newspapers, on the basis of their partisan affiliation much more than the reverse. All news media, but especially television, which is the major news source for most people, perform an agenda-setting function, and governments and parties have to react to important issues raised persistently by the media, the "fourth estate." During election campaigns this is especially important, since time is short and in some cases only a few percentage points separate winning from losing. Governments and parties attempt to mold their images and information about them in favorable ways. In recent years extraordinary efforts at crafting favorable stories in the media have been labeled "spin," or media manipulation. That has been an especially serious charge leveled against the New Labour government of Tony Blair in Britain.

Although the EU is also interested in dissemination of information, there is little news distribution that is specifically pan-European. The growing impact of the EU has enabled it to get more attention from the news media within countries, but the stories often are related to the particular concerns of that state's relationship with the EU. There also is increasing media ownership across countries. The EU has taken steps to harmonize broadcasting regulation among members in the interests of the single market and to assist companies producing "European content." There is, however, no public broadcasting authority sponsored by the EU, and private networks featuring pan-European content beyond sports and music attract only tiny audiences. Thus, information communicated to the public about the EU and pan-European issues comes through the private and public channels of individual countries and is designed accordingly. Any EU attempt to use the news media to encourage people to "think European" is sporadic and indirect.

POLITICAL PARTIES AND PARTY SYSTEMS

Political parties and party systems provide important dynamic parts of a political jurisdiction. No democratic polity has been able to function over the long term without competitive parties constituting a party system that provides options for voters and allows both stability and change in the governance of a country. Although parties and a party system exist at the EU level as well, one of the problems of the "democratic deficit" is that they are outgrowths of the party systems in individual countries. What little distinctive EU debate exists in the party systems of member states is as likely to occur within as between parties, with the notable exception of far-right parties that oppose the EU as an international bureaucracy imposing itself on sovereign states. Parties are only represented within one EU institution, the European Parliament, and there the parties tend to be collaborative rather than confrontational because they are interested in solidifying the power of the EP as an institution and are not directly responsible for formation of an EU government.

A political party is an organization with two key elements: (1) it contests elections in attempts to win governmental power for its candidates and ideas; (2) it has a permanent headquarters and staff, to maintain the party as an organization by collecting dues, arranging conferences, taking positions on issues, and recruiting candidates and voters, among other functions. A political party, particularly a well-established one, is a complex organization. Within a party, there are several different levels, including, from the bottom to the top of the organization, (1) party voters in the electorate; (2) dues-paying party members; (3) the local, often constituency, party organization; (3) regional party organizations and conferences; (4) the central (national) party conference, held periodically to debate issues and rally the membership; (5) the party bureaucracy, the organizational staff, normally with headquarters in the capital and led by a party chairperson; (6) party candidates for office, especially for the popularly elected house(s) of the central legislature; (7) the legislative party; (8) party leaders, usually in the central legislature; (9) if the party forms part or all of a government, the party in the cabinet, led by the premier.

The term "party system" refers to the relationships among political parties within a jurisdiction. There are several methods of classifying party systems. The classic way is by the number of major parties (two-party, multiparty), but one can also consider the party share of seats in the legislature; its long-term tenure in government, especially a single-party government (a competitive or a dominant-party system); party organizational structures (centralized or decentralized); and the range of ideologies in a system (degree of polarization). Over the past two decades party systems in these countries have become somewhat more fragmented, with more parties entering legislatures even though the major parties have remained the same.

The British Party System and Political Parties

The United Kingdom is most often characterized as a two-and-a-half-party system. Until recently it has tended toward long-term Conservative dominance; centralized party structures balanced by a degree of internal party democracy; and generally a considerable amount of ideological consensus, interrupted occasionally by bursts of ideological polarization, most recently in the Thatcher era when the Conservatives moved to the right and Labour went to the left. To win office, however, Labour moderated its policies.

The Conservatives, often called "Tories," are one of the oldest political parties in the Western world. Over the years they have been among the most successful parties because they have managed to adapt their policies to changing times and maintain a strong organizational basis. Originally they defended established privilege through the monarchy and landed aristocracy, but with the advent of mass suffrage, they developed more widely appealing policies, such as strong advocacy of the country's imperial mission, eventually reduced to defense of British state sovereignty and good management of the economy. Although often slow to embrace new ideas, the Conservatives have usually managed to avoid internal ideological conflict and fragmentation, remaining united in their pursuit of political power. Recently that behavior has changed, to the party's detriment. After Prime Minister Margaret Thatcher was ousted by her parliamentary colleagues in 1990, her successor, John Major, suffered from continual backbench sniping over Britain's role in the European Union. Many backbenchers and constituency activists remain suspicious of greater European integration. The moderate nature of the Labour government has compounded the difficulties. Subsequently the Conservatives have had four different party leaders and lost the general elections of 1997, 2001, and 2005 by substantial margins. Nevertheless, the ascent of David Cameron as party leader in 2005 rekindled enthusiasm for the Conservatives in many quarters.

In many ways the Labour Party in British politics has followed a path opposite to that of the Conservatives. Labour has always had a distinctive social profile in its support, has suffered several major internal ideological conflicts, and has had difficulty holding office for very long. In recent years, however, the characteristics of the two parties have been reversed, with Labour more united, ideologically moderate, appealing to a broad constituency, and successfully holding office for a decade, its longest period ever.

The Labour Party became the second major party in the British party system in the 1920s. Formerly a minor party, it benefited from the extension of suffrage to the working class and the splintering of the Liberal Party during World War I. In 1918 it adopted a socialist platform emphasizing social equality through government intervention in the economy, including public ownership of leading industrial sectors. It often has been said that Labour's socialism owed more to Methodism than to Marx, although adherents to both were included in the party. Although the party managed to form two minority governments in the 1920s, they did not last long, and the second resulted in its first major ideological split.

Until 1997, Labour's most successful term of office had occurred immediately at the end of World War II, when it formed two successive majority governments that instituted an era of social reform and helped Britain recover economically. Despite winning four general elections in the 1960s and 1970s, chronic economic problems and left-right party divisions over the role of trade unions, public ownership, and the EU led to eighteen years out of government, from 1979 until 1997. For a period in the early 1980s left-wingers gained ascendancy, leading to a formal split within the party. A few prominent, moderate former Labour cabinet members led other Labour MPs into the Social Democratic Party (SDP) which, allied with the Liberals, challenged Labour as the second party in the country. By the late 1980s, however, Labour had assumed a more moderate image and the SDP challenge had failed; eventually, in 1997, Labour regained office. By then it had democratized internally to reduce the power of its affiliated trade unions, decided to favor continued British membership in the EU, embraced the privatization of formerly nationalized sectors that the

Conservatives had initiated, and channeled its appeal more toward the growing middle class rather than toward its working-class, socialist roots. This new stance was called the "third way," based on the ideas of Anthony Giddens.

Led by Prime Minister Tony Blair, this embrace of the center allowed Labour for the first time to win three consecutive terms of office, all with substantial majorities of legislative seats. Nevertheless, discontent within the party and the electorate over Britain's joining the war in Iraq and over its generally moderate form of governing led to calls for Blair's resignation in favor of his long-serving treasury minister, Gordon Brown. Blair has said that he would resign after serving his third term of office, begun with the 2005 general election.

The Liberal Democratic Party (LDP) is a persistent, countrywide minor party in the United Kingdom with some parliamentary representation, which it has recently increased. Prior to the 1920s, the Liberals were the major challenger to the Conservatives, but party splits over the conduct of World War I and the rise of a more working-class electorate reduced their support. The increasing ideological confrontation between Labour and the Conservatives, beginning after the stagflation brought on by the Arab oil embargo in 1973, led to a Liberal resurgence as a moderate alternative, although more so in votes than in parliamentary seats. Its support has continued at a level of about 20 percent of the electorate over nine general elections since 1974. Its share was further enhanced in the 1980s by the alliance with the SDP, in which these two parties ran on a common platform and did not challenge each other's constituency candidates.

In the face of Labour's more moderate stances, the Liberal Democrats have claimed to be the most left-wing party in Britain, staunchly in favor of the EU, willing to raise taxes for education and health purposes, and opposing the war in Iraq. Although the Liberal Democrats have increased their seats in the House of Commons over the past few elections, they remain significantly underrepresented because their votes are spread across the country in a single-member-district, plurality-win electoral system. Their dream is to replace the Conservatives as the major alternative to Labour, but they are still some way from achieving that.

Other persistent minor parties also exist in the British party system, the most successful being the various nationalist parties in Wales, Scotland, and Northern Ireland. In Wales and Scotland parties advocating greater autonomy and even independence for their areas gain a few seats in the House of Commons from concentrated voting support, and even more seats in the regional assemblies set up under devolution. The Plaid Cymru (PC) is organized around defense of the Welsh language as a nationalist symbol, primarily in education and the media (there is a government-sponsored Welsh language television channel in that area), and is strongest in those areas with the heaviest concentrations of Welsh speakers. The Labour Party, however, has always been the strongest party in heavily working-class Wales. In contrast, the Scottish National Party (SNP) has broader appeal in Scotland because it is not organized around language but instead around socioeconomic issues, as well as cultural defense against English domination. Nonetheless, Labour also has been the dominant party in Scotland; the high tide of support for the SNP occurred in the 1970s when its slogan, "It's Scotland's Oil," referring to the growing production in the North Sea, had some resonance. Oil production from those reserves has now declined. In both Wales and Scotland, however, the concentrated strength of the nationalist parties makes the party system one of four-party competition.

The party system in Northern Ireland is entirely different from that elsewhere in the United Kingdom. The Unionist-Nationalist divide dominates all other issues. On the Unionist side are two parties, the more hard-line, anti-Catholic Democratic Unionist Party (DUP), whose longtime leader is the Reverend Ian Paisley, and the more moderate Ulster Unionist Party (UUP), whose longtime leader was David Trimble. On the Nationalist side there are also two parties, the hard-line, IRA-sympathetic Sinn Fein ("Ourselves Alone"), whose prominent leaders are Gerry Adams and Martin McGuinness, and the more constitutionally nationalist Social Democratic and Labour Party (SDLP), whose leading figure, now retired, has been John Hume. Attempting to bridge the divide is the cross-religions Alliance Party, whose small following bespeaks the continuing fissures in the province. Under the power-sharing arrangement in Northern Ireland, all of these parties are required to participate in the devolved government when it is functioning. Since the 1998 Good Friday Accord, however, the more extreme parties in each community, the DUP and Sinn Fein, have become more electorally appealing to voters than their more moderate rivals.

Other small parties in the British party system may generate media attention or local support for a time but usually do not achieve parliamentary representation. That has been true for the left-wing Greens; various right-wing anti-immigrant parties, especially the British National Party (BNP); and also such anti-EU parties as the Referendum Party, the United Kingdom Independence Party (UKIP), and Veritas.

The French Party System and Political Parties

The French party system is both like and unlike the British party system. The similarities are a left-right divide, multiple parties in the electorate and in the legislature, and two major parties, one on the left and one on the right, that anchor the party system. Differences exist in that the left-right divide is wider (there is greater polarization) in France and coalition governments are more likely. Even though the official names of political parties change, the persistence of the left-right ideological divide in France means that they can retain the loyalty of their core supporters.

Although by most measures France would qualify as a multiparty system, the single member plurality, double-ballot electoral system for the legislature and the creation of a powerful, directly elected president in the Fifth Republic have focused parties and voters' attention on defeating their ideological foes rather than their closer ideological competitors. Thus there is now a "two-tendency" system, even if there are more than two parties. The parties themselves are generally centralized, although the Socialist Party is composed of factions and some smaller parties are organized largely around particular personalities.

On the left there are two long-standing parties, the Socialists and the Communists, plus several others, including the Radical Party of the Left and two Green parties. Although the Socialists and Communists once were major rivals, the rise of a reformed Socialist Party since the 1960s under François Mitterand allowed it to eclipse its leftist rival. Although the Socialists only managed to hold the presidency for Mitterand's two seven-year terms, they also have secured, with aid from other leftists, a majority of the National Assembly in "cohabitation" with Gaullist president Jacques Chirac, 1997–2002, as well as during part of Mitterand's rule. The Socialists stand for secularism and socioeconomic reformist policies to benefit workers, such as the introduction of the thirty-five-hour week. They also introduced decentralizing reforms in the 1980s. The Socialists saw their attempts to operate a more government-directed economy, against the growing tide of neoliberal market forces in the international economy, frustrated in the early 1980s. Subsequently they have broadly gone along with increasing privatization, although they owe much of their domestic political fortunes to the good opinion of public workers. The party retains a more leftist orientation than many other, similar parties in other countries, including a general suspicion of "third way" policies. The current leader of the party is François Hollande, but former cabinet ministers, including Laurent Faubius, Dominique Strauss-Kahn, Jack Lang, and Martine Aubry, also see themselves as possible presidential contenders. There is even talk of a comeback by Lionel Jospin, the former premier and defeated presidential candidate in 2002.

The Communists, who in the earlier postwar period were the largest party on the left, have never recovered from their long embrace of the Soviet style of communism. They even have yielded their position as the preferred vehicle of protest against the status quo to other parties on the left and right. Now they have to compete with several other small leftist parties discontented with moderate Socialist positions, although none of them has substantial representation.

On the right, the two major parties are the Gaullists, most recently incorporated in the form of the Union for a Popular Movement (UMP; its former name was "Rally for the Republic," and in 2002, the "Union for Presidential Majority") and the Union of French Democrats (UDF; formerly called "Independent Republicans"). The difference between these parties ideologically is that the Gaullists are the more distinctively nationalist protectors of the role of the French state domestically as well as internationally, whereas the UDF is more inclined toward free market economics and moderate social policies. Nevertheless, these two parties have always found it convenient to collaborate electorally, legislatively, and in policy, even if they maintain distinct party organizations, first-round parliamentary candidates, and even presidential candidates. In 2002, part of the UDF split off to join Chirac's UMP.

The Gaullist party was founded by Charles de Gaulle when he assumed the presidency of France upon the inception of the Fifth Republic. It is a broadly conservative party embracing the principles of capitalism, French nationalism, and a strong role for the French state, especially through its executive branch. As one might expect from its origins, the party puts a premium on strong leadership, ranging from de Gaulle through Georges Pompidou to Jacques Chirac. With Chirac beset by illness and his term as president due to end in 2007, a rivalry has emerged in the UMP for the succession. The major contenders are premier Dominique de Villepin and party head and interior minister Nicolas Sarkozy.

The UDF is a center-right party that emphasizes market liberalization more than do the Gaullists. Its recent leader has been François Bayrou. With the exception of Valéry Giscard d'Estaing's presidency, 1974–1981, the UDF has served as junior partner to the neo-Gaullists in the legislature and in right-of-center cabinets. Both of these parties get their support disproportionately from the middle class, businesspeople, and the more-religious sectors of society, especially women. There are also several small moderate parties, but they are of little importance in the Fifth Republic (unlike the case in the Fourth), since the role of the National Assembly is highly circumscribed.

On the far right sits the National Front (NF), with its xenophobic policies toward immigrants and foreigners, including the EU. For most of the time since its rise to prominence in the 1980s, it has been led by one of the last holdovers from the Fourth Republic, Jean-Marie Le Pen, although his rule has come under challenge in recent years, with the National Republican Movement emerging as a splinter organization. The NF draws its voting support from disgruntled lower-middle-class and working-class people, especially in areas near where immigrants live. Le Pen's survival into the second-round runoff for president in 2002 was due less to rising support for the NF than to fragmentation among the leftist parties in the first round of voting; he won only 18 percent of the votes in the runoff. Unlike extreme-right parties in Britain, however, the NF is a long-term force in France, as it holds a number of seats in local governments

The German Party System and Political Parties

The German party system is different from the patterns seen in France and the United Kingdom. Unlike the other countries, political parties have a place in the German constitution. Article 21 "guarantees the legitimacy of parties and their right to exist—if they accept the principles of democratic government." This provision led to the Nazi Party and originally the Communists being prohibited, but the bans have been loosened over the years. Since the foundation of West Germany in 1949, there has been a multiparty system with the same dominant parties on the left and right: the Social Democratic Party (SPD) and the Christian Democratic Party (CDU), respectively. The rest of the parties are smaller but important because election results are decided through a system of proportional representation, and minor parties usually are needed to form a government. However, they must pass a threshold of 5 percent of the vote to receive seats. Because Germany is a federation, the parties are relatively decentralized, with *land* parties running their own affairs and sometimes forming governments of a different party complexion than the central one. Ideologically the two major parties have grown closer over the years, allowing room for dissident small parties to rise.

The Social Democratic Party has been a force in German politics since the late nineteenth century. Similar to socialist and social democratic parties elsewhere, it has championed social, economic, and political equality for the working class through government interventions in the economy, including both public ownership (nationalization) and welfare provisions, using parliamentary and democratic means. The "social wage" guarantees from the state, established through corporatist bargaining, have made welfare reform in Germany a difficult issue in the face of the German economy's loss of dynamism over the past two decades.

With the loss of the conservative, Protestant eastern portion of the country to the Soviet bloc at the end of World War II, the SPD thought that its moment of governance had come. But instead the Christian Democrats, espousing a strong anticommunist line, became the dominant, governing party in coalition with smaller ones. The SPD decided it had to adopt more moderate policies, and at its famous Bad Godesberg conference in 1958 the party agreed to maintain capitalism and abandoned policies of extensive public ownership. By joining the "grand coalition" with the CDU in the late 1960s, it showed itself capable of assuming responsibility for governing, paving the way for its electoral successes later. Subsequently the SPD has governed Germany over half of the time. Through its recent coalition with the Greens, the SPD has addressed environmental issues, including strong sponsorship of the Kyoto Treaty and the phasing out of nuclear power. Restarting the engine of economic prosperity has proved more difficult. The SPD has embraced the "third way/*neue mitte*" principles of a more economically liberal but socially responsible moderation. Its voter profile remains largely working class, unionist, secular, and urban. The government leader of the SPD is Franz Müntefering, vice chancellor of the cabinet.

The Christian Democrats are actually an amalgam of two distinct parties. In all states except Bavaria, the party is known as the CDU. Formally the party in Bavaria, in southern Germany, historically a maverick state, is the Christian Social Union (CSU), and it has a separate structure, including a different leader. Normally the CSU affiliates with the CDU in parliament, and together they choose one candidate for chancellor before each countrywide election, usually from the CDU. The CDU/CSU appeals to the middle class, business owners, and more-religious people—especially Catholics. It is the descendant of older Catholic-based parties formed in the late nineteenth century. Although it is basically procapitalist, many of its social doctrines follow those of the Catholic Church, which means advocacy of a family-based welfare state. Its dominant position in the party system after World War II, due largely to its embrace of Western capitalism, NATO, and the European Union against the Soviet communist bloc and the more ambivalent policies of the SPD, has now given way to an almost even balance with the SPD in terms of votes. The last two chancellor candidates for the CDU/CSU have been Edmund Stoiber, minister-president of Bavaria, in 2002 and Angela Merkel in 2005. Unusually for this party, Merkel was not only a woman, but also from an eastern, Protestant background.

The balance of power belongs to the three smaller parties in the Bundestag, as long as they can cross the 5 percent threshold. They are the Greens, the Free Democrats (FDP), and the new Left party, which is an electoral alliance of two small, regionally based parties, the Alternative Labor and Social Justice Party (WASG), which is a group of dissident, left-wing former Social Democrats in western Germany, and the Party of Democratic Socialism (PDS), composed of former Communists in the East.

The Free Democrats are the oldest of these three parties; they function as a liberal party favoring free enterprise. Although they are often to the left on foreign policy, on economic and social policy they tend to be to the right of the CDU/CSU. They traditionally receive 5 percent to 10 percent of the vote and until the arrival of the Greens in the 1980s were considered a moderating force in German politics, choosing to form a government with either the CDU/CSU or the SPD. In return, the FDP often received key portfolios, especially the foreign ministry. But with the rise of other minor parties, the place of the FDP in the party system is no longer as secure. Their current party leader is Guido Westerwelle, and the parliamentary leader is Wolfgang Gerhardt.

The Greens rose to prominence in the 1983 election, when they first entered the Bundestag, and they have maintained that presence. Not only have they managed to share government with the SPD in some *länder* ("Red-Green coalitions"), but for two terms since 1998 they joined forces with the SPD in central-level coalitions led by Gerhard Schröder. The German Greens are the most governmentally successful "postmaterial" party, but in accepting power they have faced starkly the dilemma of all parties—how much to compromise the principles for which they stand. In the Greens' case, their principles were two in particular: environmentalism, especially in the form of opposing nuclear power both at home and abroad, and anti-elitism. Both positions have had to be compromised, especially as the Greens, in the person of their party co-leader Joschka Fischer, held the foreign ministry in the recent coalition government. Claudia Roth is the other Green co-leader. For years the Greens had an internal conflict between the *Realos*, those who were more pragmatic about what had to be done to gain and maintain power, and the *Fundis*, who wanted to remain true to fundamental, radical tenets of the party at the expense of power holding. This conflict often took the form of debate about whether the Greens should have a permanent leadership cadre, in the Bundestag as well as in the party bureaucracy, or rotate those positions in the interest of being closer to the membership. The debates largely have been resolved in favor of the *Realos*, although the Greens remain, in principle, a party different from others on the left because of their concern over the environmental costs of industrialization and desire for a more sustainable pattern of economic growth.

Upset by the Schröder (SPD) government's movement toward less security for workers and greater freedom for businesses, a group of trade unionists and dissident Social Democrats, led by the former party leader and federal finance minister Oskar Lafontaine, formed the Alternative Labor and Social Justice Party (WASG) in early 2005. Its policy positions urged strong state protection of social welfare and limits on immigration while unemployment is high in Germany. Hoping to overcome the 5 percent threshold for parliamentary representation, this western-based party combined with the eastern-based PDS to form the Left party alliance to gain enough votes countrywide. With almost 9 percent between the two parties, they were successful in this.

The Party of Democratic Socialism (PDS), led by Gregor Gysi, was formerly the Communist Party of East Germany, and its support comes almost exclusively from that area. From the start of all-German elections, the PDS has been able to win sufficient votes to gain seats in the Bundestag. Ironically the PDS represents the conservative elements of eastern Germany, those that view capitalism and democracy with trepidation and are nostalgic for the security of the Communist regime. The PDS claims to represent the true interests of the working class that the SPD has shunned in its move toward moderation. The PDS is eager to appear reasonable and has joined the SPD in coalitions in a few *land* governments; with its Marxist-Leninist origins, the leaders of the PDS have no problems in maintaining central control of their members. As long as they can maintain their pockets of strength in eastern Germany, they can remain a minor figure on the central level. There has been some discussion about a formal merger of the WASG and the PDS into one party.

There also exists a far right in Germany. Recently several tiny parties were united under the banner of the neo-Nazi National Democrats (NPD), but they have achieved little legislative representation. Germany has banned the Nazi Party, but it is difficult to ban neo-Nazi parties as long as they disavow Nazism per se. During the Grand Coalition period in the 1960s, when only the FDP was in formal opposition in the Bundestag, a neo-Nazi party increased in votes, but it never achieved any legislative seats because of the 5 percent threshold. More recently, concern about immigration and economic insecurity in the East has led to growth of the NPD, and it has managed to gain seats in some *land* legislatures. Because of Germany's past, a gain in popularity for such parties is always a concern for the leaders of other parties.

The Party System of the European Union

The party system of the European Union is not distinct from the party systems of its member countries. All of the elections for the European Parliament are conducted under rules established by the particular countries, and the results in party seats are often a reflection of the relative popularity of each country's government at the time. Very few parties contest the EP elections on the basis of EU issues. Where the party systems differ somewhat for EU elections is in the greater success of minor parties, perhaps because of lower turnout, and the fact that small anti-EU parties, sometimes formed only to contest EU elections, manage to secure a few seats in the European Parliament to air their views.

While parties from far left to far right hold seats in the EP, the three leading groups are the European People's Party–European Democrats (EPP-ED), made up of Christian Democrats and Conservatives; the Party of European Socialists (PES), constituting the Socialists, Social Democrats, and Labour; and the Alliance of Liberals and Democrats for Europe (ALDE), comprising the Liberals. Although there are signs that the EU is becoming a more important issue in the domestic party systems of some countries, especially France and the United Kingdom, mostly it is an issue that generates internal debate within parties rather than one that divides parties from one another.

ELECTORAL SYSTEMS AND ELECTIONS

Elections provide one of the most dynamic elements of a political democracy. Most definitions of liberal democracy include free and fair elections as an essential element because they provide the opportunity for the citizens to choose their leaders. In a modern democracy, that usually means rearranging the party distribution in the legislature and perhaps even direct choice of a chief executive, as in France. Accordingly, the arrangements for conducting elections, as well as what transpires during the campaign and the election itself, are important for establishing the partisan and policy direction of a regime.

Technically electoral systems belong to a state's institutional, and sometimes even constitutional, structure, but because they are closely connected to elections, campaigns, and political parties, it is more convenient to discuss them in conjunction with those elements. The electoral system constitutes the basic rules of the game for the choice of rulers and may also include referendums, binding or advisory, on particular issues. The system covers such matters as parties' and candidates' access to the ballot, campaign duration and rules, financing of campaigns, the role of the media, and electoral administration of the vote—when it will occur, how voters are registered, the method through which votes are cast, how winners are determined, and how appeals can be lodged. What most analysts mean by "the electoral system," however, is what is often called "the electoral formula," that is, how votes are turned into seats in the legislature. There are two major electoral formulae, with variations: single-member-district (SMD), in which one person wins the seat, whether by plurality or majority, and proportional representation (PR), which involves multimember districts in which parties or individual candidates win election based on obtaining a certain share of the vote.

The choice of electoral formula has a major impact on the party formation of the government, as well as on the number of parties represented in the legislature. Without any gerrymandering, the single-member districts in the United Kingdom and France often allow a party winning a plurality of votes to gain a majority of seats and thus form a single-party, majority government (see Table 4-1). In contrast, in Germany, as long as a party passes the 5 percent threshold across the country, it will receive a nearly proportionate share of

Table 4-1 Recent Elections in Europe

	UK	France Parliamentary	France President	Germany	EU
Year	2005	2002	2002	2005	2004
Turnout (%)	61	64, 60	72, 80	78	46
Electoral system	SMP	SMD majority or two rounds	Majority or second-round runoff	Mixed SMP/PR	PR (various)
First party vote shares (%)	35	34, 47	20, 82 (second round)	35	N.A.
First party seat shares (%)	55	64	100	37	37
Women in lower house (%)	20	12	N.A.	32	30
Type of government	One-party majority	Coalition	N.A.	Coalition	N.A.[a]
Parties in charge	Labor	UMP/UDF	UMP	CDU-CSU/SPD	EPP/ED (Center-right)

Notes: **CDU:** Christian Democratic Party; **CSU:** Christian Social Union; **EPP-ED:** European People's Party-European Democrats; **PR:** proportional representation; **SMD:** single-member district; **SMP:** single-member plurality; **SPD:** Social Democratic Party; **UDF:** Union of French Democrats; **UMP:** Union for a Popular Movement.

[a] No government formed from European Parliament results.

seats in the Bundestag through what is called "party list" PR. The number of parties represented in the central legislature has increased from three to five in recent years. Similarly, use of PR for the European Parliament means that some parties achieve representation in the EP even if they cannot win seats in their home country SMD elections.

Each of the four entities has a different electoral system for the most popular branch of its legislature, but two use single-member districts and two use proportional representation. The United Kingdom has a classic SMD system with a plurality vote for the House of Commons. The country is divided into districts geographically, and the party candidate with the most votes in each constituency wins, even if the person gains less than a majority. The outcome in party terms is that the leading party in votes receives a disproportionate benefit in seats because it finishes first in so many districts. Since 1979 in the United Kingdom, for seven consecutive general elections, the party winning a plurality of the votes has won a comfortable majority of the seats in the House of Commons. In 2005 the gap between vote shares and seat shares was especially pronounced, with 36 percent of the voters (22 percent of the electorate) choosing Labour, which won 55 percent of the seats. A majority of the population in each instance voted for other parties, but finishing second or third, however closely, does not result in a seat. A party such as the Liberal Democrats, which receives a large vote across the country but does not finish first in many individual districts, is especially disadvantaged by this system. Thus Britain has continued to have an overwhelmingly two-party House of Commons despite having a multiparty electorate. Small parties that can concentrate their votes and win seats in particular regions of the country, such as nationalists in Scotland, Wales, and Northern Ireland, however, can benefit from the system.

Although this is still the electoral system used for Westminster parliamentary elections, under the Labour government since 1997 different electoral systems, with an element of PR, have been established at other levels, including party list PR for European Parliament elections, the single transferable vote (STV) for the Northern Ireland Assembly and Scottish local elections, a mixed system of SMD and party list PR for the devolved legislatures in Scotland and Wales, and a popularly elected mayor through the "supplementary vote" (voting for two candidates in order of preference on the same ballot, also called an "instant runoff") for London and some other cities.

In 1997 Labour established a Commission on the Voting System to consider changes to the electoral system for the House of Commons. That body recommended a mixed electoral system to give more proportional results across the country. But because Labour has been able to win majorities in the legislature based on pluralities in the electorate, the incentive for electoral reform in the House of Commons waned. After the disproportionate results in terms of votes and seats in 2005, there were renewed calls for a fairer electoral system.

Most British elections do not occur because of a loss of confidence in the government by the House of Commons or through expiration of the five-year limit on a Parliament. Instead, the prime minister chooses an appropriate time, normally about four years after the last election, to call for a new one, based on the political situation, especially the relative standings of the major parties in the opinion polls. Although this might be expected to result in incumbent governments' nearly always being returned to office, in fact, with a thirty-day campaign and sometimes a narrow range of difference in party popularity, incumbent governments have been defeated even when they called the election.

British elections are held on Thursdays. An official election campaign begins when the monarch, upon advice from the prime minister, dissolves Parliament and announces the date. Although the official campaign period is relatively short, the unofficial campaign may begin some months ahead of time in expectation of an election call. Parties may choose their candidates for Parliament, prepare their campaign themes and budgets, and behave in the House of Commons, especially during prime minister's question time, in ways reflecting this expectation.

Once the campaign is official, laws governing party advertising and media appearances come into force. There are severe limits on what individual candidates may spend on their constituency campaigns, although the parties are not subject to overall campaign spending limits. Parties receive a specified allocation of free, countrywide telecast and broadcast programs to present their cases to the voters, based on their voting support in the last general election. They cannot purchase broadcast time. Even though the voters are only choosing their local member of Parliament, or MP, the focus is on the general campaigns of the parties and the leadership teams they will field if chosen to form the government. Each party has a manifesto of detailed policies, and constituency candidates, each of whom produces an "election address," usually follow these manifestos closely in their own issue stands. Thus the winning party claims to have a mandate for the policies it has espoused during the course of the election, and individual MPs consider themselves to have been chosen on the basis of their party's standing and appeal, rather than mainly on their own characteristics.

Although traditionally the United Kingdom has been considered to display class-based voting on a relatively uniform, countrywide basis, recent elections have featured substantial dealignment of voters and parties, with fewer citizens voting for the same party in every election. This development has led to electoral volatility; more choice of parties in particular elections based on issues, including local concerns; and more voting for parties other than the two major ones.

Turnout for the general election, the one time every few years when citizens can vote for their central rulers, has traditionally been 70 percent or more of those registered, but it has declined recently, especially in 2001 when it fell to 59 percent. The drop brought alarm about the state of democracy in Britain and various officially sponsored investigations. In 2005, turnout rose marginally, to 61 percent, with about 20 percent of the voters casting postal ballots for the first time. Younger people are especially less likely to vote. That is a problem in many advanced industrial democracies, although Britain seems to be an especially dramatic case.

Britain is the home of representative democracy through candidate elections, not populist democracy through direct voting on ballot measures, or referendums. Until 1997 there had been only four referendums in the entire history of the United Kingdom and only one countrywide, in 1975 on remaining in the EU. In its first year in office, Labour held four additional referendums (in Wales, Scotland, Northern Ireland, and London). Two countrywide referendums, on ratification of the EU constitution and eventually on joining the European single currency, were promised. The one on the EU constitution was canceled after its referendum defeats in France and the Netherlands in 2005. To preserve parliamentary sovereignty, technically these referendums are advisory only, rather than binding.

The French electoral system for the National Assembly is another variation on SMD, usually called a "double-ballot runoff system." Under this electoral formula, two rounds of elections are conducted. To be elected on the first ballot, candidates must receive a majority of the votes in their districts. Because multiple parties are running candidates, however, that rarely happens.

If no candidate receives a majority, a second round of balloting is conducted two weeks later, with only those receiving at least 12.5 percent of the votes on the first ballot eligible for the second and only a plurality needed to win.

Nevertheless, because French parties have a long history of aligning themselves on a left-right basis, there is usually collaboration among the parties on each side of the ideological divide before the second round. The candidate of the left (mainly Communists and Socialists) who ran higher in the first round will get the nod of the united left for the second round, in return for similar arrangements in other constituencies in which party roles are reversed. The same arrangement occurs on the political center-right between the Gaullist party (under whatever name) and the Union for French Democracy, but not including the National Front. Without such arrangements, a less desirable candidate from the other side of the spectrum might win a plurality. Thus the outcome of the double-ballot runoff system again favors the larger parties and reinforces the French tendency toward two ideological blocs, resulting in a majority or coalition government of the left or right in the legislature, even if multiple parties manage to win seats. In the second round of legislative voting in 2002, the Gaullist party received 47 percent of the vote, but 64 percent of the seats in the Assembly. There has been some discussion, especially by the government parties on the right, about formally limiting the number of candidates contesting the runoff election to two, which would further reinforce this tendency. When France shifted to a system of party list PR for the 1986 legislative elections only, party representation was more diverse, as expected.

Presidential elections in France are also conducted under a two-ballot runoff system, but a majority winner by popular vote is guaranteed because only the two leading candidates in the first round are allowed to contest the second round. There are multiple presidential candidates in the first round, sometimes even more than one from the same party, because nomination is based on having five hundred elected officials, mainly local mayors, sign a sponsoring petition. In 2002 fragmentation of the votes on the left among several candidates in the first round led to a second-round runoff between Jacques Chirac of the center-right Gaullists and Jean-Marie Le Pen of the far-right National Front, rather than the usual left-right contest.

French parties are financed through a combination of public funding (since 1990) and private contributions and have an overall limit on spending during election campaigns. But old habits die hard. Despite public financing, there have been investigations of each of the four major parties' diverting local government funds into their party coffers. They led to the conviction of former premier Alan Juppé and to charges against President Chirac, who is immune from prosecution during his term of office. Parties also receive a limited amount of free television time, shared equally rather than proportionately, during campaigns and cannot purchase additional time.

Parliamentary campaigns take place over a twenty-to-forty-day period following the call for the election. Despite Sunday voting in France, there has been a steady decline in turnout for both parliamentary and presidential elections over the past thirty years, culminating in the lowest levels yet in 2002 for all four major election rounds except the second presidential one (see Table 4-1). French voters broadly divide in expected ways, with secular, urbanized, public-sector, unionized, and working-class voters choosing the left parties and private-sector, middle-class, older, more-religious, and rural voters selecting parties of the right. However, class voting occurs less than in Germany or Britain, and dealignment has occurred as well. Issues such as the state of the economy, crime, and immigration can also be important. Interestingly, left-right self-placement is not confusing to French voters; all but about 15 percent place themselves on one of these two poles rather than in the middle. The next elections for the National Assembly in France are scheduled for 2007, which is also the year for a presidential vote.

France has a long tradition of populistic democracy through referendums, especially during times of strong executive rule. Sometimes the referendums have been considered informal plebiscites, that is, popular votes of confidence, with the government resigning if it lost the referendum. During the Fifth Republic referendums have been occasional, usually on amendments to the constitution or on EU matters, which are considered to have constitutional importance. After losing a referendum in 1969, President Charles de Gaulle resigned, and the defeat of the referendum on approving the EU constitution in 2005 resulted in replacement of the premier.

The German electoral system incorporates elements of party list PR that make the distribution of seats in the Bundestag largely proportional, despite the 5 percent threshold for minor parties to gain representation. This again was a product of compromise between traditional German principles of PR, which led to representation for extremist parties of both the left and right in the Weimar Republic, and Allied insistence on the establishment of single-member districts to reduce such a possibility and make stable government more likely. The result on both the central and provincial levels is a "mixed" electoral system, with half of the members of the popularly elected branch chosen by single-member-district plurality vote and half by party list PR. Thus each voter casts two ballots, one for an SMD member and one for a party list that contains as many candidates as there are available seats in that *land*. The party chooses the order of the list; based on the proportion of the vote the party receives, successful candidates come from the top of the list. Since it is difficult for one party to win an overall majority of seats, this electoral system has resulted in coalition governments, usually encompassing one large and one small party. There are fewer parties in the central legislature than there were in the Weimar Republic, and anti-regime extremist parties have not been represented. The basic results are determined by the PR distribution; SMD seats are subtracted from that total, and the parties receive enough PR seats to make up the difference. Parties are allowed to keep any extra, "overhang" SMD seats if the number exceeds their PR share. On the central level, all SMD seats were won by the two largest parties, CDU-CSU and SPD, until the concentrated appeal of the former Communists (PDS) in eastern Germany after unification allowed them to gain representation in the Bundestag. Other small parties, especially the Free Democrats and the Greens, get all of their seats from the PR lists, as have far-right parties in some provinces.

Elections in Germany are held on Sundays. As in other European countries, turnout has declined, but it is still relatively high, around 80 percent, for Bundestag elections. Electoral administration is legally controlled, with electronic voting prominent. The campaigns are focused around the central party leaders and platforms. There is free, proportionate access to public television broadcasting, although paying for advertising on private stations is also allowed. In 1959 Germany pioneered public funding of political parties, including funding for campaigns, based on the votes that each party received in the most recent federal election. Although that legally can be supplemented by declared private contributions equal to the amount of public contributions, this provision has not prevented scandals involving supplementary, secret private financing, such as the one that engulfed former chancellor Helmut Kohl. Because Hitler used popular votes in the form of plebiscites (general votes of approval or disapproval in the government) to legitimize his rule, the Federal Republic has never held a referendum on any topic, even EU constitutional matters.

Since 1979 direct elections have been held every five years, in June, across the European Union. Although individual countries are responsible for electoral administration, including the exact date of the election, countries have been encouraged to adopt proportional representation so as to provide a broad representation of partisan opinion. There are, however, variations in the types of PR used. Even the British agreed to party list PR in 1999, except in Northern Ireland, which uses STV. This has led to relatively proportional results by party for country delegations in the European Parliament and representation for smaller parties.

EP elections have been plagued by low voter turnout. Except in those countries that have compulsory voting, turnout is lower than in corresponding state-level, central legislative elections. Even though turnout has been declining in the older member states, it stabilized in 2004 at 49 percent; all but two of the new-accession states had remarkably low turnout, averaging 27 percent when weighted for population size.

Why, given the opportunity to have a direct impact on EU affairs, is the electorate so apathetic or even disenchanted? First, the authority of the EP, although it has increased over the years, is still not completely coequal with that of the Council of Ministers (or perhaps even the European Commission). Second, MEPs, or members of the European Parliament, often are viewed as distant, underemployed time-servers rather than as performing a useful job of looking after their constituents' interests. Constituencies are large, and communication with voters is difficult.

Third, parties have tended to conduct EP election campaigns in familiar terms, as if they were actually votes about the popularity of the incumbent government in the country. The electorate has tended to vote according to how well they like the record of the domestic government. This is what is called a "second order" election. As long as EP elections are treated as less consequential than member state legislative elections, fewer voters will turn out, and they often will not consider the impact on the EU of their votes. In that sense, EU elections resemble lower-level elections within many member states.

POLITICAL RECRUITMENT

Although considerable attention has been paid to mass political culture, less analysis has been done of the ways that elite culture differs from it. It is the elites (those with more power) who rule on a daily basis. Elections are held only periodically, on terms that elite competition largely dictates. Thus the values of elites as well as those of the population at large are worthy of study. Especially important is how elites are recruited to their positions; the life experiences of political elites are likely to influence their political views.

Why is elite recruitment so important? For one thing, the integration or fragmentation of elites affects the balance between consensus and conflict in a political system. When elites are familiar with one another from long association, even back to university education, across party lines, that will lead toward consensus on the fundamental operating principles of the regime, for example, the constitution. On the other hand, when elites even in the same party have not had common socialization experiences, that is likely to lead to greater diversity of views and more internal conflict, even aside from the usual competitions of ambition and partisanship.

In the United Kingdom, the only road to political leadership leads through parties and Parliament. The latter is the center of political debate, through which party loyalty, speaking and administrative skills, and political support from the legislative caucus are demonstrated. Although most important political figures come from the House of Commons, a few emerge from the House of Lords, especially if they serve in the cabinet. In seeking a seat in the House of Commons, potential candidates are not hindered by a requirement of local residency. Instead, they can seek a seat anywhere in the small country, what is referred to as "parachuting." The selection of candidates is normally in the hands of the constituency party committee, which interviews them and presents a short list to the local party for final selection. Increasingly, parties have adopted "one member, one vote" criteria for parliamentary candidate selection rather than allowing only party activists to make the choice at a meeting. Central party organizations maintain lists of approved candidates, however, and have been known to intervene when the local choice proves controversial.

Candidate background experience and qualities differ by political party, with the Conservatives and Liberal Democrats reliant on the private sector for candidates while Labour is more dependent on the public sector, including local party officials. People with working-class occupations, such as trade union officials, have declined as a share of Labour candidates. Conservative candidates are more likely to come from a private school background than are their counterparts in the other main parties. After being a party member, and usually an activist, for several years, the normal progress for an aspiring MP is to start by contesting a hopeless seat for his or her party and subsequently be selected for a marginal or safe one (depending on the previous party vote distribution in the district). Once elected to the House of Commons, the MP serves a few years on the backbenches, then possibly moves to junior government or opposition spokesperson positions, then on to senior positions. A few manage to climb to the top of the "greasy pole" and become party leader and possibly prime minister. The number of years of legislative apprenticeship necessary before a politician becomes part of the senior leadership has shortened in recent years.

Many MPs remain on the backbenches throughout their careers because of lack of ambition, maverick views, lack of skills, and/or lack of support from the legislative party caucus. Advancement to senior positions, especially in government, is dependent on the choices of the party leader. Because the leader has only the members of the two houses of Parliament from which to choose, however, it may be necessary to include some powerful senior figures in the cabinet or shadow cabinet to keep the rest of the legislative party satisfied. Although the leader is the dominant figure, public division within the legislative party would be a serious problem.

All British government ministers must also be serving in either the House of Commons or House of Lords while they are ministers; most are in the Commons, to maintain more accountable democratic connections. This practice effectively limits the prime minister's choice to members of the majority party in each house.

Ambitious MPs make themselves eligible for such selection by supporting their party effectively in parliamentary speeches and developing a strong reputation within the parliamentary party caucus. In recent years selection of the principal party leader (the potential prime minister) has moved from the parliamentary party exclusively to the general membership of the party if the election is contested. Nevertheless, the road to preferment still lies through party-related parliamentary activity. The prime minister may shift ministers from one portfolio to another, depending on need and the minister's expertise. MPs normally are generalists rather than experts in particular topics, although some cultivate particular areas of interest.

Generalists predominate in the British civil service as well. Priority in civil service recruitment and promotion is given to general intellectual and management skills; successful candidates move from one department to another as their careers progress. Since the mid-nineteenth century, civil servants have been recruited and evaluated on a meritocratic rather than a patronage basis through competitive examinations and internal evaluations. Despite attempts to broaden the educational backgrounds of those entering the bureaucracy, Oxford and Cambridge ("Oxbridge") university graduates still make up a disproportionate share of those selected. Under the British doctrine of separating politics and administration, a civil servant must resign before running for political office, but few combine these careers.

Although there also is a political elite of elected officials in France, they come from somewhat different backgrounds and are more likely to have interrupted, rather than continuous, political careers. Those aspiring to such a career, especially one involving cabinet office and party leadership, often receive an undergraduate education at a prestigious university. Then they may matriculate to an elite, selective graduate educational institution (the *grandes écoles*) such as *Ecole Normale Supérieure* (for academics), *Sciences-Po* (for scientists), or *Ecole Polytechnique* (for engineers). Those desiring a career in government service, private business, or both often attend the *Ecole Nationale d'Administration* (ENA, or National Academy for Administration), an elite administrative training graduate school established after World War II. Graduates of this institution are likely to become high flyers in the civil service and sometimes in the private sector as well. Some of them later have political careers through election to parliament and/or selection into the cabinet.

France also has an unusual tradition of what is called "accumulation of positions," whereby a politician can hold more than one office at a time at different levels of government, even if one of them is a high one such as premier or a cabinet position. Since 1985 one may hold no more than two elected offices. Often major political figures, even government leaders, serve coterminously as mayors, an especially popular position because much of local administration is in the hands of the central government prefect. Jacques Chirac was mayor of Paris from 1977 to 1995, and he also served as prime minister and leader of the opposition in the National Assembly during that time.

In France parliamentary candidate selection is generally decentralized to the regional and local level in the Socialist Party, with oversight from the central organization. In all other parties, candidate selection is predominantly in the hands of the central authorities of the parties, in consultation with local party organizations and leaders. They look for candidates who will uphold party principles and who also have strong local roots in the constituencies they would represent. In some cases, local connections are more important than strong party commitment.

Unlike in the parliamentary system of the United Kingdom, cabinet ministers in France are specialists. That means that it is not necessary to hold a seat in the legislature to be appointed to the cabinet. Thus the premier (or president in a single-party executive) has a wider pool of candidates from which to choose. Once a legislator is appointed to the cabinet, however, an alternative from the same party assumes the seat to perform the legislative duties while the minister concentrates on executive ones. As with other elements of the Fifth Republic constitution, this incompatibility clause was designed to reduce government dependence on the legislature.

Nevertheless, those who aspire to the presidency and premiership usually have parliamentary as well as bureaucratic and party experience. In most parties, leaders are formally chosen by the party membership. However, as mentioned earlier, presidential candidates are nominated through the petition of local notables, and that has occasionally led to more than one candidate of the same party in the contest. Once a party has secured the presidency, as well as a working Assembly majority, however, the nomination of the premier is in the hands of the president.

Germany is closer to the French than the British system for recruiting leaders, but with some differences due to federalism and legal requirements for choice of candidates. Extensive participation in party politics, as in the other countries, is usually necessary, but federalism means that there is a parallel channel to high central office through major party and government positions in the states. Each party chooses its chancellor candidate in a party convention before the federal election, and sometimes the one selected, especially by the Christian Democrats, is the state leader of a populous jurisdiction rather than the leader of the parliamentary party in the Bundestag. The choice of party candidates for the Bundestag is in the hands of local conventions of party organizations, which often choose the same individuals to contest both the SMD and the list seats, giving senior figures with strong local roots two opportunities to be elected. Germany follows the specialist system of recruitment for cabinet ministers. With party lists of candidates, alternates to perform legislator duties are always available.

Germany does not have a centralized higher education system for recruitment of public officials into the bureaucracy. Many officials serve at the *land* rather than the central level. Nevertheless, there is no shortage of candidates who desire these prestigious positions, and the testing process is rigorous. The German civil service is not separated completely from partisan politics. German civil servants can leave their administrative posts for a period and run for political office, with the right to return to their former positions with full benefits when their political term of office is over. This is considered desirable in the interest of keeping legislatures aware of formal legal rules in the lawmaking process.

Political recruitment to major positions in the European Union relies heavily on an individual's having extensive political experience in the home country. State political leaders, of course, are represented on the European Council and the Council of Ministers. EU commissioners, including the president, normally have backgrounds as cabinet ministers in their home countries, even though they are to serve the interests of Europe as a whole while they are on the commission. Nonetheless, they are nominated by their home country, which means ties to the political elite in that country are necessary. Several former party leaders and heads of government have served on the commission; the last two presidents previously were prime ministers in their home countries, Italy and Portugal. Members of the ECJ and ECB require technical backgrounds in their respective specialties as well as domestic political ties. The only EU institution that departs somewhat from this "senior elite connections" mold is the European Parliament. Although the party list electoral system used in most countries gives central party organizations a considerable role in selecting the candidates, in most countries the EP has emerged as an alternative political career rather than one that leads to higher office either in the EU or at home.

Recruitment for the bureaucracy in the European Commission is similar to procedures for the separate member-state bureaucracies. As in other international organizations, however, meritocratic considerations must be balanced against the aim of having roughly proportional shares of citizens from the different member countries serving in each agency. There is a limited flow of officials moving their careers between the bureaucracies of individual member countries and the European Commission.

Elite socialization is a key element in understanding why the British system, although it is formally very easy to change legally and constitutionally, has instead developed through evolutionary change. For better or worse, the narrow political socialization of elites through the House of Commons and the long apprenticeships and many collective activities within parties make elites tend toward consensus rather than innovation, especially in constitutional terms. France has avoided a "deadlock of democracy" with its sometimes-divided executive in the Fifth Republic, and there also a common elite socialization through the higher education system may be part of the reason. In Germany, there is potential for elite conflict because of the distinct career paths provided by federalism, but in practice tendencies toward cooperation, even across parties and interest groups, usually have prevailed. All have stayed within the constitutional boundaries of 1949 after the searing experience of dictatorship and defeat in World War II and the need to rebuild democracy. Unlike Britain, however, legalism, including use of the Constitutional Court to settle political disputes, is the final resort. In the European Union, the elites are all, to varying degrees, proponents of the "European project," despite their national differences. This shared commitment, plus the experience of high-level politics in their home countries, makes them amenable to cooperation for common purposes.

Until recently, one of the major disadvantages of relatively closed socialization processes for political leadership was the exclusion of women from higher levels of government. Although political elites are still disproportionately male, compared to the general population, some countries and political parties have taken substantial steps to correct that. In 2005 women were 32 percent of the members of the lower house of the legislature in Germany and 20 percent in Britain, but only 12 percent in France. In the European Union, women made up 33 percent of the EP. Women recently constituted 26 percent of cabinet ministers in the United Kingdom, 26 percent in France, 38 percent in Germany, and 28 percent in the EU. All three countries have had one woman as government leader in the past thirty years (Margaret Thatcher in Britain, Edith Cresson in France, and Angela Merkel in Germany), although no woman has served as president of the European Commission. What has happened, aside from general social change, is that some political parties, starting with small parties on the left in Germany (the Greens) and the United Kingdom (the Social Democrats), have developed quotas for women candidates at the aspirant, (short list) level and sometimes at the formal candidate level. This is more readily done in party list proportional representation systems, where parties can largely determine what individuals win the multiple seats the party receives based on its share of the votes. France's attempt to legislate gender equality through financial incentives for political parties to nominate more women did not succeed in the legislative election of 2002. In Britain, the Labour Party attempt to guarantee women some safe and competitive seats through all-women short lists, although controversial and short-circuited, had some success in raising the proportion of women in 1997 and again in 2005 through the Sex Discrimination (Electoral Candidates) Act of 2002. But the practice did not spread beyond that party in Britain. In late 2005, new Conservative leader David Cameron charged his party with diversifying its candidates. In Germany, with its PR system, even the CDU earlier had adopted candidate selection processes favorable to women. Almost all member states use party list PR for European Parliament elections, and that has helped women gain such a large share of seats. More debatable, however, is what effect, beyond gender diversity, these procedures have had on the output or performance of governments.

POLICY PROCESSES

The dominant policy processes in these four jurisdictions, with some variations, are an important part of policy dynamics. Each of the three countries uses party government, controlled by the executive based on a legislative majority, as its major policy mode, whereas the process in the EU is more complex and dependent on intercountry bargaining, without a single center of "responsible party government."

The executive is either controlled by a single party with a working majority in the legislature, as normally in the United Kingdom and sometimes in France, or a working coalition government, as normally in Germany and sometimes in France. The latter has provided another variation with its periodic *cohabitation* when there is a divided executive as well as a legislature of different partisanship than the president.

The basic model is the same in all three countries. Policy comes from the executive, backed by party discipline in the legislature and the advice, drafting, and implementation expertise of the bureaucracy, with few avenues to check or block it.

Legislative party caucuses are informed and consulted about the exact shape of legislation and can sometimes act as influences on what is proposed, but once the decision is made to introduce a bill, unity of government party support is expected and normally received. The legislature is reactive rather than initiating. Except in Germany, with its strong committees, upper house, and Constitutional Court, there is little opportunity for the opposition to alter proposed legislation. If a major policy measure or the budget is defeated on a vote in the lower house, that is considered a vote of no confidence, which could lead to a new government. Usually, however, the only recourse for opposition parties is to voice their concerns in debate and hope that it resonates at the next central election.

There are certain issues that parties prefer to keep nonpartisan because of their content and capacity to create intraparty divisions based on strong but conflicting beliefs among legislators and some of their constituents. Although they may be defined slightly differently in various jurisdictions, they are what are called "moral issues," or "issues of conscience," ones that primarily concern matters of life, death, and sexual relations based on individual choice but with more general social implications as well. Included are such issues as abortion, capital punishment, homosexual rights, and in Germany, tobacco control. The Constitutional Court in Germany may also become involved in these disputes. In short, these are issues on which parties avoid taking official positions and on which parliament has "free votes," although party voting often resembles voting on other issues, with leftist parties being more sympathetic to individual human rights concerns than others. Even in systems emphasizing responsible party government, with the parties collectively responsible to the voters for their positions, on these issues party government is avoided rather than embraced.

Within the EU policymaking is more complex, even if the issues are limited in number and type. In terms of policy authority, EU competence focuses on selected economic concerns, but sometimes those have social ramifications as well. Major portions of the EU domain are trade, agriculture, fishing, transportation, consumer protection, public health, environment, regional aid, foreign aid, monetary policy, labor standards, and justice.

There have been increasing forays into foreign policy, especially policy concerning Europe and the Middle East, and even some tentative steps toward a common defense policy. EU foreign and defense policies require unanimity among member states. Several of these policy competences are either shared with the member states or are subject to substantial member-state influence through EU institutions. Each country defines it own interests and positions on matters of potential common action through the EU and attempts to influence decisions in ways favorable to its interests, not only before decisions are made but afterward, through implementation and legal decisions, for instance.

The *acquis communautaire* refers to the whole set of common laws of the EU that each member pledges to uphold once binding decisions have been made. That does not preclude delays or exceptions being formally made, the most famous case being the refusal of three members—Sweden, Denmark, and the United Kingdom—to join the European Central Bank. New members, however, have to pledge themselves to accept the full *acquis communautaire* from their entrance, although transitional arrangements are made for implementation, as in the cases of the CAP and EMU.

The following is a simplified schema of how policymaking occurs in the institutions of the EU: (1) The European Council sets the broad agenda and attempts to resolve difficulties. (2) The European Commission develops specific proposals for new laws and policies to implement the agenda. (3) The European Parliament and the Council of Ministers (Council of Europe) discuss and amend commission proposals; despite increasing powers of co-decision for the

Parliament, the Council is still the principal body in making final decisions. (4) The Commission oversees implementation through the member states. (5) The European Court of Justice interprets and adjudicates conflicts over applicable law.

This is a generally useful model, although there are exceptions, depending on the issue and circumstances. Unlike sovereign states, there is no dominant, central decision-making power in the form of a political executive chosen by, and responsible to, parliament on partisan terms. With this lack of clear accountability, varying interpretations of the European Union's current and potential future policy dynamics have been developed by both academics and political figures.

THEORIES OF EU DEVELOPMENT AND GOVERNANCE

Institutionally the EU is complex and multilayered. There is considerable debate among scholars about which interpretive theories best fit the organization. The major contenders are three: (1) the neofunctionalist theory; (2) the liberal intergovernmentalism (state-centered) theory; and (3) the multilevel governance theory. The neofunctionalist theory argues that "form follows function." In the EU context, this means that elaborate construction of political institutions is less important than having integrationist political leaders cooperate so that the organization performs its assigned tasks successfully. Through a spillover effect the organization then will be assigned more tasks, and more countries will be encouraged to join. Thus, "ever-closer union," the dream of European suprastate integrationists, will develop over time. Neofunctionalists see the key institutions of the EU as those that are most "European-oriented," namely, the Commission as it develops and implements EU policy, and increasingly the European Court of Justice, as it acts to make the implementation of EU policies more uniform across member countries.

The second major interpretive theory of the EU is "liberal intergovernmentalism," which argues that EU success depends fundamentally on member states' seeing it as in their individual interests to allow the EU to have more authority in certain policy sectors. This view, unlike that of the neofunctionalists, sees EU integration largely as a negotiated process among the member states (intergovernmentalism). States are willing to give up part of their sovereignty if they are convinced of the overall positive gain for their interests, even if those benefits occur through trade-offs on other issues. Within states, interests can attempt to influence policy both through the positions of their governments and through lobbying EU institutions directly. For liberal intergovernmentalists, the key institutions of the EU are the Council of Ministers, where each state's interests are represented, even if now under increasing qualified majority voting (QMV) decision rules, and the European Council, the periodic summit meeting of the chief executives of the member states.

The third, and increasingly influential interpretation of EU developments is multilevel governance. This view denies both that the EU is becoming a super-state, in which member states are clearly subordinate to the broader organization, and that it remains exclusively a negotiated, state-centered organization. According to this perspective, what has developed is a permanent system of multilevel governance. Some policies are controlled by EU institutions; others remain largely in the hands of the sovereign states. But critically, lower levels of government, particularly provinces in federal systems such as Germany and regionally autonomous areas in officially unitary systems such as the United Kingdom, also have significant roles in the EU, both as lobbyists for policies favoring their interests (regional aid) and as participants in the Council of Ministers, when issues arise in which these jurisdictions have authority. The 1992 EU recognition of the principle of subsidiarity means that levels below the member state have legitimacy within the organization. Which institutions are most influential depends on the issue.

POLITICAL VIEWS OF THE EUROPEAN UNION

Politically, views differ about the desirability of "ever-greater union" through the EU. Euroenthusiasts (federalists) see more policy authority for the EU over both domestic and foreign policy as desirable, as Europe would function in a more coordinated fashion, solidifying its international role and dampening frictions on the continent. They prefer EU competence in more policies, QMV rather than unanimity in decision making, and more power for the European Commission and European Parliament. Their champions have been former president of the European Commission Jacques Delors and, in terms of member countries, Germany, Italy, and smaller members. In recent years, however, all of these normally EU-supporting countries have become less predictable. On the other hand, Euroskeptics (intergovernmentalists, antifederalists) favor maintenance of the traditional sovereign state, restricted policy competence for the EU, less use of QMV, and keeping decision-making power in the hands of the Council of Ministers and European Council. Their champions have been individual political figures on both the left and right of the ideological spectrum, such as French president Charles de Gaulle and British prime minister Margaret Thatcher. Some groups and countries see the EU as potentially burdensome in social policy, for example, the United Kingdom, even under a Labour government. On the other hand, some countries with strong domestic welfare states, such as Sweden and Denmark, have been concerned that the EU is becoming too economically neoliberal and may erode their capacity to make internal policy choices. These contradictory views, along with complaints against the internal economic policies of the state governments and fear of economic competition from the new member states, also led people to vote against the EU constitution in the French and Dutch referendums in 2005.

Nevertheless, for member states these are tendencies rather than fixed camps, as all countries act in EU councils to advance and protect their particular interests.

The need for extraordinary majorities of member states to make policy within the Council of Ministers, plus the involvement of multiple institutions in the process, has led some analysts to consider the EU a primary example of what is called "consensus" decision making, as exists among institutions in such countries as Germany, the Netherlands, Belgium, and Austria. Other analysts contend that there have been two dominant countries in EU decision making—the two most populous original members, France and Germany. The so-called Franco-German axis arose from their mutual need to make the EU successful to maintain peace between these two dominant continental powers, which had gone to war three times in less than one hundred years. The EU served other purposes as well. Germany needed the organization to legitimize its reemergence as an economic and political power within the constraints of a united Europe, after its military aggressiveness, especially under the Nazis. France wanted the EU to enhance its status as semi-independent from U.S. influence. Thus Germany was willing to make economic sacrifices in terms of the EU budget, especially CAP payments, to gain political legitimacy among other members and more generally in the world (see Table 3-2). France used the CAP to benefit its own agricultural sector and attached itself more generally to the German economic engine within the EU to improve its own economic and political standing. In recent years, however, that cooperative relationship has faltered, without becoming entirely defunct.

The current period marks a turning point in the development of the EU. An enlarged and reconstituted EU could emerge with enhanced power in the world. Largely through the EU, Europe is more peacefully unified than ever before in its history. Whether that condition will continue and deepen, or weaken and perhaps even dissipate, has been thrown into doubt by rejection of the EU constitution, especially by one of its largest and founding members, France. In addition to the alternatives of greater or less integration, a "variable speed" European Union could also develop, with some members moving ahead on coordinated policies more than others.

CONCLUSION: BRITAIN, FRANCE, GERMANY, AND THE EUROPEAN UNION

Within these four jurisdictions—the United Kingdom, France, Germany, and the European Union—are different internal dynamics, as we have discussed. But the major question facing Europe today is what the role of the European Union will be in the domestic and foreign policies of its members. "Europeanization" refers to the convergence of policies and institutions in the member countries through their mutual interaction, especially within the European Union. The EU can facilitate Europeanization through voluntary emulation or make it coercive through EU mandates. Member states can also initiate Europeanization by influencing the EU to endorse their preferences, which then are disseminated more widely across countries. Because countries have diverse interests, Europeanization is inevitably a contested process.

Although recent British prime ministers have indicated that they want Britain to be at the heart of Europe, the United Kingdom has continued to be closer to the edge than the center of the EU. Its approach has been intergovernmentalist and oriented toward market neoliberalism. Even Tony Blair has maintained Britain's defensive engagement with the EU. He has continued to argue for the special British budgetary rebate first negotiated two decades ago by the Conservative government of Margaret Thatcher and also successfully defended a series of "red lines" against further centralization of the EU in the negotiations over the EU constitution.

Britain remains one of only three older EU members not to join the European Monetary Union and its currency, the euro. If Britain were to join the EMU, then control over its monetary policy would effectively pass into the hands of the European Union. The chancellor of the exchequer (treasury secretary) periodically announces whether current economic conditions meet the "five tests" necessary for him to recommend that Britain should converge with the euro zone. Tony Blair has indicated that this step would only be taken if a countrywide referendum demonstrates public support. Thus Britain continues to be a leading member of the "awkward squad" of countries within the EU who want to maintain strong state sovereignty within the organization and limit common EU endeavors.

France has been ambivalent about its role within the EU. Many of the most enthusiastic supporters of greater European integration, from its founding, have been French, including Jean Monnet, Robert Schuman, and Jacques Delors. The position of the French government has shifted from periods of intergovernmentalism under Charles de Gaulle toward a later willingness to have the EU operate more frequently as a superstate, as long as France can maintain a central role in the organization. The Franco-German axis allowed this to happen, but now economic weakness and the expansion of EU membership threaten to dilute the power of that alliance. France has defied the constraints of the stability and growth pact that limit government budget deficits within the EMU, which endangers the whole institution. The rejection of the EU constitution in 2005 revealed doubts in France about whether it can continue to influence the direction of the EU as strongly as it has in the past. It would not be entirely unprecedented for France to assume a more intergovernmentalist role.

The role of Germany in the European Union is shifting as well. For a long time Germany was willing to be net contributor to EU budget because of the political benefits it received from incorporation into the EU, as well as the economic trading opportunities provided for the largest economy in the organization. But over the past decade Germany has become reunified, has become less central to an expanded EU, and has had a weak rather than a strong economy. By defying the stability and growth pact underlying the European Central Bank, an organization founded on German sound money principles, and increasingly balking over its budgetary contributions, Germany has shown itself to be quite willing to pursue its own short-term interests. Yet it has not moved as far as France, much less the United Kingdom, along the intergovernmentalist path, as shown by the German parliament's approval of the EU constitution in the week before the French referendum. Germany is a more wary but still committed European integrationist.

Foreign policy continues to divide EU members. Several European countries see their goals and strategies as not in harmony with those of the United States. That was the case even before the administration of U.S. president George W. Bush and its policies on such issues as Middle East peace, human rights, foreign aid, and the balance between social provision through the state and free enterprise. There have also been some significant trade disputes between the EU and the United States. The crisis over the Iraq war and the policies and style of the Bush presidency have deepened those divisions. There is increasing recognition in the United States of the economic power of the EU, although less recognition of its capacity in "soft power" diplomacy since the U.S. position is still based on the "hard power" of modern, high-technology military capacity when diplomacy fails. A more united Europe probably would accelerate the divergence in policy from the United States. A less-united or even fragmented Europe would make it easier for the United States to continue its dominance in foreign and defense policy.

Already these three countries, as well as others, have made major changes to accommodate European Union membership. Whether they are willing to adjust even more to the prospect of a united Europe, with the enhanced economic and political position that would represent but at the cost of less decision-making sovereignty for themselves, is the major question of the near future. Many observers think it will take a more united Europe under the European Union to make Europe more independent of the United States, but it is not clear that all states desire such a future or even that those who have heretofore been more integrationist will continue to be.

Suggestions for Additional Reading

Books

Bale, Tim. *European Politics: A Comparative Introduction.* New York: Palgrave, 2005.

Bartle, John, and Anthony King, eds. *Britain at the Polls 2005.* Washington, D.C.: CQ Press, 2006.

Bulmer, Simon, and Christian Lequesne, eds. *The Member States of the European Union.* New York: Oxford University Press, 2005.

Cole, Alistair, Jonah Levy, and Patrick Le Gales, eds. *Developments in French Politics 3.* New York: Palgrave, 2005.

Conradt, David. *The German Polity.* 7th ed. New York: Longman, 2000.

Dinan, Desmond. *Ever Closer Union.* 3rd ed. New York: Palgrave, 2005.

Farrell, David M. *Electoral Systems: A Comparative Introduction.* New York: Palgrave, 2001.

Gallagher, Michael, Michael Laver, and Peter Mair. 2005. *Representative Government in Modern Europe.* 4th ed. New York: McGraw Hill, 2005.

Geddes, Andrew. *The Politics of Migration and Immigration in Europe.* London: Sage, 2003.

Giddens, Anthony. *The Third Way: The Renewal of Social Democracy.* Cambridge: Polity Press, 1998.

Hix, Simon. *The Political System of the European Union.* 2nd ed. New York: Palgrave, 2005.

Hooghe, Lisbet, and Gary Marks. *Multilevel Governance and European Integration.* Lanham, Md.: Rowman and Littlefield, 2001.

Inglehart, Ronald. *Culture Shift in Advanced Industrial Democracies.* Princeton: Princeton University Press, 1990.

Leduc, Larry. *The Politics of Direct Democracy.* Peterborough, Ontario, Canada: Broadview Press, 2002.

Lewis-Beck, Michael. *How France Votes.* Chatham, N.J.: Chatham House, 2000.

Lijphart, Arend. *Patterns of Democracy: Government Forms and Performance in Thirty-Six Countries.* New Haven: Yale University Press, 1999.

Marx, Karl, and Friedrich Engels. *The Communist Manifesto.* 1848. Reprint. New York: Signet Classics, 1998.

Norton, Philip. *The British Polity.* 4th ed. New York: Longman, 2000.

Piper, J. Richard. *The Major Nation-States in the European Union.* New York: Pearson/Longman, 2005.

Putnam, Robert D. *Bowling Alone: The Collapse and Revival of American Community.* New York: Simon and Schuster, 2000.

Rosamond, Ben. *Theories of European Integration.* New York: Palgrave, 2000.

Rose, Richard. *What Is Europe?* New York: Longman, 1997.

Smith, T. Alexander, and Ray Tatalovich. *Cultures at War: Moral Conflicts in Western Democracies.* Peterborough, Ontario, Canada: Broadview Press, 2003.

van Oudenaren, John. *Uniting Europe: European Integration and the Post-Cold War World.* 2nd ed. Lanham, Md.: Rowman and Littlefield, 2004.

Webb, Paul, David Farrell, and Ian Holliday, eds. *Political Parties in Advanced Industrial Democracies.* New York: Oxford University Press, 2002.

Zeff, Eleanor E., and Ellen B. Pirro, eds. *The European Union and the Member States.* 2nd ed. Boulder: Lynne Rienner, 2006.

Web Sites

British Broadcasting Corporation, www.bbc.com

British Politics Group, www.uc.edu/bpg

CIA World Factbook, www.cia.gov/cia/publications/factbook

The Economist, www.economist.com

Election Process Information Collection, www.epicproject.org

European Union Studies Association, www.eustudies.org

Freedom House, www.freedomhouse.org

German Information Center, www.germany-info.org

German News, www.germnews.de/dn/about

Information on France, www.france.com
International Institute for Democracy and Electoral Assistance, www.idea.int
The Inter-Parliamentary Union, www.ipu.org
Richard Kimber's Political Science Resources, www.psr.keele.ac.uk
World Press Review, www.worldpress.org

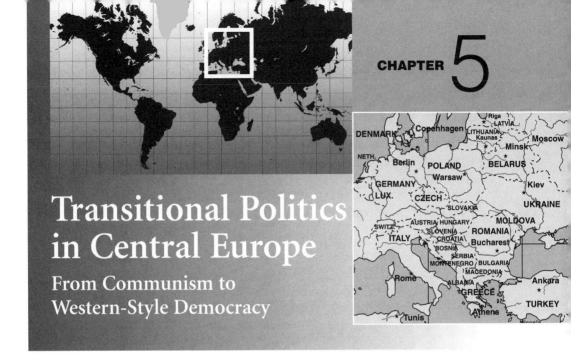

CHAPTER 5

Transitional Politics in Central Europe

From Communism to Western-Style Democracy

In the realm of comparative politics through most of the twentieth century, one political system stood in sharp contrast to the others. Four generations of American and global leaders contended with images and stereotypes of the so-called communist political systems. Communist political systems claimed a distinct ideological heritage, a contrasting goal culture (meaning what societies say they want to achieve), a poignantly different institutional structure, and a pattern of political behaviors (mass and elite) unlike other political systems. In many ways, that legacy is what makes the former communist countries such interesting cases for comparison today. They share elements of the same recent political heritage and are struggling with deciding what to change and how to change in the special conditions of the twenty-first century.

With changes that caused the disintegration and collapse of Soviet-style communism between 1989 and 1992, all of the ideological conflict and most of the political antagonism stemming from systemic differences vanished. The fundamental characteristics of the political and economic systems in Central and Eastern Europe changed in the 1990s. It is that process and those changes that draw our attention. In comparative politics it is important to remember that we strive to use social scientific means to examine how systems organize themselves, adapt, and manage. It is also important to remember that, like all living systems, societies can become ill and even die. In today's language such political systems are called "failed states." Lessons from the communist era in Central and Eastern Europe are instructive in this way. Nonetheless, the larger and more intellectually valuable task is to take a close, comparative look at

Table 5-1   European Postcommunist Political Systems

Large, non-EU	Small, EU	Small, non-EU, *conflicted*
Russia	Hungary[a]	Serbia
Ukraine	Poland[a]	Bosnia
Belarus	Bulgaria[a]	Montenegro
	Romania[a]	Kosovo
	Slovakia	Macedonia
	Czech Republic	Moldova
	Slovenia	Croatia
	Latvia	Albania[a]
	Lithuania	
	Estonia	

[a] Same political boundaries as under communism.

transitional systems. Can these countries implement the West's ideological pre-scriptions? We need to understand the implications if the answer is yes, and if the answer is no. These countries are experiencing a metamorphosis. We know what they looked like; we are observing their transformations. Crucially, we watch as the political leaders outline objectives and try to enlist their publics. Less clear is just how manageable the transition is. Social scientists have recognized that because no political system has ever been through this particular process—that is, from communism to something else. It is an illuminating and instructive political experiment whatever the outcome.

The task of comparing and contrasting postcommunist political systems presents many options. As a point of departure, in the next two chapters we create three clusters of these postcommunist political systems (see Table 5-1). The first identifies Russia and Ukraine as two very large countries with very new political systems that have *not* gravitated to the European Union. Both of those cases will be examined in chapter 6. In the second group are generally smaller countries that have already entered the EU—Hungary and Poland, two countries that existed under communism in their present geographic form, and two others, Slovenia and the Czech Republic, that have been newly created from the disintegration of larger countries that existed before and under communism. The third cluster comprises small states that have emerged from the breakup of a larger state and that have not yet made the decision to accede to the EU. In the present chapter we focus on select cases from the second group. Among the European postcommunist states, only Albania, in the third group, is an aberration in that it retains its original communist-era boundaries and is not currently an active candidate for EU membership.

To detail all the challenges that present themselves to postcommunist political systems would require volumes. The notion that once the limitations and inhibitions of communism were jettisoned, Central and Eastern Europe would be able to duplicate the standard of living, the security, and the political stability common in mature democratic and market systems has lingered both in the postcommunist countries and in Western Europe and the United States, resulting in ever-spiraling frustration.

Before delving more deeply into these political systems, it is wise for us to create a framework that will enable us to sort through the myriad factors that one might use to compare and contrast. Simply stated, to emerge as democratic political systems, weather the storms associated with transition from a nondemocratic system, and survive the long-term strains of maintaining a democratic political environment, a political system must acquire or establish three things:

1. A generic *value system* shared by the bulk of the governed—ideas and expectations that enable the leaders to communicate with, and anticipate the behavior of, the publics they are attempting to lead
2. *Political machinery*—structures or mechanisms institutionalized to the point that they are recognized and can produce the outcomes (policies) that the leadership is aiming toward
3. *Leadership*—a cadre of persons able to pursue goals by making rational policy choices, accounting for costs, payoffs, and consequences

A bit more explanation is required. Values are the platform for both attitudes and behavior. Casual political rhetoric in democracies often leaves one with the impression that everyone in society "does their own thing" or can go in whatever direction they wish. Political systems wishing to become democratic are essentially saying that they wish to take the society where the masses themselves say they want to go. The tough question becomes, What happens in societies in which both government and governed are inexperienced with democratic relationships when the public comes to believe that each person in society can really set his or her own agenda (or destination) for government? This level of naïveté is evident in Central and Eastern Europe. Imagine a new leader genuinely committed to taking the society where it wants to go. He or she asks the public to point toward that destination, and what follows is the unpatterned response of a free public: Everyone points in a different direction—up and down, right and left, forward and back. How can the leader take the system in all those directions at once? It is not possible. The system then has the unenviable choice of either abandoning the notion that it will take the masses where they want to go, or pretending that there is a consensus about direction coming from the masses. The point is basic but important. Functioning democratic systems require a consensus about direction, about destination, even if broad or vague. Established democracies have this. Transitional systems typically do not. Constructing that consensus is the first, critical task for postcommunist systems.

If a consensus emerges from the public about where they want government to take them, the next task is the construction of a vehicle that the public can board for the journey toward the destination. This turns our attention to the political machinery and the political architecture for that machinery. Imagine this as the bus that could move a large mass of people toward a common goal.

Naturally, reaching the destination is less critical than making progress along the path toward it. A student thinking through this analogy might ask, Why is it necessary to have a bus? Can't folks in a society walk toward their destination and implicitly set their own individual pace? Of course that can be, and when one examines many of the political systems in our world, it looks as if that is often what is happening. But the twenty-first century is a keenly global, competitive, and transparent era, in which many societies have already embarked on their own journeys using political machinery that gets them along their paths more quickly and effectively. People in one society are likely to be displeased with their progress, just as one walking along the side of the road is displeased when a bus zips past toward a similar destination. What all this means for our political look at Central and Eastern European systems is that we must be careful to examine how assembled and functional the institutional parts of the political and economic system are. "Transition" implies that the bus is only *partially* assembled.

Completing the model, the leadership of a society functions as the driver of the bus. The driver will certainly play a major role in defining the speed, path, and maneuvering essential to move the society toward its goals or destination. The skills of the driver must not be presumed. Transitional systems are driving along new paths, slick, untested, and fraught with hazards and unanticipated detours. As irony would have it, "drivers" in established democracies need fewer skills because institutional ruts in the road more clearly guide their journey. Furthermore, they evolve in systems that teach and test their driving skills before they take on driving the bus. Transitional systems have no such advantages. Their paths are without institutional pattern or grooves, and most of the leaders find themselves in positions of great authority without previous experience—certainly without experience in a democratic context.

THE OLD SYSTEM IN A NUTSHELL

Communism advocated a goal of economic equality, or "economic democracy," which in practical terms meant a leveling of the society economically. These values, coupled with the government's control of prices and distribution, created a belief that many goods and services should be guaranteed by government. Functionally, this was the value consensus for that system.

There was also an elaborate political machinery. The single Communist Party was designed and refined over time to perform one primary function: to maintain its exclusive hold on power. If the machine's effectiveness were judged only in those terms, it functioned well until Mikhail Gorbachev began tinkering with the machine. In comparative terms, the political machinery of the communist system was as extensive, bureaucratized, and penetrating as any in the twentieth century. Setting aside for the moment what one may think about a system designed to keep itself in power, there can be little doubt that both a broad value system and a developed political machine existed in communist systems.

It is far less clear that the system generated a minimum level of leadership that could direct and manage those societies. The recruitment system, the inadequate education system (in terms of policy-relevant studies), the propensity to quash issue-oriented debate, the minimal relationship between rulers and ruled, and the very vertical nature of the political system combined to ensure mediocre leadership. The leadership in Central and Eastern Europe was generally detached, non-innovative, and passive. It failed to acknowledge that political systems, as all living systems, must adapt to inevitably changing circumstances and environments. It ultimately revealed itself incapable of calculating the costs, payoffs, and consequences of major policy decisions. Simply, the pattern of politics produced leadership that was the weakest link in the political system. It was characteristically inept, narrow in its thinking, and timid in the post-Stalin era (after 1953). It committed more energy to maintaining illusions than to solving problems. The political landscape in the Gorbachev era (1985–1992) was dominated by uncertainty and unsolidified change.

The new systems, from Lithuania to Albania and Moldova to Slovenia, share a number of concrete and complex problems. By 1994 there were twenty-five political systems where five years earlier there had been just nine. Pressures for disintegration persist, especially in struggling systems that contain ultranationalist groups.

COMPARISONS

Students of comparative politics always need to remain keenly aware of the rationale for the comparisons that they make. For example, if one opts to look at communist versus postcommunist systems, a positive sense emerges from the realization that the old system was nonadaptive, had poor leadership, and had educational, economic, and political structures that stifled initiative and results. This approach suggests comparing the past with the present. Certainly one could argue that off-loading that burdensome and unproductive system was a good thing. At least, a greater potential exists in the new system for solving problems.

A less-common view, but one that arguably is more analytically productive, suggests examining the educational, economic, and political systems that exist today and comparing them to what will reasonably be needed to face the future. The emphasis here would be on systems that can be effective in twenty-first-century terms, in essence, comparing the present with the future. Political scientists and especially university students, whose lives lie ahead and whose vision is most often fixed on the future, should consider this second strategy. Much of what follows is built from this second kind of comparative focus: Are the Central and Eastern European states developing political systems that will enable them to face and meet challenges that lie ahead?

FRAMEWORK APPLIED

All of this frames a very challenging reality for the transitional political systems that are trying to move rapidly from communism to Western-style democracy. What lies ahead in this chapter is an effort to broach the key questions and elements of political transition. Although some partial answers will surface, the reader should never lose sight of the fundamental value of this enterprise: You should be able to think about future developments in politics anywhere by thinking about the questions raised here.

VALUE CONSENSUS

Principal Agents

Of central concern is who is contributing to the formation of a value consensus in these transitional political systems. Leaders play some role. Vladimir Putin, in Russia, has promulgated order and the fight against terrorism as his desired theme. Aleksander Kwasniewski, in Poland, has emphasized Poland's need to shape its future linked to Western Europe. Viktor Orban (of the Fidesz Party) and Ferenc Gyurcsány (Socialist Party), past and current prime ministers in Hungary, frame a consumer culture. Apart from leaders, external dynamics help crystallize a consensus. Television, the Internet, and the European Union all have key roles in bringing a common future into sharper focus for the public in these transitional societies. Beyond them are international agencies, the International Monetary Fund (IMF) and the World Bank prominent among them, that have as their explicit task to guide societies toward a prepackaged model or destination. Although there is significant debate about the wisdom of this or that destination, the only point being offered here is that political development in these societies, at this stage, requires that there be a destination defined by a broad and general consensus. Some political theorists call this a "common story" or "narrative," but whatever it is called, political societies in the twenty-first century will have great difficulty drifting toward democracy.

Two other agents play roles with varying levels of effectiveness: religion and education. Poland and Russia are two examples of places where organized religion has joined the dialogue about the society's destination. Ukraine, Hungary, Slovenia, and the Czech Republic are considerably less homogeneous in religion, and that has muted the voice of religion in framing a consensus.

Education is another powerful element in the dialogue. The Czech Republic, Hungary, Poland, and Slovenia all have engaged their educational resources to enhance the study of society and to nurture academic and public discourse on society's direction. In other systems, notably Russia and Ukraine, the reformatting of the education system has been halting and modest, producing little dialogue about the future that could guide or challenge leadership.

The education infrastructure in Bosnia was so thoroughly destroyed or compromised by the violence of the 1990s that it is impossible to recognize it as an actor in the effort to create a consensus. A study generated by the *Times Higher Education Supplement* (November 5, 2004), a very reputable source, ranked the world's two hundred top universities, and only one postcommunist university made its list—Lomonosov Moscow State University in Russia (at number 92). Not a single Central European university was listed.

How Refined?

The next key question is how congealed are the efforts at consensus? Public opinion polls from the region suggest that although they are certainly not solidly formed, patterns are beginning to emerge. Generally, the number of Central and Eastern Europeans who say that they have "some trust" or "a lot of trust" in government hovers at around 40 percent, significantly below the global average. Only Latin America and the Middle East have lower levels of trust in government. Trust in "the media" is around 50 percent, a figure above the global average and on a par with the highest levels in the world. When the World Economic Forum sponsored a survey in 2003 on the extent to which the public trust the legislature to operate in the society's best interest, 65 percent of Central and Eastern Europeans indicated little or no trust, and only 27 percent indicated some or a lot of trust. When asked if their country is governed by the will of the people, 70 percent of Central and Eastern Europeans said no; 17 percent said yes. Curiously, significantly more people of the region living in countries not committed to EU membership indicated confidence that their countries are governed by the "will of the people"—47 percent ("Voice of the People" survey, Gallup and Environs International).

What Values?

The last question is, What are the values around which a consensus is forming, if indeed one is forming at all? Polls also reveal deep schisms about goals in the public's mind. One way to encapsulate these differences is to highlight the tension between prosperity, income, risk, inequality, and insecurity on the one hand, and security, social services, income leveling, and equality on the other. Increasingly these are not seen as continua but as dichotomies that polarize politicians and the public along what are perceived as ideological lines. There is also an apparent division between those that see the future as the destination and those that see the destination in terms of the past, of returning to former glories. (More about this later in the chapter.)

Another key value that raises concern about democratic development in Central Europe is the centrality of tolerance. From one considered perspective, tolerance is the absolute cornerstone of functioning democratic and capitalist systems. Tolerance is the conceptual platform that enables the debate that is requisite to compromise. It is the glue that holds together societies that are just beginning to work through issues that come naturally with heterogeneity and political debate. Most Central and Eastern European societies have very little experience with tolerance. Hallmark periods of power in the region have been associated with intolerance and exploitation. Russia and Ukraine suffer from this absence of historical experience. The histories of Poland and Hungary include embarrassingly long episodes of harsh intolerance. The Czech Republic and Slovenia have more passive histories. Bosnia has the most poignant recent pattern of intolerance, and it is evident in nearly every aspect of politics today.

The most significant development that accelerated the search for common values was the emergence of the European Union. By 1992, just as communism was disintegrating in the region, Western Europe was raising its level of integration from the European "Community" to the European "Union." In essence, that made the relationships in the region more binding and involved some sacrifice of political sovereignty by member states. As political systems in the postcommunist region began foundering, the European Union provided an elaborated set of societal goals and an organizational destination for these countries that are best captured in the requisites for formal membership (it should be added that these conditions are negotiable and flexible given sundry interpretations and situations):

- A stable system of democratic government
- Institutions that ensure the rule of law and respect for human rights
- A functioning and competitive market economy
- An administration capable of implementing EU laws and policies

These should be understood as setting the destination for aspiring member societies past, present, and future.

The absence of a consensus in Central and Eastern Europe in the early 1990s was a function of the process by which communism ended. Large numbers of persons and groups in communist countries (including some Communist Party members) concluded that the communist regimes were not meeting the minimum obligations that they had laid out. In a nutshell, broad and diverse movements began to grow quickly in Central and Eastern Europe that shared a vision of what people were against. Solidarnosc (Poland), the Civic Forum (Czechoslovakia), the Democratic Forum (Hungary), and Yeltsin's *ad hoc* effort to save Gorbachev (Russia, August 1991)—all reflected a strong sense of what was *not* wanted. However, each disintegrated when the time came to establish what the public did want. The point is that a consensus did not grow out of these movements. The task of establishing one fell on the subsequent governments. The difficulty was apparent, and some still are unable to frame a constructive consensus.

The so-called Orange Revolution in Ukraine (2004) is yet another example of a movement rejecting established directions but soon recognizing that it lacked a mandate for setting a new destination.

POLITICAL ARCHITECTURE OF THE STATE

Basic Constitutional Framework

The architectural design of a political system is often reflected in its constitution. Though with markedly different levels of flexibility and specificity, every constitution sets out the following:

1. The component parts of the political system
2. The discrete functions of each part
3. The nature of the relationships among the parts

Commonly, a few other issues are addressed, including the mechanism to change the design, the boundaries (if any) of government activity, and a set of ideals that establish a model and/or destination for the society.

In many political systems, describing the constitution is relatively simple because of the longevity and stability of the document. In systems experiencing or that have recently experienced profound change, often traumatic change in human terms, describing constitutions is more tentative. It requires caution because of the absence of a historical record that could provide insight into the critical relationship between what is supposed to happen and what does happen in the system. Naturally, sharpening our view of this discrepancy is never easy, and generalizations need constant reevaluation. Where patterns have barely had time to emerge, extreme caution is warranted.

We can separate the communist political systems that were, technically speaking, federal systems from those that were unitary systems. The difference is the degree to which the central government can overrule policies made in the parts—whatever they be called—in that system. Unitary systems make it possible for any decision made by lower authorities to be overturned, but federal systems insulate some policies from such action. It should first be said that as they actually worked communist political systems did not function as federal systems. All were unitary by the definition above. The only reason that the distinction is significant at all is that all of the so-called federal systems from the communist era—the Soviet Union, Czechoslovakia, and Yugoslavia—have disintegrated, broken into a number of separate sovereign states, whereas all of those that were unitary have retained the same political boundaries. Perhaps the fact that they were nominally federal systems indicated the disintegrative pressures that existed when the three systems were formed. In any event, it does strongly suggest that communist systems were particularly inept at forging new bonds and identities that could hold a diverse political system together under stress.

Compounding this problem in postcommunist states, communism made no effort to create a public understanding of the workings of the political system. Guiding one's behavior in it based on the constitution would have produced great frustration or worse. In simple terms, constitutions did not and do not clarify for individuals what they can and cannot do or what they could expect from government in communist or postcommunist states. Political experience in communist systems simply taught people to frame political expectations by other means and to seek other logics by which to engage themselves with government.

The European systems emerging from communism set their constitutional direction toward participatory, representative, and open governments, with varying measures of oversight, limitation on authority, and transparency. The variations are significant, but the thrust was decidedly toward Western-style constitutional systems. All have written constitutions (see Table 5-2).

Volumes can be, and have been, written about Central and Eastern European constitutions. It is perhaps wise to raise just a few comparative questions:

- How new are these constitutions?
- How much do they reflect, or build on, the old constitutional order?
- How refined is the political machinery created?
- What are the key issues that define the effort to create effective government?

How New? The issue here is subtle. To what extent did the architects of the new, postcommunist political systems choose to build on the constitutional foundations of the past? They had options. In all cases there were older constitutions and documents that could be used. Some of them had been superseded by later communist constitutions, and others simply lay dormant under the de facto operation of communist political routines. The story is interesting, and the systems we have chosen reflect very different behaviors. We find examples of simple duplication of earlier designs. In other cases, the old constitution was used as a template, and significant changes and additions were made. In still other cases an effort was made to import a document that had worked effectively elsewhere. Then there are the examples of conjuring a constitution from scratch. Most constitutional processes in these countries involved a combination of approaches, most often directed by a constitutional commission appointed by the new government. That procedure had the advantage of committing more time and thought to the task, while distancing the design process from the day-to-day political struggles that dominated the political landscape.

Of our examples, Slovenia and the Czech Republic acted most quickly, drafting and ratifying their new constitutions in less than three years from the collapse of Communist political authority. That had the advantage of quickly establishing rules—both political and legal—upon which the public and commercial interests could premise their behavior. Both constitutions were modeled on ones that existed in other politically developed states.

The Russian case exemplifies what can go wrong in hasty constitutional redesign. In 1991, an awkward series of political events caused the collapse of the Soviet political system. Boris Yeltsin held the position as leader of the part of the Soviet Union called the Russian Republic and simply assumed that when Russia became an independent country he was the legitimate leader of the new

Table 5-2   Constitutions

Country	Date	Distinction
Slovenia	Dec. 1991	• Fastest production after communism.
Czech Republic	Dec. 1992	
Russia	Dec. 1993	• Never ratified by legislature; vague referendum.
		• Drafted by Yeltsin and his inner circle.
Bosnia		• The Dayton Agreement, signed Dec. 14, 1995, included a new constitution now in force.
		• Each of the entities also has its own constitution.
Ukraine	June 1996	
Poland	April 1997	• Modest redesign of 1921 constitution.
		• Drafted by commission led by Kwasnievski.
		• Most elaborate in region with 243 articles.
Hungary	Sept. 1997	• Modest redesign of 1949 communist constitution.
		• Drafted by commission.
Serbia and Montenegro	April 2003	• Newest.

political system. At that point, the structure of the old Soviet system was simply brought forward into the indeterminate future. Before long, in October 1993, a violent crisis arose in which the legislature confronted the executive branch over the rules (or absence of rules) of the political system. In the outcome of that violent episode, in which Yeltsin and his executive branch cohorts defeated the side comprising the legislative leadership, the vice president, and a significant portion of the Moscow public, it became apparent that a new set of rules (a new constitution) was needed to advance Yeltsin's interests.

Yeltsin and a small circle of close advisers retreated to draft a document that would both look like a democratic schema and enable Yeltsin to manage (or manipulate) the legislature. It was written in two weeks and announced as the new constitution in advance of the December 1993 elections for the Duma, the lower house of the Russian legislature. Those elections generated a legislature far from Yeltsin's liking, and he declined to submit the draft constitution to it for ratification. Instead, Yeltsin included a question in an April 1994 referendum seeking to have the public legitimize the document. The constitution was not the central focus of the referendum, and each element of the referendum process was open to considerable criticism. In spite of the fact that most Russians admitted that they had not read the proposed constitution, the voters endorsed it by a slight margin. It is also true that American funds were poured into the campaign for a positive vote on the referendum items including the new constitution. In a very technical sense, the Russian constitution has never been ratified explicitly by either the public or the legislature. The 2003 Duma elections were the very first to produce a legislature that would even consider approving the Russian constitution, which is heavily tilted toward a powerful and dominant executive. Russia, then, is an example of creating a constitution hastily and "from scratch."

In contrast, Hungary, Poland, and Ukraine took more measured and patient steps through the mechanics of creating new constitutions. Those systems invested more than five years into the issues, challenges, and implications of their backbone documents. Commissions were created, and although progress was slow and sometimes halted by political infighting, the process was more transparent and seemed to benefit from critical scrutiny by the news media and a range of political groups.

In sum, there were advantages and disadvantages to the relatively fast and the slow paths to constitutional design and approval. All of the postcommunist constitutions are less than two decades old, and the transition has put great strain on all of them. Limited resources, ambiguity, complexity, and thin public knowledge have hampered the patterned growth of predictable behavior by both government and nongovernmental actors in these political systems. In essence, they are not yet institutionalized constitutional systems.

Key Constitutional Issues Three basic issues have drawn, and will continue to draw, the attention of political scientists as they scrutinize the theory and practice of the new constitutions. The first is the effort to define the "community." That is, who is entitled to be a part of the society, and what protections are afforded the majority and minority? The effort is seen in provisions about official language, eligibility for citizenship, and minority rights. These are particularly thorny issues in Estonia, Latvia, Slovakia, Croatia, Ukraine, Romania, and Moldova. The most significant minority populations affected by such provisions in these countries are Hungarians and Russians.

The second issue is the impulse away from pluralistic, federal styles. The communist legacy and the inexperience and anxiety of new leaders, coupled with the breakup of all of the systems that had been formally federal in design, caused many makers of new constitutions to tilt away from decentralization of political power.

The last issue is, in many ways, the most crucial and the most enduring: the issue of sovereignty. Sovereignty is the ultimate authority to make decisions binding on a population. The new Central and Eastern European constitutions faced, and continue to face, political strategies linking them to the European Union, which necessarily abridges that sovereignty. In fact, there is no such thing as partial sovereignty. EU member and candidate states effectively join a macro-state that has, even if it chooses not to exercise it, sovereignty over the populations in the member states.

More Political Architecture

The political architecture of a society is a core element in its ability to serve the public. In politics, the machinery produces policies, decisions of all sorts, judgments and prescriptions. These are the things that come out of the back end of the political machinery. The raw materials, that is, what goes into the front end, include information, opinion, strategies, calculations, and more—all filtered by the design of the machinery. Both elements should be kept in mind as we frame opinions about, and assess the performance of government. The array of factors that one would want to examine to fully understand a political system is nearly endless. We will focus here on just three structural characteristics.

Before doing that, however, let us think for a moment about who the architects were and are in Central and Eastern Europe. The communist system did not permit study of the political system in any genuine way. It argued that there was no need, since the Communist Party had the single, correct, and indisputable vision for society and its development. Case closed! Surely, in this course, you are learning that managing a political system is not simple, nor can it be achieved simply by employing basic common sense. Public management is complex and challenging. In many ways it can be more challenging than corporate management, given that the interface with the public is always delicate and resources are in some ways harder to predict and allocate than in a business.

So, who were the political architects as these systems sought to redesign themselves? The answer: They were politicians from the old system, academics, and imported "experts." All brought biases and liabilities to the task. Politicians from the communist period had trouble conceptualizing liberal systems and generating faith in the political public. Academics brought disciplinary principles from their own, nonpolitical realms that often did not mesh with the real political world. Imported experts from other regions of the world with established political systems and routines had never had to deal with the peculiar nature of the transition from communism to something else.

An added problem was the simplicity with which American experts especially dived into providing prescriptions for these countries. American political parties, legal associations, management consultants, and the U.S. government itself all injected notions that on reflection were of modest use. The principal reason was that all of them assumed the existence of a value consensus and a stable environment. Judges, political operatives, stock market experts and many others produced unworkable suggestions or, at best, partially effective ideas. On balance and on reflection, they often complicated the allocation of human and financial resources as the design process went along, and as a result, most new systems stumbled on the path to system redesign.

Legislative-Executive Relations The first specific challenge of redesign was how to delineate and institutionalize the relationship between the legislative and executive branches of government. The design of these two components literally defines a democracy in that it guards channels of input for public views and creates boundaries for the use of authority by those two key institutional actors. And, unfortunately, designing the relationship is just half the battle. It is as essential that the design process generate a genuine appreciation for, and commitment to, actually behaving according to the design. The subtle point here is that the respect of each part for the role and responsibility of the other is as important as the structural design itself. One way to achieve that mutual respect is to make the design process and the logic that underpins it as transparent and publicly accessible as possible. In this way suspicion, distrust, and skepticism can be minimized.

Russia, the Czech Republic, Slovenia, and Bosnia, for different reasons and in different ways, neglected to embrace this consideration. Poland and Hungary did. Ukraine appears to have tried and failed.

Russia, Ukraine, and Poland created presidential systems, that is, systems that directly elect (that is, the voters elect) an executive separate from the election of legislators. Hungary, the Czech Republic, and Slovenia created parliamentary systems, though with many different features. Parliamentary systems ask the public to elect legislators who, based on the levels of electoral support they received, elect one of their own to serve as the executive. Bosnia had imposed on it a system that nearly defies description. Its presidency consists of three individuals none of whom is directly elected by all the people. It has two legislatures, which function spasmodically. Russia anchors the end of the continuum in that it places the most sweeping powers in the hands of the executive.

Centralization The next design feature that draws our attention is the center-periphery question: How will power be distributed between the central authorities and the various levels of authority in regions and districts? This is often raised as the centralization-decentralization issue. The trade-off should be clear to students in political science. With centralization comes a concentration of power, which could be abused but also brings consistent policy to the whole system. With decentralization decision making is closer to the people who are likely to be affected by policies, but there is also some inconsistency or unevenness in what, or how much, government does area by area. There are of course many more implications. Add to that the reality that the bureaucracies associated with the old communist systems did not simply go away when communism collapsed. Vast numbers of bureaucrats, with their tendencies to do things the way they did them yesterday, remained. They fought for their own survival and resisted reform or change. The common discomfort of democratic political leaders in transitional systems stems from the belief that to "break the stranglehold of the bureaucracy" leaders must have more centralized power and authority, even if their ultimate goal is to decentralize power.

Russian reformers, including Gorbachev, Yeltsin, and now Putin, have all reasoned that to effect any change, especially of the sort that will reinvigorate the political system by decentralizing power, one must first centralize authority. Naturally, they see themselves as benevolent actors in this process. The pattern is clear: These Russian leaders believed and believe that they had to centralize power in order to decentralize power.

It is likely that we will see the same pattern in Ukraine, though with many years' lag time because the major reform push is just beginning under the new president, Viktor Yushenko. It is likely that his reasoning will be similar and that the criticism that he will endure will also be similar. Other leaders in our sample have often been indicted for being "insensitive" and "arrogant," but few have been charged with structurally altering the system to centralize power. The Fidesz Party in Hungary, which is currently out of power but is poised to win the next election, has said that it wishes to create "superministries" to streamline policymaking, but which would necessarily centralize power as well. Bosnia again is an outlying example, given that it is an ultimately decentralized system that suffers from an inability to exercise any central (systemwide) authority.

Law and Politics Finally, there is the matter of creating a new legal framework. A legal system obviously becomes the guide to behavior for the general public, for commercial activities, and even for the government. Without it, there are no rules of the game by which to judge risk and reward. Without it, the environment is unpredictable and vulnerability rules. "Corruption"—whatever meaning is given to it—finds operating space in such a setting.

In this realm of the transition one encounters the greatest levels of misunderstanding. The form of social control under the communist system was so misunderstood that efforts to assess the challenges associated with the transition of the legal system are quickly frustrated.

The reason is that the old communist system was built on an altogether unfamiliar premise: that laws should be as ambiguous as possible so that people are unclear about exactly what they can and cannot do. Under these conditions people shrink from testing the system because it has promised a harsh and arbitrary response. Western legal systems, in contrast, try to construct rules as specific as possible, but that carries the added burden of implying that all behaviors that are not explicitly prohibited are legal. The most obvious benefits of the communist system for managing, controlling, or manipulating people were not apparent to the public but certainly must have been clear to those governing. It was efficient and effective.

All of the transitional states have committed themselves to create new systems in which laws are specific, understandable, and applied in a nonarbitrary way. That means that they are developing legal frameworks like those found typically in liberal, democratic, developed political systems. The result for most Central and Eastern Europeans will be that most will have more, not fewer, encounters with police and the government, as people probe the limits of the new and specific rules. More, not fewer, police will be needed to deal with the pressure from the public to find the new limits, especially in economic behavior. More court cases, attorneys, regulations, and visibility for legal considerations have already resulted. It is reasonable to assume that these conditions will generate negative feedback for the regimes. The new legal systems are having to deal with public pressure and resentment that may articulate itself in challenges to incumbent leaders at the ballot box.

Table 5-3 shows ratings produced for the World Economic Forum in Switzerland in 2004. It enhances our ability to see that legal development is not uniform in Central and Eastern Europe. Though certainly open to interpretation, the data suggest that Slovenia, Hungary, Estonia, the Czech Republic, Latvia, and

Lithuania have managed more than the others to flesh out a working legal system. Of those rated, Romania, Bulgaria, Russia, and Ukraine fared poorly in terms of legal development.

Corruption may be another telling signal in our effort to understand how these countries are doing in the transition. Lithuania, Estonia, Slovenia, Bulgaria, Hungary, and Slovakia perform reasonably on that measure. Campaigns to reduce corruption in Russia, Poland, Romania, and Ukraine have been ineffective.

Poland presents the only real surprise in the data. The unrated countries should be understood to be so deficient in data and performance as to be neglected by the researchers for the World Economic Forum. They include Macedonia, Bosnia, Serbia/Montenegro, and Albania.

Economic Architecture

Postcommunist systems are also distinguishable by size. The data suggest interesting kinds of analysis as one learns more about the systems in Central and Eastern Europe.

Does Size Matter? The simple answer is yes. At least in this context, and perhaps everywhere in the twenty-first century, a country with a small population, a small market, difficult or yet unpatterned relations with its neighbors, low investment appeal, or a politically fluid environment may have fundamental difficulty pooling the resources—financial and human—to perform up to the expectations of modern Europe. The compelling logic for the creation and expansion of the European Union was based on the notion that larger markets, with more homogeneous policies, more coherent management, and fewer politically motivated barriers to economic activity will serve all peoples. Size ensures diversity (economic and human), requires cooperation, and nurtures stability. It follows that government, given its principal task in a democracy of serving the public, can retain its authority and legitimacy best in a service-producing or service-supporting environment. However, that is a long-term perspective. It may be that in the short-term, transitional setting, small size has some advantages.

On at least one scale of competitiveness, Estonia, Slovenia, Hungary, Lithuania, the Czech Republic, and Latvia were assessed as most competitive, and Russia, Romania, and Ukraine as least competitive in the region. This draws our analysis in that other direction. The data seem to indicate that small countries have been more effective in renovating their economies and making themselves over into viable, competitive markets. It is perhaps also salient that all of the best-performing systems have folded into the EU as new member states. It would be wise to study carefully the data in Table 5-3 to get a grasp on just how uneven the information is, as it pulls our thinking in different directions.

One forward-looking variable is the percentage of businesses that have access to the Internet: Slovenia leads the list with 96 percent. The Czech

Table 5-3 Regional Comparisons: Rankings among European Postcommunist Systems

Political system		Size rankings			Institutional rankings[a] (Only 13 countries rated by World Economic Forum)		
Post-1989 –1991	Pre-1989	Rank by population	Rank by area	Rank GDP per capita	Competitiveness	Corruption	Law
Russia	USSR	1 (143.5 m)	1	10 ($9,800)	11	9	12
Ukraine	USSR	2 (47.5 m)	2	15 ($6,300)	13	13	13
Poland	Poland	3 (38.5 m)	3	7 ($12,000)	8	11	7
Romania	Romania	4 (22.3 m)	4	11 ($7,700)	12	12	10
Serbia and Montenegro	Yugoslavia	5 (10.8 m)	6	17 ($2,400)	Unrated		
Czech Republic	Czechoslovakia	6 (10.2 m)	8	2 ($16,800)	5	8	4
Hungary	Hungary	7 (10.0 m)	7	3 ($14,900)	3	5	2
Bulgaria	Bulgaria	8 (7.5 m)	5	13 ($8,200)	10	4	11
Slovakia	Czechoslovakia	9 (5.4 m)	13	4 ($14,500)	7	6	8
Croatia	Yugoslavia	10 (4.5 m)	11	9 ($11,200)	9	7	9
Bosnia	Yugoslavia	11 (4.0 m)	12	14 ($6,500)	Unrated		
Lithuania	USSR	12 (3.6 m)	9	6 ($12,500)	4	1	6
Albania	Albania	13 (3.5 m)	15	16 ($4,900)	Unrated		
Latvia	USSR	14 (2.3 m)	10	8 ($11,500)	6	9	5
Macedonia	Yugoslavia	15 (2.0 m)	16	12 ($7,100)	Unrated		
Slovenia	Yugoslavia	16 (2.0 m)	17	1 ($19,600)	2	3	1
Estonia	USSR	17 (1.3 m)	14	5 ($14,300)	1	2	3

Source: The Global Competitiveness Report 2002–2003 (Davos, Switzerland: World Economic Forum, 2004).

[a] In all cases a lower number is a "better" ranking.

Republic and Estonia follow at 90 percent. Poland, Lithuania, and Hungary are above 75 percent.

Emerging Markets Although framing the political architecture of a society is crucial to the behavior of both the government and its public, the design of the economic system is equally important. In many ways it is even more complex because a country necessarily makes decisions and designs structures for its economy in an international economic framework. Economists cluster and label economies by their nature. Popular labels are constructed reflecting a system's recent past and how far along the path of development it is. To that end, the systems we are examining are called "emerging markets."

Emerging markets are societies that have been committed by leaders or circumstance to developing economic markets in a capitalist or mixed (government and private) environment characterized by private ownership, profit motivation, relatively free prices, and a fluid labor market. As the term also implies, these economies are understood not to have reached that goal. In fact, they are judged to be in the early phases of the journey. They typically experience high rates of growth and dramatic fluctuations in their economies, which are reflected in economic data. Because of that, it may be misleading to provide economic figures for a single slice of time. Instead, this chapter will offer some patterns and groupings of the states under examination. Regionally, annual growth rates average around 4.5 percent. Deficits are higher than a decade ago, and some argue that the costs associated with accession to the EU are the reason. In most of the countries, economic prospects are buoyed by optimism, but unemployment and declining foreign direct investment are worrisome.

EU membership will mean shifting some resources to Brussels, and spending cuts will be unpopular. Most Central and Eastern European publics already suffer from what is called "reform fatigue"; if it results in political instability, crises could result. Most of the countries have, with advice from the EU, focused on strengthening growth by emphasizing trade and foreign direct investment. A study commissioned by the World Economic Forum concluded that of seventy drivers influencing the flow of foreign direct investment to particular countries, the top three accounted for 60 percent of the variation, and all three were directly related to government policy. Emphasizing this point, observers noted that when the subject of investments was discussed at the World Economic Forum 2004, more than 50 percent of the discussion focused on politics and "political burdens."

Central and Eastern Europe has become one of the fastest-moving consumer goods markets in the world. This accentuates the interest of the international business community. By a standard used in economics, emerging market systems today include China, India, Indonesia, Taiwan, Argentina, Brazil, Mexico, Peru, Egypt, Israel, South Africa, and Turkey, to name just a few. The postcommunist systems in Central and Eastern Europe represent a special subset of countries from the category. The special features that set them apart from other emerging markets are (1) the abrupt and recent nature of the economic change they experienced and (2) the shared experience with centrally planned and hierarchical economic policymaking under communism.

Both elements create quite distinctive challenges for these societies. Many other emerging market systems have been at the task of becoming competitive market systems for much longer. Many also have emerged from mixed economies and authoritarian or semiauthoritarian political systems that have not created the behaviors and characteristics in both government and the public that communism did. In this sense, Central and Eastern European societies face additional and somewhat peculiar challenges.

The postcommunist transition will require a long inventory of economic changes, among them the following:

- Establishing *a consumer logic* to serve as a platform for consumer behavior that conforms to market concepts. Price (or cost) sensitivity to basic purchase decisions is key.
- Establishing a link between *worker productivity* and wages.
- Establishing a consumer and commercial *credit system,* in which people, and especially entrepreneurs, embrace risk for the goal of long-term business performance and success.
- Establishing a basic understanding of *competitiveness,* especially in an international market environment.
- Establishing an *investment* and savings mentality that could nourish and sustain investment.
- Reconceptualizing the *role of government* to one other than sole provider of essential services and living conditions.
- Establishing a *philanthropic mode* of behavior that could ease pressure on government to provide all services.

As one can readily see, these are changes in *culture*—changes that refocus public thinking and behavior in postcommunist societies. It should be clear as well that these are hard to measure; different countries responding to different leadership will display very different levels of success. Even in places where efforts have been focused on the points in the above list, scholars understand that it will take time to transform thinking. In a sense, the acceleration of thinking and behavior in Central and Eastern Europe has been remarkable. Students of political science should understand that these changes are keys to the way the political system will unfold and therefore must draw their attention.

Economists also remind us that there is a significant inventory of structural changes that are necessary, including changes in the legal and banking systems; in government fiscal and monetary policy, including the tax system; and in mechanisms for trading equities/stock/commodities.

It should be added that the dramatic transition from communism also has resulted in a significant population in many of the countries who do not accept the wisdom of the path toward the market system or toward liberal and participatory democracy. That factor, however, does not distinguish postcommunist systems from other emerging market states.

Table 5-4 The "Good," the "Bad," and the "Ugly": Central European
Political Systems

"Good"	"Bad"	"Ugly"

• Routinized political mechanics
• Executive, legislative
  legitimacy
• Partial economic recovery
• "Limited" convertibility
• NATO membership
• Foreign investment weak
• Immigration destination
	• Authoritarian leadership
	• Ethnic politics/intolerance
	• Inadequate legal systems;
	  crime
	• Economic decline continues
	• Acute economic problems
	• Soft currency
		• Violence
		• Systemic collapse
		• Multiple political authorities
		• Nonfunctioning courts,
		  education, and tax systems
		• Borders not secure
		• Black market commerce
		• "Super-soft" currency
		• Emigration to other post-
		  communist states

Poland Hungary Czech Republic Estonia Lithuania Latvia Slovakia 　　　　Romania 　　　　Bulgaria 　　　　　　Croatia	Russia Ukraine 　　　Belarus	Serbia Montenegro Macedonia 　　　　Bosnia 　　　　Kosovo 　　　　Albania 　　　　Moldova

The four postcommunist systems that have attracted the greatest international attention from business are Russia, Hungary, Poland, and the Czech Republic. Other systems that warrant close attention based on their recent performance are Ukraine, Slovenia, Slovakia, Romania, and Bulgaria. Still others draw our attention because of their poor records and very modest movement along the path to market development. They include Albania, Macedonia, Serbia and Montenegro, Kosovo, and Belarus.

To help understand these dynamics, it has been useful in the university setting to cluster the postcommunist states into three categories. A scholar would label them "types A, B, and C," and one is encouraged to think in those neutral terms. But students seem more prone to remember the clusters by thinking of them as the "good," the "bad," and the "ugly" (Table 5-4).

POLITICAL AND SOCIAL DYNAMICS

Students of comparative politics have learned that structures induce behaviors by both the governors and the governed. But it is also true that behaviors stemming from culture and circumstance influence the evolution of structures. This is the standard "form and function" relationship. We examine the political dynamics in a system as a way to understand how behavior and attitudes affect the journey toward a society's goals.

We examine three elements of the political environment that provide us with some predictive ability for these countries: (1) How "forward-facing" is the system? (2) How do the countries expect to meet the resource needs associated with governing? and (3) How much and what kinds of legitimacy are found in each system?

Forward- versus Backward-Facing

Identity and loyalties are essential to understanding any political environment. Given the range of examples with which comparative politics must deal, it is important to distinguish nation from state. American students can find this awkward because American political rhetoric has evolved without making this distinction. Simply, the sovereign state is a political entity, and one's identification with that political entity (in whatever form) is patriotism. The nation is an ethno-cultural phenomenon. It is a group, often calling itself a "people," who in their mind are different from all others around them on a number of bases, such as race, history, language, religion, various concrete and amorphous cultural characteristics, physical traits, and preferences for food, colors, or music. If that inventory is not enough to distinguish a "people," myth fills the void: Something is made up to distinguish "our people."

Since the state (the government) is assigned the task of providing for society, or at least providing the framework within which this can be done by other actors, one can make the case that it is naturally forward-facing. It has to think about tomorrow. In Central Europe, most of the societies are said to be "young"—that is, a very large percentage of the citizenry are not yet middle-aged. Most of them face formidable demographic problems: low or negative population growth rates, high death rates, and susceptibility to major diseases. Recognizing these hazards, some countries, Poland most prominent among them, have made a systematic political effort to get the public to face forward. This involves placing much less focus on historical grievances and much more focus on what needs to be done to improve tomorrow. The attitudinal response to EU membership in the region has hinged on the ability of Central European leaders to bring their publics to ask the key forward-facing question: Will our future be brighter and safer in or out of the EU?

Anyone familiar with the history of Central and Eastern Europe knows that the past is fraught with conquest, manipulation, and abuse by countries of their neighbors. It would be difficult to make a case that any country was without times when it was abused or without times when it did the abusing. History has been tangled and ugly for this region of relatively small countries. With that backdrop, nation and nationalism become important. Given a history where some "peoples" have made efforts to eliminate other "peoples" and in which political boundaries have never matched ethnic boundaries, everyone has an inventory of grievances! However, to address those grievances is to face backwards. It requires arguing the rightness of our position and the wrongness of theirs. It requires advocating "solutions" that can only be embraced at the expense of other groups, and which in turn create more grievances. A focus on nation is always about the past. It is a feeling that binds "our people" together but only at the expense of isolating others, and in Central and Southeastern Europe, that means driving the "others" out or eliminating them. Today, that has been called "ethnic cleansing." One is thus led to conclude that nation and nationalism are negative political phenomena. They block the political integration of a society and, building from an emotional identity, make political violence easier to rationalize.

What this all means to our comparative analysis is that it is useful and illuminating to gauge the level of nationalism (often labeled "ultranationalism" in Central Europe) by focusing on how forward-facing or backward-facing a society is. The more the focus is on political performance and results, the less the public is likely to succumb to emotional arguments and backward-facing prescriptions. Although this phenomenon can be demonstrated in virtually every system in the region, the best illustration and the most devastating example is the nationalism that accompanied the breakup of Yugoslavia. That political arena has been gripped by violence and hatred from 1991 to this day, growing out of nationalist themes and the quagmire of history. Bosnia, Macedonia, Kosovo, Serbia, Montenegro, and Croatia today suffer in varying degrees from the legacy of recent violence. Russia, Ukraine, Moldova, Estonia, Slovakia, and Hungary all have witnessed strong nationalist arguments that are most easily recognized when the political rhetoric dwells on the past. However, that nationalism is an unproductive political phenomenon in the twenty-first century is a controversial proposition, especially among those embroiled in the recent violence.

Resource Needs

The next insight into these political systems comes from comparing their awareness of and strategy for garnering the resources necessary to enable government to perform the functions to which they have committed themselves. Governments have revenue and other resource needs. In most cases, as communism was set aside a most significant void emerged. Communism had provided itself with resources by controlling prices and wages. Its ability to generate funds to do what it wanted to do was a matter of manipulating the cost of goods and the money paid to workers. In this way it raised revenue without elaborate taxing schemes and collected revenue in an unobtrusive, invisible way. The arrangement has often reminded me of a skilled pickpocket who can take from you without your knowing it, until, of course, you notice that you have nothing left.

When new political systems were created, the need for revenue was out of focus. No one had experience judging the financial requirements. In fact, few had any idea of what government was going to try to do. At that point legislatures and executives were established at many levels in each country, each facing revenue needs. The process that followed was random and uncoordinated. Various legislatures began creating taxes to cover immediate cash flow needs. Rather than create a strategy that might have prevented overlap and redundancy, they proceeded independently and incrementally. Bit by bit they imposed taxes to a point that gave businesses in many systems three unappealing choices: don't create a business; avoid paying taxes altogether and hope you won't get caught; or become engaged in the gray world of corruption and organized crime as a form of protection. In a number of these countries, after just a couple of years of plodding and spiraling taxes, a business faced paying more than 100 percent of its revenue in taxes were it to pay all of the levies. Such unworkable and irrational tax levels were common.

Only with the specific prescriptions of EU membership was the trend reversed. Coherent systems modeled on the Western European experience were introduced in the member countries including Poland, the Czech Republic, Slovakia, Hungary, Slovenia, Lithuania, Latvia, and Estonia, as well as the candidate countries of Romania, Bulgaria, and Croatia. Significantly, in the other countries of Central Europe the tax revenue mess persists. The EU has added much-needed expertise to budgeting processes as well. One can be much more confident that realistic calculations are being made regarding the actual costs of governing and providing services in the systems that are following the EU formulas.

Legitimacy

Legitimacy is yet another key basis for comparing and contrasting the Central European cases. Authority is the power to get someone to do something. Authority has many sources, some constitutional and routinized, others not. In political science, "legitimacy" is given a special and narrow meaning. It is the sense among the governed that the person(s) having authority achieved that authority by established, proper means. In essence, they followed the rules and have power as a result. In this narrow sense there is but one source of legitimacy—the people—and it is fluid since the people can change their views about it as time passes.

Central European political systems obviously experienced the unsettling and abrupt collapse of the communist system. In this context, old and new elites scrambled to establish a grip on authority. Every political system went about creating new authorities, but very few understood enough about democratizing to make establishing legitimacy a priority. In the old, communist system, legitimacy was presumed, and many in the new environment were inclined to take for granted that it could be presumed in the new system as well. On reflection, this was a predictable but unfortunate failing. Political scientists and public policy experts in even the most advanced of the Central European countries suggest that little time or effort was invested in building a foundation for legitimacy. The general comparative literature tells us that legitimacy can be built

- By procedure(s),
- By results,
- By habit,
- By identity.

The reader can surmise that most new political elites anticipated legitimacy by habit. Those playing on ultranationalist themes nurtured legitimacy by identity. Those with greater focus on political development in the Western tradition began to work on legitimacy by procedures and results. Poland, the Czech Republic, Slovenia, and Hungary made serious efforts in this direction.

Elite Accountability

Legitimacy by results may imply a strong measure of elite accountability. Many students, when thinking about the meaning of democracy, focus on elite accountability as a characteristic. A more fundamental balance that must be struck in any democratic or aspiring democratic system is that between elites' shaping public opinion and elites' responding to public opinion. It is not helpful to be too simple about this dimension. Clearly, both dynamics exist, and the balance can change from moment to moment and certainly from administration to administration. If a pattern exists in Central Europe, it would seem to be that leaders subscribe intellectually to the notion that they should be responsive both to situations and to public opinion. However, their political gut pulls them in the direction of skepticism about the "wisdom of the majority," which is reinforced by a very real inexperience with civil society and participatory politics. The problem is exacerbated further by the absence during the communist period of political and civic education that would motivate and energize the public to engage themselves in civic affairs.

Transparency Transparency receives a great deal of lip service in Central European politics. It is a pivotal criterion for EU qualification. Nonetheless, little has been attempted and still less has been achieved in firmly establishing transparency as a valued elite goal. The tendency has been to see public scrutiny as an impediment to efficient governing—an element that delays and muddies the policymaking process. That perception, of course, is not unknown in established democratic systems. In Central European politics, transparency is understood largely as a requisite for effective opposition party politics rather than as a generic advantage for the public's understanding of political processes. Whichever master it serves, in those political systems outside the realm of EU politics, transparency will be one of those variables that can only gestate slowly and likely with fits and starts—advances and reversals. In contrast, EU member states will have little choice but to conform to the rigors and norms of political experience with transparency.

Elite-Mass Interface This brings us to elite-mass interface—the dynamic between the governed and those governing. For Central Europeans and many others, this discussion begins and ends with elections. This is a particularly dangerous notion.

Elections as Political Art

The salience and sheer weight that political analysts ascribe to elections are formidable. That is surprising given the voluminous literature on election irregularities and manipulation in new political states.[1] The mainstream argument is that any alternative to elections is less constructive and less democratic. Perhaps so, but the reality that must be acknowledged in Central Europe is that elections are more clearly art than science. In the worst cases they reflect the normative and prescriptive thinking of those managing the transition. In the best cases, they represent warning signals to those same elites. What the world sees and what Central Europeans see certainly does vary with the experience and political sensibilities of each population.

First among the problems is the designation of constituencies. Where and how the boundaries are drawn and how the electorate is defined or qualified predestine the outcome. Post-Dayton elections in Bosnia come to mind as keen examples. Even in classic, established democracies, the preelection identification of constituencies is a partially visible process at best and is a locus of significant power struggles.

Second are the choices. The range and representativeness of the candidates and the policy choices color the attractiveness or acceptability of the elections. Given the absence of civil society and the reality of thinly rooted pluralism, the menu is, at the very least, directed by those with power. In the worst cases, war-validated political groups (most often paramilitary groups) and externally sponsored groups, especially in Southeastern Europe, tend to generate the electoral choices.

Third, in the absence of pluralism, political parties have abbreviated and uncompromising platforms. "Ideological" parties reject pragmatism and the mass appeal that it could generate. The texture of some of these political elements is intimidating and aggressive. The tone is often polarizing rather than accommodating. The most strident elements of political parties portray an "only truth" aura that will serve democratic development very poorly.

Fourth, voter turnout is problematic. The overall pattern in the region reflects a decline in voter turnout with each passing general election. Aside from common boycotts of the sort seen in recent Montenegrin and Kosovar elections, a more elemental issue exists. Elections are understood as the *moment* when the people's voice identifies the direction for the country and chooses who will wield authority. While not absurd, the missing perception is that of elections as one stage of an ongoing, participatory *process*. Many countries in the region have a record of electing persons who behave after the election in an authoritarian way. A political psychology emerges in which successful candidates imagine themselves as "super-trustees," as opposed to delegates with continuous links to the constituency. The super-trustee perception draws policy-making away from compromise and real dialogue.

Representativeness is another of those dimensions that Central European systems seem to have to work out in their own way. The experiences of many established democratic systems, including the United States, are unhelpful in marking the path. A delegate is a person selected by a constituency to mirror the views and perspectives of that constituency. The task in this mode is to reflect the vision and preferences of the segment of the public "represented." A trustee, in contrast, is also selected by a constituency, but perceives that the election was an endorsement of his or her vision of the issues, and presumes to make decisions based not on the public view but upon his or her own view. Such politicians often use the term "mandate" to signal their independence from public attitudes. Trustees often argue that this is "leadership."

Patterns of leadership in Central Europe indicate that the trustee interpretation is by far the most common one among elites, although this should be understood as a matter of degree. Slobodan Milosevic (Serbia), Franjo Tudjman (Croatia), Alija Izetbegovic (Bosnia), and Alexander Lukashenko (Belarus) can only be labeled "super-trustees." By many measures they were authoritarian in their political behavior. But many others, including Viktor Orban (Hungary), Lech Walesa (Poland), Vaclav Havel (Czechoslovakia and the Czech Republic), have demonstrated an arrogance that can best be understood as a trustee mentality framed by an electoral mandate.

Such arrogance is hardly warranted. Since the transition from communism began, the collection of new political systems have held fifty-nine general elections. Fifteen of those were "first" elections. Of the forty-four elections in which incumbents were running (i.e., second or third elections), thirty-four resulted in the opposition winning. In one sense, this could be interpreted as a good thing. That elections have come to be a reliable mechanism by which to change leadership is the good news. The bad news is that such pendulum-like swings from party-in-power to party-out-of-power and back again derail strategic policymaking and interrupt step-by-step construction of a societal design. More subtly, it may be that this pattern is a function of a kind of transitional logic: Many analysts have speculated that in the more politically developed countries in the region, there is a constituency for those in power, a second constituency against those in power, and a third constituency that remains skeptical that elections will actually bring a change of leadership. To be clear, they aren't sure that those in power will give up power even if voted out. For those voters, their only option is to vote for the opposition because only then will they be able to test the system. That is the only way to know if those in power will give up power. Some speculate that this subset of voters ranges from 5 percent to 15 percent in the countries of Central Europe and as such may tip the scales consistently to the opposition vote.

Fifth, following from the above point, the gaps between elections are characterized by closed or narrowly constrained input mechanisms in the system. There is a view that a voter, by voting, buys a ticket and sits back and experiences the ride. A more constructive view, but one that is hard to find in Central Europe, is that elections are one kind of input but that democracy requires *reg-*

ular elite-mass interaction and significant efforts by leadership to account for both popular and minority interests.

The overarching point here is not that elections are counterproductive. To the contrary, they forge some support and are certainly a part of democratic political evolution. But without evolving awareness of the limits and imperfections of elections, and without genuine interest on the part of the leadership in unpopular views, elections remain a less-central feature of politics than the commitment to developing civil society. Elections are art in the real sense that Central Europeans will see what they want to see in them—positive and negative. They will not assuage political anxiety. One man's masterpiece is another's ugly picture.

None of the above argues for ignoring elections. Rather it suggests an approach that anticipates the limits of elections and the likely public response to them. Former U.S. deputy defense secretary Paul Wolfowitz (current president of the World Bank), after a May 2003 trip to Bosnia and Kosovo, suggested that those places hold lessons for American efforts to bring postwar stabilization and the transition from dictatorship to democracy in Iraq and Afghanistan. He concluded, "The experience in Bosnia shows the danger of rushing to hold elections . . . simply as a show of democracy taking root. The threat is that dangerously divisive leaders may be the first to take power. . . . By holding elections so early, it became impossible to remove some bad actors, because they now had electoral authority," he warned.[2]

Doors and Windows

Another dynamic part of this political picture concerns the points of access for public input into government deliberations and policymaking. As the political architecture changed fundamentally, Central Europeans were told that they now had access. They now had a role to play. But the political systems generally did not provide maps of the political system. In essence, the public was left unclear about where the doors and windows are for gaining access to government. Besides the channels for access, the public needs to know where powers and responsibilities lie within the government, so that access to the right person or agency is possible. Unless those who wish to advance interests know which part of government is responsible for particular functions, the result is likely to be access without impact. That is a prescription for frustration.

Civil Society

The overarching challenge to nurture grassroots political activity in Central Europe could become the basis for widespread, genuine public participation that would pressure each system to become more responsive. It could rebalance the delegate-trustee pattern of representation. The concept of civil society is very much in vogue today, but it suffers from some ambiguity as a concept. First, there is considerable debate about which actors can be said to be a part of civil society. Do business interests fall in the mix? Do organizations that are created or supported by commercial interests fit? Do religious organizations come under this rubric? Do organizations initiated with or receiving significant public funds fit the label? More crucial to the political development of the region is the question that stems from the very creation of these actors. When the EU surveyed the Central and Eastern European countries that have recently become members, it concluded that much more needed to be done to enhance and nurture civil society and committed resources to the task. But the new member states mostly responded by using the resources to provide local organizations and movements with a menu of items and services that could be provided or financed by the central government using funds already provided by the EU.

The fundamental problem was that simply by generating the menu, the central government was conditioning the form and nature of the issues at hand. An alternative view argued that this was counterproductive. What was needed was for the local constituencies themselves to decide on what their issues are and what they think they need to further their interests—a genuinely grassroots, bottom-up process. But that would likely produce (1) some inept requests for support, (2) some very localized and insignificant efforts, from both the central government and EU perspectives, and (3) some efforts that could become a challenge to the plans and directions of the central government. For these reasons the more manipulative approach was commonplace. Perhaps the more neutral term "guided approach" would better represent the establishment vision of this dilemma. There is evidence that all of the new Central European EU member states wrestled with this question and resolved it in a standard and uninspired way. Civil society in Central Europe today thus appears more robust than it actually is. Many genuine efforts are evident, but they are narrow and thin. The lesson from Central Europe is that there is no way to meaningfully accelerate the development of civil society without castrating the effort. It must be a self-generating and self-perpetuating phenomenon if it is to contribute meaningfully to democratic development.

In terms of the kinds of participation and the kinds of interests that one finds developing in Central Europe, the overwhelming pattern in the public's mind is to anticipate that government will solve problems and provide services. Very little evidence is yet apparent of groups forming to activate their own energy and resources to solve problems. This should be interpreted as a part of the legacy of communism. Rare exceptions stand out. The Democratic Youth Alliance Initiative in Hungary is a rather unorthodox example of raw and energetic young people simply doing what they think is needed locally without turning to government for assistance or guidance.

The issues around which most local energies are focused include social services, schools, minority rights, unemployment, and economic development zones. Most such efforts reflect a general disaffection from political parties as a vehicle for promoting these interests.

LEADERSHIP CADRE: "DRIVING SKILLS"

As suggested near the beginning of this chapter, it is this requisite for political development—a leadership cadre—that was so sorely lacking in the communist system. To reiterate, leadership then was timid, poorly skilled in policymaking, and without incentive to pursue systemic goals. What sort of generalization is possible given the new echelon of postcommunist leaders? The range of leadership skills and abilities found in Central and Eastern Europe is vast, as is the range of commitment to real democratic development. The electoral turnover cited earlier in this chapter has hardened and polarized many of the political environments, making political careers especially unstable work. Nonetheless, there is little doubt that these new systems have managed to identify, if not embrace, a large number of bright, polished, and articulate leaders whose personal dedication to the task, as they see it, is impressive. They still tend to fall into two broad groups, which are keenly recognized by the general public in Central and Eastern Europe.

With the collapse of communism, two-and-a-half types of persons aspiring to positions of authority emerged. The first were what can be usefully called "born-again democrats." They were some of the political leaders and players (called *nomenklatura* in the old system) from the communist era. They politically survived the collapse of communism and most often suggested that they had "seen the light" (that is, the error of their ways and those of the old system) and were prepared to promote the new values and institutions of the fledgling system. In essence, they are reborn and committed to the new politics, including the efficacy of elections and pluralism. In many cases, this new posture was largely rhetoric, and when impulses and gut politics took over, these politicians revealed that they were markedly unable to deal with criticism or compromise. Yeltsin (Russia), Kuchma and Kravchuk (Ukraine), Lukashenko (Belarus), Milosevic (Serbia), Tudjman (Croatia), Meciar (Slovakia), Iliescu (Romania), and Berisha (Albania) are examples. To be fair, others did manage to renovate their thinking and have adjusted to the new political environment. Kwasniewski (Poland), Horn (Hungary), Zhelev (Bulgaria), Kucan (Slovenia), and Mesic (Croatia) are arguably in this category. Many of the latter group made the argument that if they were to effect any change in the old system, there was only one game in town to play, and they opted to play it in spite of their ideological skepticism. The persistent problem for these political leaders was and is that a very significant segment of the general population did not and do not believe that such a transformation by a politician is possible. They imagine this as a thinly veiled, self-serving grab for power.

The second group might be labeled "rookies." In sharp contrast to the first group, they argued that their inexperience with political leadership was an asset! They claimed that any connection to the old system is contaminating and that as "virgin" politicians they are untainted by any previous political experience. Some even argued that their credentials for leadership were established simply because they had been persecuted by the old regime. This was initially quite appealing until the realization dawned that inexperience is not an asset, especially when policymaking demands sophisticated solutions to very difficult problems compounded by limited resources. Among this type were Walesa (Poland), Havel (Czechoslovakia), and Antall (Hungary). An electrician, playwright, and librarian, respectively, these men had no practical or conceptual experience to draw on when faced with complex policymaking. All had confrontations with the previous, communist regimes in their personal histories.

Generational Change

In the very early days of postcommunism, the rookies and the born-agains tended to be of similar generations. Today there is a clear generational gap. The born-agains are older and are increasingly marginalized or disappearing altogether with the passage of time. Rookies, on the other hand, had by the mid-1990s become markedly younger, more assertive, and more confident. The Poles Leszek Balcerowicz and Bronislaw Geremek are solid examples.

The last subset also comprises rookies of a sort, but they are imports. Generally they are established and accomplished in professions other than politics in a country to which they or their families migrated (see Table 5-5). Canada and the United States were the most common sources, but France and Britain also contributed some of these want-to-be politicians. The president of Lithuania, Valdas Adamkus, was a U.S. federal housing administrator. The prime minister of Serbia, Milan Panic, was a California businessman. A Polish presidential candidate, Stan Tyminski, had been a Canadian/Peruvian businessman. Boris Miksic, a Minnesota chemical company CEO, ran for Croatian president, finishing third. Even Zbigniew Brzezinski, former U.S. national security adviser had been unsuccessfully recruited by some Poles to run for president. Hungary tapped a longtime American businessman as its first ambassador to the United States and an economics professor from the United States to become a prominent member of parliament. Imported, and in some cases reimported professionals were assumed to know about effective leadership because they had led companies successfully or simply because they had lived in the kind of system that Central Europe was seeking to create. All such imports have struggled in their pursuit of political power though the stories differ with each example.

Confidence

Born-agains understood best the system from which society was distancing itself. In cases where their personal political transformation was incomplete, they hampered reforms. They also found that they were largely unprepared for the rigors of democratic and pluralistic politics. The public also recognized quickly that rookies were ill-equipped to appreciate the complexity of what they were trying to do, that inexperience was not an asset. The learning curve for many was steep, and the impact on both regimes and society was costly.

Table 5-5   Leaders of the Postcommunist European Countries

Country	Power-laden executive office	Current leader	No. of previous leaders since communism
Russia	President	Vladimir Putin	1
Ukraine	President	Viktor Yushenko	2
Belarus	President	Alexander Lukashenko	0
Poland	President	Lech Kaczynski	2
Hungary	Prime minister	Ferenc Gyurcsány	5
Czech Republic	Prime minister	Jiři Paroubek	5
Slovakia	Prime minister	Mikulas Dzurinda	2
Latvia	Prime minister	Aigars Kalvitis	9
Lithuania	Prime minister	Algirdas Brazauskas	9
Estonia	Prime minister	Andrus Ansip	6
Slovenia	Prime minister	Janez Jansa	4
Croatia	President	Stjepan Mesic	1
Serbia/Montenegro	President	Svetozar Marovic	1[a]
Serbia	President	Boris Tadic	2
Montenegro	President	Filip Vujanović	1
Bosnia	Tri-presidency	Ivo Miro Jovic	(Too nuanced for a number)[b]
Macedonia	President	Branko Crvenkovski	6
Albania	Prime minister	Fatos Nano	6
Kosovo	Prime minister	Bajram Kosumi	2
Moldova	President	Vladimir Voronin	2

Source: Data collected and prepared by Chase Crucil and Valerie Paulson.

[a] Serbia and Montenegro have both joint and separate leadership.
[b] Bosnia has three presidents and a chairman of the presidency.

Imports, by and large, were revealed to be out of touch and suffered from the same ills as the rookies—which, after all, they tended to be.

Hope lies in the generation of new but not inexperienced leaders who are developing backgrounds colored in with education, international exposure, and an awareness of the sophistication needed to be effective. Youthful confidence is giving way to measured clarity of purpose. Whatever one might think of the ideological texture of the evolving, middle-aged leadership in Central and Eastern Europe, it is clear that these are the people in whom power will be vested. Their education tells them that the EU and Europe is the safest framework for their own society's development. They will try, with varying levels of success, to convince their respective publics.

The major difference between the leadership dilemma of the early 1990s and today is the emergence of leaders with a sound basis for their confidence. Today they can and do use the external advice and guidance that they get, measure it against a growing pool of internal advisers and experts, and remain committed to a political process involving public input, turnover, transparency, and compromise. To frame the general situation in terms of our analogy, most leaders are still far from experienced drivers, but they understand better than ever before that driving a bus is tough, that it demands all of their focus, and that turning the task over to another driver at some point is normal and necessary.

PROGNOSIS

The approach suggested in this chapter is one of many possible ways of studying a political system. You should by this point be impressed by how challenging it is for leaders and masses to live through and manage a societal transition of the sort that Central and Eastern Europe has faced over the last two decades. If you can embrace this complexity and see how intriguing it is, you will understand all of politics much better. Politics is about half-measures, fits and starts, noble efforts that can fail, and pragmatic efforts that can produce glowing successes. All this means that it is a mixed bag that demands of you (the student) cautious and measured language.

Those countries that emerged after being dismembered from larger political systems faced added challenges. The ones that experienced spiraling violence are still debilitated. Others have moved to recognizing that the idealism of having one's own state must be offset by the problems of economic and political development that come with small size. Aware of this, most have moved voluntarily to incorporate themselves into the European Union, which holds out the long-term prospect of enhancing security and prosperity. The future for those unwilling or unable to turn toward this twenty-first-century solution will be rough for some and disastrous for others.

Consistent with this view, one finds that the process of forming a consensus of values has been difficult but is much more advanced in places that have chosen to conform to the EU's vision of the future. In terms of political architecture, the picture is more mixed, with significant variations in both form and function. Those in, or aspiring to be in, the EU have had to accept boundaries to the designs they have chosen. For Central and Eastern Europeans, the EU is the template and ultimate guarantor of a consistent direction. It is also not lost on the Central Europeans that it is the source of many resources that can ensure and accelerate change. Finally, the EU provides a peer group for aspiring and actual political leaders, making it possible to incrementally overcome the legacy of communist-style leadership. The mobility of people, information, ideas, and goods in the EU provides a firm foundation for future development in those member states. On balance, the societies that have become part of the European Union or will do so will have the opportunity and the tools to address their problems and move toward their goals.

The picture is far less clear for those not moving in this integrating direction. Those places will be examined in some greater detail in the next chapter. They tend to be struggling with direction (values), machinery (vehicle), and leadership (driver). Each of these is an imposing problem, but when experienced in combination, they are crushing. As irony would have it, the largest and the smallest political systems fall into this next category. All but one share the experience of spinning off from a larger political system under socialism and of various forms of violence in the process.

Conventional wisdom in the region, as well as the larger global dialogue about these issues, suggests that even these reluctant and ill-prepared political systems will gravitate in time to the EU. That would require change to a constructive direction, and it assumes both a significant transition in public thinking and a new clarity for political leadership. For the life span of this text, it is far more likely that analysts will see in Eastern and Southeastern Europe instability punctuated by spasmodic hostility and even violence.

Suggestions for Additional Reading

Baker, Peter, and Susan Glaser. *Kremlin Rising.* New York: Scribner's, 2005.

Cohen, Leonard. *Broken Bonds: Yugoslavia's Disintegration and Balkan Politics in Transition.* New York: Westview, 1995.

Gorbachev, Mikhail. *Perestroika.* Harper and Row, 1987.

Institute for War and Peace Reporting, www.iwpr.net.

McFaul, Michael, Nikolai Petrov, and Andre Ryabov. *Between Dictatorship and Democracy.* Washington, D.C.: Brookings Institution Press, 2004.

Whitmore, Sarah. *State-Building in Ukraine.* London: Routledge, 2004.

Wolchik, Sharon, and Vladimir Zviglyanich, eds. *Building a State: Ukraine in a Post-Soviet World.* New York: Oxford University Press, 1995

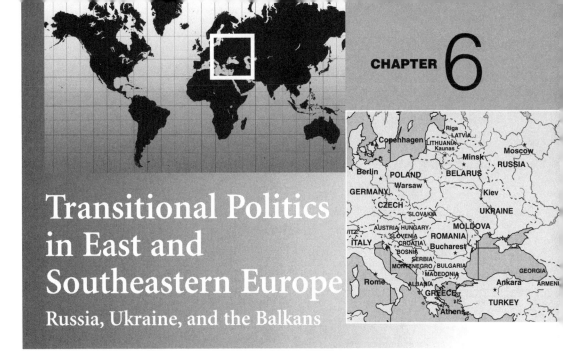

CHAPTER 6

Transitional Politics in East and Southeastern Europe

Russia, Ukraine, and the Balkans

The previous chapter shared a great deal of information about the challenges associated with transition in general and focused on cases of postcommunist politics in Central Europe. The very different choices that other postcommunist systems have made and their consequences are the focus of this chapter. Three examples of systems that have set themselves on a path that does not, for the foreseeable future, include European Union membership are Russia, Ukraine, and the new Balkan countries. The implications and consequences of their choice not to pursue EU membership are profound. Not only have these countries expressed little or no interest in membership in the EU, but the EU has been very reluctant to offer discussions leading in that direction for these political systems. As suggested in chapter 5, that means that these countries intend to take on the challenges of designing and managing their own systems with their own human, financial, and intellectual resources. In an increasingly interdependent world, characterized by global communication and financial networks, this independent path of development will face critical challenges to both domestic and foreign policy.

The focus of this chapter is the set of countries that have differentiated themselves from the general, mainstream pattern (see Table 5-1 in the previous chapter). We will employ the same conceptual framework we did in chapter 5 to examine and compare these political systems, again focusing on their needs to (1) form a consensus on values that can give the society direction—a destination; (2) embrace a political architecture for the political machinery that can produce policies and decisions—a vehicle; and (3) identify political leadership that can guide the system toward its goals—a driver.

RUSSIA

Russia is certainly the most powerful and significant of the cases we examine here. It inherited much of the capability, territory, money, prestige, social organization, infrastructure, and modes of politics of the old Soviet Union and along with them much of the anxiety that the rest of the world feels about its place and future in the world as a nuclear power. In this way Russia warrants our attention to understand both what is happening in the political system and what is likely to happen.

Value Consensus

There is an old and revered passage attributed to Anton Chekhov that states, "Russians idolize the past, hate the present, and fear the future." Most area specialists find reality in those words. Their implication for our concern about values in contemporary Russia and where they come from is that many Russians are prone to search for consensus in the past. Russia, in its many incarnations, has often perceived itself as a great power, both respected and feared by others. The Soviet period warranted that respect and attention if only because of the USSR's awesome nuclear military power. However, none of the tsarist or Soviet eras reveals a foundation for democratic values, democratic political architecture, or democratic leadership. None was built on values that could reasonably support democratic, market-focused actors in the system. Perhaps most important of all, there is no historical experience with tolerance as a society-framing value. That means that as long as Russians look to their own history for values that they wish to support and promote, it is unlikely that democracy can result.

Vladimir Putin has made some effort to shape a public consensus that would give him a more consistent signal about direction for his leadership. Such the-

Russia Timeline

Fall 1917	Bolsheviks overthrow government
1918–1921	Civil war: Reds vs. Whites
1918–1924	Lenin in power
1927–1953	Stalin in power
Oct. 1956	Krushchev changes political rhetoric
Fall 1964	Krushchev pushed from power
1964–1981	Brezhnev in power
1985–1991	Gorbachev in power
Jan. 1992	USSR disintegrates: 15 countries
1992–1999	Yeltsin in power; resigns Dec.1999
Spring 2000	Putin elected president
Summer 2003	Electoral reform changes political landscape
Dec. 2003	Duma elections give Putin control
Spring 2004	Putin reelected

matic values sketch in broad terms what the people want government to do and what they want society to look like. It is hard to establish whether Putin has attempted to read the Russian people or has decided to try to shape the consensus as he thinks it ought to be. In either event, his theme is clear. He understands the destination to be a society in which people feel more secure and in which there is a high level of order. Without criticizing the wisdom or integrity of these two values, it is clear that neither is central to the development of a democratic system. Order is inherent in any social system (sometimes called social "order"). Security, while it is something that most people would like to have, is also not an essential characteristic of democracy. After some careful thought, one might conclude that security and order are actually less characteristic of open, pluralistic, and participatory political systems than they are of more authoritarian systems.

In his own defense, Putin has frequently said that Russians will need to develop their own style of democracy. That is, they will seize the opportunity to give their own definition to the term. The analysis of political events in this chapter will present a view of this "Russian democracy" that will not seem at all familiar to most American students.

The practical realm of political values is largely about expectations. Past experience conditions people living in a society to what they think can and should be. Many people living under Communism emerged from that experience believing that government should be able to provide extensive goods and services to the masses. Furthermore, they believe that people living in society should feel safe from all sorts of violence and uncertainty. These expectations drawn from communism were formed largely without reflection on their costs or problems.

To understand how perplexing the transition is, one must add to these carryover expectations about government the notions that were promoted by ideological democrats in Europe and the United States. Ideas exported to Central and Eastern Europe encouraged people to believe that after communism, there would be more prosperity, "freedom," and mobility. In reality those notions are often in direct conflict with one another. Prosperity in a capitalist sense also means insecurity, uncertainty, and unevenness in wealth. More power in the hands of individuals—freedom—means that there is a much greater chance of conflict and violence. Mobility means that one can rise up through a system but drop down as well. There is no simple way to seamlessly combine the old values with the new.

Those living in postcommunist societies are beginning to learn that the values underpinning democracy involve efforts to level the political power of people in the society—that is the sense in which many talk about equality as the core value in democracy. But the market capitalist system is inherently about inequality. Inequality is the engine that drives the productivity and many of the accomplishments of this economic system. No single value serves both masters. Democracy and capitalism are predicated on two different sets of values. People living in institutionalized, democratic societies have become accustomed to shifting between sets of values as needed to pursue their objectives in the two realms.

The complexities of this effort by postcommunist societies to emulate democratic systems are many. For example, a market system will not infuse the marketplace of a transitional economy with goods and consumer choices unless there is abundant capital in the system to make entrepreneurship possible. Without investment capital, manufacturers, retailers, inventors, and entrepreneurs will not be able to contribute by doing what they do.

Compromise and tolerance are more central to a functioning democracy than are freedom and self-interest. In fact, expectations about freedom and self-interest could lead some to expect that government was *not* going to actively manage society, that laws were not going to inhibit behavior, and that regulations were not going to limit choices. Adjusting to new political realities and accepting new lessons about government are difficult for those living in postcommunist transitional societies.

As established democratic systems exported ideas to Russians (and others), people living in Russia were encouraged to judge governments by their performance. The alternative is for people in a society to support their system based on faith. Superficial thinking seems to draw one into believing that democracy is a tough-minded political system in which people support the system only when it continues to perform for them. But reality is a long way from that. Comparative politics recognizes that, in fact, most democracies function on the basis of "system affect," which is the fundamental idea that the system is so good that it deserves public support even when it performs badly. The "output affect," encouraged by classic democratic rhetoric, induces especially new systems to struggle because they are the least able to perform consistently.

Finally, the search for a set of core values in which the bulk of people in a society can believe raises the issue of allegiance or identity. When a person tells you that he or she is a Russian, it is not clear exactly what that identification includes. It could mean he or she is a citizen of Russia. That would mean that the label is essentially political. Such a person has identified with Russia as a political entity. If one acted in support or in defense of this Russia, one would be a patriot. Alternatively, being a Russian could mean that he or she is ethnically Russian. That means something quite different in Europe and, indeed, in most other parts of the world. It may mean that one sees himself or herself as a member of a people, an ethno-cultural group with shared historical, linguistic, physical, behavioral, and cultural characteristics. Those often include music, colors, symbols, legends, and idiosyncrasies. In comparative politics, this phenomenon is most accurately labeled "nation." "A nation" and "a people" are reasonable synonyms. One's support, identity, commitment to, and defense of the nation is "nationalism."

This distinction is critical. Political boundaries and sovereignty define the state (the political entity), and those within can choose to identify with it. Nation is different. It is something "in the blood." You are either in the group or you are not. You cannot choose to join. You have the requisite characteristics or you do not. The reason this is so important stems from the fact that Central and Eastern European countries all suffer from having been buffeted by one another over time to the point that political and ethnic boundaries no longer match up. For this reason, one persistent political issue seems always to be nationalists pressing, sometimes violently, to have ethnic and political boundaries match. Curiously the argument for this, though not often made clear, is that if "our people" were to have our own political system, life would be prosperous and conflict would vanish. Although this rationale is common, there are to my knowledge no examples of this warm and fuzzy political reality. In fact, of course, given the real demographic world we live in, the only way to make this happen is to eliminate the "others" from "our place." The contemporary term for that is "ethnic cleansing." Perhaps a better term is "genocide."

In the special context of democratic development, nationalism seems unable to accept the wisdom of tolerating and giving voice to minorities. The purity that defines the nationalist's destination cannot embrace the value of diversity nor the very practical argument for maximizing human resources through heterogeneity.

Russians, like many of their cohabitants in Eastern Europe, find it easier to find pride and accomplishment in their nation than in their state. The Liberal Democratic Party, led by Vladimir Zhirinovsky, is the clearest example of ultranationalist sentiment in Russia. It promotes "recapturing" all of the land ever controlled by Russia and zealously touts the superiority of the Russian people.

Perhaps the best example of nationalism finding its way into public policy in postcommunist Russia was a policy promoted and implemented in the Boris Yeltsin period. It clearly underscored the degree to which Russians are disinclined to consider tolerance a strength. A policy was created that sought to identify the four traditional religions of Russia. These would be able to conduct themselves actively and with few constraints, while all other religions would be severely limited in their right to own property, their activities, and their ability to proselytize.

The four religions were Russian Orthodoxy, Judaism, Islam, and Hinduism. One should see in this the thinly veiled advantage for the Russian Orthodox religion and the modest gesturing to three very much smaller faiths. More critically, those eliminated from operating in a pluralistic setting were the Ukrainian Orthodox, the Roman Catholic, and all of the Protestant denominations.

Overall, where does this leave today's Russia in terms of direction? What, if anything, have Russians settled upon as the consensus on values that would define a destination for the society and the kind of leadership expected? Whether one looks at public opinion polls, legislative policies, or presidential behavior and rhetoric, the signals all seem to point to values that are not characteristic of a democratic direction or destination. Order, control, and security are certainly known objectives in democratic societies, but they are not the driving forces that define society. They are not the ultimate destination that democratic societies aspire to reach.

Political Architecture of the State:
The Constitution as an Issue

The postcommunist Russian experience with creating a constitution was fundamentally flawed by the self-serving behavior of Yeltsin and his colleagues. They had their own agenda, and it influenced the design process to the point of making the resulting constitution dysfunctional. Their central consideration at the time of design was to ensure that the legislature would be weak and the executive would have the power to prevail in virtually all situations. Other structural issues were ignored or made secondary to that goal. Even with those power assets, the Russian president did not have the political muscle to press the Duma (the lower and more powerful legislative body in Russia) to ratify the constitution. The president's own strata of support not only did not have control but did not approach the level of support needed to engineer legislation except by executive decree. That changed in December 2003 when the broad-based movement promoted by Putin achieved a preeminent position in the Duma.

Rather than guiding policy or functioning as a vehicle for resolving issues, the Russian constitution has itself become an issue. Its status as an unratified document is but one aspect of the controversy. Another is the provision that presidents can serve just two terms. That was a key issue for Yeltsin, but it vanished abruptly when he resigned in December 1999. It has resurfaced with Putin. Elected in March 2000 and reelected by a huge margin in March 2004, Putin and/or some of his inner circle are unhappy with the term limitation. As a result of elaborate policy maneuvers, and reinforced by the outcome of the last Duma elections, Putin now has the power to change the constitution in whatever direction suits his interests. There is broad speculation about whether he intends to use that power. From Putin's perspective, if stability, control, and order are the real destinations, it is easy to rationalize a change that would permit him to remain in power as long as the public continues to elect him.

Perhaps as important as the explicit issues associated with the constitution are the omissions in the constitution's structuring of the government's political behavior. The crucial relationship between center and periphery, that is, the central issue of federalism, is left unclear.

We will return to many of these points in the section on elections.

Economic Architecture

The economic difficulties Russia faces are traceable to the early stages of the transition. It is fair to say that mistakes were made, but to do so veils the reality that the choices were very difficult and the advice received both from within the system and from outside was self-serving. Today's malaise has a number of elements:

- Public skepticism
- Inadequate investment
- Oligarchs, the *nouveaux riches,* and privatization

- Disincentives to manufacture
- Inadequate government revenues (ill-conceived tax systems)
- Corruption

Behind each of these is a nagging design problem. That is, had the economic architecture of the system addressed these challenges, it is reasonable to suggest that they would be more manageable today.

Public skepticism is traceable to the simplicity and exaggerated promises characteristic of the early years of the transition. Yeltsin and his economic adviser, Yegor Gaidar, publicly promoted a plan that claimed to be able to transform the Russian economy in just five hundred days. Scholars, and perhaps politicians, knew better, but the public did not. In August 1998 the Russian economy collapsed altogether in response to mismanaged economic policies. All bank accounts were frozen, and people who had invested heavily in Russian enterprises and in so-called GKOs (short-term Russian government bonds) lost everything. The result since has been a dramatic outflow of capital from Russia.

Those events are part of the reason that Russia today has insufficient investment capital for business and industry. Put most simply, you cannot build or sustain capitalism without capital. Money must be available for those with initiative who are prepared to embrace risk to do what they propose to do. Economies cannot grow without this fuel. Rich Russians understand that investment capital is drawn to environments that generate yields sufficient to balance risk. Under today's conditions most Russian investors, as well as most international investors, are deciding to place their funds elsewhere.

The so-called oligarchs achieved their vast wealth either by seizing opportunities as they emerged from the haze of the first days of the transition or by using their connections stemming from the old system and its bureaucracies. In any event, they recognized that a system with massive economic and industrial assets would have difficulty monitoring the privatization of those assets. Stepping into this gray area where the law was nonexistent, they became super-rich by moving quicker, more brazenly, and often more viciously. They then astutely recognized that protecting such assets required them to engage in politics, which they did. The Yeltsin regime, especially in the years 1995–1998 when Yeltsin himself was not healthy, was steered by the "family." That group included Yeltsin's daughter, some bodyguard-advisers, and a prominent circle of oligarchs. Boris Berezovsky is the most famous, but many others played roles.

Many believe that the root of the long-term economic problem lies in the reluctance of those Russians most knowledgeable about the system and most able to take financial initiatives to invest in manufacturing. Business logic does not support serious, medium- or large-scale production for a host of reasons. Investing in bricks-and-mortar projects is relatively expensive, quality construction is hard to organize, and the Russian work ethic is problematic. Moreover, such enterprises would surely draw the attention of government tax authorities. Money could be made more quickly and hidden more readily in retail and services.

The effort to escape taxation claimed some legitimacy given that legislatures at all levels of Russian politics had simply piled taxes upon taxes to the point where most businesses would be crushed under the burden if they paid all of their taxes. But paying only *some* of the taxes was an unworkable strategy. Reporting to one agency could mean that the information would be shared. Worse still, it could expose one to prosecution for avoiding the other taxes. Many reasoned that if they were guilty of tax evasion whether they paid some or none, they should do the sensible thing and pay none. The result is devastating for the government. Some statistics suggest that revenue fell to less than 20 percent of projections for some years and less than 50 percent for others. Compounding the revenue problem, after the 1998 economic collapse, government borrowing was a problem, especially in international circles. Leadership support for providing government services declined steadily. By the end of the 1990s most government employees (bureaucrats, teachers, the military, and a vast number of workers still employed by nonprivatized Russian firms) had their wages reduced and often deferred.

Putin took dramatic action in the face of this problem. In response to advice from economists, he reduced taxes for firms and individuals to a flat tax of roughly 13 percent. Although that has improved revenues somewhat, reluctance among taxpayers is still evident. Some believe that this is a ploy by government to get persons and firms with profits to declare those profits, after which the government will step back in with new and higher taxes. Compounding the problem, tax police, rather infamous in Russia, operate using clandestine and abrupt police techniques and are seldom placed under any scrutiny themselves.

Finally, there is the "corruption" element of the economy. This is often discussed in tandem with "organized crime." The problem with both terms is that they assume that there exists an established pattern of legal and ethical behavior and that behaviors that lie outside those patterns are thus "corruption" or "organized crime." In transitional systems, however, the law is not yet elaborately detailed. Gaps and voids are commonplace. In established democracies, systems promote the idea that one is at liberty to do whatever one wishes unless the law prohibits it. It is with this perspective that corruption must be understood in Russia and other transitional systems. If it is not against the law to embezzle funds from my own company, and I do it, am I a criminal? If the law does not differentiate insurance and extortion, and I intimidate a customer into buying protection, am I a criminal? The questions demonstrate how much new thinking needs to go into the effort to understand transitional political systems. There can be little doubt that many persons, firms, and organizations both in and out of government in Russia are engaged in activities—most often for profit and without sensitivity to those that may be harmed—that would in the European democracies be illegal or unacceptable. This affects Russia as a business environment, making it markedly less attractive for conventional businesspersons and intriguing for more flamboyant ones.

Political and Social Dynamics

One of the most significant implications of the economic malaise has to do with the ability of the government to do things for people. Ironically, since the collapse of communism most Russians would claim that the new system is *not* doing more *for* them and less *to* them, compared with their experiences under communism. Students might ask, How could this be?

Consider for a moment that there is always a balance in society between what the government takes from you and what it gives to you. Political scientists call this the "extractive" and "distributive" functions of government. It follows that if this equation seems to advantage the citizen, the citizen will be more favorably disposed toward the government than if it does not. In the communist era, government did not have to tax people because it controlled their wages and the prices they paid for things. By manipulating those factors central planners in the government could ensure adequate funds to provide services and run the government. The citizen had no way to opt out of this pattern. Taxing companies would be absurd since they were state run and the system would be taxing itself.

On the distribution side, the Communist system provided a wide range of mass organizations sponsored (read, financed) by the system, whose membership was generally open to those who wished to belong. These organizations provided goods and services of the sort that were consistent with their organization and membership. For example, opera lovers could join an organization that provided performances, tickets, and contact with performers. Youth organizations provided activities of special interest to young persons. In this way the system limited and guided choice, to be sure, but affordable options were always available. Add to this day care, meals, and vacations provided by one's workplace, and you had at least an adequate menu of services available to all workers.

Communism collapses and vanishes. The transition replaces it. Governing routines are incrementally built into the new, partially formed system. The result is that governments decide to generate revenue the typical way—taxing the people and organizations in the society. To many citizens this seems new and imposing, much as an obtrusive pickpocket would be. But the equation could still be balanced if government does a great deal with this money and the citizen sees the result. But, in fact, what happens in Russia and elsewhere is that services are cut. Mass organizations disappear or have to be self-financing. Those opera tickets now cost a great deal more. Child care must be paid for. Meals, vacations, tuba lessons, and lectures all cost. The government shrinks from providing services and goods; prices rise, and wages and jobs are uncertain. The picture is one of shrinking benefits and higher apparent costs. The result is public aggravation and dissatisfaction. These conditions reinforce the inclination of Russians to think about the past in nostalgic ways. They can begin to account for the behavior of the Russian electorate.

Elections Russian elections provide cautionary—and perhaps the clearest—insight into the dynamics of Russian politics. The elections illustrate the ebb and flow of political thinking, the distance between elite and masses, and the structural flaws in the system. The story begins with the first Duma election in December 1993. It came right after a violent episode when the executive, Yeltsin, and the legislature, led by vice president Aleksander Rutskoi and prime minister Ruslan Khasbulatov, each tried to unseat the other. The two-week crisis, in October 1993, ended when Yeltsin used the power of the military to crush the rebellion and remove the legislators. A month later, in haste, Yeltsin and his colleagues drafted a constitution that he expected would be ratified by the new legislature that was to be elected in December. In spite of the obvious power at his disposal, the people elected a new Duma that was even more abrasive to Yeltsin than the one he had fired on. Yeltsin's candidates fared very badly in the election. The party with the largest level of support was the misnamed Liberal Democratic Party. Led by an ultranationalist, Vladimir Zhirinovsky, it is a neo-fascist party of the extreme right. The Communist Party ran second in the election. Both results came as a shock to the regime.

Two years later, in December 1995, the next Duma election saw the Liberal Democrats fade and the Communist Party win the greatest number of seats, though not nearly a majority. After another four years, another Duma election was held in December 1999, and the Communist Party again gained the greatest level of support. These are pluralities hovering around 20 percent. The parties did not control the legislature in any sense, and their inability to form coalitions discounted their power still further. Through the 1990s it became clear that political parties were not forming around platforms, nor were issues bubbling up from the general public. Rather, the so-called parties were merely organizations to promote the candidacy of a particular individual. Every party in Russian politics is described in this way. Some forty-nine "parties" were registered, half of them garnering sufficient electoral support to be taken seriously. Many fade, some grow, but few remained persistent political players.

Before the December 2003 Duma election, Putin maneuvered some changes that appear minor on the surface but in fact represent a formidable redesign of the political landscape. Putin attempted to create a dialogue with the executive leadership of the "republics" of the Russian Federation. These leaders are analogous to U.S. governors. Putin proposed that they be appointed by the Russian president rather than elected. Some balked, and the idea appears to have been tabled. The move was seen as an attempt to centralize power and give Putin control over politics and resources in the regions. Putin's other "reform" was passed by the Duma. It made the next Duma election a watershed by giving those political parties that achieved the 5 percent threshold for gaining seats clear advantage in a number of ways from that point forward. Parties that did not get 5 percent of the vote had, under the Yeltsin constitution, been prevented from assuming seats in the legislature. With the December 2003 Duma election, the parties that attained 5 percent or more of the vote would be endowed with many more privileges, which would be denied the parties that failed to get to that threshold. Most important, the privileged parties would be able to place their candidates on ballots throughout the Russian Federation without cumbersome stipulations. The others, effectively made second-class parties, would need to struggle with petitions and election bonds and even then could be prevented from placing candidates on ballots under certain circumstances.

Before the 2003 Duma election was held, Putin and the political establishment created what they called a "movement" (in their minds, in contrast to a political party), which was fleshed out with candidates who were already members of the Putin administration. They called it "United Russia," "Unity," or "Medved" (meaning, "bear"). It became what is known in Russia as a "party of power," which roughly means what we call "the establishment." All other parties were portrayed as nay-saying, opposition parties with nothing positive to offer.

At this point we should mention that Russia was at that time reeling under pressure from Chechen terrorist activity even in Moscow. The election produced fairly shocking results, especially in the context of previous Duma elections. Remember, Yeltsin was never able to marshal public electoral support for his legislative candidates. Putin, however, clearly did. Of the 60 million votes cast (of 109 million eligible), 37.5 percent were for United Russia, the highest vote total yet achieved by any party in postcommunist Russia. The Communist Party finished second with 12.6 percent. The Liberal Democrats, who had virtually disappeared in the previous election, finished third with 11.5 percent, and a new party called "Rodina" (alternatively called the "Homeland" or "Motherland Party") finished fourth. The really big news was that no other party made the cut! From a transitional perspective, it may be most important that the two genuinely democratic political parties, Yabloko and SPS (Union of Right Forces), led by the impressive young politicians Yavlinsky, Chubais, and Nemtsov, were eliminated. The "Against all" option on the ballot pulled more support than either of the democratic parties.

As a result of the 2003 election the political landscape in Russia seems to have narrowed significantly. But on closer inspection, it is even worse. After this election the Communists replaced their recognized leadership with unknowns who have created a record in the Duma of critical rhetoric but grudging vote support for Putin. The Liberal Democrats (far-right party) attack legislation differently but, more often than not, vote with the Putin establishment. The most interesting of all is the Rodina Party. Created by Putin strategists to siphon off support from the Communists, its spokesmen are the most strident critics of the Putin regime, but if ever needed, they can be manipulated by their original sponsors, the Putin administration itself. It is a tangled but remarkable story. It means that Putin has largely undisputed control of the Duma. This control requires some finesse, but the ability of Putin to get the Duma to do as he wishes is clear. After the Beslan terrorist attack on a rural school on opening day (September 1, 2004), Putin reintroduced his idea of appointing republic presidents (regional governors), and the Duma passed the legislation easily as an antiterrorist measure. Today, much speculation exists that if Putin wishes to seek another term, he will certainly be able to gather the votes to change the constitution—some say, replace the constitution with one that will enable him to retain the presidency.

It is hard to imagine a more fundamental shift in political power in a transitional setting. The Russian experience stands out as the preeminent example of centralizing power; to what end remains a question and a controversy. Following the Duma election of 2003 and its fallout, Putin ran for reelection in March 2004 and managed to eliminate most competitors by the implementation of the new regulations. The competitors that remained were beset by problems that are suspicious in nature. Mikhail Khodorkovsky, a rich oligarch, expressed interest in running for president and was indicted for tax evasion. The system claimed he owed $32 million in back taxes. Ivan Rybkin, formerly a high-ranking official in the Yeltsin administration, declared his candidacy and during the campaign went missing for nearly a week, after which he claimed to have had a breakdown. He had the unlimited financial backing of the maverick oligarch Berezovsky. Putin declined to campaign or debate and won with 73 percent of the vote.

Elite Accountability If elite accountability is a serious condition for democratic development, Russia has been moving in an inconsistent direction. As suggested in the previous chapter, many political elites in Russia believe that accountability is a nuisance. We may want to concede something to them because accountability does slow the process, it does siphon off energy from the immediate task of solving problems, and its does advantage the opposition, who may or may not have the system's interest at heart. Still, functioning, mature democracies have uniformly concluded that for the system to survive in a democratic form, it must make a diligent commitment to accountability to both the opposition and the general public. Russia is far from that commitment.

Transparency in Russian politics is evident for most Russians in the personality of Putin himself. Unassuming, highly visible, mild mannered, intelligent, and a "counterpuncher," he seems to most Russians "like the person he seems to be." That does not make most political analysts happy, but it has worked for Putin in his meteoric political career. His image is aided by the story, apparently true, that he did not want or seek the job of president that was forced on him by Yeltsin.

The elite-mass interface that is an essential texture in democratic politics is missing in contemporary Russian politics. Russian elites seem too preoccupied to devote any attention to public dialogue. If one is looking for some bright spot, there is some evidence that such a relationship between governed and those governing is taking shape in the regions. One finds grassroots politics nurtured by some democratic leaders but also by some populist demagogues. As with other aspects of Russian politics, the fallout from such contrasting motives is debatable.

Doors and Windows Have the Russians managed to build a political system in which people feel that they understand enough about how government is organized, and about who does what, to enable them to effectively make requests, lodge complaints, or offer support? The simple answer is no. The bureaucracy remains thick and intransigent. The legacy of the old system suggests that if you want to get anything accomplished, the only way to be effective is through informal connections. This perception permeates the system. As long as it prevails—and it will, without explicit political effort to dispel it—the notion that a citizen has rights, voice, or responsibility will not take root. It follows that civil society is not an active model for broad-scale public engagement in politics. There is, however, a rather firmly established and prolific record of small groups' engaging at the most local level. Their efforts are most often frustrated, but the socialist system in its post-Stalinist years did experience a good deal of this anomic (i.e., single-issue) pressure directed at the lowest levels of authority. It has carried over and could indicate how very limited is the information that is actually available to the Russian public about the functional responsibilities of political offices, agencies, or departments. The system lacks the "map" that citizens could follow to attempt to articulate their interests.

Leadership

The Russian political elite are mostly what we called in the last chapter "born-agains." They have maneuvered their previous experience into their current positions perhaps owing to the timeworn tradition of connections. The oldest generation of born-agains are disappearing quickly. Rookies with 1990s experience enter the picture regularly now. Putin has an established record of reaching into the ranks of the intelligence services for advisers. With this generational change, leaders display a greater polish and sophistication, but qualms remain about their own level of confidence in their policy choices. Fits and starts are common. Policies lurch ahead, and then the administration pulls back and watches for reaction. This might best be explained as a leadership who, at the same time they are making today's public policy, are trying to establish in their own minds what their ideology really is. Without an ideological compass—a sense of where you think the system should be going—it is virtually impossible to steer a steady course.

Vladimir Putin's time in the KGB in his early adult years did not encourage such personal philosophies. In fact, a well-defined set of personal political beliefs could negatively affect the career of any person in an intelligence organization anywhere. Agents collect information. They are not asked to judge the assignment or analyze its meaning. Putin is dealing with at least two learning curves: (1) the grit of everyday politics at the top of the system in Russia and (2) searching for his own sense of "destination." Without such a compass, he cannot gauge the degree to which a particular policy advances the system toward, or diverts it from, its objectives. Remember too that Putin regularly receives poignant advice from economic elites who may not give systemic interests priority but instead recommend policies serving the business elite. The inconsistency that so many scholars find in Putin's behavior is best understood in these terms.

How would one judge the driving skills of Vladimir Putin and his aides? Perhaps like those of a rookie driver at the Indianapolis Speedway. His skills are better than those of the average man-on-the-street, better than those who went before him, but he is racing with the world's best drivers in an unforgiving, competitive world in a partially designed vehicle. He might add that he has unforgiving fans. Not an enviable role in spite of the prestige.

Prognosis

Russia is a political system in turmoil, partly because of the awkward and incomplete design of the system. The architecture is dangerously flawed, unless democracy is not the destination. In that case, values may be forming that support the direction of politics. Leadership, although vastly improved, may not be up to the imposing task that lies ahead.

The system has a penchant for facing backwards. Resources to govern are not at hand. Legitimacy is nurtured by habit and identity. Tolerance is ignored as a system-valued foundation. Expectations persist that government can and should provide for the substantial needs of citizens. Political issues and political participation are understood as someone else's realm.

Those interested in politics tend to become "Putineers"—believers who share the youthful discipline of the old Soviet "pioneers," the zeal of the 1950s Disney "Mouseketeers," and the passionate desire for a political savior. This phenomenon cannot last long. Russians will begin to debate the destination, the machinery, and the driver. This may take so much time to evolve that Russia will be left a broken and failed state.

UKRAINE

Ukraine is a very interesting example of a political system struggling with both its identity and its problems in the twenty-first century. Like Russia and the thirteen other parts of the old Soviet Union, Ukraine found itself with new dimensions and new sovereignty in 1992. Historically and culturally, Russia and Ukraine have been linked. In the USSR, their economies and political leadership were elaborately intertwined. Yet Ukrainian nationalists lingered in the hope that an independent Ukraine would materialize and miraculously sweep away society's problems. Political leaders in Ukraine in 1991, along with Yeltsin and their Belarussian counterparts, were primarily responsible for creating the tensions that Gorbachev could not manage. In essence, they engineered the breakup of the Soviet Union.

Since that time Ukraine has drawn much attention. It has many assets, including both geographic and population size (comparable to France), extraordinarily rich agricultural land and environment, a developed industrial base, owing to Soviet investment, and access to the Mediterranean via the Black

Sea. For some, Ukraine is interesting because of its parallels with the Russian experience; for others, it is interesting because of the key differences.

Value Consensus

In one important sense Ukraine is quite like Russia: Patterns of thinking about politics are still confused and without much dialogue or focus on the future. Some Ukrainian analysts insist that Ukrainians are much more inclined to see political values and economic values in some sort of balance, that is, to see the linkage between the political system they seek and the prosperity that they seek. To put it another way, Ukrainians might be less willing than Russians to sacrifice democratic political routines and rights in exchange for promises of economic improvement.

The dramatic political events of 2004, called the "Orange Revolution," have been simplified and generalized by the news media and by European and U.S. authorities to a point that goes well beyond reality. Many are saying that the Orange Revolution has produced a president and a government committed to broad "common European values." This exaggeration—perhaps better called a hope—veils Ukraine's real struggle as it searches for a value consensus. Generalizations about values, orientations, and expectations in contemporary Ukraine are often framed by the notion that Ukraine has three parts. The western part (once part of Poland) faces west and is the most fiercely nationalistic. The eastern part is rich in raw materials and is populated by a significant number of ethnic Russians; it has often felt less anxious about Russian-Ukrainian relations. The center section of the country is portrayed as the mainstream, owing perhaps to its mixture of people, economic interests, and cultures. It is often represented as the balancer of the two other parts. It has much of the industry nurtured in the Soviet period and is also often presumed to be the most politically astute part of Ukraine.

All this implies that Ukraine has not found a consensus of values that would define a destination for people or government. A crude but poignant illustration of this uncertainty is former president Leonid Kuchma's (two-term president from 1994 to 2004) favorite label to describe the direction of policy—"multi-vector." This term should conjure up in your mind's eye leadership pointing and moving in all sorts of different directions.

The Orange Revolution (November–December 2004) is another of those cases identified in the previous chapter as political movements that solidify public opinion around what people are against, without capturing what people are for. In this important sense, the Orange Revolution is like the Yeltsin movement in August 1991 and other movements in Central Europe—Solidarnosc (Poland), the Civic Forum (Czechoslovakia), the Democratic Forum (Hungary,) and even the OTPOR movement (Serbia). Although they represent politics in a dramatic moment, they often do not contribute to the task of finding a value consensus for a fledgling democracy.

Ukraine
Timeline

1921	Ukraine part of USSR
1932	Famine
1941–1944	Nazi occupation
1945	USSR annexes Western Ukraine
1986	Chernobyl nuclear accident
1988	Opposition forming
1991	Ukraine breaks away from USSR
1991–1994	Kravchuk in power
1994–2004	Kuchma in power
1996	New constitution
2001	Last nuclear weapons destroyed
Nov. 2004	Presidential election scandal
Dec. 2004	Election rerun: Yushenko wins
Sept. 2005	Yushenko dismisses prime minister

Political Architecture of the State

The Ukrainian constitution of 1996 creates what it calls a "semipresidential" system. Analysts suggest that the constitution's greatest shortcoming is its inability to prescribe the working relationship between the legislative and executive branches. Since its inception, the executive has followed its own interests by extending its own political power. Like the Russian legislatures, Ukraine's Rada has been populated by multiple political parties unable to achieve a working majority coalition. That regularly empowered the executive to use a default provision permitting executive decrees in lieu of legislation. The first two presidents, Kravchuk and Kuchma, found it useful to "connect" with new Ukrainian oligarchs (newly super-rich entrepreneurs) and moved legal and economic reforms ahead much more slowly than their political rhetoric would suggest. Scholars speculate that this course was followed because it maintained a system in which those with connections could create and retain fortunes. Conventional wisdom sees this as policymaking spurred by self-interest.

In his second term Leonid Kuchma and his new prime minister, Viktor Yushenko, gained considerable support from the center and right. Nonetheless, the legislature never did learn how to forge coalitions and continued to face manipulation by the executive. Kuchma wielded the power of appointment without constraint.

The only major constitutional or electoral reform that has been made specifies that beginning with the 2006 elections, all legislative seats will be filled on the basis of proportional representation. This means that voters will vote for a political party. Each party will have provided a list of its candidates that presumes that it will receive 100 percent of the vote. When the party receives just a percentage of the votes, say, 28 percent, 28 percent of that party's list of candidates will assume seats in the legislature. This represents a major change from the original procedure, which elected half the legislators with this system and half by single-member-district, plurality elections. This latter form is the one most familiar to Americans; in the United States the candidate who gets the most votes in a local district is elected. The political implication is that opposition politicians with a locally concentrated power base will not play a role at the central government level.

Political parties in Ukraine suffer from many of the same problems they face in Russia. Most are candidate centered rather than issue centered. The public has a generally low opinion of parties and their effectiveness. Most parties are vague about their commitment to genuinely democratic institutions and mechanics. They are also rather easily cast as negative forces in the political system. You should recall that under communism this sort of criticism and public political dialogue did not exist. Upbeat political cheerleading was the norm. The 2002 Rada elections were the first in Ukrainian politics in which another party—Yushenko's centrist "Our Ukraine"—won more votes than the Communist Party. It was an early signal that the center of the political spectrum was increasingly unhappy and was gaining courage.

Legislative-Executive Relations The struggle over the legislative-executive relationship has to do with the most basic elements of the institutional design of the political system. Ukraine's long-term destiny depends on an accommodation evolving between these key elements of government. But especially during the Kuchma years (1994–2004), the open rivalry and hostility between the two destructively affected economic policy, foreign economic relations, the provision of social services, the (unsuccessful) effort to deal with abuse of power and wealth, and reforms of all sorts. It is telling that no fewer than thirteen presidential candidates emerged from the legislature to challenge Leonid Kuchma in his bid for reelection in 1999.

Centralization As suggested earlier, the penchant of political leaders to believe that they need to centralize power, even if their ultimate objective is to decentralize power, lingers in the behavior of most postcommunist leaders. It is difficult to sort out the true motives in such political actions. The man who dominated postcommunist Ukraine is former president Leonid Kuchma. He served two terms as president and conducted himself in the mode of a super-trustee. With increasing frequency, he ruled by presidential decree. Kuchma was most prone to this centralizing tendency around his own reelection time. He tightened control over the media and sacked governors (regional political leaders) when he did not receive electoral support from their constituencies. He regularly revealed a willingness to alter or reinterpret the constitution when it would favor his position.

Economic Architecture

One of the central political contests between the legislature and the executive in the late 1990s concerned the power to tax. Each tried to expand its own mandate and limit the other's authority to impose taxes. The contest of power ended in a draw. Both sides continued to impose unworkable taxes that stifled business, encouraged nonpayment of taxes, and strengthened the relative position of connected and corrupt officials and entrepreneurs. A number of budgets were adopted after contentious political fights, but both revenue and expenditure specifications were ignored. Budgets became unreliable guides to government financial behavior.

Typical of emerging market systems, and especially characteristic of post-communist economies, is the mixed performance that various indexes and variables reflect. By the late 1990s Ukraine's gross domestic product (GDP), international trade, and incoming foreign investment were in free fall. All of them declined so fast that the figures were hard to monitor. In just the year from 1998 to 1999, the rate of decline was nearly 50 percent. Much of the decline was caused internally, but some was attributable to Russia's economic collapse in August 1998. Currency problems and debt plagued the system. The IMF and World Bank both became queasy about what had been a pet project—the rebuilding of the Ukrainian economy. Default on foreign loans, which had become the very foundation of the economy, was a constant policy option. Ukraine's dramatic energy dependency on Russia complicated politics, given the politically correct and popular misconception that Ukraine was strong and did not need Russia. No leader wanted to concede the awkwardness of that dependency and the foreign relations and regional negotiations that it forced on the system.

The dramatic swings in the statistical picture can be demonstrated by the fact that in 2004 Ukraine recorded the fastest rate of growth in GDP in all of Europe. A student should see this as evidence that great caution is warranted when generalizing about emerging markets.

The privatization process initially made some well-connected Ukrainians super-rich. Whole industries came to be controlled by single individuals or small business circles. The abuse of the process by the powerful was obvious. The legislature saw the solution to the problem in very simple terms: resist further privatization. That turned out to be a bankrupt strategy, given that millions of workers remained mired in inefficient and unproductive state-run factories and businesses.

In Kuchma's second term he opted to nominate a "respected reformer" to be prime minister. That was Viktor Yushenko; he had experience as director of the national bank and had the will to become Kuchma's point man on the economy. The move was designed to deflect responsibility away from Kuchma. With a flair for the dramatic and considerable zeal, Yushenko introduced two economic programs that respectively promised to turn around the economy in one hundred and one thousand days. This was a classic misstep, quite like the Russian Gaidar's five-hundred-day plan for turning Russia's economy around. There was little realistic hope for either program. The promised improvements in government administration and the fundamental changes in economic behavior were supported neither by the legislature nor by the executive. Yushenko, like most reformers, discovered that political will was not enough to change society, or even the part of government that manages it.

Political and Social Dynamics: Elections

In the same sense that elections and the politics surrounding them in Russia provide keen insight into the political dynamic there, Ukraine's elections illuminate Ukrainian politics. The Orange Revolution is another story of elections gone off-track. It may be useful to build the story chronologically. When communism and the Soviet Union suddenly evaporated in Ukraine, a former Communist, Leonid Kravchuk, became president. People in and out of power, in and out of government, had little basis for anticipating what would happen. Most Ukrainians simply waited and watched.

In 1994 a presidential election was held without a great deal of international scrutiny, and another former Communist, Kuchma, won. Expectations had not crystallized, and Ukraine was struggling. The national military was in disarray. The monetary system had not been established. Coupons were being used in place of money. Both agricultural production and industrial production were declining, and international trade was massively disrupted. The picture was grim.

Kuchma enlisted liberal democratic rhetoric but seemed unconvinced of the real utility of those ideas. Nonetheless, the rhetoric seemed to generate the desired international aid. When it came time to run again, Kuchma's record was weak, but a strategy was gleaned from Yeltsin's "reelection" in 1996 in Russia. It involved the following:

- Casting the opponent as bound to return Ukraine to communism and thus enlisting all those that the old system had abused, as well as the zeal and money of all the new rich
- Portraying a vote for the incumbent as a vote for stability—a broadly popular, if vague, desire in transitional societies
- Controlling the media and embracing the candidate who finished third in the first ballot by adding him to the administration before the second and final ballot (In Russia this was Lebed, a popular general, and in Ukraine it was Yevhen Marchuk, former prime minister and chief of the Security Service.)
- Ensuring that European and American authorities would buy the notion that the other guy would bring back communism

The strategy proved successful. Kuchma won a second term on the second ballot, with 56 percent of the vote. International scrutiny of the election produced harsh criticism.

It was at this point that Kuchma sought a new prime minister who would deflect some criticism from him. His first choice was rejected by a newly invigorated legislature. His second choice was Yushenko, whose five years as director of the national bank gave him establishment credentials. Yushenko had been able to maintain his image as a genuine reformer, a Western-facing, pragmatic economist untainted by any apparent connections to crime and corruption. He was able to move ahead with some economic changes because he had the support of many in the legislature both personally and politically. He marshaled support for a new currency and generated policies that curbed inflation. His popularity grew in the shadow of Kuchma's leadership.

By April 2001 Yushenko had outlived his usefulness to Kuchma. He may have become too popular with center and right elements of the legislature, threatening Kuchma's preeminence. He was replaced when leftists and centrists loyal to Kuchma voted him out. Yushenko then joined the opposition and created a new political bloc called "Our Ukraine." In the 2002 parliamentary elections Our Ukraine emerged as the most popular opposition party.

As the 2004 presidential election approached, Kuchma endorsed Viktor Yanukovych. He became the establishment candidate, and Yushenko the "democratic opposition" candidate. The election was intense and was ultimately marred by such obvious vote fraud that Ukrainian election officials and international watchdog groups forced a re-balloting. This time masses of Ukrainians were mobilized—some by their disapproval of Kuchma's policies, some by the apparent link between Kuchma and Yanukovych. Some were outraged by the corruption of the first election and some by Russian efforts to endorse Yanukovych. As in other cases, the only thing solid about the movement of these masses was their view of what they did not want. Volunteers, activists, and young people in large numbers took politics to the street. Ukrainian security forces remained passive, just as the Serbian forces had when street demonstrations challenged Milosevic in Serbia four years earlier. Both Ukrainian and international news media became fascinated with Yushenko and the opposition, openly or inadvertently enhancing the Orange Revolution by the nature of their portrayals. It was captivating TV and reinforced many in the United States who wanted to believe that democracy was indeed an irresistible force spreading across the face of the Earth. There is also some mystery associated with the poisoning that nearly killed Yushenko during the campaign.

Yushenko won the presidency. There was dancing in the streets, and the newly elected president was pictured with his American wife—all apparent proof that democracy lives in Ukraine and that Americans should feel warm and fuzzy about Yushenko. Students of transitional politics in our world know that much more caution needs to be exercised.

Leadership

Ukrainian leadership reflects the pattern suggested in other postcommunist systems. Born-agains (former Communists recasting their political images) dominated and are still significant. Even the Yushenko leadership circle is not without its carryovers. It is true that in 2005 Yushenko put together a team of technocrats who have some expertise in the policy arenas that they manage. Reading Yushenko's popularity at this stage is challenging. He has a base in rural Ukraine and in the professional class of Ukrainians. He does reasonably well among some urban, working-class elements and demonstrates rather even support from various religious groups.

The track record of those who come to power on the back of a movement shows that they struggle desperately searching for that illusive value consensus that tells them what people want, especially from government. Yushenko's electoral following has splintered in the face of this task. As he encounters the institutional and systemic barriers to effective governing in a transitional setting, we will see him turn, as so many others have, to centralization as a way to promote change.

Yushenko brings a major advantage in his considerable postcommunist political experience (two major positions) in the Ukrainian system. He may be able to avoid some of the chronic mistakes made elsewhere. He may have more refined "driving skills." Generational leadership change has had more time to occur in Ukraine, but it is unlikely that this new Ukrainian leadership group will be any more confident about their strategy than those that have stumbled through transition elsewhere.

Prognosis

Ukraine is one of those places that tempt one to think that because it has so many assets, so many resources, it is destined to become a healthy political system. In fact, Ukraine is beset by all the problems common to transition and has been slower to deal with them than many other transitional states. U.S. and European assistance to Ukraine has been significant but mostly thwarted by the narrow, self-interested behavior of those in government and business. Ukraine does not have a consensus that identifies a destination. It has a vehicle whose design has some decidedly dysfunctional parts that frustrate its movement down a path. Whether it has found the leader to drive the society toward a brighter future is debatable. It may be that after five years in the Ukrainian presidency Yushenko will be targeted with the same criticisms currently directed at Putin, five years being about the time lag between the start of the Putin era and the beginning of the Yushenko era.

BOSNIA AND SOUTHEASTERN EUROPE

The political systems that have emerged from the breakup of communist Yugoslavia are case studies of just how challenging establishing new political systems can be, especially in the accelerating reality of the twenty-first century. To begin with just a brief word about labels, the classic way to refer to the countries in this region is "Balkan." To this day it is the most common name for Romania, Bulgaria, Greece, Macedonia, Bosnia, Croatia, Albania, the Federation of Serbia and Montenegro, and Kosovo. In everyday politics in Europe, "Balkan" has come to mean "entangled" or "backward" and to connote confrontational politics. The name did not acquire that meaning by accident. The history of the region reflects those characteristics. Increasingly, as analysts and organizations search for ways to help these societies deal with their circumstances (the EU, the

UN, and development agencies in particular) it is common to encounter suggestions that the label itself is part of the problem, as it not only describes the past but serves to predict and rationalize a chaotic future. For that reason, many suggest that "Southeastern Europe" replace "Balkan" in our thinking and our lexicon. The change also makes sense because Greece is now a member of the EU, and Romania and Bulgaria are on a firm track toward membership. That leaves a subset of countries that we will refer to as "Southeastern Europe." Bosnia is perhaps the most poignant example of the malaise in the region and will become our central example.

Value Consensus

The political systems of Southeastern Europe are far from establishing a consensus about values that can support democratic destinations. In virtually every case, they are societies that are mired in their violent and coercive histories. They dwell on the goal of righting the wrongs of the past, which are legion and which, depending upon the epoch chosen, can be pinned on any of their neighbors. Each has conjured its own historical rationale for intolerance of the "others" in this rather small geographic region. In essence, all of written history has been very unkind, and probably the period before that as well. To make matters worse, when history has left some opening for cooperation and kinship, myth and legend have reinforced intolerance and animosity. The modern manifestation of this pattern is called "nationalism" (whose definition we developed in the previous chapter). Southeastern Europe is affected by a virulent strain of the phenomenon. In any other place it would be called "ultranationalism," given its strident ideas leading to inflexible conclusions.

As you study politics, you will discover that many people prefer feeling about politics to thinking about politics. Feeling is easier. It makes it easier for people to bond, to agree. But such "agreement" overlooks the implications of that togetherness—it is built around those that we hate or those with whom we cannot live. Stop and think about that.

Nationalism drives us to divide society. It eliminates some measure of the human resources that our society has. It then paints one or more groups as evil and the source of all our problems. People are induced to believe that if "they" were simply eliminated from our society, we would be happy, prosperous, without anxiety or fear, and able to accomplish all of our objectives individually and collectively. To my knowledge there is no example of this prediction actually being borne out anywhere in the modern world. Perhaps more important is the reality that for this to happen, someone else must be displaced. And without any doubt, the displaced will then sharpen their commitment to reclaiming their place and displacing those who displaced them. In a nutshell, this is the history of the region. It is the reason why history does not offer the solution for any of the peoples of Southeastern Europe.

In fact, no constructive destination—or value consensus—is possible without literally ignoring the region's history. This is a radical idea, however, and one that those enmeshed in the tangle of politics in the region are unable or unwilling to see.

One must remember the distinction between nation and state. The state and allegiance to it can be constructive. People can become a part of the state because they want to or because they have something to contribute. In this way, the contrast is sharp. Commitment to the state can be inclusive and forward-looking; commitment to nation is exclusive (you are born into our people) and backward-facing. You cannot join. In its most aggressive form, even those with some identity of blood with nation but who are not "pure" (that is, whose parentage or ancestry is not entirely Serb, Kosovar, Ukrainian, etc.) cannot be included. They are viewed as "others" as well.

In Southeastern Europe today, ire is so sharply focused in politics that Greeks and Macedonians, Serbs and Croats, Kosovars and Serbs, Albanians and Macedonians, Montenegrins and Serbs all manage to claim that they are unable to deal with or live with the other. Bosnia is even more curious. Geographically in the center of the region and vexed by all the swirling hostility, Bosnia is even more torn. Ethnic Serbs and Croats living in Bosnia, especially in its population centers, found themselves "converted" to Islam by the Ottoman Empire that controlled the region for centuries. Their religious conversion did not change their ethnic heritage, but with the passage of time, many cultural traits did evolve. When in the early 1990s violence erupted in a political void, not only did Serbs fight Croats, but Serbs also fought against Bosnian Moslems. Croats fought Bosnian Moslems as well as the Serbs. This became a three-way, no-holds-barred, ethnic struggle, even though Bosnians cannot easily establish that they are a distinct and separate ethnic group. Religion became shorthand for ethnicity, even without any scientific foundation. All of the groups in that war spoke the same language. All had lived in practical political and economic harmony for many decades in communist Yugoslavia. The only way to get them to kill one another was to dig up historical grievances that had progressively been laid to rest in the political development of communist Yugoslavia.

If you are an American, you should be particularly cautious when you read that the conflict and breakup of Yugoslavia were inevitable or that ethnic groups have always fought with one another. Ask yourself if other political systems you have been studying—the United States, the United Kingdom, and the European Union—don't squarely challenge that notion, especially when the people in society can be encouraged by their political leaders to face forward. In what ways do past grievances and divisions dominate U.S. political relationships? Ask not how we rectify the past but how we construct the future. American society, perhaps because of its immigrant history, has evolved as a compulsively forward-facing society. We all think a great deal about tomorrow—our lives, our society. Canada, Brazil, and the EU are also cases that suggest that history and its grievances do not have to guide development. The Southeastern Europeans and many others in the broader region need to imagine searching for and establishing a value consensus that builds toward a future destination. That is requisite number one.

Former Yugoslavia

T i m e l i n e

1919	World War I peace creates Kingdom of South Slavs
1929	Name changed to Yugoslavia
1941–1945	World War II: German and Italian occupation
1945	Joseph Broz "Tito" emerges as Communist leader
1948	Stalin-Tito confrontation
1950s	Tito consolidates power
1961 and 1964	Yugoslavia leader of nonaligned movement
1965	Decentralizing political reforms: "workers' self-management"
1970s	Collective presidency created
1980	Tito dies
1980s	Political system moves ahead without charismatic leadership
1989 and 1991	Communism collapses in Eastern Europe
1991	Republic leaders create ethnic conflict
1991–1994	Violence and civil war in Croatia
1994–1995	Violence and civil war in Bosnia
1999	Violence and civil war in Kosovo

Political Architecture of the State

Basic Constitutional Framework The Bosnian constitutional framework is an awkward example because it was quite simply imposed on Bosnia by external actors. The 1995 Dayton Accords brokered by the United States (in Dayton, Ohio) managed to stop the fighting in Bosnia and attempted to impose a political structure on the society. A process not unlike the one Bosnia experienced may be just ahead in Kosovo and indeed in other parts of our world. The three warring elements were brought together and pressed to accept a political redesign of Bosnia. This architecture created an extremely weak federal system of government. Calling it a "government" may be stretching the term. Two geopolitical areas were created that very roughly reflected the concentrations of Bosnian Serbs, on the one hand (the Srbska Republic), and concentrations of Bosnian Croats or Bosnian Moslems on the other (the Federation of Croats and Moslems). The rationale was that the two weaker elements need to be combined to balance the political power of the Bosnian Serbs. One can imagine how awkward it was for the two warring elements—Croats and Moslems—to be thrust together politically.

The "presidency" was to be a three-headed executive with Serbs, Croats, and Moslems each electing a "co-president." Decisions were to be made by consensus among the three. Two legislatures were established—one for Bosnian Serbs, the other for the Confederation of Croats and Moslems—to make policies for their respective territories. Elections have been held twice since the accords, both times marred by an array of problems described in chapter 5. The questions of who had a right to vote and where were never resolved. To no one's surprise, candidates from the dominant ethnic group won in all constituencies. In fact, in most of the polling places the voter turnout was more than 100 percent. Think about how that might happen.

More Political Architecture The design, then, is flawed, dysfunctional, and not viewed by Bosnians as legitimate. It fails to address such major issues as the relationship between the legislature and the executive. It does not frame a central government that has any capacity for generating public policy that might be uniformly applied in the state. It has proven altogether inadequate to the task of producing a legal platform for the society. As such, it has not routinized the behavior of people, businesses, or government itself in contemporary Bosnia.

Efforts to make even the simplest decisions have been protracted and seldom successful. Two examples may illustrate how basic the problem is: When the political system attempted to establish a flag for itself, so much controversy erupted over the colors and symbolism that the Spanish ambassador to Bosnia was ultimately asked by the *de facto* governor (the UN high representative in Bosnia) to design the flag. Similarly, creating license plates for vehicles may seem like a simple administrative decision. However, the ability of people in the society to move about and return to their homes in areas where other ethnic groups are the majority is precluded unless Bosnia has a single style of license plate. If my license plate identifies me as a Moslem, Croat, or Serb, as is the case today, I am in some measure of danger in some parts of Bosnia. The Bosnian government has struggled with such elementary matters.

Students must recognize that the institutions and routines that they often take for granted are not givens. Functioning schools or hospitals, postal service, public transportation, banks, and utilities are just some of the government-provided or government-supported services that do not come into existence automatically. Bosnia and Kosovo, the most war-torn areas in the region, lack many of these government functions.

Political machinery and the architecture that it reflects are crucial to a society. Bosnia and Kosovo have no "vehicle" to carry them toward their goals. Macedonia, Albania, Montenegro, and Serbia have partially assembled vehicles that break down regularly. Croatia seems much farther along, in terms of a vehicle ready for the road.

Economic Architecture

It must be clear that without some basic elements of political architecture, the economic environment in Southeastern Europe is difficult. Some mining and small industry has existed, but the communist period caused many such enterprises to become outdated and inefficient. Privatization is difficult because foreign direct investors are wary of the political environment and instability. Locally financed privatization invites dominance by suspect groups of entrepreneurs that many label "organized crime." Furthermore, the war exacerbated the problems by destroying a great deal of infrastructure.

International organizations and agencies are active in the region, but when projects have been turned over to internal leadership, the result has consistently been a decline in services. There are even cases of selective delivery of services along ethnic lines.

Virtually all of the countries are industrially weak, technologically backward, and agriculturally small-scale. They are also dependent on outside sources for energy. In sum, this means that large-scale exports are nonexistent and dependence on imports is common. That relationships with neighbors tend to be poor makes those import dependencies all the more difficult. Macedonia, Serbia, and Bosnia are essentially landlocked. Albania and Montenegro have ports, but they are badly deteriorated and in need of modernization. Only Croatia has an easy time importing and exporting. The various currencies are weak and unstable. The most stable currency is the Croatian kuna. In the worst case, people in Kosovo, parts of Bosnia, and elsewhere use euros (the currency of the EU) in place of their own everyday money. Bosnia itself is peculiar in that it uses as its official currency the "deutsche mark," which is no longer used by the Germans themselves. Inflation is a major problem in Serbia, Montenegro, and Bosnia.

Political and Social Dynamics

It is perhaps useful to review the factors that set Central European political systems apart from these in Southeastern Europe. In Central Europe the numbers of those in government and of those being governed who see the wisdom of facing forward are much greater. Many in Southeastern Europe do not yet see the complexity and implications of asking government to right the wrongs of the past. They do not see the wisdom of sketching goals for tomorrow and asking government to focus on those objectives. Were they to understand how limited government is, in terms of both human and financial resources, they might be more inclined to press the notion that the future must be the first priority.

Recognizing that government resources come from people and businesses in the society would also be a major step forward. There is a persistent notion that others need to contribute to government revenue, but people tend to avoid acknowledging that the public plays a major role by accepting and paying taxes. To date, the norm is for people to see the entire process as illegitimate and to not pay taxes, rationalizing that corruption abounds. No pattern of public responsibility is evident. Communism left these publics with no realistic sense of what government costs and how much revenue is needed.

Legitimacy is very low. We have said that legitimacy can be built by identity, results, habit, or procedures. The only clear form of legitimacy in this region is legitimacy by nationalist identity. As stated earlier, this is not a healthy basis for legitimacy because it is not available to all of those in society but only to those in the dominant ethnic group.

Tolerance is the casualty in a political system framed by nationalism. Tolerant values and behaviors have no place. Anyone arguing for tolerance in policymaking, lawmaking, or administration is presumed to be weak and is politically suspect. Without tolerance, however, political systems that form will be guided by the crude promotion of the interests of the majority and the elimination or marginalization of minorities. It is likely that all of these systems will find themselves unable to compete with larger, more diverse, and more inclusive political and economic systems.

One of the toughest transitions for those living in Southeastern Europe has been the reorientation of people away from the expectation that the government will provide and toward the sense of personal initiative and responsibility. It is certainly the case that there are some large-scale functions that only government can perform. But a wide range of activities must increasingly be embraced by individuals. Paying taxes has already been mentioned. With added choices characteristic of market capitalism, housing, education, and employment will fall more clearly into the hands of individuals. Pensions, health care, and the individual's role in the application of the law (civil and other individually initiated cases) are also realms where more nongovernmental initiative will have to evolve.

Elite Accountability The recent pattern of violence and hostility has made elite accountability a distant dream for those promoting democracy in Southeastern Europe. War and the threat of war produce a mentality that urges falling into line, supporting the cause, or being a good soldier. Strong leadership is portrayed as not having to ask for guidance and taking vigorous and stalwart decisions. Transparency is often represented as weakness and vulnerability. The tenor of politics is hierarchical. The "threat" can be internal or external, often both, as it is presented to the public. It is argued that elite accountability is a luxury for peacetime. Even in this region, where postwar accountability is a major issue before the International Court of Justice (Hague), Southeastern Europeans are generally not ready to see their leaders (past or current) subjected to scrutiny.

Elections Elections in nationalist environments are simply symbolic exercises. They do little to advance (1) the real choices or preferences of the masses for leadership, (2) legitimacy based on procedures, or (3) the perception that leaders and masses are linked by elections. By and large, elections in the region have been comic in their mechanics and manipulation. As Paul Wolfowitz claimed in the passage quoted in chapter 5, elections in this atmosphere do little more than contribute to the authority of leaders who do not have democratic objectives at heart. In this region, elections will continue to be of little constructive value until political parties form as real reflections of public interest, until minority rights and roles are institutionalized, and until issues about the future direction of the society become the central dialogue in the campaigns.

Doors and Windows The notion of establishing doors and windows to enhance access by the public to the people and agencies running government is not yet evident in the systems of Southeastern Europe. Croatia has made a conceptual commitment to this feature but has done little to map the system for public access. That said, all of the other governments have done much less and do not seem poised to see public access as a necessary objective. The region has a broad cultural bias, reinforced by decades of communism, that posits that nothing is done for you in politics unless you have connections. This is not the familiar notion that knowing people and networking are good things; it goes much beyond that. The premise is that the doors and windows are never open to just anyone—their location is secret and they are opened only to those in the powerful person's most immediate circle. If they are in positions of authority, they are obligated to do for you or you for them. This sense that connections are king is so pervasive in the region that it does not normally occur to elites or masses to broaden access. The implications of that are profound. First, little effort is made to institutionalize access for everyone. Efforts are often made to create better access for special groups or individuals. Second, and more subtly, if everything is based on connections—jobs, services, privileges, and so on—then by implication, nothing is based on performance or principle.

Civil Society "Civil society" has come to mean the grassroots engagement of the citizenry in defining issues for themselves, organizing, and articulating their interests to political authorities and the society at large. It follows that civil society is a level of private activity that has little meaning and less likelihood of effect in the political environment we have been describing. Why would individuals promote a collective goal if it is likely to undermine their special access? The evolution of civil society depends on the ability of groups to define their interests beyond ethnic dominance or ethnic persecution. Until issues are defined by community (rural), gender, generation, economic group (business, labor), environmental impact, or other such categories, and not by ethnic identity, civil society will have no meaning in these political systems.

Leadership

The top echelons of leaders in Southeastern Europe have been prone to authoritarian behavior wrapped in popular and sometimes democratic rhetoric. Most visible among these leaders and responsible for the bulk of the violence that accompanied the breakup of Yugoslavia were Franjo Tudjman of Croatia and Slobodan Milosevic of Serbia. The world press seems not to focus on the others, but they, too, have limited democratic credentials. Most of them are gently labeled "illiberal" in an attempt to recognize their other-than-democratic political positions without acknowledging that little political development is occurring in the region. The executive and legislative leadership picture in many of these states is so fluid (not institutionalized) that many U.S. and European authorities use the euphemism "emerging" democracies or "emerging" republics to describe them. Consistent with earlier suggestions, this means that the journey is just beginning for these political systems or, in the cases of Kosovo, Montenegro, and Bosnia, has not yet begun.

Franjo Tudjman (Croatia), Slobodan Milosevic (Serbia), Alija Izetbegovic (Bosnia) and Sali Berisha (Albania) are classic born-again democrats. Ibrahim Rugova (former president and professor of literature) and Bajram Rexhepi (former prime minister and a surgeon) are Kosovo's crop of classic rookies, though they were not young.

Executive leadership positions in the region are not usually attained through general election. Most executives are elected by the legislature. Macedonia, Serbia, and Albania are examples.

Stipe Mesic (Croatia) has fashioned a personal political transition that may place him in a more favorable light. He is a born-again with the advantage of having seen the mistakes made by Franjo Tudjman. In this sense he is advantaged in the same way that Yushenko (Ukraine) is. Mesic's greatest leadership challenge has been deciding to actively assist the International Court of Justice in finding and trying a suspected Croatian war criminal. Mesic's doing so is unpopular with the Croatian people, but it is a requisite for continued discussions with the EU about membership for Croatia. The EU suspended and reinstated Croatia's candidacy for EU membership over this issue. General Ante Gotovina has now been captured outside of Croatia. Mesic now faces the dilemma of cooperating with the court in the face of widespread popular disapproval. If he does so, is he acting democratically?

Serbia's leadership posture is especially crippled and contorted. Milosevic was recently reelected to the Serbian parliament, although he is now on trial in the Hague for war crimes. Voter fraud in the first round of the presidential election in 2000 was so blatant that the Serbian population mobilized. Milosevic was forced from office as president by strong electoral opposition backed by a confrontational youth movement (OTPOR) and a general strike. Two rookie leaders emerged, both with academic backgrounds: Vojislav Kostunica and Zoran Djindjic. The successful democratic opposition that had joined together to defeat Milosevic soon began quarreling, and Milosevic supporters made a partial comeback. Efforts to purge the system of old politicians and the corruption that surrounded their circle of leadership resulted in the assassination of Djindjic. He was a political lightning rod because he was the politician responsible for turning Milosevic over to the War Crimes Tribunal. Kostunica remains politically active but is a strange combination of populist, nationalist, and intellectual democrat. He has been replaced as president by Svetozar Marovic.

Macedonia had begun to emerge on a path toward democracy when its young and pro-Western president, Boris Trajkovski, was suddenly killed in an accident. His replacements and the current leadership, Vlado Buckovski, prime minister, and Branko Crvenkovski, president, have been markedly less successful in managing nationalist pressures and a sinking economy.

Bosnia remains the ultimate example of disarray. Each of the two *political* parts of Bosnia has its own constitution. All three *ethnic* parts have their own elections for a co-president, and the three then serve together in a collective presidency. The powerlessness is perhaps best illustrated by the fact that the high representative of the secretary general of the United Nations in Bosnia is much more politically powerful than any of the country's elected leaders. In the last election, a Croat elected to the presidency was judged by the UN rep to be unacceptable. That elected official was removed and replaced by an edict of the top-ranking UN official in Bosnia.

Leadership in Southeastern Europe faces so many impediments to effective policymaking that it is difficult to sort out whether it is possible. For many, the only realistic course is to try to look as if they are successfully driving the bus. Leaders suffer from lack of legitimacy, resources, bureaucratic collaboration, and experience. Each is a different story, but none has distinguished himself as able to gauge the situation and negotiate the journey. As a group they are near-sighted and consequently prone to incremental policymaking.

Prognosis

As Southeastern Europe creeps toward its goals, Central Europe is pressing ahead toward its future. Scarred and perhaps crippled by the violence that accompanied the breakup of Yugoslavia, the region is adrift. The countries are without infrastructure, capital, or robust human resources. Politically they seem unaware of the problems of micro-states in this century and are still enraptured by nationalism. They revel in the feelings associated with "discovering" their past. Most who study the region believe that in time recognition of the advantages of EU membership will drive these political systems toward European integration. It is tougher to predict that the EU will be very interested in these mismanaged and ever-poorer systems.

COMPARING REVISITED

In comparative politics we face a number of interesting analytic challenges. We can compare the political systems described in this chapter with one another. We can compare this group with those in Central Europe dealt with in the previous chapter. We can compare postcommunist systems with other transitional systems, and we can compare transitional systems with more established ones. We can and should also try to compare the present and the future, if our efforts are to be as useful as possible to succeeding generations of university students. Needless to say, in an introductory text we can only point to some possibilities and hint at conclusions. But a serious student should see the intrigue in this. Comparing is not something that we need to learn to do. We do it quite naturally in all aspects of our thinking. What we do need to focus on is the care and rigor with which we do it.

The selected cases in this chapter are the ones that are struggling most and succeeding least with the challenges of transition. Two are very large, and many more are very small. They are quite different in terms of resources—natural, financial, and human. They share a number of critical experiences. They are very new sovereign states. They emerged from a communist system that left behaviors, routines, expectations, and mechanics that are proving not only useless but debilitating. They are all struggling with catching up in a globalizing, competitive world in which many others are well ahead and accelerating. These countries suffer from the detour on which they find themselves while they decide where they want to go. If they resolve that dilemma they face assembling a vehicle that can take them there. If they experience too much trial and error, dissent could sabotage the journey. And if all else is in place, destination and vehicle, there is still the challenge of identifying and enlisting the most able "drivers." The sovereign states in this chapter have a long way to go to make this journey. They have a long way to go to manage the transition and emerge as institutionalized and developed societies in our twenty-first-century world.

In very gritty terms, the political systems identified in this chapter have not recognized the challenges they face or searched constructively for help. That is the key contrast with the political systems discussed in the last chapter. Facing many of the same problems and issues, those countries have opted to use the resources and intellect of the EU as a means to accelerate their passage through transition. Doing that does not magically solve problems or overcome deficiencies, but it does nurture public confidence that solutions will be found. And it does bring vastly more experience to each of the challenges: destination, vehicle, and driver.

Transition is tough. The competitive world is just that—competitive. If transitional states get help, the reason is that other systems find it in their own interest to help. Transition does not ensure democratic development. It might be reasonable to suggest that democracy complicates transition. Hard decisions in the face of ill-specified values and goals can cause leadership change and other forms of instability. These chapters have discussed how instability can affect virtually all aspects of development.

As a student just setting out on your academic journey, it may be most useful for you to take away from all this reading that politically managing a society is not easy. When Americans look at the world they often naïvely ignore the differences in experience, resources, confidence, and behavior that make each society's political story different.

Suggestions for Additional Reading

Cohen, Lenard. *Serpent in the Bosom: The Rise and Fall of Slobodan Milosevic.* Boulder: Westview Press, 2002.

Drakulic, Slavenka. *Café Europa.* New York: Penguin, 1996.

_____. *How We Survived Communism and Even Laughed.* New York: HarperCollins, 1993.

Gill, Graeme. *The Dynamics of Democratization.* New York: St. Martin's Press, 2000.

Glenny, Misha. *The Fall of Yugoslavia: The Third Balkan War.* New York: Penguin, 1996.

Gros, Daniel, and Alfred Steinherr. *Economic Transition in Central and Eastern Europe.* New York: Cambridge University Press, 2004.

Kapstein, Ethan, and Michael Mandelbaum, eds. *Sustaining the Transition: The Social Safety Net in Post-Communist Europe.* New York: Council on Foreign Relations, 1997.

Radio Free Europe, www.rferl.org.

Tanner, Marcus. *Croatia: A Nation Forged in War.* New Haven: Yale University Press, 1997.

White, Stephen, Judy Batt, and Paul Lewis. *Developments in Central and East European Politics #3.* Durham, N.C.: Duke University Press, 2003.

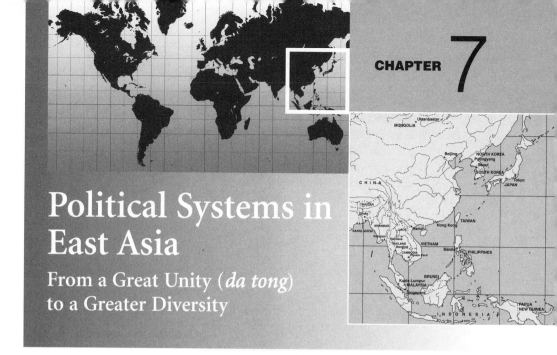

CHAPTER 7

Political Systems in East Asia

From a Great Unity (*da tong*) to a Greater Diversity

A sia," like "Europe," is a collective term that encompasses immense diversity in social conditions. While one may find threads of commonality in cultural, political, religious, ideological, linguistic, culinary, artistic, architectural, and literary practices, these manifestations of humanity are far more varied—both within and among states—than consistent. There is no single manner of governance or preferred political system that operates throughout Asia.

Even within East Asia—a region differentiated from South Asia or Central Asia—one notices stark differences among political systems, not uniformity. If one's aim is to learn about the variety of solutions societies have devised to govern themselves in the early twenty-first century, one could consider as case studies only the states of East Asia, and one would have a sample in which are represented most of the systemic variants present around the globe.

Before focusing on the political systems of East Asia, however, one must ask, What, precisely, is East Asia? The term is ill-defined. There is no consensus about which states are, and which are not, part of the region. Indeed, "East Asia" is a label associated with states that are identified in some sources as the Far East, Pacific Asia, Asia Pacific, or the Pacific Rim.

In an effort to establish greater specificity, some writers refer to yet smaller subregions within East Asia, such as Northeast Asia and Southeast Asia. Ordinarily, the two states on the Korean Peninsula, Japan, and the People's Republic of China (PRC) are considered Northeast Asia. Brunei Darussalam, Cambodia, Indonesia, Laos, Malaysia, Myanmar (Burma), Philippines, Singapore, Thailand, and Vietnam are usually considered Southeast Asia and are all members of the Association of Southeast Asian States (ASEAN). In December 2005, when ASEAN organized a conference trumpeted as the first East Asia Summit, it included Australia, the PRC, India, Japan, the Republic of Korea, and New Zealand, in addition to its own members.

Looking at a map, though, one may wonder whether Russia, which has a long Pacific coast extending far north of the Korean peninsula, ought to be considered an East Asian state. Indeed, the government of Malaysia, host of the first East Asia Summit, invited Russia to attend as its guest expressly because the question of Russia's status in the region could not be resolved.

There are other vexing issues. To some observers the vast, landlocked state of Mongolia is too far east to be part of Central Asia, yet too far west to be considered East Asian. With no Pacific coast, should Mongolia be labeled part of Pacific Asia or the Asia Pacific? Taiwan, the large island off China's southern coast governed since 1949 as the Republic of China (ROC), suffers from multiple ambiguities about sovereignty and national identity. One more ambiguity is whether a place so far south should be part of Northeast Asia or whether its history as part of China means that it cannot be considered part of Southeast Asia. The same definitional question might be asked about those states on the Himalayan ridge, Nepal and Bhutan. Are they Central, East, or South Asian?

The point is that terms such as "Asia," "East Asia," "Northeast Asia," and "Southeast Asia" are crude distinctions governed by convention, not precision. They are barely adequate as guides to geographic boundaries and should by no means be seen as delimiting social, cultural, or political realities. There is not a single Asian way of doing anything. There is no uniform set of values to which all Asians subscribe, as some political leaders suggested there was in the 1990s. There is not a single Asian identity.

Leaders and elites in various states within East Asia have attempted to establish links among themselves, and between themselves and states in other parts of Asia, to serve as the foundation for regional coherence in the pursuit of commercial, ideological, or security objectives. Those efforts have occasioned the emergence of transitory regional or functional identities but have not bound the states to common attitudes, values, or beliefs that one might mistake for a single political culture. So, as one looks to Asia, or even just to East Asia, one should dislodge the notion that one will find there much that makes the states of the region collectively more like one another than like states in other parts of the world.

DIVERSITY IN EAST ASIAN POLITICS

One finds in East Asia—including both the states of Northeast and Southeast Asia—political systems that concentrate power in the hands of a few and others in which power is distributed to many in a skein of checks and balances. One finds systems in which there is widespread participation in regularly scheduled and highly contested elections, others in which elections are engineered from above for predetermined outcomes, and still others in which there is no pretense of participation by the governed.

One finds in East Asia systems in which supreme power is passed from one generation to the next as a function of heredity and others in which the current political structure was built on the ashes of past systems overturned and demolished in revolutions, both bloodless and bloody. One finds one-party, authoritarian or totalitarian states and multiparty democracies. Some states are led by monarchs, some by civilians, and some by military officers. In some states, power is intentionally segmented on the basis of religion, ethnicity, or regional origin; in others power is distributed without regard to, or to overcome, such subnational distinctions. Some states are guided by a foundational constitution that is the touchstone of political principle and legal process; others are governed without respect for legal restraints, constitutional or otherwise.

For instance, Cambodia and Thailand are both parliamentary democracies with a constitutional monarchy. Nepal was a multiparty democracy and a constitutional monarchy until 2002 when, following years of instability and a menacing challenge to authority by a left-wing insurgency inspired by Mao Zedong, the king staged a "royal coup" and wrested control of the government from elected officials, to rule directly from the throne as chairman of a council of officials he has appointed. The Philippines is a multiparty democracy with a presidency, a two-chamber congress, and a supreme court that looks to a foundational constitution. However, in 2001 the vice president staged a "democratic coup," with military support, to oust the president and was subsequently elected, in 2004, for a six-year term. Myanmar (Burma) has been governed since 1988 by a military junta. Mongolia—long dominated by Moscow as a socialist, one-party state—established itself as a multiparty, democratic state in 1990 with a directly elected president and national assembly. Singapore is a parliamentary democracy that has been dominated since its founding by a single party and a single family. The present prime minister, Lee Hsien Loong, is the third to hold that office and is the son of Singapore's "founding father," Lee Kuan Yew, who served as its first prime minister from 1959 until 1990. Vietnam is a one-party state that is governed by a ruling coalition guided by an ideological orthodoxy.

Nowhere is ideological orthodoxy as rigid or power so concentrated as in the Democratic People's Republic of Korea—North Korea. It is a totalitarian, one-party, military-dominated state, ruled by Kim Jong-il, the "Dear Leader," who inherited his paramount position and is the object of a "cult of personality," as was his father, Kim Il-Song, the "Great Leader." By contrast, the Republic of Korea—South Korea—is a pluralistic, multiparty, constitutional democracy headed by a president who is directly elected for a five-year term. Korea was divided by civil war, but it is united by history, culture, language, and other markers of commonality. One might expect there to be some comparability in the Korean systems of government, but the political systems north and south of the common border are radically different.

Another East Asian state divided by civil war is China. The People's Republic of China is a one-party state governed by a ruling oligarchy that emerges from the consensual elevation of bureaucratic peers. Bodies that, according to the constitution, are intended to legislate are ordinarily used to rubber-stamp policy decisions made by the ruling party leadership. The constitution is more a lofty slate of ideals than a living document that sets the parameters for political behavior. By contrast, the Republic of China—Taiwan—is a multiparty, intensely competitive democracy with a directly elected president and legislature and an independent judiciary. Interparty rivalries in Taiwan's notoriously contentious parliament have been known to spill over into occasional bouts of fisticuffs, food fights, and other excesses of pluralism.

Hong Kong, a former British colony on China's southeastern coast, and Macao, a former Portuguese possession nearby, have been governed as Special Administrative Regions (SAR) of the People's Republic of China since Beijing "resumed" sovereignty over them in 1997 and 1999, respectively. Each is governed by a Basic Law—represented in some publications as a "mini-constitution"—that entitles them to their own legislature and judicial systems. The chief executive in each place is elected—some say approved—by a committee appointed by Beijing.

Finally, there is Japan: a multiparty, representative democracy with a directly elected, two-chamber parliament (the Diet) that has been dominated for decades by a single party, the conservative—and therefore inaptly named— Liberal Democratic Party (LDP). Japan, like Great Britain, has a prime minister who is chief executive and a monarch who is head of state. Japan's emperor now has only ceremonial duties, but he is a vital symbol of national identity and— for better and worse—a link to the past.

Indeed, if one is seeking evidence of some commonality in the political life of Asia it is that "the past" is not so long in the past. That is to say, the political systems by which most of the aforementioned states are now governed are relatively recent concoctions. Most states in East Asia underwent some tumultuous political transition in the twentieth century by which a deep-rooted system of governance was supplanted by a new system. For several states of the region, the nineteenth and twentieth centuries were periods of rapid, cataclysmic, and repeated change.

Although it is difficult to discern much uniformity in the systems by which Asian states now govern themselves, greater comparability might have been detected in the recent past. For example, rather than imagine Asia divided in geographic terms, one might view it as divided along ideological lines. For much of the twentieth century one could easily divide Asia into those states that were adherents of communism and those that were not. Before Marx and Lenin, one could have divided Asia on the basis of which states venerated the values of Confucius and which did not.

Both the principles of Confucian thought that originated in China during the fifth century BC and those of Marxist-Leninist thought, which emerged from Europe and Russia much more recently, have left legacies in the political systems of Asia. In fact, several states in East Asia—notably the PRC, North Korea, and Vietnam—were shaped by both Confucian and communist ideologies.

All that is to say that the political systems that now exist in East Asia were built on the foundations of other systems and that the building process is ongoing. It also means that the great variety of political systems one finds in the early twenty-first century is comparatively novel. Until recent decades, dictatorship of some sort was the norm throughout the region.

Most states in the region have a long and embedded tradition of rule by law, not rule of law. In other words, law has been used to justify the political preferences of a ruling elite that is not, itself, subject to legal restraint. In most East Asian states power was concentrated in the hands of a tiny few, who viewed power as a private prerogative not a public trust.

The states of East Asia are not in any way unique in having such political traditions. Looking back on the history of civilization, public participation, contestation for political office, constitutional order, legal processes regulating power and establishing rights, and the idea that the state serves the people—not the other way around—are all relatively recent innovations.

Most states in Asia have only in the past few decades begun to grasp at these systemic features and ideals as ambitions to guide political transformation. Some states have thus far resisted doing so. Rather than view the relinquishment of dictatorial traditions in Asia as surprisingly late in coming, readers in the United States might wish to consider how long, in the context of human history, it took for Western Europe and America to reach the same political threshold. Indeed, an honest appraisal of the political transformations of Europe and the United States would have to admit that some unsavory ingrained political traditions have proved stubbornly resistant to change.

Asia's political past is still within very recent memory. Elderly citizens of Korea, Japan, and the PRC can recall several substantial transformations of the political system by which the state where they live has been governed. The imperial system, by which China was governed since 221 BC, survived until 1911. From then until 1949, the state was in political disarray, governed locally more than centrally. The first three decades after the establishment of the PRC were punctuated by periods of political turmoil and ideologically induced fervor. In many respects, the present political order and system of governance emerged only after the death of Mao Zedong in 1976, though it was built on fundamental structures that he and his revolutionary cohort created earlier in the century.

Japanese who lived before the end of World War II in 1945 may recall that the emperor was regarded as a divinity. Although Japan first adopted a constitution in 1889, the present constitutional system was established in conjunction with—some say was imposed by—the United States, which occupied Japan for seven years after the end of the war. Accepting the emperor as a mortal was part of a fundamental reorientation of Japan's political system that brought it into concert with the political ethos of the occupying power and of Japanese pacifists and internationalists who had objected to the virulent nationalism and militarism of the previous era.

As to Korea, elderly citizens on either side of the border between north and south undoubtedly recall growing up in a unified state that was, from 1910 until 1945, a colony of Japan. The division of their state into two opposing and quite different political systems occurred only thereafter. While the political system in the north appears unreformed and unapologetically dictatorial, the Republic of Korea (ROK) in the south was governed in an authoritarian manner for much of the period after decolonization, experienced a brief democratic hiatus, reverted to authoritarianism, but has in recent decades established and apparently consolidated democratic reforms.

That rapid political transformations are so prevalent in the modern political history of Northeast Asian states prompts one to see that transition is, in fact, the norm. Political systems constantly change. At times and in certain places, systems evolve gradually and in such incremental ways that observers may not even perceive the transformation. At other times or in other places, political change can be revolutionary and swift, leaving people disoriented and uncertain about whether the changes—for good or ill—will endure. It is understandable that the political establishment in some states continues to reflect habits and attitudes inculcated by long experience with whatever system it was that came before.

Transformation, then, is rarely complete. It is not reasonable to expect that, as a state develops new systems of governance, adopting and adapting what it gleans from the values and practices it sees around it, it can divest itself of all ties to its political past.

CHINA'S INELUCTABLE INFLUENCE

Considering the foregoing emphasis on diversity in East Asian political systems, one must assert some rationale for choosing the Chinese case(s) as a focus. Why emphasize China rather than Singapore? This, after all, is a volume devoted to comparative politics. It is the significance of the political system of the state that should determine its selection as an illustrative case, not the size of its population or its territorial reach, or its recent economic growth rates or prospective military might. Why single out China? To be sure, it is not because the political system of the PRC is a model that others emulate.

There is, one must confess, the temptation to highlight China for reasons having little to do with the nature of its political system: That is, if the influence of the PRC is likely to be felt ever more widely in world affairs, perhaps it makes sense to use the opportunity afforded by a text on comparative politics to smuggle in for readers a bit more instruction about an entity that few can be assumed to know well. That, though, is a thin justification for distracting the reader's attention from this volume's principal concern, which is the variation in political systems around the globe, not foreign policy or international relations.

A more defensible rationale is this: It is not the PRC, *per se,* that is the focus of this chapter but the varied responses of political systems that are rooted in approaches to statecraft informed by Confucian thought and Chinese bureaucratic practices. During periods of cultural florescence, commercial cosmopolitanism, and political power, China exerted a palpable influence on its neighbors in Northeast and Southeast Asia. It was, during phases of greatness, a source of inspiration and instruction—a model of sorts, to which other states looked for clues about how to make their own nations more prosperous and powerful.

How China's political and cultural influence was transmitted to other states deserves much greater attention than this brief comment can provide. Suffice to suggest that by territorial expansion and imperialism, by imposing its will in asymmetric political or commercial relations, by drawing to its centers of learning students from abroad, and because smaller and weaker states envied and admired China's superior wealth, organization, and power, Chinese modes of thinking and doing things spread.

This is not to say that Korea, Japan, and Vietnam aped Chinese ways so thoroughly that they became precisely like China. Distinct political cultures in each place served as lenses through which the ideals and practices of China were filtered. The results were hybrid political systems that reflected both imported political values and indigenous ones. Yet in each of those places the imprint of Chinese political values—Confucian and otherwise—remains.

CONFUCIAN AT THE CORE

Here a few words—and, regretfully, only a few—should be offered about the content of the Confucian values that were so influential on politics within and beyond China's borders. First, Confucius (551–479 BC) is believed to have been a historical figure. Revered as a great sage, he was known as Master Kong (*Kong Fuzi* in Chinese). "Confucius" is a Latinized version of the man's name and honorific title.

Confucius emphasized the importance of learning from an ethical "golden age" long past, when social, political, and cosmological order were maintained because of attention by the rulers to propriety and virtue. Indeed, Confucius claimed that his role was to transmit what was already known about how to establish order, not to create a new body of wisdom. Yet it was his teachings that became the focus of scholarly debate for all the centuries that have followed. Texts associated with Confucius have been the touchstones for an intellectual tradition that is reflected, refined, and disputed in each generation.

The political ramifications of Confucian thought come from its reinforcement of social hierarchy. As a social inferior—child, younger sibling, student, or citizen—one owes allegiance and obeisance to those in superior positions—parent, older sibling, teacher, or ruler. In Confucius's day, this extended to marital relations, in which the wife was inferior to the husband. People in socially superior positions were expected to provide for the welfare of—to nurture and protect—those who offered loyalty and submission. Even more important was the notion that if the ruler—and by analogy, anyone in a socially superior position—abided by certain central virtues, the governed—and by analogy, anyone in a socially inferior position—would be led by example to do the same. If everyone played their social roles properly, families, villages, regions, and the state would fall into good order.

Naturally, there is much more to be said about what Confucius meant by playing one's roles properly and what virtues he promoted. The foregoing is a grievously superficial overview of Confucian thought. The point is that, with social relations at its core and an emphasis on hierarchy and mutual obligation, Confucian thought lent itself well to self-serving misinterpretation and distortion by power-hungry men at all levels of society. One result was the emergence of a rigidly hierarchal social order in China that was justified by the intellectual elite in terms of a reverence for deeply rooted Confucian values.

Confucius and his followers were by no means the only commentators about social order. Other intellectual traditions coexisted among China's literati, including the "Legalist" school of thought, which valorized strict laws and swift punishment for violators as effective means of maintaining social order. Within each of these intellectual traditions—and there were others—there was vigorous debate about how best to govern and what should be the ultimate aims of good government.

Thinking politically, it is easy to imagine how the Confucian emphasis on hierarchy and the Legalist focus on law and order blended to justify dictatorship, the absolute power of rulers, scant concern for individual liberties, and lack of interest in due legal process. It is not surprising that a civilization that gave rise to both the Confucian and Legalist traditions is one in which the populace served the interests of the state (as defined by its rulers) rather more than did the state concern itself about the interests that the populace might have articulated as their own.

To be sure, Chinese society was not the only one where this attitude flourished. One should dismiss as hokum the idea that China's despotic tradition makes it impossible for the political system of China to be more tolerant of pluralism and political competition. In fact, it is difficult to identify a pluralistic democratic state today that does not trace its political lineage to an authoritarian or dictatorial past. Beyond that, the cases of Taiwan, South Korea, and Japan make evident that political liberalization and democratization can emerge from states in which the political system has flowed from dictatorial practices informed and justified by Confucian ideals.

There was, though, a conservative, self-reinforcing vision of China's role on earth that may have been distinctive. The emperor of China was imagined to be the "son of heaven"; he was served by a cohort of civil servants selected by examination on their mastery of a canon of Confucian classical texts. Their expertise as scholars was believed to imbue them with the wisdom to administer a portion of the emperor's realm in his name. If the emperor and his carefully chosen functionaries were able to maintain good order in the Chinese domain, it was understood that the empire would be prosperous and powerful. Less-civilized states on China's periphery would naturally be drawn to associate with and emulate China—a reflection of the idea of teaching by example—and China's civilization would spread. As it did, the influence of the "son of heaven" would radiate outward until he governed "all under heaven" in a "great unity" (*da tong*) of all peoples. Thus by his own rectitude and attention to proper virtues, the emperor would set the earthly domain in order, and so the entire cosmos would operate in accordance with *dao* (or *tao*—the correct, heavenly ordained way).

Obviously, this is a highly idealized vision of China's role that diverged greatly from reality. China was not always governed by virtuous men any more than any other society was. It was not always great and powerful. It certainly has enjoyed long periods of cohesion, security, prosperity, and magnificence, but also long periods of disorder, vulnerability, deprivation, and decrepitude. Its path to wealth and power was not guided by any heavenly way but by the same political machinations and application of violence that have led other states to become empires. Yet for those intellectual and political elites who embraced the idealized conception of China's civilizational superiority, political and cultural imperialism was interpreted or justified in terms of grand cosmological objectives.

During historical chapters of power and greatness, social values and notions of statecraft were transmitted from China to its neighbors, affecting their political development. That influence waned in moments when China's neighbors or adversaries were stronger than China. By the nineteenth century, the Qing dynasty—established by Manchus who invaded and took control of China in 1644—was in decline. Domestic disintegration was exacerbated by pressure from foreign imperialist powers that exploited China's political and military weakness for their own commercial advantage. The court resisted advice from Chinese social reformers about ways to restore order and revivify the empire. Finally, in 1911, the Qing dynasty collapsed.

China was governed thereafter by a sequence of weak rulers, who established the Republic of China (ROC) but did not even exercise effective control over the entire territory they claimed as the Chinese state. For one thing, the Manchus had created an empire by conquest. They greatly and swiftly expanded the borders of the Chinese realm in the seventeenth and eighteenth centuries to encompass Taiwan, a western region called Xinjiang, Tibet, and Mongolia. The end of the Qing dynasty signaled the breakup of that empire. None of the four major territories that the Qing had brought into the realm sat firmly or permanently under the control of the government of the Republic of China that was established in 1912.

Even within the core territories of what had been China prior to the Qing dynasty the rulers of the ROC were not firmly in control. In some regions of China, local holders of power who maintained private armies were able to exercise actual control. Indeed, the period from 1912 to 1949 was one of prolonged struggle for domination of the Chinese state by rivals to power.

From its founding in 1921 with assistance from the Soviet Union, the Chinese Communist Party (CCP) became the most vigorous challenger to the legitimacy of the ROC government. It captured and held territory in northern

China that it governed in the 1930s and early 1940s as a state within a state. Its efforts to take control of all China were impeded by Japan's invasion and occupation of Chinese territory beginning in 1931. Following Japan's defeat in 1945, civil war erupted between the CCP and the ROC government, resulting in the defeat of the government and the establishment of the PRC by the communists on October 1, 1949.

THE POLITICAL SYSTEM OF THE PRC

In politics, everything that is must be built on what was. The governing structure that the CCP established after 1949 was influenced by China's imperial and Confucian traditions, the experiments in republican government of the period after 1911, and the principles of socialism that flowed from Marxist-Leninist thought. It did not reflect one stream of political tradition only, but was a blending of several streams.

The PRC, with the CCP at its core, was also a response to three persistent problems that plagued China in the nineteenth and early twentieth centuries: poverty, social inequity, and vulnerability to exploitation by foreign powers. Consequently, the PRC was intended to be a "New China," in which wealth and privilege would be more evenly distributed to those who labored, social classes and the inequities that they implied would be eliminated, and the state would become strong enough to defend its sovereignty and territorial integrity. From Marxism the CCP derived notions of class struggle and the merits of egalitarianism. From history it derived notions of China as a regional power deserving of national glory. The era of "New China" began with heady idealism flowing from both communism and nationalism.

Combined with the Chinese expectation that political authority will be vested in the hands of a few, who demand unquestioned subordination, the ideals were ultimately perverted. The political history of the PRC from 1949 to 1976 was dominated by ideological rigidity coupled with the overbearing, capricious, and often malevolent influence of Mao Zedong. Although Mao was not the only political leader with influence on what the CCP did, his role in some spheres of political activity was paramount. In 1949, when the PRC was established, Mao was the first among equals, in a system that still demanded consensus among a small cohort of political elites at the very peak of the CCP hierarchy. Over time he eliminated rivals, cultivated loyalty among followers, encouraged the cult of personality that was created about him, and became a ruler with unchecked powers.

Mao Zedong led the PRC through twenty-seven years, during which national construction and efforts by the professional bureaucracy to rationalize governance were intermingled with self-inflicted destruction and political turmoil. The period in which Mao dominated was punctuated by ideologically inspired political campaigns—the Great Leap Forward (1958–1960) and the Great Proletariat Cultural Revolution (1966–1976) may have been the most widespread and devastating—and wars abroad aimed in part at mobilizing support at home for his vision of socialist revolution. Although chauvinistic Chinese in the PRC today (many born after Mao died) may venerate him as the avatar of Chinese national power and international status (during the cold war, Mao led the PRC to oppose both superpowers), millions who suffered and survived Mao's years in power undoubtedly harbor less-romantic sentiments about him and the CCP.

After Mao's death the PRC essentially cut loose from the ideological moorings to which Mao and the radical wing of the CCP elite had tied the state. Deng Xiaoping and the PRC leadership that emerged in 1978 embarked on a process of gradual economic, social, and even tentative political reform. By the start of the twenty-first century, Deng's program of "reform and opening" can be seen to have yielded extraordinary and, for the most part, welcomed developments—especially in the economic and social arenas. The political reform undertaken by the PRC has likewise brought about some change, but not nearly as fundamental or thoroughgoing as the changes in other spheres.

In a word, the CCP has jettisoned its role as defender and promulgator of ideological orthodoxy in favor of unapologetic authoritarian rule justified in terms of maintaining the social order needed to sustain rapid economic growth. A party that had devoted itself to socialist revolution and a leadership that claimed legitimacy on the basis of its capacity to guide China to realize the egalitarian ideals of communism have become the engine of Chinese capitalism. The transformation is both paradoxical and astonishing.

Looking back on the twentieth century, concerted efforts to transform China's political system were the norm. It was a century of rapid, revolutionary, and often brutal change. If one were to have visited China once every twenty-five years during the twentieth century, one would have found a radically different political system in place on each visit. The political systems by which China was governed in 1900, 1925, 1950, 1975, and 2000 were all quite different. In 1900, China was still part of the Qing empire. By 1925, the ROC had been established but had crumbled into internecine power struggles. By 1950, the PRC had been established and was consolidating control. In 1975, however, the system the communists had devised had been so drastically distorted by the Cultural Revolution that it bore little resemblance to its earlier self. Reforms begun in 1978 had born luscious fruit by 2000, and the PRC—still communist in name, still authoritarian in practice—was swiftly modernizing and rationalizing its style of governance.

The question is, Has this period of speedy change ended or slowed? At this writing, the political system of the PRC appears to be changing in a measured way, governed by reflexively conservative and cautious political leaders fearful that their party's legitimacy, to say nothing of their own necks, is on the line. One does wonder, though, whether the political system described below will have been supplanted or transformed by the time these words are read.

The central cause for uneasiness is that the PRC leadership, for all its recent attention to, and success with, economic and social reform, has been peevishly defensive about the pace of political reform. It operates from a view that a vast and largely uneducated population cannot be entrusted with decisions that affect the welfare of the state. Hence, political participation is still severely constrained and democratization a professed, but distant, aim. The leadership in Beijing worries about the eruption of social disorder and believes that until the PRC has reached a higher level of prosperity that is more evenly distributed the party must maintain a firm hand on the population to ensure stability.

Beijing's anxiety about instability is not unfounded. While the world gawks in admiration and envy at the apparent "rise of China," measured in annual economic growth rates, magnificent new buildings in cities exemplified by Beijing and Shanghai, increasing signs of prosperity, and spreading commercial and international political influence, these are not the only indices that the leadership in Beijing considers. As the policy of "reform and opening" has brought wealth and opportunity to some regions of China, in others poverty and despair prevail.

Just as the PRC's new wealth and development are astonishing, so is its poverty. In the PRC, the depth of deprivation finds people working as beasts of burden, stoically performing menial tasks in hazardous factories, living without plumbing or electricity, or eking out an existence on an unforgiving patch of land. In some regions, old age appears quickly and death comes early to those who survive childhood. Even for those whose existence is not quite so dire, life can be physically taxing and emotionally harrowing.

Whether in rural or urban settings, life for many Chinese is one prolonged effort to ensure subsistence in a state that offers few avenues for advancement and precious little hope that anything significant is likely to improve. Perhaps the most palpable national change resulting from, and contributing to, economic growth is the steady flood of laborers who have been leaving rural communities since the 1990s to seek greater opportunity in the cities. This trend, which has already dramatically altered the rural-urban population balance, persists and carries economic, social, and political consequences.

Although politics and ideology are, for most Chinese, realms with which they do not concern themselves, equity and fairness are very much issues that matter. In the first years of the twenty-first century, one reads ever more frequently of social disturbances, mass public protest, and occasionally violent clashes between protesters and state authorities. In almost every case, the issues arousing the public outcry are injustices perpetrated by, or done with the connivance of, local officials, whom the populace judges to be corrupt, uncaring, or inept. Some conflicts emerge from the dislocations associated with the very economic development that is otherwise so vaunted.

So, while the government prides itself on policies and practices that have led to the "rise of China," it is also increasingly alarmed by evidence that it takes little to provoke some segments of China to rise up in protest. Considering that the CCP was, itself, established to combat economic and social inequality and derived its legitimacy as the ruling party from the promise of doing just that, it is now concerned that its credibility is under assault.

Development has reintroduced extreme economic disparities; some Chinese have become much more prosperous while others feel left behind. Change in the scope of services that the government is prepared to underwrite has also withdrawn social welfare safety nets, such as job security, housing, health care, and pensions, on which some portions of the population have depended. Yet the means to voice dissatisfaction, to contribute to deliberations about policy, and to signal distress about gaps or injustices in the delivery of services are underdeveloped or ineffective.

The central government's wish to keep the lid on society while steering a course to greater national wealth and power has resulted in occasional outbursts of mass frustration, most notably the protests of mid-April to early June 1989. Whether the CCP will succeed in continuing to constrict the expression of political views and restrict the scale of public participation in, and genuine contestation of, policy is a matter of speculation. If it does, then the formal structures and practices outlined below may continue to merit attention.

Political Party Structure

There are nine political parties in the PRC, but the CCP is the only one with any significance. It has utterly dominated the political life of the PRC since it established the state in 1949, reserving all political power for itself, stifling dissent within its ranks, forbidding challenges to its authority, and infusing itself into the governing structure in such a way as to make the party and the state overlapping and entangled domains. Indeed, many of the individuals who hold high-ranking posts in the CCP concurrently hold powerful positions in the state apparatus. In sum, the PRC functions as a one-party state.

Just as the emperor and his Confucian scholar-officials sought to inculcate virtues in the people they ruled to transform society, so the CCP has fashioned itself the "vanguard of the proletariat," or leaders of the working class, with the aim of inculcating "New China" with socialist values. Indeed, for much of the past half-century, the primary objectives of the CCP have been to instruct, mobilize, and control China's populace, not to represent it.

Although the political culture of imperial China may have engendered attitudes that the CCP capitalized on as it rose to power, the party's approach to governance is modeled on the party of Lenin, the Communist Party of the Soviet Union. As a Leninist party, the CCP has been headed by political elites who are not accountable to the population at large or even to the full membership of the party. To the contrary, a key feature of such a party is that its leaders are regarded as unimpeachable authorities on doctrine; thus they determine policy and transmit it downward to the membership and from the membership to society at large.

Leninist parties, such as the CCP, also expect all members to respond to centrally generated directives with unquestioning discipline. In principle, the CCP operates according to the notion of "democratic centralism," by which party members are at liberty to discuss and debate issues—the democratic component—but expected to uphold the collective decisions of the party without further dissent or complaint once they have been made—the centralist component. One can imagine, though, how such a principle lent itself to abuse by strong party rulers.

Another hallmark of Leninist parties such as the CCP is the thorough penetration of society for the purposes of organization and mobilization, the means by which the party's revolutionary aims are to be attained. After defeating the forces of the ROC government during the Chinese civil war of 1947 to 1949, the CCP worked to consolidate its political control over all Chinese territory, inculcate the people with what it saw as the correct ideological perspective, and establish a system for governing China's vast population. To enforce its authority and maximize its capacity to control the populace, the CCP placed in every level of government, every institution, and every urban *danwei* ("work unit," or place of work) CCP representatives whose duty it was to serve as the party's watchdog.

In an elaborate, hierarchal structure, information, regulations, and ideological instruction could be transmitted from the central authority down through the party structure to every village, city, school, factory, hospital, shop, and office. This system enhanced political uniformity. Beyond that, the party representative could effect a preferred social order by regulating behavior with rewards and punishment. When it chose to, the party, through its agents, regulated not only political acts but the most intimate aspects of what elsewhere would be seen as private matters. For instance, party representatives in each place were authorized to give, or refrain from giving, permission for such personal matters as marriage, pregnancy, divorce, change of jobs, and travel, as well as access to social services such as health care, and housing. The CCP was also the source of mass campaigns in which citizens were prompted to act in prescribed ways to root out "counterrevolutionaries," "rightists" and other "enemies of the people," many of whom were publicly vilified, roughed up, tortured, imprisoned, ostracized to bleak labor camps, or even murdered in excesses of ideological zeal.

At the start of the twenty-first century, when the population of the PRC is calculated to be about 1.3 billion, the CCP is thought to have about 68 million members (officially, party membership has only increased since 1921). The CCP is headed by Hu Jintao, who was elevated to the post of general secretary in 2002. Technically, it is the CCP Party Congress—a body of about 4,000 party representatives, who meet once every five years for a few days—that is charged with selecting the general secretary. The Party Congress also approves the membership of the CCP Central Committee—about 200 people who function as the party's legislative organ during the years between the plenary sessions, at which all representatives are expected to gather.

The Party Congress is also responsible for approving the formation of the Politburo—the elite group of about twenty that guides policymaking and approves the Standing Committee of the Politburo, which is the highest echelon. That group has had six or seven members in the past; as of 2002 it was expanded to nine people. Although the institutional structure suggests that power is held by the Party Congress, in fact the membership of the Central Committee, Politburo, and Standing Committee is determined from the top, not the other way around, and very much behind closed doors.

It is characteristic of the CCP is that political power seems to flow from attention within the party to personality, patronage, and factions. Although the precise manner in which people are chosen for high office is not publicized, close observers have suggested that competition has taken the form of jockeying for influence behind closed doors by a group of party luminaries, each of whom may have a stable of protégés and followers, rather than open contestation and transparent, institutionalized processes. Succession politics, potentially explosive under such *ad hoc* conditions, was relatively seamless as Jiang Zemin succeeded Deng Xiaoping (in 1989) and Hu Jintao succeeded Jiang (in 2002). It is anyone's guess how the CCP will manage the transition from Hu Jintao to his successor.

Another uncertainty is how the CCP will evolve in an era when capitalism and market forces, not communism and a planned economy, are clearly ascendant. Although the CCP has tried to finesse the ideological transformation from communism to capitalism, one cannot know whether it will continue to succeed in monopolizing power, as it has since 1949. There are, after all, other political parties. Indeed, an elaborate display of interparty cooperation has been the objective of the Chinese People's Political Consultative Conference (CPPCC).

The CPPCC, whose members serve five-year terms and which convenes in plenary session once a year, is described as a "patriotic united front organization" that is neither an official organ of government nor a state-sponsored civic organization. Its role is to showcase the capacity of the CCP to consult with a wide range of "patriotic" opinion leaders from more than thirty other political parties, "mass organizations," and representatives of various segments of society. It has no legislative power but is a forum for deliberation about matters of national importance and ostensibly the transmission of views to the central leadership of the state. Still, at the start of the twenty-first century, it is the CCP alone that wields power. Its highest echelon is nearly all male and "Han" (the nationality of China's vast majority, who claim descent from the original inhabitants of the earliest Chinese state in the third century BC), even though Mao Zedong once proclaimed that "women hold up half the sky" and the PRC comprises fifty-five officially recognized ethnic minority groups (approximately 7 percent of the population) in addition to the Han.

The State

Formally, the PRC is governed by a constitution that provides for something like a parliamentary system. Legislative power rests with the National People's Congress (NPC), a body comprising about 3,000 deputies who, in principle, represent each administrative unit within the PRC and the military. However, popular participation is limited to direct elections at the township and county levels for representatives who serve on local People's Congresses. Local congresses elect deputies to congresses at the next level up to represent the provinces, autonomous regions, key municipalities, and special prefectures. Those congresses and the military, in turn, elect the deputies who serve on the National People's Congress. It is worth observing that at all levels nominees who have stood for election as deputies have been approved first by agencies of the CCP. Reforms and some liberalization notwithstanding, the electoral system has been controlled, presumably to ensure "stability" and the continued domination of the CCP.

The NPC holds annual plenary sessions that, like the meetings of the full Party Congress, last for only a few days. Between sessions, a smaller Standing Committee of about 150 members exercises power on behalf of the NPC. Ordinarily, the chairman of the NPC Standing Committee is a powerful member of the CCP who is one of a small group of political elite who genuinely determine the direction of policy.

Until the 1990s, the NPC provided a forum for a symbolic expression of popular consensus about the wisdom of proposals submitted to it by the central leadership of the state. In essence, the NPC provided a rubber stamp of approval for the central leadership. In the 1990s one began to see hints that the NPC was taking its constitutional role a bit more seriously. Although it has largely conformed itself to the wishes of the central leadership and approved proposals and programs submitted, it has not done so with the routine unanimity of the past. The NPC has sought to shape, not just affirm, the policies it considers, and some deputies have been prepared to stand out by objecting.

Formally the NPC is the body that elects the president and vice president of the state, and it selects the State Council, which is the PRC's executive "cabinet" of ministerial-level officers who oversee the state commissions and ministries. In practice, however, the senior posts in the state hierarchy are filled by individuals whose status is established by the CCP and who are simultaneously party and state leaders. The interpenetration of the state by the CCP has been a hallmark of the PRC's political system.

This interpenetration operates at all levels of government: central (national), provincial, municipal, and county. Although there have been proposals to decouple the party from the state in certain spheres, to date the two remain intertwined down to the most remote and local political entities. At every level and throughout the bureaucracy one finds CCP officials assuming overlapping roles as state officials.

The State Council is headed by the premier—a prime minister—who since 2002 has been Wen Jiabao. There are four vice premiers and five state counselors. The State Council oversees the work of twenty-eight ministerial-level departments.

The Constitution of the PRC

Since the PRC was established it has promulgated four constitutions, in 1954, 1975, 1978, and 1982. In the same period, the CCP has had five constitutions.

The present constitution of the PRC has been amended four times and probably should not be confused with the kind of social contract by which a populace holds its government to account, delimits state power, and defines a scope of liberty that all can expect to enjoy. It is much more an assertion of the state leadership's present political platform than a foundational document that serves as a statement of principles to which succeeding generations agree to be bound.

In addition to providing a historical context for the state and the basic structure of government, the constitution lays out the economic, social, and political ambitions of the leadership for the PRC. For example, in its chapter 2 the constitution asserts a range of "fundamental rights and duties" of citizens that the state has committed itself to protect and impose. However, few citizens of the PRC would be likely to say that they enjoy what, for instance, article 35 promises: "the freedom of speech, of the press, of assembly, of association, of procession and of demonstration."

Indeed, one is left with the impression that the document is a statement of admirable ideals toward which the most cynical political leaders would like to imagine that the PRC is moving, however gradually. More enlightened and cosmopolitan members of the political elite undoubtedly understand, however, that the duties side of the ledger seems to be more fully realized than is the side that offers extravagant assurances of rights and liberties.

The Limits of Party-State Control

The formal organizational charts of the CCP and the PRC offer only a notional structure of power. The impossibility of identifying precisely how the political system in the PRC operates is compounded by the sense that it is not fixed and is always on the brink of potentially significant change. For example, China has always been a place where regional differences generate distinctive perspectives on national policy. Economic reforms and commercial liberties have exacerbated this factor by sharpening the inequalities between localities that are conspicuously benefiting (mostly along the east coast) and those that are not. Inequalities have a tendency to inspire protest.

The liberalization of commerce has also empowered certain individuals to expand greatly the influence they have over their economic welfare. There is in some cities a growing middle class, with increasing expectations of enjoying the sort of materialism and consumerism that not long ago would have been condemned in the PRC as "bourgeois." Greater control over economic decisions, greater mobility, and rising expectations have, in other times and places, been harbingers of demands for greater opportunity to exercise choice in the political arena. In other words, economic reforms can provoke demands for political liberalization, although there are instances in which power holders manage to restrain pressure to change.

To date, the PRC leadership has evinced little will for widespread political reform. Certainly the PRC is a far more open place in 2005 than it was in 1995 or 1985 or 1975. However, its political system is still one in which liberties are doled out sparingly by a political elite that believes it is able to regulate the valve. Organized dissent is crushed mercilessly, as are social organizations that have the potential to serve as bases of alternative political power—whether social protest movements, the Catholic Church, or the Falungong.

So long as they do not venture into political acts or challenge the authority of the state, people are now much freer to do or say what they please, as compared with even the recent past. However, the leash of tolerance is short. The authorities monitor and intervene at will. Self-regulation and self-censorship are habits ingrained from earlier days, and only a brave or foolish few are prepared to risk the consequences of pushing the edge of the envelope too far.

The PRC leadership is highly alert to the specter of inflamed public opinion. What it wants most is to deter people from resorting to the street to express political dissatisfaction. The PRC leadership knows it confronts a legitimacy crisis. It knows that the transitions under way are as disorienting and disruptive to some as they are rewarding and welcome to others. It understands well that it governs a society with legions of discontents. The leadership still has the authority and power to control the state, but it worries that the cost of using that authority and power is rapidly rising.

Yet there has been a growing tolerance for limited, but pointed, debate about matters of policy in certain media outlets and on the Internet. Scholars, think tank analysts, and officials in the PRC attest to the increasing attentiveness of the central leadership to views expressed on the Internet. That, in part, explains efforts by the PRC to regulate the Internet, monitoring and censoring views that run afoul of the accepted range of deliberation and planting views that it hopes to propagate. Thus far, the formless, decentralized, malleable, and pervasive capacity of the Internet has proved a very tough adversary for the PRC authorities.

Of course, expressions on the Internet cannot be seen as a valid measure of public opinion, as its users are a source redolent of what statisticians would label a "sampling bias." Even though the number of Internet users in the PRC is certainly staggering in absolute terms, as a percentage of the total population early in the twenty-first century it is still in single digits. Moreover, most users are urban, coastal, economically privileged, young, and male. To the political leadership, this is an important and potentially influential elite cohort. That cohort's views may not be representative of the majority, but brazen criticism of government policy, on one hand, and the strongly nationalistic character of much that appears as private opinion on the Internet, on the other, are viewed as likely to inspire an active few.

In the PRC, even an active few can stir up trouble. The CCP leadership worries that a protest by activists focused on a single issue could quickly escalate, drawing into the streets people with frustrations about a range of matters, and rapidly create a referendum on the party's legitimacy. The CCP leaders understand that their grip on power depends, in part, on party unity and social stability. Unity within the CCP depends on the maintenance of a delicate balance of personal and factional interests. Stability depends on ensuring that most citizens are either sufficiently content, or sufficiently intimidated, that they will not protest—and also on snuffing out dissent immediately whenever it emerges. The CCP recalls its own past. It knows, as Mao Zedong wrote in 1930, that a "single spark can ignite a prairie fire."

THE POLITICAL SYSTEM ON TAIWAN

Just such a fire was sparked on Taiwan. Until the late 1980s, the Republic of China (ROC)—the official name of the government on Taiwan—was an authoritarian, one-party state, in which the Nationalist Party of China (the Kuomintang, or KMT) reigned with impunity. Although it was decidedly anti-communist, in form and function the political system of Taiwan bore some similarity to the political system of the PRC. Indeed, the KMT had been a Leninist party, too, with the same social penetration intended as a means of organization and control of the populace.

That is not to say that the KMT was modeled after the CCP, or vice versa. Rather, both emerged from the same social and cultural milieu of the early twentieth century. Both were influenced by the Soviet model and by Chinese political culture. The Leninist dimension of social control and mobilization dovetailed well with preexisting political habits in China and with attitudes about such things as the role of supreme leadership, social conformity, dissent, and the instrumental function of law. The CCP took the Leninist form and moved to the left on the political spectrum, and the KMT took the form and moved to the right.

Like the CCP, the KMT was capable of ruthlessness, repression of opponents, self-righteous paternalism, and arbitrary enforcement of laws to ensure its continuance in power. Moreover, from 1978 to 1988 the president of the ROC was Chiang Ching-kuo (Jiang Jingguo), the son of Chiang Kai-shek (Jiang Jieshi), who had been president for most of the period from 1928 until his death in 1975. In this respect, the ROC under the KMT had something in common with both North Korea and Singapore. Chiang Ching-kuo's status and selection by the KMT elite had everything to do with heredity, rather than with a transparent election that he stood as good a chance of losing as winning.

The ROC became synonymous with Taiwan after the titanic battles of the Chinese civil war. Before then, the ROC was the government of all China, with the KMT as the ruling party. When the ROC lost to the communists, those KMT loyalists who could do so fled to the Chinese island of Taiwan. As they considered themselves the legitimate government of the ROC and the island a part of China's national territory, from their vantage point they were simply displaced from one portion of China to another. They continued to rule with the hope that eventually they could muster the forces to reclaim control over the rest of China's territory.

The Chinese who fled from the mainland in the shadow of civil war found themselves a minority on an island largely populated by the descendants of Chinese who had migrated there centuries before and by politically marginalized, non-Chinese "aborigines." For four decades, the KMT ruled Taiwan in a politically oppressive, authoritarian manner, under a form of martial law that was not lifted until 1987. It dedicated itself to retaking control of the Chinese mainland and justified the suspension of constitutional liberties as necessary during the prolonged struggle with communism.

In the 1970s and 1980s, the KMT oversaw the "Taiwan miracle" by which the island was greatly enriched and developed. In that same period, political opponents of the KMT were emboldened to make ever more creative and piercing challenges to the regime. Opponents of the ruling party were mostly people whose families had been on the island long before the KMT arrived. They considered Taiwan their only home and objected to the political repression they endured, especially as they had no interest in affairs on the Chinese mainland. They and others demanded political reform and greater opportunity for participation in a political system dominated by the minority that had come with the KMT in the 1940s.

With opponents of the regime increasing their demands for reform, human rights abuses tarnishing the KMT's image, and a confluence of international pressure from both the PRC and the United States, Chiang Ching-kuo authorized limited liberalization of the system. By the time he died in 1988, Taiwan was embarked on a course that led relatively rapidly to democratization. Restrictions on the establishment of political parties and on the press were lifted, making it legal to voice dissent and organize an opposition. In swift succession, the KMT greatly reformed the way it conducted its internal business and released its stranglehold on the legislative bodies, opening them to genuinely competitive elections.

In 1996 Lee Teng-hui—who was Chiang Ching-kuo's vice president and immediate successor—was elected president of the ROC for a fixed term, in a popular election with universal adult suffrage, the first time in the history of any Chinese polity that the chief executive was selected in such a manner. In 2000, Chen Shui-bian—a candidate from the opposition Democratic Progressive Party (DPP)—was elected, relegating the KMT to the role of opposition party in the ROC for the first time since 1928. Chen was reelected for a final four-year term, with a narrow and contested majority, in 2004.

The contrasts between the ROC on Taiwan and the PRC on the mainland are stark in many ways, but especially when one juxtaposes the political systems of the two places. By the twenty-first century the political system in Taiwan was utterly democratic. Checks and balances are carefully monitored by a feisty press and a bombastic legislative branch. The judiciary is as free as any, public participation is widespread, and contestation at all levels of government is fierce and genuine. The 1947 constitution of the ROC has remained the foundational, legitimizing document, setting forth the structure and powers of government as well as the rights of citizens, although it has been significantly amended and the subject of great controversy. Civil society is vibrant and thriving in part because of a highly literate and educated populace.

There are problems, to be sure. The constitution specifies a five-power government devised by Sun Yat-sen as a mode of governing all China. As in many political systems, it comprises the executive, legislative, and judicial branches. In addition, perhaps reflecting imperial traditions, it has a "control" branch, intended to serve as a government accountability agency, and an "examination" branch, responsible for recruitment into the civil service.

Reforms have made the Legislative Yuan (parliament) more influential than it had been when it offered no more than ritualized consent to presidential and KMT decisions, but the system as a whole still suffers from a lack of clarity about lines of authority and therefore is highly inefficient. In some respects, Taiwan's is a semipresidential system with characteristics of a parliamentary system, similar to that of France, which features both a president and a premier. Constitutional amendments intended to streamline and rationalize the cumbersome structure have not succeeded in resolving the question of how the president, premier, and legislature should share power.

Still, laws, not men, now rule. Parties compete. Power is limited. Voters are confronted with genuine choices in regular—some say too-frequent—elections for every office from the presidency down to the proverbial dogcatcher. Indeed, whatever changes are to be made, there is universal expectation in Taiwan that they will be made by the ballot, not the bullet. That is one reason why the contest with the PRC about sovereignty over Taiwan is so terribly thorny. Beijing asserts, and wishes to impose, its sovereignty over Taiwan, which it still claims as China's territory. Most voters on Taiwan—now accustomed to democracy and attached to a separate political identity—prefer to retain their political autonomy from the PRC.

THE POLITICAL SYSTEM OF JAPAN

One reason why Taiwan may have so quickly habituated itself to elections as the basis for its democratic system is that from 1895 to 1945 the island was a colony of Japan. Although Japan was not, in that period, fully democratic, and it ruled its colonial possessions quite differently than Japan itself was governed, it did introduce elections at local levels on Taiwan in the 1930s.

Indeed, Japan had been engaged in wholesale transformation of its own political system since the feudal structure based on rule by a clan-based military leader, known as the *shogun,* was ended with the restoration of the Meiji Emperor in 1868. Japan's first constitution was introduced in 1889 and was aimed at bringing Japan into conformity with other "modern" powers. Sovereignty was vested in the emperor, and civil liberties, such as they were, were bestowed by him. However, the constitution did provide for an elected national legislature (the Diet), which was established in 1890 and may be seen as the institutional seed for the subsequent growth of Japan's democracy.

There occurred in the first decades of the twentieth century a protracted struggle between civilian leaders who wished Japan to emulate Western democracies, and militarists who sought a dominant and autocratic role in the nation's political system. The defeat of Japan in 1945 brought an end to World War II and to more than a half-century of Japanese expansionism in East Asia that had been provoked by militarism in the name of nationalism and development. A new constitution was implemented in 1947, during the seven years when Japan was occupied by the United States. That document, from which Japan's current political system flows, was very consciously intended to enhance civilian control in a parliamentary, multiparty, representative democracy. Indeed, in an effort to prevent the recurrence of military adventurism of the sort that had taken Japan down the path to war with its neighbors, the prime minister was required to be a civilian, and the document's article 9 renounces war as a tool of foreign policy.

The constitution is also explicit in offering guarantees of basic human rights, about sovereignty resting with the people, and about gender equality. It established an independent judiciary, with a supreme court as the final legal authority, and has operated from the principle of judicial precedent, reinforcing the rule of law and insuperability of the constitution.

Japan has a bicameral parliament, elected by universal adult suffrage, in the form of a (lower) House of Representatives (since 2000 comprising 480 representatives, ordinarily serving four-year terms) and an (upper) House of Councilors (since 2004 comprising 242 representatives, elected for staggered three year terms). A majority of seats in each house are directly elected, and a minority assigned on the basis of proportional representation of certain preestablished constituencies.

The House of Representatives selects the prime minister, who is chief executive, but much of legislation is drafted by the professional civil service, giving the bureaucracy in Japan a much greater role in lawmaking than is the case in many other parliamentary systems. This, in part, reflects both a "revolving door" between the bureaucracy and the Diet and historically close ties between the professional bureaucracy and the LDP.

From 1955 to 1993 the LDP was able to dominate as the ruling party. In 1993, the LDP prime minister lost a no-confidence vote and his government fell. Although the LDP remained the party with the greatest number of seats in the Diet, it was for the first time out-maneuvered by a coalition of other parties and was unable to retain its status as ruling party. After nine months, the LDP recaptured its position and has retained it since, despite being a much weaker force than it had been. After 1993 there were a flurry of short-lived governments headed by a sequence of ten prime ministers. Then, in 2001, the popular maverick Junichiro Koizumi was first elected prime minister, apparently breaking the political free fall into which the LDP had stumbled.

Japan has a highly literate, highly educated population and the longest life expectancy of any state. It is ethnically homogenous, economically stratified, and comparatively wealthy. Civil society flourishes freely, but interpersonal and social relations are still characterized by a certain rigidity and inclination to conformity that reflect Japan's pre-democratic social mores, many compatible with, and expressed in terms of, Confucian values that Japanese adapted from China. So, while Japan's political system is democratic, its social system emphasizes communitarian harmony and consensus rather more than individualism and contestation.

That may appear to American readers as a contradiction, but it makes evident the lesson that democracy is an approach to decision making. It determines the means by which decisions are made and the principles by which the political system is structured, not the outcome of decisions or the social values that the societies that employ it embrace. Democracy is a process, not a product. Moreover, it coexists in every society where it is adopted with preexisting political and cultural values that create systemic hybrids, not purebreds. Hence, democracy can thrive in a civilization like Japan's, where consensus and conformity trump individualism, and Confucian values can be esteemed in a democratic state, like Taiwan, that has forsaken despotism and authoritarianism for popular sovereignty, free choice, and individual liberty.

Suggestions for Additional Reading

Chao, Linda, and Ramon H. Myers. *The First Chinese Democracy: Political Life in the Republic of China on Taiwan.* Baltimore and London: Johns Hopkins University Press, 1998.

Charlton, Sue Ellen M. *Comparing Asian Politics: India, China, and Japan.* 2nd ed. Boulder: Westview Press, 2004.

Cohen, Warren I. *East Asia at the Center: Four Thousand Years of Engagement with the World.* New York: Columbia University Press, 2000.

Dickson, Bruce J. *Democratization in China and Taiwan: The Adaptability of Leninist Parties.* Oxford: Clarendon Press, 1997.

Dreyer, June Teufel. *China's Political System: Modernization and Tradition.* 5th ed. New York: Longman, 2006.

Fewsmith, Joseph. *China Since Tiananmen: The Politics of Transition.* Cambridge: Cambridge University Press, 2001.

Rigger, Shelley. *From Opposition to Power: Taiwan's Democratic Progressive Party.* Boulder and London: Lynne Rienner, 2001.

———. *Politics in Taiwan.* New York: Routledge, 1999.

Rozman, Gilbert, ed. *The East Asian Region: Confucian Heritage and Its Modern Adaptation.* Princeton: Princeton University Press, 1991.

Saich, Tony. *Governance and Politics of China.* 2nd ed. New York: Palgrave, 2004.

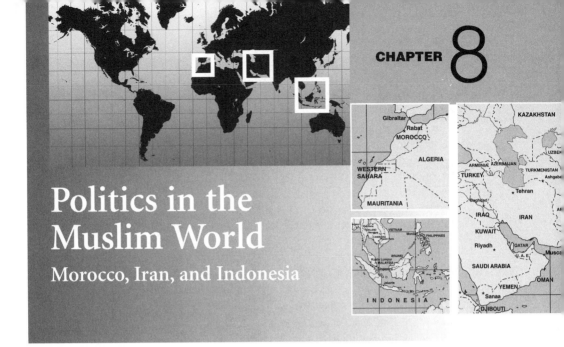

CHAPTER 8

Politics in the Muslim World

Morocco, Iran, and Indonesia

Behind the political process in the United States and Europe, there is a normative assumption that the sovereign power of a state formally resides within the community that the state represents, thus ensuring popular engagement in the political process that controls communal affairs. The assumption may be explicit in countries—the vast majority—where a constitution defines the political process or implicit, as in Britain, where no written constitution exists. Communal power is usually expressed in an indirect fashion because elected institutions exist to sanction government action, although in Switzerland, for example, referendums provide unusually direct participation in the legislative process. This mode of expression depends on a convention, inherent in the general political culture, that elected representatives do not abuse the power granted to them and do indeed reflect the interests of those who elected them, either directly or through political programs that a majority within the community have endorsed through the electoral process.

This concept of participatory political processes through the communal manipulation of sovereign power—the essence of democratic governance—has other assumptions built into it as well. For instance, there is a common acceptance that political disagreement should be resolved by established procedures, accessible to all, within the formal political arena and that popular support for representative government should be regularly and periodically tested through the electoral process. Political institutions, the political process, and communal order are sanctioned by an independent judiciary—the rule of law, which ensures equal treatment for all. Public space, that arena between the private world of the family and the formal activities of the state, is mediated by civil society, which also serves to restrain the ambitions of the state.

In democratic countries, such statements seem self-evident, for they form the very substance of what Alexis de Tocqueville, when he analyzed the political system in nineteenth-century America, described as the "habits of mind" that determine the democratic political process. They even lie behind Friedrich Hayek's cynicism when he described democracy as a temporary dictatorship of the majority redeemed only by its regular renewal through the electoral process. They are not, however, the sole way in which societies and communities achieve effective, acceptable governance, in terms either of the institutions they describe or the objectives they proclaim. This is important because in, for example, the Muslim world, different assumptions traditionally have held sway, and modern political systems reflect such differences even when they appear to mirror the paradigms of the developed world. Social justice, for example, might occupy a place above popular participation, and consensus might be more important than the accommodation of dissent within the formal political space.

TRADITIONAL PRINCIPLES OF GOVERNANCE

Such differences reflect differences in the ways political institutions and processes have developed historically, as well as differences concerning the purposes for which political processes were conceived. The traditional Islamic state embodied the principles on which the initial Muslim community, that created by the Prophet Muhammad at Medina, was based. Its principles reflected the needs both for communal defense against a hostile external world and for internal coherence and submission around the principles inherent in the Islamic message that the Prophet had revealed—an ideological concept of the state. The political manifestation of this embryonic state was typified by a series of annual agreements, drawn up to regulate relations between those who had come from Mecca with the Prophet and those who had invited them, known collectively as the Constitution of Medina. It also defined the nature of relations with the external, non-Islamic world, later known as the *dar al-harb* ("the land of war," where Muslim law does not apply). The constitution emphasizes the unicity— the uniqueness and unity (*tawhid*)—of the Muslim community, the *umma* or *dar al-islam*; its external obligation for collective defense (*jihad*),[1] and its internal imperative of egalitarian religious practice, as well as the role of the Prophet Muhammad as its leader and arbiter.

Traditional Institutions and Political Culture

The early history of the Islamic world entrenched these principles and expanded them. The disruption that followed the death of the Prophet elevated the importance of political order, rather than chaos, alongside unicity. In addition, the rapid expansion of Islamic conquest promoted the elaboration of law derived from the Qur'an (*shari'a*), which had been at the core of the embryonic state, to order the growing Muslim community under a ruler, the caliph. His authority, formally as the deputy for Muhammad *(khalifa)*,[2] derived from his kin relationship to the Prophet and his election by the new Muslim community-at-large *(bay'a)*.

The Prophet's authority and power, of course, derived from the Divinity, such that sovereignty (*hukm*), too, was a divine attribute. That principle also passed over to his successors, the caliphs, whose right to exercise authority and power was subject to an implied contract: If they failed to mirror the immaculate qualities of the Prophet as *imam*—leader of the community—their right to exercise this delegated power might no longer be uncontested. In divine terms, of course, this meant enabling proper Islamic observance; in temporal terms it meant consultation (*shura*) to achieve consensus (*ijma'*) on the ways in which that might be achieved.

After the death of the fourth caliph—the last of the *rashidun* ("the rightly guided"), those who had actually known the Prophet Muhammad and the system he had created—the elective process became predominantly contractual, in that communal obedience to the caliph was, in theory, dependent on the latter's ability to guarantee consensus on social justice and communal order, in accordance with Islamic precept and, particularly, the *shari'a*. There is a tension here between the idea of conditional loyalty and the imperative of political order even if the ruler was unjust and tyrannical. That tension is evident in later political culture. It has never been fully resolved because of the importance accorded to political order, on the one hand, and the normatively immaculate quality of the imamate on the other.

An alternative vision also emerged at this juncture, as a result of the great sectarian split inside Islam between Sunni and Shi'a. In essence this was a dispute about who should take up the caliphate after the death of 'Uthman, the third of the "rightly guided" caliphs of the early tradition. The fourth and last *rashidun* caliph was Ali, the cousin of the Prophet and the husband of his daughter, Fatima. His rule as caliph was, however, disputed by Mu'awiya, the governor of Damascus. After Ali's assassination, Mu'awiya assumed the caliphate, and his descendants effectively transformed it into a hereditary office. As part of this process Mu'awiya's successor, Yazid, ensured the elimination of Ali's son, Husayn, whom the Muslims in Iraq had selected as caliph after his twin brother, Hasan, who had renounced the caliphate in favor of Mu'awiya, had died, probably from poison.

Thereafter, those Muslims who had supported the claims of Ali and his son Husayn to the caliphate looked to Ali's descendants as the true leaders of the Muslim community. They therefore became know as the *Shi'at Ali*, or the "supporters of Ali," while the remainder of the Muslim community were called the *Sunni*, "those who followed the traditions of the Prophet." Yazid and his descendants imposed their rule on the rest, although they preserved the fiction of the caliphate as an elective office. Legitimate authority, for the Shi'a, however, was hereditary, not elective, and each of Ali's direct descendants was regarded as the immaculate *imam* for the community, even though their temporal authority was circumscribed by Sunni persecution.

In another pivotal event, the twelfth imam, Muhammad al-Mahdi, disappeared in 873 CE, maintaining contact by a series of alleged emissaries, in what has become known as the "lesser occultation." Seventy years later he ceased contact, direct or indirect, in what has become known as the "greater occultation." According to Shi'a theology, he remains hidden from human view until he emerges to lead Shi'a Muslims as the *mahdi* to millenarian justice.

A further problem emerged from the expansion of the Muslim world, that of delegation. The simple model of a caliph as supreme ruler, legitimized by his descent from the Prophet and by communal endorsement, could not cope with geographic expansion and social complexity. Inevitably political complexity, in the form of separate states, emerged, thus disrupting the political integration of the *umma*, although the ideological fiction of unicity was preserved.

In these separate political entities the principles governing the caliphate still formed the ideological base for the exercise of power. Those in authority, however, were no longer seen as *imams* but rather as examples of a temporal concept of power, kingship (*mulk*), who lacked divine sanction for their authority, even if the principles governing their legitimacy as rulers remained the same. Loyalty to them, therefore, was more contingent on their behavior, such that religious sanction could legitimize their removal.

In addition, managing an expanding state required new measures if effective political control was to be exercised. Thus a theory of delegation (*tafwih*) developed, legitimizing the roles of ministers (*wazir*) and governors (*wali*). Their authority was a reflection of that of the *imam* or caliph, the theoretical leader of the unitary Islamic community, and was legitimized by their ability to match its moral and ideological demands. At the same time, the imperative ideological and cultural demand for the preservation of order preserved their power.

Of course such principles of political organization would not survive a thousand years of history in such pristine purity, and a plethora of different political structures and processes were to emerge, not least after Islam was exposed to the variegated traditions of India and Southeast Asia. There Hindu and Buddhist political traditions were absorbed into the Islamic corpus, particularly as Islam spread more through trade than by conquest. There was a similar development in Africa, too, and even in Southern Europe, where seven centuries of Islamic presence in the Iberian Peninsula affected Islam as a political culture and praxis. Yet the core ideas drawn from Islam did inform the generalized political culture in much of the Islamic world. Sovereign power was a divine attribute delegated to temporal rulers; order was always to be preferred over political chaos; the Islamic world was an ideological—and preferably a political—unit; consultation and consensus lay at the core of the political process. These are ideas that constantly reappear in political discourse.

They appear in the legitimating discourses of the great Muslim empires of the Ottomans, the Safavids, and the Mughals and are shared by both the Sunni and Shiʿa religious traditions. Indeed, the Ottoman sultans felt constrained to produce a genealogy showing their kinship to the Prophet Muhammad to justify their adoption of the title of "caliph." The principles are even repeated in smaller political entities such as Morocco, one of the oldest states in the Muslim world with a continuous political tradition, where the sultan (now king) is, even today, *amir al-mu'minin* ("commander of the faithful"), which is one of the traditional titles of the caliph.

The Colonial Experience

By the end of the eighteenth century the Muslim world could no longer ignore the intrusive reality of imperial Europe. Indeed, this awareness at the Muslim periphery had been explicit and brutal much earlier. Imperial Russia had begun to encroach on Ottoman and Iranian territory as early as the start of the eighteenth century, and Britain had defeated the last remnants of the Mughals in India at the Battle of Plassy in 1759, two years after the empire itself had been dismembered by Afghan invaders. The Dutch had appeared in Indonesia as early as 1596 and had been preceded by the Portuguese, although Dutch control over the archipelago was only complete by the mid-eighteenth century. The date at which Muslims suddenly became aware of the aggressive technological superiority of Europe is conventionally set as 1798, the date of Napoleon's invasion of Egypt and his destruction of the Mamluk dynasty there. The early part of the nineteenth century for the Muslim world was an uncomfortable period of adjusting to this new challenge, either by internalizing it or by trying to confront it.

It was apparent that technological superiority was also linked to an intellectual and ideological vision, ostensibly secular and scientific but derived from a complex cultural and intellectual inheritance. It is true that Islam was important as a vehicle for the transmission of knowledge from the ancient world and, in the medieval period at least, for the innovative development of that intellectual heritage. Yet Europe had subsequently developed its own intellectual and ideological patterns, through the Renaissance and the Enlightenment, on which its newfound power was based. Furthermore, it was evident that the structure of the European state had fostered scientific development, as well as contributing to the dynamic aggressiveness of its commercial and military aspirations.

Muslims therefore reacted to the challenge in two ways: States sought to internalize the structures and mechanisms that made the European paradigm so powerful by transforming administrative and fiscal systems, importing new technologies to modernize economies, and developing military power along European lines. Thus the Ottoman Empire introduced the "Tanzimat" reforms and eventually, in 1876, a constitution that paralleled European models. Egypt—ostensibly part of the Ottoman Empire but effectively independent under Muhammad Ali—had earlier, in the 1820s, created a European-style modern "Nizam" army and transformed the fiscal and economic systems of the country to support it. Even Tunisia, in the 1830s, did the same, and in 1856 it introduced the Arab world's first constitution—largely because of European pressure to grant foreigners property rights. Iran was to follow much later, with the 1906 Constitutional Revolution, although the Qajar dynasty that ruled it began to seek modernization without succumbing to Russian or British pressure.

Indeed, European pressure became ever more overt as the century wore on, with the first directly administered colony being created by France in Algeria in 1830. In India, too, the often corrupt and often indirect administration of the East India Company gave way to direct British administration after the Indian Mutiny of 1857. The same occurred in Tunisia and Egypt in 1881, as European colonialism moved into high gear. Muslim Africa was divided up at the end of the eighteenth century, and the First World War provided the excuse for the colonization of the Middle East, partly to guarantee British access to India. Other European states—France, Italy, and Spain—also satisfied their own imperial aspirations. Morocco fell under Franco-Spanish control in 1912. In the Indonesian archipelago, the Dutch in 1816 began a determined move toward establishing a colonial empire that lasted through the nineteenth century and included the Java War in the 1820s and the Acheh War from 1873 until the dawn of the twentieth century.

The First World War itself was a profound formative experience for the Islamic world, particularly in the Middle East, where the mandates created after the war formed the embryonic entities that were to become its contemporary states. It also brought an end to the Ottoman Empire, which was replaced by colonies and the modern secular state of Turkey. The Ottoman caliphate was consigned to history in 1927, although it left behind, particularly in South Asia, the Khalifa movement, which still seeks to re-create the caliphate as the unifying pole of the Muslim world. And, because of the British government's Balfour Declaration in 1917, promising a Jewish homeland in Palestine, which was to become a British mandate, it introduced one of the longest-lasting political and diplomatic problems facing the Muslim world, one that it has not yet resolved.

Yet these experiences also brought Muslims into direct contact with the constitutional, administrative, and fiscal implications of the European model, either through emulation or domination, profoundly influencing the subsequent indigenous political cultures, informed as they were by the essential Muslim paradigm described above. That contact in itself forced a reevaluation of Islamic doctrine and ideology as they applied to the temporal world, an attempt to derive within the Islamic intellectual corpus a dynamic to match that of Europe and create a vibrant, self-sustaining culture capable of addressing the modern world.

It took time to develop, but by the 1860s a new intellectual movement was sweeping the Islamic world, offering paradigms for state and society designed to challenge Europe's secular intellectual hegemony. This was the Salafiyya movement, named after the "ancestors," those at the pristine core of the Islamic experience in the seventh and eighth centuries. In other words, the Islamic intellectual experience itself contained all that was necessary for the construction of a modern political theory and the creation of a system embodying all the virtues claimed by European experience. It only required intellectual imagination to develop and apply it. Thus the writings of Jamal al-Afghani and later those of Muhammad ʿAbduh resonate with this intellectual challenge and their response to it, creating the impetus for political change and reconstruction. Their ideas lay at the roots of the initial Muslim response both to the European intellectual challenge and to colonial occupation, for they informed the early nationalist movements that emerged at the start of the twentieth century.

Thus European political concepts such as sovereignty, constitutionalism, popular consent and participation in the political process, and independent legal sanction for political action all had their Islamic counterparts which, in turn, were also conditioned by the contact, sometimes consensual, often violent, with Europe. This has been particularly important, for it has enriched the political culture of the Muslim world, which has internalized these concepts and integrated them. Not all of them have been beneficial, for the European and wider western experience, too, has not always been progressive, and colonialism itself was based on a concept of domination and exploitation in which benefit to its subjects was incidental, even accidental. The secular and holistic lessons of fascism and communism are evidence of that.

In addition, European colonialism had created discrete political and geographic units out of the vast empires of the pre-colonial Muslim world, anticipating its contemporary states. The original boundaries were ones between the possessions and spheres of influence of different colonial powers and defined administrative zones within them. It was only after independence that the boundaries hardened into international frontiers—often against ideological attitudes seeking to reassert a sense of unity within an increasingly disparate and fragmented Islamic world. Unity was, after all, the essence of Arab nationalism and is today one of the abiding themes of political Islam.

EXAMPLES OF GOVERNANCE

It is out of these extraordinarily variegated traditions and experiences that the contemporary political process in the Muslim world has emerged. The original Islamic ideal has been profoundly modified, but to a greater or lesser extent it remains at the core of the political culture of the modern states. The states also have institutions and processes that reflect their individual historical experiences.

Thus, to appreciate the range of responses that the Muslim world has produced to the problems of creating legitimate governance, it would be best to consider some specific cases in detail rather than try to draw a set of principles from across this complex and diverse political arena. The case studies below offer a sampling of the range of solutions that have grown from the complex heritage of Islamic paradigm, historical experience that may even predate the discovery of Islam, and colonial imposition. They are by no means the only examples that exist. They reveal, however, the essential Islamic experience that separates them from governmental processes in other parts of the world.

MOROCCO

Morocco's contemporary system of governance reflects one of the best-preserved traditional political systems in the Islamic world. Yet at the same time, it has proved to be one of the most malleable in adapting to modernity and has become, in many respects, a paradigm, rather like Turkey, of how political culture and tradition can be integrated into participatory governance. In part, that has been a consequence of the way the country was administered during colonial occupation, from 1912 until 1956. In part, too, it has depended on the astuteness of its rulers in appreciating contemporary realities and on the cohesiveness of a political culture linked to a state tradition stretching back nine centuries.

The Sultanate

The traditional Moroccan state reflected some of the dualities one finds in the ideal theocratic image of the state described above. It was headed by a *sultan* (as an embodiment of power) who claimed legitimacy as caliph because of his descent from the Prophet Muhammad. His claim was authenticated by communal approval through the *bay'a* when his reign was inaugurated, which in Morocco was a contractual document issued by urban elites and power centers—the *ahl al-hall wa'l-'aqd* ("those who bind and unbind" power by legitimating it through their consent)—and by powerful rural leaders and tribes. Interestingly enough, there was also an element of kinship involved, for a new sultan was usually a son or close relative of his predecessor, and he was considered to have inherited the qualities—the *baraka*—that had characterized his predecessor. That, of course, reaches back to the immaculate figure of the Prophet Muhammad. The term means "divine favor" or "blessing." It refers to the serendipity of descent from the Prophet and thus the transmission and incarnation of the quality that rendered him immaculate and appropriate to act as the intermediary between the Islamic community and the Divine.

Yet in traditional fashion, in those areas (the *bilad al-makhzan*) where he could impose his authority (and his powers of taxation) through direct force, the sultan required unquestioning obedience to preserve stability and order. As the Moroccan *'ulama* (religious authorities) claimed, "To him who holds power, obedience is due!" In the more distant regions, where direct power could not be applied so effectively, if at all (the *bilad as-siba*),[3] the sultan either had to depend on tax-raising military columns, whose predatory power was effective only when they were physically present, or on the tacit support of the local power centers—tribal leaders or the *zawiyas* (lodges) of religious orders. They would only offer such support if they were in accord with its objectives, such that consensus formed the basis of the tacit and often temporary alliances that could be formed to ensure stability.

Sovereignty, then, could not be articulated merely through the direct application of force; it also required prestige and consent. Inevitably, there was a constant tension between the three requirements, for the sultan sought to articulate control by applying military power when and where he could, whereas those on whose support he depended sought precisely the opposite approach. The sultanate, in short, was inherently weak as a vehicle for the articulation of temporal power.

Yet paradoxically enough, this weakness was to be one of the main causes of its survival. In the largely acephalous society that made up much of rural North Africa, centralized authority outside the regions the sultan could control directly had little meaning or effect. As a result rural society, organized tribally, developed spontaneous mechanisms for defusing political tension and violence.[4] In general, these depended on certain kin-lineages acting as mediators when disputes arose. Often such lineages claimed legitimacy as mediators through genealogies connecting them with the Prophet Muhammad.

The caliph-sultan, whose lineage descent was unquestioned, could act as the ultimate mediator because of his innately weak status. Thus he became essential to a political system based on a normative hierarchy of power legitimated by descent from the Prophet but which required consent and consensus on its objectives to operate because of the relative powerlessness of the pinnacle of the hierarchy—the sultan. The sultan's military power waxed and waned in geographic terms, depending on his ability to mobilize armed force through tribal levy or by a standing army. Because standing armies were expensive, he increasingly depended on tribal levy, which of course also depended on consent, so that the elective and contingent principle behind sultanic power was reinforced.

Colonial Legacy: From Ruling to Reigning

The advent of the colonial era was to transform this situation. France preserved the institutions of the traditional Moroccan state while constructing the attributes of modern state power around it. Yet the traditional political culture, based on the combination of submission to direct power and contingent consent to indirect power, persisted even within the nationalist movement that emerged in the 1930s. Allied with the sultanate from 1944 onward, it was to achieve independence in 1956. Yet when Morocco became an independent state, it was the sultanate that inherited the power structure France had created. It then needed the consent not only of autonomous traditional institutions, but also of political parties and the structures of a modern state.

The sultanate, now transformed into a monarchy (*mulk*), responded to the new challenges in a traditional fashion. It continued to seek absolute power where it could and to mediate where it could not. The difference, of course, was that it was now in control of an instrument that was infinitely more powerful than the precolonial predecessor—a modern state in which the police, gendarmerie, and army ensured that power could be equally expressed over the totality of its territorial extent. That power, furthermore, was now the property of a political system centered around the person of the king in the institution of the *makhzan,* the royal court as an administrative and coercive apparatus to express the royal will, in contradistinction to formal government.

Yet this, too, offered its own dangers, for if the new monarchical state could impose itself, then seeking to exploit a consensual relationship with it had little meaning, and the only alternative would be to replace its controlling personnel. Thus in the 1970s King Hassan II had to face three attempted coups d'état, a popular clandestine political movement challenging his political legitimacy, and a rural rebellion that was intended to seed countrywide upheaval. Hundreds went to prison in the clampdown that followed, and the formal political system created at independence, involving political parties, elections, and a unicameral parliament, was marginalized.

It was to his credit that the king realized that the monarchy had become too powerful to survive, both in the modern world—where patterns of democratic consent were increasingly seen as the norm—and in a traditional political culture that considered the imposition of central authority outside a context of consent and consensus unacceptable. The solution would be to transform the role of the monarchy from ruling to reigning. In other words, the monarchy should abandon its engagement in and domination of the political process and seek instead to legitimate the political system and act as the ultimate repository of power should the political process fail. Prestige and mediation, rather than the articulation of repressive power, should become its instruments.

King Hassan also realized that such a system, if it were not to fail, could not be installed by decree. It would have to evolve, stage by stage, as politicians learned the responsibilities of power as well as its institutionalization. Finally, he realized that he himself, schooled as he was in an absolutist tradition, would find it very difficult to observe the self-constraint inherent in such a system and that the system he constructed would eventually be put into operation by his successors. Accordingly, over the last fourteen years of his reign, which ended in 1999, institutional reforms were put into place increasingly rapidly, alongside changes in administrative, judicial, and penal practice. The *makhzan,* or royal court, however, continued to be the "dark heart" of the regime.

Reform and Institutionalization

There was also external pressure to encourage Morocco along the path of reform. After 1973, and particularly after the Moroccan occupation of the Western Sahara in November 1975, European and American nongovernmental organizations increasingly questioned Morocco's human rights record. Individual states in Europe, together with the United States, also fitfully applied similar pressure, although this was often moderated by Western perceptions of Morocco's geopolitical utility. With the end of the cold war, however, considerations of governance came to the forefront of diplomatic relations, and when, in November 1995, Morocco joined the European Union's Euro-Mediterranean Partnership it formally agreed to be bound to respect human rights and practice democratic governance.

The construction of the institutions of government begins in 1962, when the current constitution went into effect. Alongside the *makhzan*, by then rapidly becoming the real instrument of power as it absorbed the repressive administrative and legal structures constructed by the French, the constitution created a unicameral legislature, partly directly elected by universal suffrage and partly indirectly elected by representatives of local administration and professional organizations. Its authority, however, was totally dependent on the king and his parallel administrative system through the *makhzan*.

It was only in 1974, as Morocco began the process of seeking international support for its annexation of the Western Sahara, that Morocco's political parties were granted some space to participate meaningfully in the political process in return for their support for the kingdom's foreign adventure. Even then, however, the constitutional political system could only operate within the confines marked out for it by the arbitrary power of the *makhzan*, itself answerable only to the king. Despite four constitutional amendments in 1970, 1972, 1980, and in 1992, the system remained substantially unchanged until the constitutional reforms of 1996.

These provided for the institution of a bicameral parliamentary system, based on a House of Representatives (*majlis an-nuwwab*) and a new upper chamber, the House of Counsellors (*majlis al-mustasharin*). The 325-member lower chamber is directly elected, by simple majority, in single-member individual constituencies, for a term of five years. In 2001, 10 percent of the seats in this chamber were reserved for women. The members of the upper chamber are elected for nine-year terms, 162 of them by local and regional administrative councils and the remaining 108 by industrial and agricultural associations and the country's trade unions.

Twenty-nine political parties participate in the legislative institutions, the major parties grouped into electoral coalitions—the *Kutla* or bloc of left-wing and nationalist parties; the *Wifaq*, bringing together conservative movements; and the remainder forming a bloc of independent parties. The monarchy was anxious to establish a pattern of dominant power oscillating between the two major blocs, in a system of what it called "altérnance," for the party winning the largest number of seats in a legislative election normally expects to propose the prime minister.

The king is not, however, obliged to accept the nominee, for he appoints the prime minister and appoints all other ministers on the prime minister's recommendations, which he is not obliged to accept, either. The king also presides over cabinet meetings and has absolute powers to prorogue or dissolve parliament or rule by decree, or even to change the constitution by referendum without parliamentary consent. He is also head of the armed forces and, as *amir al-mu'minin*, the country's religious leader as well.

The monarch is, in short, still effectively absolute, although now institutions exist through which, in theory, consultation and consensus can be achieved if he so wishes. Over the past fifteen years, however, growing substance has been given to the parliamentary process as a result of royal indulgence, as—in a parallel move—restraints on freedom of expression and on individual rights and freedoms have been removed. The result is that Moroccans today enjoy substantial rights and freedoms, compared with the situation in 1990, when political liberalization really began. Those rights and freedoms are still conditional and not absolute, even when guaranteed by law, because of the status of the monarchy, which is outside law as the embodiment of legitimacy—an authority acquired through divine sanction.

That status is highlighted by the contradiction in the constitution whereby royal descent is now through primogeniture, even though royal authority has to be legitimated by the traditional *bay'a*, annually renewed in a traditional ceremony called the *tajdid al-wala'*. This is sanctioned by dignitaries of state supposedly representing communal interests against sultanic power—the traditional *ahl al-hall wa'l-'aqd*—except, of course, that today they are functionaries of the state and pensioners of the *makhzan*. Once again, it is difficult to resist the conviction that the improvements in political participation and individual rights that characterize Morocco have been the king's gift and not functions of constitutional government. The contradiction inherent in the Islamic ideal, in short, has not yet been resolved.

Political Stability

Although much of Morocco's rural population has, over the years, been prepared to accept the idea of absolute monarchical power, a significant minority and an increasing urban majority have not. However, whereas in the past the innate weakness of the monarchy provided space for autonomous political action, based around royal mediation or the practice of consultation and consensus, this is not the case in the circumstances created by colonialism. Since the end of the colonial period the monarchy, in exploiting its absolutist tendencies and potential, has bought off potential opposition by incorporating it into the *makhzan* system. This has been done either by incorporation into the political structure or by access to economic advantage.

In other words, absolutist power has been partnered by economic corruption—widely used to neutralize the traditional elites that might, in the precolonial environment, have challenged the innately weak sultanate—or by political co-option, the phenomenon of monarchical "récuperation," which has been extensively and effectively used to neutralize potential opposition. This was a technique used to bring both ultra-left-wing opponents of the monarchy and its Islamist opponents back into the political arena in the 1980s and 1990s. Those at the extremes of political opposition had the alternative of outright repression through the apparatus of the modern state.

In many respects, the constitutionalization of the political system and the role of the monarchy proposed under the Hassanian system in the 1990s has sought to add a new weapon to the Moroccan state in its search for political stability. The challenge is to determine to what degree such an experiment will be allowed to develop, and must develop, in the search for that objective. King Hassan himself had little intention of carrying it forward; there were great hopes at his death that his son, Muhammad VI, would do so.

To some extent, such hopes have been realized. Individual human rights have been largely entrenched inside the political system, as has freedom of expression. The last legislative and municipal elections, in 2002 and 2003 respectively, are generally recognized to have been transparent, free of political interference, and fair. There have been significant improvements in the legal protection of individual rights, as through Morocco's new personal status law, the *muddawana*, which has, in effect, given women rights equal to those of men in marriage, although in principle the normative inferiorities innate in *shari'a* law have been preserved. Moroccans have also been able to address the injustices of arbitrary repression in the past through an "equality and reconciliation commission," although none of those identified as responsible have had to confront their behavior or face punishment.

At the same time, there have been areas of regression. Morocco passed a ferocious antiterrorism law in mid-2003, just after terrorist attacks in Casablanca. After that incident, Morocco's major Islamist political party, the Justice and Development Party (*Hizb al-Adala wa'l-Tanmiya*), was pressured to reduce its representation in the municipal elections. In addition, although torture has been outlawed, there are fears that, in the context of terrorism, the prohibition is not being observed by the police and security services. Although the courts, rather than the executive, are now responsible for addressing excesses by the media, journalists and newspapers can still face arbitrary repression, particularly if they criticize the royal family. The issue of the Western Sahara is still excluded from critical analysis in the news media.

Despite the obvious and significant improvements in human rights observance, the structural changes essential to make the Moroccan political system meaningfully participatory have not occurred, even if the culture and institutional traditions that could make this possible exist. The failure lies both within the Royal Palace, which has not yet been prepared to abandon its effective monopoly of power, especially its ultimate control of the political process and its status outside formal legal sanction beyond *shari'a* principle, and with the political parties. The political parties are often criticized for failing their members and the political system itself by not modernizing or demonstrating the maturity necessary to successfully operate a participatory political system.

In addition, the massively powerful system of absolute power within the structure of the *makhzan* must be formally dismantled before those objectives can be fully achieved. It is not just the *makhzan* as an institution that will have to be transformed; it is also the system of subservience and loyalty to royal power (*khudama*) that must change. Morocco cannot hope to achieve an effective participatory political system with a duality of power in which unaccountable subservience to arbitrary power supersedes multiparty parliamentary transparency and accountability.

IRAN

Similar problems to those of Morocco beset the political system in Iran. The tension between the Islamic ideal of consultation and consensus, on the one hand, and legitimate authority vested in an immaculate leader, or one rendered immaculate by his understanding and knowledge of Islam, on the other, has not been resolved. The Iranian system of governance, enshrined in the constitution that was approved by referendum in 1980, draws on a complex mixture of constitutional concepts based on French constitutionalism, involving democratic participation, and the ideas of Ayatollah Khomeini as developed in a series of lectures that he gave in Najaf during his exile there between 1964 and 1979, which dominate within the system. Those lectures described an innovative Islamic political system in which Shi'a doctrines of noninvolvement in secular government were reworked along Sunni lines, to allow for political activism in the temporal sphere, but in terms of fundamental Shi'a principles.

Interestingly enough, the underlying justification for such a novel political approach parallels the Islamic-Marxist agenda popularized by Dr. Ali Shariati, one of the most important ideologues of the Islamic revolution in Iran. He argued that the world was divided into oppressors (*mustakbarin*) and oppressed (*mustadafin*) and that the duty of the true Muslim was to struggle against the oppressors to restore justice to the oppressed. Not only did this neatly align Iranian Shi'a against the Shah's repressive regime, but it also reflected the Marxist doctrine of proletarian revolution and the Shi'a vision of millenarian justice transposed from the metaphysical world into the contemporary arena.

It was the latter vision that Ayatollah Khomeini adopted when he argued that true Islamic government, dedicated to social justice—and thus the interests of the oppressed—should be monitored and guided by a jurisconsult who reflected the perfection of the Shi'a *imam*, otherwise occulted until the Day of Judgment. He did not, of course, endorse the radical political program proposed by Shariati, for his political vision was intensely conservative and linked to the primacy of the *mullah* (clerical) class within organized political life. Yet the parallel between two thinkers from opposite ends of the political spectrum illustrates why the Islamic revolution, led by conservative clergy, found such a wide echo inside Iran at the time.

Dual Governmental System and the Power of the Jurisconsult

Thus the Islamic republic of Iran is based on the concept of *hukumat-i Islami* (Islamic government) under the guidance of a jurisconsult. This specially qualified leader is versed in *shariʿa* (Islamic) law of the Jafaʿari (twelve Shiʿa) school of jurisprudence, the *velayat-i faqih* (the way of the jurisconsult), and effectively acts for the occulted *imam* of Shiʿa tradition. It is also participatory in that some of its ancillary institutions are elective, either directly or indirectly, although some of them are only consultative in nature. This means that they enjoy restricted power and that the supposedly democratic components of the political system are subordinate to the control of the religious authorities.

Thus Iran also has a dual governmental system. On the one hand it has executive and legislative arms that operate as most formally democratic governments do, under a president who takes the role normally associated with a prime minister but also enshrines Iranian sovereignty, as a president would normally do. Yet overarching these governmental structures is the role of the jurisconsult and the institutions associated with his office. Sovereignty itself is once again formally a divine attribute, and therefore the president can only act in a sovereign fashion as a vehicle of divine authority and intent. This means that he can be open to criticism by the clerical authorities on grounds of interpretation, particularly by the jurisconsult who, as substitute for the *imam* and in his role as supreme legal interpreter, embodies the divine delegation of sovereignty.

The president presides over a ministerial cabinet appointed by himself and approved by the directly elected legislative body, the single-chamber *Majlis-e Shora*. The name itself is interesting, for it reveals the real purpose of the body, which is consultation, not decision making. Both the president and the *majlis* are directly elected for four-year terms. Cabinet ministers fulfil functions that are ultimately monitored by the *majlis*, which can call them to account, and *majlis* members enjoy legal immunity. The *majlis* also has reserved seats for members of minority communities—Jews, Christians, and in theory, Zoroastrians, who are "people of the Book" and who therefore enjoy restricted formal political rights under the constitution.

As mentioned above, the *majlis* only has consultative, not legislative powers; its decisions have to be formally approved by a superior body, the Council of Guardians (*Shora-e Nejahban*), before they can become law. The *majlis* may, however, introduce legislative bills designed to become law. Political parties exist. They were only authorized during the 1990s and must be approved to ensure their conformity with religious principle to operate as legal political movements—and they reflect political currents. The most important parties, each associated with a faction within the overall administrative structure, are as follows:

- The *Doveme Khordad* (the "Second of Khordad") movement. It is moderate, the party of Mohamed Khatami when he was president up to mid-2005. It is traditionally supported by the *mu'talafat* (the moderate clergy association), in contradistinction to the *mu'talafe* movement (see below).
- The *Kargozaran-i Sazandagi* (the "Servants of Construction") movement. They are pragmatic conservatives and supporters of former president Ali Akbar Hashemi Rafsanjani.

- The *mu'talafe* (the "Coalition of Islamic Associations") movement. It is conservative and today the real embodiment of power.

There are other parties, such as the Freedom Movement, the successor to the National Front created originally by Mohammed Mossadegh and now in eclipse after thirty of its former activists were arrested at the beginning of 2002. There are also the illegal parties—the *Tudeh* (Communist) Party; the *Mojahedin-e Khalq,* a radical opponent of the clerical regime, based in Iraq and now under American control; and the *Fedayin-i Khalq,* now split into pro- and anti-regime factions.[5] None of these parties now takes part in formal politics.

Despite its limited power the *majlis* plays an important role in conditioning the political scene. During the two presidential terms of Mohamed Khatami, the *majlis* was dominated by moderates linked to his political party, and it initiated many liberalizing laws. Most were blocked, but they set the scene for the considerable liberalization of Iranian society between 1997 and 2005. Yet a relentless conservative campaign, possible only because of the protection afforded it by the jurisconsult, wore away at public conviction that reform could really occur, thus reducing the turnout at elections, and allowed the conservatives to monitor and exclude many moderates from elective office. The result of both factors has been that the 2004 legislative elections brought in a wave of conservative *majlis* members, as a preparation for the election of a conservative president a year later.

In fact, as mentioned above, this formal democratic system is only half the government equation, for it is overseen by the parallel and dominant structure headed by the supreme leader—the *faqih* or jurisconsult. This post was created for himself by Ayatollah Khomeini, who designed the parallel system. It is now occupied by Ayatollah Ali Khamane'i. His role is to survey and monitor the governmental process to ensure that it is in accordance with Islamic constitutional principle—the famous *velayat al-faqih* ("guidance of the jurisconsult"). He has three councils to assist him in this process.

- The first, which was part of the original Islamic constitution, is the Council of Guardians (*Shora-e Nejahban*). Its role is to monitor all legislation passed by the *majlis* and ensure that it conforms with Islamic precept. It thus acts as an upper house of the parliamentary side of the constitutional system and enjoys the advantage of being, in effect, an actual legislative body, whereas the *majlis* itself is purely consultative and advisory. The Council of Guardians must also monitor and approve all persons who wish to stand for elective office. It thus stands as guardian of the constitution's requirement that politicians be of recognizable Islamic character. It is indirectly elected: three of the six members are sanctioned by the *majlis,* and three are appointed by the supreme leader.
- The second, the Council of Expediency (*Majma-eTashkhis-e Maslehat-e Nazan*), was created by Ayatollah Khomeini at the end of his life and reflects his realization that the interests of the state have priority over all other considerations—a principle that appears to run directly counter to

his fundamental belief in the primordial role of *shari'a* law in determining the operation of the Islamic republic. The opposites are reconciled by the dictum, "My people will never agree upon an error," which is one of the *hadith* (traditions) of the dicta of the Prophet Muhammad. Its members are appointed by the supreme leader, and its major task is to adjudicate between the Council of Guardians and the *majlis* should they find themselves in chronic disagreement. It is headed by the former president, Ali Akbar Hashemi Rafsanjani.

- Article 176 of Iran's constitution establishes the Supreme National Security Council and charges it with "preserving the Islamic Revolution, territorial integrity, and national sovereignty." Today the Supreme National Security Council is headed by the supreme leader's direct representative, Hassan Rowhani, a cleric with a long and very close personal relationship to Ali Khamane'i. With responsibility for maintaining Iran's security, Rowhani's main public role has been as chief negotiator with Europe and the United States over Iran's desire to have a nuclear research program—it claims for the development of peaceful uses of nuclear energy, but others suspect for military purposes. Since 1997 Rowhani's position has strengthened considerably within the shadow structure of government, and he now is involved at all levels of decision making. Outside government control and with its own sources of funding (through private companies jointly held with members of the bazaar), the Supreme National Security Council formally includes key officeholders such as the president, the ministers of foreign affairs, interior, and intelligence; and the commanders of the Islamic Revolutionary Guard Corps (the *Sepah* or *Pasdaran*) and the regular military (the *Artesh*). However, in a consolidation of conservative power inspired by a desire to restrict President Khatami after his election in 1997, the council has increasingly focused power in its special committees dominated by hard-line clerics and the leadership of the Islamic Revolutionary Guards. After the election of President Ahmadinejad in mid-2005, the Supreme National Security Council now provides a forum in which the conservatives who dominate the democratic side of the government now find their natural allies among the conservative clerics around the supreme leader, the jurisconsult.

The Supreme Leader: Military, Judicial, and Security Power

In short, the political system has been rendered even more complex by the fact that certain functions that should normally belong to the presidency are now reserved to the supreme leader, who is elected for life by the Assembly of Experts (the *Majles-e Khebregan*), an eighty-six-member, directly elected body that exists solely for this purpose and which is the only body that can remove him from office. As a result, the supreme leader's office (the *Daftar-i Imam*) has become a key and parallel element of government outside the control of the president, even if ministers also exist to carry out these functions as well. Its branches tend to parallel the administrative and security functions of government, just as the Communist Party in the former Soviet Union used to do before 1989 and the end of the cold war. His office thus conducts oversight and acts as a court of last resort, a position that provides it with opportunities to apply arbitrary and unaccountable power against the accountable actions of the parliamentary components of the system.

Thus, control of the armed forces, the judiciary, and the security system ultimately resides with the supreme leader, not the cabinet or the president. The supreme leader also controls the two great foundations, the *Bonyad Shaheed* (the Martyrs Foundation) and the *Bonyad Moztazafin* (the Destitutes Foundation), that manage the abandoned properties of the Shah and of other Iranians who fled the revolution after 1979. He thus directly controls 80 percent of Iran's non-oil economy, as well as its security organs. The ministers involved therefore only have executive functions under the supervision of both the president and the supreme leader, and the supreme leader plays the dominant role.

The key arena of control, perhaps, is the supreme leader's control of the security organs the *Sepah* and the *Etalaat*. Linked to the *Sepah* are the police service, the *baseej*—a paramilitary levy that was originally used during the Iran-Iraq War to increase the size of the Iranian armed forces through provincial recruitment (the provinces were responsible for raising, victualling, equipping, and paying these levies)—and the informal but very powerful *hizbollahi*. Both groups, which are essentially informal in terms of their locus within government, are part of the so-called parallel institutions that have now become the core of the unaccountable, repressive arm of the state.[6] They run intelligence services and prisons that lie outside the formal structures of the state. It is crucial that, apart from formal control of the police and the ministry of intelligence and security, the presidential arm of government does not exercise direct control over any part of the security system.

The extraordinary complexity of constitutional government in Iran, which is paralleled by the security system—for the *Sepah* and the Iranian armed forces, the *Artesh,* although they ostensibly cooperate are in reality fundamentally opposed to each other—reflects the fact that the Iranian revolution was never completed, largely because of the outbreak of the Iran-Iraq War in 1980, just a year after the Islamic revolution took place and only months after the clergy had asserted its political dominance. In essence, institutions, such as the army, that stem from the previous regime have been retained and serve functions similar to those they originally discharged. Alongside them have emerged new, radical, and revolutionary entities, but their areas of competence remain to be properly constitutionally defined. It is at the boundaries of these institutions, particularly in areas where they intersect, that the governmental process breaks down and can be exploited by powerful individuals.

This is particularly true of the judiciary, which is a repository of conservative values and power and now even has its own intelligence service, the

Hefazat-e Etelaat-e Ghovey-e Ghazai-e. It also runs its own prisons separate from the government-run prison service, as part of the parallel institutions—the *nahad-emovazi*—of the state. The judiciary is its arbitrary and repressive core. Iran's judicial system was profoundly reformed on May 1, 1983, four years after the Islamic revolution, by a new law introducing a court system based on Islamic *shari'a* law. Typically, the ministry of justice only administers the court system, under the authority of the Supreme Judicial Council, which appoints and dismisses judges and selects the minister of justice. The council itself is supervised by the supreme leader, Ayatollah Ali Khamane'i.

There are special courts as well that essentially deal with political offenses. The Islamic Revolutionary Courts, for example, handle only crimes threatening domestic and external security, theomachy (opposition to God), and "corruption upon earth" (*mofsed,* or Islamic lapsus). These very wide, catchall categories are extended to cover activities in opposition to the current political system that may not involve violence, as well as actions that would generally be construed as criminal, such as assassination attempts on politicians; drug dealing or smuggling; murder, detention or torture designed to restore the Pahlavi regime to power; plundering the treasury; and hoarding or overpricing.

Since 1993 judges have also combined the function of prosecutor—a feature of the judicial system that reformers around President Khatami swore to change but which continues, mainly because of the protection of the supreme leader. It also continues because it reflects the true position of a judge under traditional Islamic legal systems, which is to apportion punishment and to investigate offenses that are considered sinful, in which it is assumed that an accused person would wish to purge a sin for the sake of his immortal soul. This is the reason that confessional evidence is so readily accepted by the courts and also the reason why, until recently, legal representation was not permitted in the Revolutionary Courts. Now defendants may, in theory, have legal representation, although in practice they frequently do not. Other methods of legal proof involve evidence, testimony under oath, and the experience of the presiding judge.

It is the control of the court system by conservative elements within the regime that has been the crucial factor in ensuring their continued control over Iran's political and collective life, despite the decisions of the electorate since 1997 and the continued severe restrictions on basic human rights. This control of the courts has been articulated through the security services, which the conservatives also control and which, because they are themselves controlled through the supreme leader's own office rather than through the government, have become the major instruments for the repression of personal freedoms.

Hizbollahi Counters Reform

Law alone, of course, is inadequate either to protect or abuse the rights of the population; for this the state must be able to exert power and create domestic security. Quite apart from the police force or the gendarmerie, which are organized centrally for the country and integrated into wider security institutions, the two major components of the security system are the informal and unofficial *Ansar-i Hizbollah,* which is linked to the Law Enforcement Forces, the *Entezami.* The *Entezami* comprise the *Sepah* and the security service, the *Etalaat.*

The term *hizbollah* is used in two senses in Islamic Iran, for it identifies both a state of mind and a specific organization. As a state of mind, it reflects the commitment of individuals to the underlying, conservative Islamic principles upon which the Islamic republic is based. Politically this implies a rejection of moderate and liberal positions for support in principle for the role of the *mullahs* within the regime, although it does not necessarily mean that the abuses of the regime are endorsed.

The *hizbollahi* or, more correctly, the *Ansar-i Hizbollah*—the companions of the Party of God—was an apparently spontaneous movement that emerged in the revolution in 1978–1979. It was financed by the *bazaari,* the traditional merchant class in major cities, which was also the major financial support base of the revolution and of the clerics' role in leading it. In the aftermath of the revolution in 1979, the *hizbollah* became the shock troops of the revolution, providing cadres to the *Sepah* and an executive arm to the *komitehs,* the revolutionary administrative committees that spontaneously emerged in every municipality and became the main enforcers of the new public morality that the Islamic revolutionary regime introduced. They continued to act in this capacity throughout the Khomeini period, but under President Rafsanjani in the 1990s their activities were curbed when the *komiteh* system was repressed, so that they made an appearance only at moments of public tension to reassert the interests of the conservative factions within the clerical regime.

Since 1997 that role has been enhanced, as the struggle between reformers and conservatives intensified. There are believed to be covert links between the informal *hizbollahi* leadership and conservative strongholds within the judiciary and the *Sepah,* such that, when the *hizbollahi* intervene to break up meetings and demonstrations, as members of a parallel institution they enjoy immunity from arrest or even interference by the normal forces of law and order. The movement also enjoys the protection of the Office of the Supreme Leader, who controls the security forces and religious institutions. Thus the *Ansar Hizbollah* is, in a very real sense, a reflection of the core attitudes of the Islamic regime in Iran, whatever reformers around President Khatami may have sought to achieve.

The essence of *hizbollahi* behavior is that its members are unaccountable. Evidence of this emerged in July 1999 when the *hizbollah* were deployed to counter a peaceful student demonstration in favor of the freedom of the press. The demonstrations were turned into scenes of mass violence by the behavior of the *hizbollah,* who enjoyed protection from the police and the *Pasadaran.* In June 2003 student protests against the privatization of the university system spilled over into popular demonstrations against the regime. The *hisbollahi* were initially unleashed on the demonstrators, until international protest at their behavior, particularly from the United States, forced the authorities to arrest some of their leaders—the first time that has ever happened. Those arrested were soon released without charge, however, which is hardly surprising given their very powerful clerical backing.

A political system of this type, whose political and administrative processes are extremely complex, with authority and power split between elected and appointed authorities, and in which the elected bodies are subservient to the appointed bodies, is both opaque and easily corrupted. It also has immense potential to act repressively because accountability is so diffuse and ideological justification is so accessible. Public officials, such as provincial governors, may well be appointed by the government, but they are also answerable to the supreme leader. Even here, of course, corruption is also rife, as the fate of the mayor of Teheran, Ghollamhossein Karbashi, in 1998 made clear. His arrest and imprisonment for corruption were the first steps in a conservative campaign to recover control of power after the overwhelming popular victory of the moderates in the 1997 presidential elections. This was soon followed by a sustained campaign against the free press in Iran, which still continues. More than eighty newspapers and journals have been banned since 1997.

The effective hegemony of the *mullahs* over the political process is also paramount, with the result that access to clerical support is far more important than the rule of law, since religious prestige and power guarantee protection. There is virtually no redress against the abuse of power, and the authorities, despite the democratic safeguards in the Iranian constitution, can be and are as repressive as they wish, sanctioning their behavior by reference to Islamic precept and tradition.

INDONESIA

Unlike Morocco and Iran, Islam has not been at the forefront of the political process, in terms of determining its structure, in Indonesia until very recently. Even now that it occupies a more prominent place within political culture and social discourse, it is still not the dominant assumption behind either culture or institutions. In Iran and Morocco, after all, the vast majority of the population is Muslim, even if in Iran only 6 percent is Sunni rather than Shi'a. The uniformity of religious belief in Iran to a large extent conceals ethnic tension, for the Farsi community is only 35 percent of the total, alongside significant Azerbaijani (16 percent) and Kurd (13 percent) minorities. In Indonesia, however, some 23 percent of the population is not Muslim, most of those being Christian or Hindu. The diversity includes significant ethnic division among Javanese (36 percent), Sundanese (14 percent), Malay (9 percent), Madurese (7 percent), and Chinese and Minangkabau (4 percent each).

The political system, therefore, has had to cope with both confessional and ethnic tension. Ethnic tensions have tended to predominate, even after independence, although governance has not been able to ignore the massive Muslim majority in what is the world's most populous Muslim state. As a result, Indonesian politicians, both in the anticolonial struggle against the Dutch and since independence, have mobilized concepts of nationalism to galvanize the political system. In theory, that should have made it possible to develop a hegemonic political discourse that would straddle the ethnic and religious divides. In practice, of course, that has not always occurred, and three major transitions in Indonesia's political system have been accompanied by violent and brutal ethnic unrest. It is only in the last five years that political Islam has apparently added to the complexity of the Indonesian political scene.

Nationalism and Islam

The tacit alliance between Indonesian nationalism and Islam that has characterized the Indonesian system goes back to the beginnings of the anticolonial struggle. Three different strands of views about the future were welded together in the period from 1920 to 1945. Secular nationalists, aiming for independence, mobilized European ideas of the modern nation-state, democracy, and self-determination. Radicals close to communism sought social revolution and a socialist state. As such, they were really radical nationalists, since they concurred on the territorial state in which their radical ideas were to be applied. Muslims, on the other hand, argued for Islam as the unifying principle for the diverse ethnic and religious groups making up Indonesia, proposing an Islamic state or at least a political system involving *shari'a* law for Muslims.

Formal movements articulating these views were eventually reduced to two—the Sarekat Islam (Islamic Union), created in 1912 as a nationalist organization using Islam as the shared identifier of the Indonesian nations (few of its adherents actually sought an Islamic state), and the Communist Party of Indonesia, created in 1920 by radicals from the Sarekat Islam (which in any case split the following year, with a new group, Red Sarekat Islam, being created). An attempt at a communist-led rebellion in 1926 and 1927 led to the disappearance of the Communist Party, whose remaining supporters returned to the Sarekat Islam, giving it a permanent radical tinge. Other Muslim nationalists drifted to a nonpolitical, modernist Islamic movement that had also been created in 1912, the Muhammadiyah, which sought to create an Islamic society through education.

It was only in 1927 that a proper nationalist party emerged, the Partai Nasional Indonesia (Indonesian National Party), founded by a young nationalist, Sukarno (Indonesians often do not have first names). It sought to bring together the three strands of the early nationalist movements—nationalism, socialism, and Islam—and saw in Japanese regional resurgence a potential ally against the Dutch. The Dutch administration, perceiving the danger, outlawed the movement three years later, arresting Sukarno and exiling him. During the Japanese occupation of the Indonesian archipelago, between 1942 and 1945, the nationalists were encouraged to reform and cooperate through the Putera, an advisory board set up by the Japanese administration.

Nationalist leaders, led by Sukarno, used the Putera to regroup and strengthen their party both to dominate the growing sentiment for national liberation and to integrate the different political strands within it. Once again, Sukarno's primary aim was to incorporate all strands, as he demonstrated in the Jakarta Charter of June 1945, in which he laid out the unifying principles he proposed for a single Indonesian nation-state. This was the ideology of "Pantja Sila" ("Five Pillars"): nationalism (unity through a single nation); internationalism (a sovereign nation within a community of nations); representative democracy (so that all elements of the nation were represented); social justice (to share prosperity among all); and belief in one God. It sought to satisfy nationalists through pillars one through three, communists through pillar four, and Muslims in pillar five. Originally they had demanded specific reference to *shari'a* law for Muslims, but this was dropped so as not to offend Christians and Hindus—thereby antagonizing Muslims.

The republic declared by the nationalists in 1945 had, however, to deal with attempts by the Dutch to reimpose colonial control, in which they exploited ethnic differences, in effect creating a federal system in place of the integrated nation-state that the nationalists had sought. Although the ideal of a unitary state was revived after Dutch forces were forced to leave in 1950, the legacy of their attempt to reconstruct the colonial empire led to powerful challenges to it. Christian groups resisted integration in Ambon and South Maluku, and communists tried unsuccessfully to revive the Indonesian Communist Party. Muslims in West Java sought an Islamic state through the Darul Islam movement, an attempt that persisted in Aceh and Sulawesi until the end of the decade.

Nonetheless, despite these challenges the concept of a unitary national state around the principles of Pantja Sila (although the principles were never written into either the 1945 constitution or the 1950 amended constitution) was generally accepted despite Muslim misgivings. Political parties avoided ethnic organization, although religion proved to be an important organizing principle. Secular nationalism prevailed, with Islam and communism marginalized in the democratic parliamentary system that emerged.

However, the contradictions inherent in the Indonesian state—the three strands that had been at the roots of the nationalist debate at the start of the century and which had not been reconciled by Pantja Sila—reasserted themselves at the end of the 1950s. As early as the 1955 elections, for parliament and for a new constituent assembly to draft a definitive constitution, Pantja Sila and Islam confronted each other as alternatives for a future political system. Added to this was resentment at Javanese dominance of the political process, which combined with Islam to trigger rebellions in Aceh, Sumatra, and Sulawesi. By 1958 the army had fragmented; rebel commanders emerged and an alternative government was proclaimed.

"Guided Democracy"

The Sukarno regime responded with force and imposed a centralized government, which abandoned its democratic traditions and instituted "guided democracy" instead. That meant increasingly personalized rule by President Sukarno in alliance with the Indonesian army. After 1960 Sukarno also turned to the revived Communist Party. But within five years the army had turned on both Sukarno and the Partai Kommunis Indonesia. Hundreds of thousands died in the resulting struggle, the Communist Party was banned, and Sukarno was replaced by Major General Suharto.

The new regime was unabashedly based on the army, which now had a formal role in preserving the integrity of the state from both external and internal threats. The unitary state was confirmed, "guided democracy" formalized, and Pantja Sila installed as the ideology of the new order. The administration was centralized and strengthened, political life was restricted, and the political parties were reformulated by the regime. Political Islam was marginalized and ethnic groups favored by the previous regime, such as the Chinese, were targeted. The driving ambition of the new order became development.

Despite secessionist movements in Aceh, and later in Irian Jaya and East Timor, the new order proved to be a stable base for development, although patronage, the political role of the army, and the process of depoliticization encouraged widespread corruption and the development of crony capitalism. The system was also dependent on the person of the president, and the uncertainty engendered by his age encouraged instability. These factors combined with the 1997 Asian financial crisis and the growing rejection of centralized control by the periphery to provoke, first, widespread ethnic violence and, second, a change of political system, when the army failed to stem the chaos and the president was forced to resign in May 1998, just months after he had been reelected.

The new political regime that has emerged in the past decade has been characterized, strangely enough, by continuity. The army has been removed from political life, and there is now a vibrant, multiparty democracy in which, although now unstated, the principles of Pantja Sila continue to be influential. Ethnic violence has largely been dissipated by acceptance of secession where necessary and greater autonomy elsewhere, although tensions persist in Aceh and Irian Jaya. The temptation to install an Islamic state by reviving the Jakarta Charter was resisted in 2002, although the political role of Islam remains an acute issue and violent extremist groups, linked to the *salafi-jihadi* movement, have emerged.

The three strands of Indonesian nationalism are now reduced to two with the global disappearance of the socialist alternative. Secular nationalism, favoring a unitary state, and political Islam seeking the creation of an Islamic state continue to exercise their fascination in Indonesia. Yet they and the associated traditions of ethnic separatism and conflict seem to have been largely diffused within a multiparty democratic tradition. This, ironically enough, since it formed part of the original independent Indonesian state, seems to have provided a sufficiently elastic framework to contain these tensions and to offer hope that the violent transitions of the past will not be repeated.

Suggestions for Additional Reading

Ansari, A. *The History of Modern Iran 1921: The Pahlavis and After.* London: Longman, Pearson Education, 2003.

_____. *Iran, Islam and Democracy: The Politics of Managing Change.* London: Royal Institute of International Affairs, 2004.

Bertrand, J. *Nationalism and Ethnic Conflict in Indonesia.* Cambridge: Cambridge University Press, 2004.

Bowie, A., and D. Unger. *The Politics of Open Economies.* Cambridge: Cambridge University Press, 1997.

Coulson, N. J. *A History of Islamic Law.* Edinburgh: Edinburgh University Press, 1964.

Geertz, C. *Islam Observed: Religious Development in Morocco and Indonesia.* Chicago: University of Chicago Press, 1968.

Lambton, A. K. S. *State and Government in Medieval Islam: An Introduction to the Study of Islamic Political Theory—The Jurists.* New York: Oxford University Press, 1981.

Mawerdi, A. H. A. Trans. E. Fagnan. *Les statuts gouvernementaux.* Paris: Editions le Sycamore, 1982.

Pennell, C. R. *Morocco since 1830.* London: Hurst, 2003.

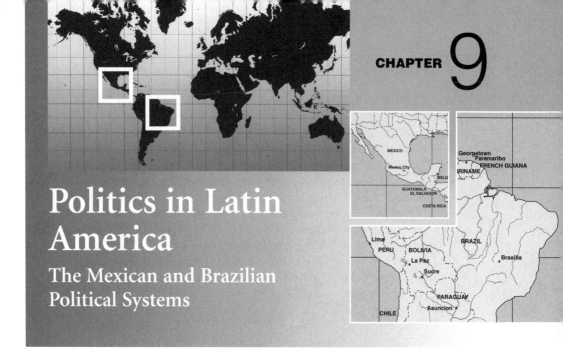

CHAPTER 9

Politics in Latin America

The Mexican and Brazilian Political Systems

At a time when so much of the attention of Europe and the United States is focused on Asia and the Middle East, one should not forget Latin America. Like the United States and Canada, Latin America is very much part of the westward extension of the European world into the Americas. The nation-state idea and democratic norms are embedded in its politics. As in the United States, questions of nation and state were for the most part decided long ago, but in Latin America the struggles to sustain democratic regimes and economic growth have been less successful as well as very different from country to country. Major differences are to be found in size, ethnicity, experience with political and economic reforms, and proximity to the United States. For example, Brazil is larger than the continental United States, whereas El Salvador, in Central America, is one of the smallest republics. Southern-Cone Argentina is an immigrant society, most of whose inhabitants are European in origin, whereas Guatemala is essentially a mestizo (*ladino*) an indigenous (Maya) nation, and Haiti, in the Caribbean, is predominantly Afro-American. Costa Rica, in Central America, has long been a consolidated democracy, but the Andean republic of Bolivia has had the most frequent changes in government and regime of any country in the region. Chile, on the southwest coast of South America, has been the most successful in installing and sustaining market reforms, while Ecuador, to the north, continues to suffer from endemic economic and political crises.

In contrast to the South American republics, many of which are far removed from direct U.S. influence, Mexico, with its 105 million inhabitants, shares a long border with the United States and is today thoroughly incorporated into the dynamics of North America. In this new world in the making, the United States, Mexico, and Canada are now joined together in what has become a complex transborder economy, continental in nature and characterized by enormous human dislocation, as millions of people move across the region despite political demarcations separating the three countries. It is here that our discussion will be centered, juxtaposed with Brazil, which is the core of an alternative attempt to structure a very different kind of regional market in South America. Through examination of these two country cases, the reader can become more sensitive to shifts in the global economy and society, which are the subject of the final chapter of this book, and enabled to understand that the developing world, with all its problems of poverty and social and political upheaval, is for Americans no farther removed than the frontier extending from Texas through the U.S. Southwest to California.

MEXICO

Of the developing countries, the closest and most important to the United States is Mexico. The two-thousand-mile common frontier extending across the southwestern United States is the source of this contact. It was never an effective barrier, and today the affairs of the United States and Mexico are becoming more intertwined than ever. Already to the north, where the border between the United States and Canada is even longer, trade barriers have been reduced, and there is an increasing flow of population, goods, and services between the two countries that defies all attempts to separate the two nations. But although the close Canadian-U.S. relationship is not without its tensions and conflicts, the economic disparities are far less between those countries and Mexico. Given these realities, it should surprise no one that the move to broaden the economic convergence to include Mexico in a larger economic arrangement called the North American Free Trade Agreement (NAFTA) has engendered enormous controversy and uncertainty. To the south, differences in culture and levels of living are much more noticeable, for despite all its progress Mexico remains a poor country. Then, too, there is the inescapable fact that what was fully one-half of Mexican territory at its independence is now an integral part of the United States.

The image that most Americans hold of themselves is not one that easily finds a place for the fact that U.S. expansion westward in the past century entailed the conquest of the northern tier of Mexico and treatment of its Spanish-speaking population as a conquered people. Granted, the population was sparse in the nineteenth century, and far more Spanish-speaking people live in the southwestern United States today than was the case before 1848 (when the Mexican-American War ended and the territory was lost to the United States). But Mexican schoolchildren cannot study the history of their country without becoming aware that the independence of Texas in 1836 and the loss of

Mexico's northern territories to the United States were traumatic events. Today, almost two centuries later, the psychological implications of that legacy, in which one nation was the victor and the other the vanquished, are compounded by the fact that despite the Mexican Revolution of 1910, Mexico is more dependent than ever on its economic relationship with the United States.

The Mexican economic crisis of the 1980s and economic changes since, however, have marked an important shift in U.S.-Mexican relations from dependency to interdependency. In 1986, for example, a substantial part of Mexico's debt ($98 billion at the time) was owed to the private banks of one country, the United States. When economic restructuring of that debt began, it became as much a U.S. problem as a Mexican one. Likewise, although the fluctuation in oil and gas prices has had a different impact on each economy, the economic effects produced in each have had consequences for the other. The devaluation of the Mexican peso, coupled with inflationary pressures in the 1980s and major economic restructuring in the 1990s, led to severe economic dislocations and reduced job opportunities in Mexico. More recently, increased violence along the border, linked to drug trafficking, has become a problem for border communities in the United States from Texas to New Mexico and Arizona. Discussions of the social consequences of structural adjustment and market reforms in developing countries may sound theoretical, but they describe concrete realities with real consequences for the U.S. labor market and trade between the United States and Mexico. Neither can one separate from these issues the increased flow of migration northward, since the poor in Mexico and Central America—now more than ever before—see in employment in the United States, illegal or otherwise, an escape from economic hardship and unemployment at home. Not surprisingly, the free flow of labor within the developing North American market remains an issue of great sensitivity, despite all attempts to ignore it or avoid its ramifications by creating barriers between the two countries.

However one assesses this situation, one thing is certain: The U.S. and Mexican economies have become so closely interrelated that actions on either side of the border can no longer be handled as self-contained. Economic and social policy in the United States or Mexico has great impact on the other. Consequently, it has become increasingly difficult to separate internal domestic affairs—labor legislation, welfare benefits, education, interest rates, sales and services, or the drug traffic—from diplomatic relations between the two countries and from foreign policy concerns.

A major cause of the changing U.S.-Mexican relationship is economic. Since World War II, Mexico has undergone fundamental transformation, ceasing to be a rural society and becoming instead a semi-industrialized country with a rapidly growing urban population. In 1940 two-thirds of the labor force was to be found in agriculture; by 1970 that fraction had declined to a little more than one-third. Then stagnation set in, and with the devaluation of the Mexican peso in 1982, economic crisis replaced sustained growth rates of over 6 percent. During those years, on the U.S. side of the border the loss of

Mexican purchasing power not only led to a recession in the regional economy but produced an overall decline in trade with Mexico. Then in 1989, when Carlos Salinas de Gortari assumed the presidency, major structural adjustment was undertaken, with extensive privatization and reduction of controls over the private sector (domestic and foreign), all at enormous social cost.

In this respect Mexico is a microcosm of many of the patterns characteristic of the developing world. Rapid modernization; continuous change and uncertainty; and extensive social, political, and economic transformations have had a major impact on the developing world over the past forty years. The same conditions exist in Mexico in that, despite the aggregate progress being made at present, conditions of life for the majority of Mexico's citizens have shown little improvement. Regardless of an external image that frequently leads to Mexico's classification as an institutionalized elected government and as a country with increasingly democratic politics, the realities are such that "the good life" belongs to a restricted political and economic elite, whose stake in society is defended and maintained by the primacy of hierarchical relations designed to marginalize the poor.

At the same time, Mexico has unique characteristics and is an excellent example of why facile generalizations about the developing world must be followed with specific cases explaining individual political system differences. More important, its example can be used to make a more general point regarding comparative analysis; why the U.S. case has been dealt with as an integral part of this text on politics and government, at the beginning; and why, here as we approach the end, we turn to the United States' most important neighbor to the south. There is a whole body of literature that deals with what is called "American exceptionalism," that is, the viewpoint that the U.S. experience is so different from that of the rest of the world that it must be dealt with apart and on its own terms. There are important reasons for holding such a view. But from a wider comparative perspective, the same is true of all political systems— each has its own distinctive characteristics and experiences, which set it apart from other countries. Whereas this point has been made in the past and has been seen as relevant theoretically but not practically, the current reality of the primacy of world markets and increased interdependency among all countries, regardless of differences in levels of economic development, requires of all of us greater capacity to see how our own society fits into a larger international setting, without sacrificing our understanding of what makes it unique.

In contrast to the evolution of government and politics in the United States, the Mexican experience was for a long time authoritarian. Yet compared with the authoritarian experiences of other countries (such as Chile under General Pinochet, 1973–1990) it was never as oppressive, nor was it after 1940 a regime maintained essentially by force. Even more important, Mexico has long been a political system in transition, in which old-style mechanisms of political control have become less and less effective. Even during the era of single-party dominance under the PRI (*Partido Revolucionario Institucional*, the Institutionalized Revolutionary Party), 1940–2000, military officers did not participate in politics and were clearly subordinate to civilian authority. Elections were held regularly, and even though they frequently resembled plebiscites designed to ratify the choices of the dominant party, an elaborate and complex process of internal ratification and consultation for many years fulfilled the function of legitimizing the selections made for major sectors of Mexican society. Also, every six years there was sufficient turnover in appointed and elected officials to ensure that no single clique could continue to dominate national politics to its own exclusive advantage beyond the six years of rule accorded to each president, since no president may serve a second term. Finally, there was sufficient differentiation between political and economic elites, and competition within and between each of these groups, to ensure that no single, coherent power structure could sustain control. In a very real sense, Mexican government became the domain of the middle sectors of society after World War II.

For many years there was a debate over whether Mexico was a quasi-democratic system or a quasi-authoritarian one. All this is now clearer in hindsight. The first wave of liberalizing reforms in Mexico was administrative. These began in 1980, during the government of Miguel de la Madrid, with the creation of a National System of Fiscal Coordination (SNCF) and were followed by constitutional reform in 1983 designed to strengthen municipalities. But political liberalization *per se* did not begin until the administration of Ernesto Zedillo (1994–2000), when more meaningful, competitive elections began to be held and the national government lessened its controls over state and local governments. Relaxation of political controls over local elections was followed by more competitive elections for the congress, until in 2000 Vicente Fox, the candidate of the opposition PAN (*Partido de Acción Nacional,* the Party for National Action), was elected president, ending the hegemony of the PRI with its control of the presidency.

Constitutional Development

The first step in understanding Mexico and how its constitution differs from those of the United States and Europe is to become familiar with its basic constitutional document: the constitution of 1917. The embodiment of ideals coming out of the Revolution of 1910, this constitution is first and foremost a statement of Mexican nationalism. It clearly establishes control over the country's natural resources and promises land to the peasantry. Equally important is its defense of effective suffrage for all and rejection of reelection of officials to executive offices. These were the slogans with which Francisco Madero initiated the revolt against the dictator Porfirio Diaz in 1910. In addition, there are provisions for advanced social legislation, demonstrating a concern for the masses that comes out of the popular social movements that swept across Mexico after the initial political revolt. The document also contains principles that have become an accepted part of U.S. constitutionalism: guarantees of political freedoms and liberties, federalism, separation of powers, and a bicameral national legislature.

In many respects, the Mexican constitution states political values and principles that have come out of Western experience in general and the United
States in particular. Yet it is also different and illustrative of how constitutionalism outside Western Europe and the United States reflects fundamentally different experiences. The Mexican constitution is above all a statement of political and social ideals, not political and social accomplishments, brought into
existence by the revolution and guaranteed uniformly to all Mexican citizens.
In this regard it reflects a different set of philosophical premises and a way of
thinking about the state that is common to Iberia and Latin America. Such
political traditions emphasize the importance of writing into the nation's basic
charter the *desiderata* of advanced political and social thinking and leaving to
future generations the responsibility for implementing those ideals through
legislation. These traditions also embody two assumptions alien to U.S. experience: (1) Government should take an active role in the nation's political,
social, and economic life; and (2) the constitutional document should spell out
governmental goals, as well as establish the political and administrative institutions to carry them out. As a consequence, constitutions such as the Mexican
are frequently hybrid documents that seek to embody the framers' view of
what is best from universal experience with national grievances and expectations developed out of the prevailing political context. In this century, that has
come to mean as much attention to socialist precepts (taken from Marxist
experience and emphasizing collective rights) as capitalist ones (coming out of
Western experience and designed to guarantee individual rights of life, liberty,
and property).

In contrast to Anglo-American constitutionalism, Ibero-American constitutionalism emphasizes the value that when individual and collective interests
come into conflict, the interests of the community, as defined by the state, take
precedence over individual rights and liberties. Thus, for example, when the
constitutionally elected government of Lopez Portillo chose to nationalize all
private Mexican banks in 1982 before it turned over power to the incoming
Miguel de la Madrid administration, it was acting fully within the norms and
expectations of Mexican constitutionalism. Mexican nationals may well have
questioned the wisdom of this action and attacked the government for the arbi-
trariness with which it implemented its decision, but the legality of the action
could not be challenged, as it certainly would have been if such an occasion
were to arise under U.S. constitutionalism. An important difference in these two
variants of constitutionalism can be seen by contrasting that action with the
U.S. Supreme Court's action in 1946 when it found unconstitutional President
Truman's decision to intervene forcefully in a steel strike and send in federal
troops. The Mexican supreme court has no comparable right to declare actions
of the president illegal. At the same time, the Mexican constitution does make
provision for what is known as the writ of *amparo*, whereby individuals may
seek redress in the nation's courts when individual rights and liberties have
been violated by arbitrary state action. (Incidentally, in the case just cited, a
political solution was worked out later, in the administration of Carlos Salinas

de Gortari [1988–1994], through economic reforms linked to privatization of state-owned enterprise.)

One of the most salient examples of the gap between constitutional ideals and political realities in Mexican experience is to be found in the practice of federalism and the separation of powers. The constitution of 1917 is definitely a federalist document, with a strong commitment to the separation of powers. Yet the realities of Mexican political life were such that for generations there was a high degree of centralism, to such an extent that the Mexican political system really functioned as a unitary form of government under executive supremacy. State governments had little or no autonomy. Of course, all of that has now changed. But what is important to understand is that it was accomplished within the existing constitution and occurred within the framework of respect for the rule of law which, while different from that in the United States, permitted change to take place without rupturing the basic institutional framework established for Mexican governance.

Like the United States, Mexico has a bicameral legislature and a separate court system, but neither served effectively as a constraint on presidential power for many years. Now that Mexico has a congress that is no longer under the control of a single party that also controlled the presidency, that has begun to change. Because this is a new experience in Mexico, it should surprise no one that it has created turbulence in Mexican political life. The idea of a president lobbying individual members of congress to gain support for his programs has been very difficult for many people to understand. For example, in the past it was always assumed that the required approval by congress for the president's absence from the country, prior to his departure, would be granted automatically. But when Fox proposed a trip to the United States at one point during his administration, without first making certain that he had the goodwill of his legislative colleagues, he had the unpleasant surprise of seeing that request turned down and then having to explain to his U.S. counterpart that he did not have the authorization necessary to leave the country.

For all the difficulties and reforms that Mexico has undergone over the last decade—and that includes the increase of violence along the U.S.-Mexico border—one fact stands out: the stability of the system. This sets Mexico apart from many of countries elsewhere in Latin America as well as developing countries outside the Western Hemisphere. There can be no doubt about the existence in Mexico of a common body of rules regulating politics and succession in government. There is a fixed set of government institutions designed to process conflict, make economic policy, and implement social policy. Since no president may succeed himself, every six years a new governing team takes over. Accompanying these changes is considerable turnover of public officeholders, which ensures that an incoming president will be able to manage his own programs and to staff senior positions in the administration with individuals who can be entrusted to carry out those policies to which he is committed.

If this is the case, then how does one account for the difficulties encountered during the Fox administration in making this system work under a non-PRI administration? That remains a contested issue, with some questioning the competency of those nominated and others questioning Fox's judgment in not appointing more individuals identified with those who elected him. The answer lies, however, in the novelty of competitive party politics and the need to structure a governing team that can work behind the scenes to accomplish the president's agenda, while also working to sustain the president's image as an effective leader.

Social Forces

In the building of modern Mexico the revolution marks a fundamental dividing line. Before 1910 Mexico was a society fragmented along class, ethnic, and regional lines. Rather than a single nation, it was a series of self-contained communities. The social structure consisted of a small upper sector that identified itself closely with Hispanic values, many of whose members prided themselves on their Spanish heritage. In the larger society, where by far the majority of the population was mestizo or Indian, the *gachupín* (the hispanophile) was seen as the most visible part of a generally disliked, privileged minority. Whether of the upper or lower sector, individuals identified themselves predominantly with their region of origin and, within the individual states into which the Mexican federation was divided, with the local community above all else. In such a context Mexico was an amalgamation of *patrias chicas,* "little countries." Few people before 1910 readily identified themselves with the larger political unit we know as Mexico.

The Revolution of 1910 changed that dramatically. Social, ethnic, and regional differences continue to exist, but a larger sense of national identity has emerged within which people take real pride in identifying their Mexicanness (their *mejicanidad*). A core concept linked to this sense of nationhood is the perception of Mexico as a mestizo culture, an amalgam in which European and Indian influences have become fused into a new and distinctive national culture. Whereas before the revolution Mexico's Indian past was generally looked down on by elite groups, postrevolutionary Mexicans take pride in cultivating an awareness of the nation's Indian past. With this self-discovery and consciousness of the creativity of its popular culture has come a flowering of the arts—in painting (especially murals), dance, music, architecture, and literature.

In this setting, poverty continues unabated in rural and urban areas without creating the conditions for mass protest. That does not mean that protest movements have not occurred or that there is an absence of strikes and demonstrations. On the contrary, state politics in Mexico has often been turbulent. Urban protest movements, strikes, and demonstrations have also taken place from time to time, as when violence broke out in Mexico City in 1968 at the time of the Olympic Games. But those events have remained confined to the immediate arena where protest has emerged, without becoming national in scope. Furthermore, political authorities have always responded to these occurrences with a great deal of effectiveness, either by a show of force, by accommodation, or by a combination of the two.

At the national level, in plotting the course of presidential leadership from 1929 to 1999, one can identify movement back and forth from one administration to the next, between progressive policies designed to respond to mass needs and conservative ones intended to maintain order, stability, and a favorable climate for economic development. For example, one can single out the administrations of Lázaro Cárdenas (1934–1940), Lopez Mateos (1958–1964), and Luis Echeverría (1970–1976) as progressive in their appeal to nationalism, improved social conditions for the masses, and flexible wage policies. Offsetting them are the administrations of Calles (1929–1933), Miguel Alemán (1946–1952), and Diaz Ordaz (1964–1970), which were much more conservative in character and given to assertions of state authority.

There are also administrations whose actions have been decidedly mixed and oriented to the political center—for example, those of Avila Camacho (1940–1946), Ruiz Cortinez (1952–1958), and Lopez Portillo (1976–1982). Whether or not the earlier pattern of contrasting administrations has been changing since the crisis of 1982 remains to be seen, for one can argue that Miguel de la Madrid (1982–1988) and Carlos Salinas de Gortari (1988–1994) preferred this alternative pattern and used it to undertake a fundamental transformation of the system. This is especially the case with Salinas, given his extensive reforms, beginning with a significant privatization initiative and extending through the opening up of Mexico to foreign investors and an accommodation with the church.

Whatever the way one interprets presidential behavior, two facts stand out. First, Mexican presidential leadership has shown a great capacity over the years to respond to changing conditions in Mexico and to guide the country in new directions when shifts in the country's national and internal context have required adjustments. Second, when one moves beyond the national level to the states, one can identify wide variation in the response of the political leadership to regional, social, and economic conditions.

In this regard Mexico remains today, as in the past, a society divided between privileged sectors (comprising at present approximately one-third of the population) and those who, because of their poverty, do not participate actively in national life politically or economically (about half). Yet this is far from a static society, for the whole postwar era is marked by tremendous social and economic change. The most notable shifts in the distribution of Mexico's social forces have come in the expansion of the middle sectors of society. Although the figures vary greatly, most counts indicate a doubling of the size of the middle-income group since the 1940s.

As Mexico has shifted from a rural to an urban society, a corresponding increase in population has occurred. Whereas in 1900, 70 percent of the population lived in communities of fewer than 2,500, by 1970 the proportion had dropped to around 40 percent. What had been a population of 19 million in 1940 had become an estimated 92 million in 1990, as Mexico has ceased to be an economy based on agriculture and the extraction of raw materials and has become increasingly industrialized. From the 1940s through the 1970s, economic growth was centered on an import substitution model of economic development. And even though economic growth slowed in the 1970s, from more than 6 percent per annum to around 3 percent, the oil boom—both internationally and in the expansion of national production—contributed to a continued positive image at home and abroad regarding Mexico's growth potential.

The economic crisis of 1982 had its most immediate impact on the urban middle sectors, those people in Mexican society who had been the primary beneficiaries of the economic growth of the previous forty years. In political terms the rapid deterioration of economic conditions, which led to frequent devaluations and eventually a floating peso exchange rate and acute internal inflation, cut directly into two of the three major social sectors on which the PRI was based: labor and the "popular" or middle-income strata of Mexican society. During the 1980s, however, what was notable about this crisis, in comparative perspective, was the stability of the Mexican system and the way in which government went about responding.

In contrast to the turbulence that has accompanied major economic and political adjustments elsewhere in the developing world and in the postcommunist states, the government's ability to inaugurate major policy change through revamping its presidential teams each six years and to implement economic and social policy stands out. The nationalization of private Mexican banks and the imposition of strict exchange controls in 1982 by the Lopez Portillo government, shortly before the transfer of power to the new Miguel de la Madrid administration, permitted the government to establish immediate and direct control over internal and external markets in areas where it was most vulnerable to fluctuation: the flight of domestic capital and Mexican private-sector indebtedness. Such action was taken in the name of Mexican nationalism, and although attacked by the domestic and foreign business communities, it generally received wide popular support in Mexico. The accompanying shift to the de la Madrid administration and the inauguration of a much more conservative set of economic policies removed the incoming government from responsibility for the previous government's actions and permitted it to negotiate a new set of international accords with the International Monetary Fund (IMF) and the private U.S. banks to which the loans were mainly owed. When foreign banks and businesses questioned the propriety of the bank nationalizations, the new administration explained that conditions—in terms of both the inability of the Mexican private sector to meet its external obligations and Mexican nationalism—were such as to preclude the banks' return to private ownership.

Equally important was the acceptance by urban labor and the middle sectors of Mexican society—the groups linked most closely to the PRI's urban base—of economic austerity measures during the 1980s. Pressures were brought on the de la Madrid administration to permit wage adjustments, but the extent to which this administration was able to guarantee and enforce commitment to the IMF program is most notable. The program imposed severe constraints on the domestic economy that required an immediate reduction in domestic consumption and changes in patterns of living based on easy credit, to which union and middle-level professionals had become accustomed.

By the 1990s all this was changing, as social groups, especially new and independent interest groups in civil society, broke with the PRI and as instances of corruption and electoral fraud, especially during the Salinas de Gortari administration and afterward, became public. By 2000 this new transparency in Mexican politics meant that the PRI, too, could now be held accountable for its actions. Thus, while the PRI remained the dominant party in congress in the opposition-dominated Fox administration (2000–2006), its actions in the past, which guaranteed control of the presidency and congress, could now be openly questioned and challenged. The consequence was that the PRI was no longer hegemonic.

Interest Groups

During the years when the PRI was hegemonic, interest groups in Mexico were organized in a way very different from those in the United States and Western Europe. Although they were as numerous as in any Western country, Mexico's interest groups were much more likely to be organized and licensed by the state. Whereas interest-group pluralism is characteristic of institutionalized parliamentary and presidential democracies, and such groups enter and exit from the political process according to the issues at stake, analysts of Mexican politics for years called attention to how interest group behavior in that society was much more likely to be subject to state control and influenced by governmental action. That is no longer the case. Although there are residual instances of what is called "corporatist" behavior by PRI-affiliated organizations, Mexican interest groups today are increasingly pluralist in their actions and free of government control.

This twenty-year transition (1980–2000) from authoritarian to democratic practices can be tracked by examining interest group behavior. Although on the one hand, there was a list of officially organized interest group associations, in which membership was often required by law, groups organized and involved in politics outside the purview of the state increased in number and in voice until finally, in the elections of 2000, PRI control of Mexican politics was ended. Accompanying these political changes was Mexico's economic transition from a state-controlled to a free market economy.

During the years of PRI hegemony, when it was the official governing party, three major sectors or groups of interests served as the mechanisms for ensuring its hegemony: the peasantry, urban labor, and the middle sector of society. Each sector had formal organizational status, within which individual groups were organized on a local and regional basis; these were banded together into confederations at the national level. Accordingly, representing the interests of the peasantry within the official party was the *Confederación Nacional Campesina,* the CNC. Complementing it in the urban sector was the

Confederación Nacional de Trabajadores Mexicanos, the CTM. The third official organization, the *Confederación Nacional de Organizaciones Populares* (CNOP), embraced a wide range of middle-class groups—schoolteachers, governmental employees (municipal, state, and federal), small businessmen, small landowners, and urban neighborhood associations.

None of the three confederations represented all interests within its sector. Major segments of society, such as landless agricultural workers, nonunionized labor, and more affluent upper- and middle-income groups always remained outside the organizations. Furthermore, frequently the national confederations found it difficult to speak with a single voice because of individual, regional, and local differences on issues that affected their constituencies, such as wage policies, social security benefits, price controls, and inflation. By far the most amorphous of the three confederations was the CNOP because of the wide range of interests that needed to be represented within the middle strata of urban Mexican society. These were the sectors most directly affected by inflation and spiraling increases in the prices of consumer commodities. As major economic adjustments had to be made in Mexico during the 1980s, and the government opted for a policy of economic liberalization in advance of political liberalization, the structure through which political and interest group organizations were merged unraveled. More and more social forces organized themselves outside government and in opposition to continued PRI dominance of politics.

In contrast to the decline and disappearance of the CNOP, the CTM was able to remain a major force in the labor movement far longer and continues to be active in Mexican politics. This illustrates how divergent interests can be within the same social sector and still operate under a single umbrella organization under stable authoritarian rule, and what happens in the transition to more democratic procedures. For example, petroleum workers employed by the state-owned oil company, PEMEX, continue to enjoy a privileged status accorded no other labor group and retain their affiliation with the CTM. Also, not all labor unions necessarily fell under the CTM umbrella in the past; for example, the FSTE (the Federation of Unions for State Workers) was originally assigned to the CNOP. Others, such as unions for electrical workers and railroad workers, maintained separate and independent status and continue to operate today as independent labor organizations

The institutional history of each of the three major sectoral organizations is illustrative of the co-optive mechanisms common to corporatist interest group representation, which is a very important ingredient in stable authoritarian systems, and also of how the groups become unglued in the transition to more open, pluralist politics. The original alliance that led to the formation of a national labor organization took place outside the official party and predates its formation. In 1918 the government assisted in the formation of the first national labor organization, which was known as the CROM, the *Confederación Regional Obrera Mexicana.* Even then, the CROM played an independent role in subsequent elections—in 1924 as well as 1928. Relations with the state were not always peaceful, as was the case in the late 1920s when Luis Morones, its leader, mounted a campaign to become president. In 1936, during the Cárdenas presidency, CROM was reorganized as the CTM, and Vicente Lombardo Toledano became its president. In 1938 Cárdenas incorporated the organization into the official party, as a means of solidifying closer relations between the government and organized labor.

Consideration of organized labor in Mexico over time, even in the encapsulated history just stated, illustrates that one cannot assume that the close relationship between the state and these semiofficial sectoral organizations necessarily means manipulation and automatic acceptance of the dictates of an incumbent administration. From time to time, individual unions called strikes independently of the government's preferences. For example, the 1983 economic austerity policies of the de la Madrid administration did not automatically generate quiescent labor support for the government.

An even more dramatic instance is how economic and political liberalization affected the rural sector. For years the CNC was essentially an organization representing that portion of the peasantry that benefited most from land distribution, either through receiving small parcels of land or rights to work the land under communal arrangements, and it was key to PRI control of the rural vote. Although an estimated two million families received land over the years while Mexico was under authoritarian rule, many rural inhabitants remained outside the system, and they periodically protested the failure of the government to meet its promises of land for them. In the mid-1960s this led some of the peasants to form an independent peasant confederation, the CCI. Although the CCI eventually joined the CNC, independent organization of interest groups outside the confines of state regulation was not unknown during these years and occurred when the national government failed to respond to mass demands in one social sector or another. For the CNC, its close relationship with the government through the PRI was especially tense during the Salinas administration. As Salinas extended privatization and economic reform to embrace the countryside, the peasantry found itself increasingly at odds with the government. It pressed the CNC to take a stance more independent of Salinas administration policies designed to enhance private, commercial agriculture and to defend the rural poor's right to own the land they worked, under either individual or collective arrangements supported by the state. That did not occur, and in its abandonment of those concerns not only did the CNC become irrelevant and disappear from the political arena, but the PRI, in effect, abandoned its rural constituency.

Other important state-regulated interest associations were those organized for the business community, although they lay outside the confines of the official party. Three in particular warrant mentioning: the *Confederación de Cámaras de Comercio de México* (CONACO), the *Confederación de Cámaras de Industrias* (CONCAMIN), and the *Cámara Nacional de Industrias de Transformación* (CANACINTRA). While CONACO and CONCAMIN date back to the early years of the revolution—to 1917 and 1918, respectively—and received state support for many years, they have become increasingly autonomous in action and critical of government policies, as their interests no longer matched those of the PRI and Mexico opened up economically and politically. This is especially true of the association of industrial producers, CONCAMIN, and that for manufacturing interests, CANACINTRA. Regulation of business interests and the presence of these state-sponsored organizations should not lead one to conclude automatically that they were subservient to the state, even at the high point of the PRI's power and influence. On the contrary, the Mexican private sector constitutes a very independent and different set of interests from other groups in Mexican society, enjoying more direct and official representation. Just as there are instances of independent, rural and urban labor organizations, the same is true of business interests. Illustrative of the latter would be COPARMEX (an employers' organization), the Mexican Bankers Association, the Mexican Association of Insurance Institutions, and the Mexican Council of Businessmen, all of which today are independent organizations in what has become a pluralistic society.

Finally, the church, the military, and private commercial agricultural interests (which are much more substantial than is apparent on first examination) all make their interests known informally, effectively, and independently. Neither the church nor the military has been officially recognized as a power contender since the revolution, but no one who is knowledgeable about the Mexican scene will deny that both constitute powerful, autonomous institutional interests. Although less formalized, commercial agricultural interests (which cultivate fresh produce for the U.S. market and thereby bring in important foreign currency earnings) must be recognized as an equally influential group. Their significance becomes particularly clear when the Mexican government makes strong representations to the U.S. government about U.S. agricultural interests that lobby for restrictions on imports of Mexican produce, which competes with U.S. production.

In similar fashion, although many political analysts have underestimated the importance of the military, today the revival of rural violence, especially in the south, and violence along the border with the United States linked to drug trafficking and small arms acquisition have made the military and its interests, especially when joined with internal security concerns and police operations, an important if poorly understood actor in Mexican politics. There are also numerous church-related groups, some linked closely with the institutional church and others with independent-minded lay groups. As interest group activity by church-related associations has increased, it has coincided with a waning of the strong anticlerical stance of the state, originally identified so closely with the revolution.

Political Parties

In the past Mexico was dominated by a single official party, the PRI; today it has a competitive multiparty system. Two parties in particular have become significant forces in Mexican politics: the *Partido de Acción Nacional* (PAN) and the *Partido de la Revolución Democrática* (PRD). The PAN is the party of the right and has received strong support from the Mexican private sector and church-related groups. Generally speaking, PAN campaigns on a platform arguing for a stronger role for the private sector in the Mexican economy and against the political corruption that has become endemic in the PRI. It is in the north, the southeast (Yucatán), and the center (to the west of Mexico City, in the agricul-tural region known as the Bajío) that PAN has developed its strongest support. PAN is quite visible as an alternative party along the northern frontier, espe-cially in the states of Nuevo León (with its industrial capital of Monterrey), Chihuahua, and Baja California, where an independent-minded business com-munity has emerged. In contrast, in the Yucatán peninsula, a region where the impact of the revolution was minimal, PAN draws its support from conserva-tive social forces. In the Bajío the strength of the PAN resides in its appeal to conservative Catholic forces (those elements that supported so strongly the *cris-tero* revolt in the mid-1920s and vehemently opposed the revolution's anticler-icalism) and to the business community that is centered in the city of León, Guanajuato, but is present throughout the Bajío in cities and towns where com-mercialized agriculture is a key component of the economy.

Since the 1988 elections, the major political organization of the left has been the PRD. An amalgamation of disparate elements, it has attempted to gather groups on the left into a united front. The older organizations would be the *Partido Popular Socialista* (PPS); the *Partido Comunista Mexicano* (PCM); the *Partido Socialista Trabajador* (PST); the *Partido Mexicano de los Trabajadores* (PMT); and the *Partido Auténtico de la Revolución Mejicana* (PARM). In the 1982 election the PCM called on all left parties to form a united front, the PSUM—the Mexican United Socialist Party. Several smaller parties and factions were willing to do so, but the PPS, the PST, and the PMT opted to retain their independent organizations. In the 1988 elections, Cuauhtémoc Cárdenas was more successful in bringing together opposition groups in the center and to the left of the PRI under the banner of the *Frente Democrática Liberal* (FDN). It is out of the FDN that the PRD has emerged. While Cárdenas made an impressive showing, with 31.06 percent of the vote, and the other opposition candidate, Manuel Clouthier of the PAN, received 16.81 percent, their votes combined still did not produce a plurality. The PRI reported a victory with 50.36 percent of the vote, with Carlos Salinas Gortari as its candidate.

Up through the election of 1994, although the size of the opposition vote increased and opposition parties continue to report important gains (despite PRI-initiated attempts linked to fraud and manipulation of results), none of the parties had the capacity to displace the PRI from the centers of power. The PPS and PSUM were able to pick up support in peripheral areas disaffected with the PRI, such as the Tehuantepec isthmus in Oaxaca, and conservative opposition forces continued to grow in the north, but none of these was able to build a coalition of sufficient size and force to challenge PRI hegemony. The PPS, which was founded by the labor leader Vicente Lombardo Toledano in 1948, attempted to change that, but as the party moved into the 1980s and 1990s, it was unable to retain what little support it had. The PST and the PARM looked to disaffected PRI elements—the former identified with the 1968 political movement that led to the demonstrations in Mexico City, and the latter with retired army generals of the 1950s. Likewise, while Cuauhtémoc Cárdenas was able to build up sizable support by appealing to the PRI's traditional mass base in 1987 and 1988, and again in 1993 and 1994, the outcome was the election of the PRI's Ernesto Zedillo for the 1994–2000 *sexenio.* Despite the failure of the opposition to displace the PRI from power during those years, what is significant is the way in which opposition to the PRI continued to increase after 1988, culminating in the election of 2000 that brought the PAN candidate, Vicente Fox Quesada, into office.

Critical election theory, which, based on the work of the U.S. scholar Walter Dean Burnham has been used to explain major realignments in U.S. politics, warrants attention here. It has major explanatory power in accounting for the enormous shift in Mexican politics that took place in 2000. The contrast between 1910 Mexico and 2000 Mexico is enormous. The former regime change, in which political protests against a manipulated election triggered a mass upheaval in Mexican society, culminated in the Mexican revolution that swept away the old order. The latter was a peaceful, democratic revolution in which 64 percent of the eligible electorate voted for major change in Mexico's presidential system, and it was followed by congressional elections in 2003 that confirmed Mexico's new political pluralism.

In the presidential election Vicente Fox Quesada, the candidate of the *Alianza por Cambio* and the *Partido Acción Nacional,* was elected president with 42.5 percent of the vote, against 36.1 percent for the PRI candidate, Francisco Labastida Ochoa, and 16.6 percent for the *Alianza por México* and the PRD's candidate, Cuauhtétmoc Cárdenas Solórzano. In the congressional elections that followed in July 2003, the PRI and its allies (either in shared lists with the Greens, the *Partido Verde Ecologista de México* [PVEM], or with independent PVEM candidates) captured 241 seats in the chamber of deputies, which gave it a working majority. The PRI stood alone in the senatorial campaign, obtaining a majority of the seats, 60, to the 51 seats captured by the pro-government coalition, the *Alianza por Cambio* (PAN, with 46, and PVEM, with 5). The left coalition, the *Alianza por México,* won 17 seats (the PRD won 15, and the *Partido del Trabajo* and the *Convergencia por la Democracia* got one each).

Governmental Institutions

Like the United States, Mexico has a presidential form of government, as does the rest of Latin America except for Cuba (which continues to follow a system of government similar to those in Eastern Europe before 1989). Unlike the United States, however, one institution has reigned supreme: the presidency of the republic. While the Mexican congress historically was a secondary institution, subordinated to the wishes of the president, that began to change with the midterm elections of 1997, which produced a more pluralistic legislature with greater representation of the PRD and PAN. The 2003 midterm elections confirmed even more clearly the changes under way in Mexican politics, and the assertion of congressional autonomy and power severely hampered the ability of the president to exercise his accustomed authority.

Prior to the Fox presidency of 2000–2006, executive-centered power combined with a high degree of centralism had produced a system of government in which the federal bureaucracy had greater voice in determining public policy than has been the case in the United States. In the past the PRI's hegemonic status produced a system of governance in which most key issues in politics and questions of public policy were debated and resolved inside government, either in the executive offices of the president or the *salas* of government ministries. Only after the interested parties reached an accord within these private corridors did public discussion occur, either through the announcement of an executive decree or the introduction of the appropriate legislation in congress. Consequently, although legislation was discussed in congress and the budget had by law to be passed by the legislature, such discussion was largely symbolic and had the function of rendering public support for government decisions already arrived at.

The Fox administration faced a radical change in Mexican politics as a consequence of the new realities of political pluralism, greater transparency in government and politics, and new emphasis on the rule of law. It is not surprising that the change has produced stalemate in government and charges of presidential ineffectiveness because no one knows exactly how to operate in this new environment, in which the presidency and the congress have become coequals.

Old-style decision making has not been entirely superseded by new, more democratic procedures, however. The source of the tension between bureaucratic decision making inside government and more transparent public policy debate within congress is twofold. First, divided government, with a PAN president and a PRI-dominated legislature, has led to stalemate in the public struggle between *Los Pinos* (the Mexican White House) and congress to control legislation. Presidential prerogatives give *Los Pinos* the authority to propose policy initiatives, but congress must vote to authorize the actions proposed. Given the standoff between the two institutions, votes in congress against the president or legislative actions tying up his initiatives in committee or debate are not uncommon. Second, after an initial attempt to produce party government by naming *políticos* to head government secretariats, either *panistas* (PAN supporters) or others playing key roles in putting together a winning electoral coalition, Fox backed off and sought to gain greater clout by appointing nonpartisan professionals (*técnicos*). But this, in turn, contributed to an image of ineffectiveness and drift in pressing public issues, such as increased violence along the U.S. border, uncontrolled corruption, growing public security concerns, and inconclusive actions in economic and social policy.

Given the stalemate in public discourse between the presidency and congress, much bureaucratic decision making so prominent during the era of PRI hegemony has continued in place, especially in issues and domains that have not been subjected to public scrutiny. As a consequence, offsetting the indecisiveness of the Fox administration is a public bureaucracy at the federal level that continues with the routine processes of government and can implement economic policy. Although this governmental apparatus is cumbersome, and corrupt in some quarters, generally its economic institutions have worked well over the years under sustained *técnico* leadership. The contrast between informal and formal mechanisms for handling public policy and confusion over who is in charge are best captured by examining the budgetary process. Preparation of the budget has long been initiated within the bureaucracy, with each public organization drawing up an estimate of its individual needs for the next fiscal year. These estimates are pulled together into budget documents by sector, according to the major administrative units. These are the *secretarías* and *departamentos,* which are the equivalent of ministries in other governmental systems. Complementing these organs of the central administration are numerous commissions, public enterprises, agencies, and other public entities, which enjoy considerable autonomy; these parastatal organizations number in the thousands.

Because of the size and complexity of the government bureaucracy, beginning during the Lopez Portillo administration a separate staff unit called Programming and Budget (*Programación y Presupuesto*) was set up, independent of the finance department, to rationalize the whole process. The unit was abolished in the Salinas de Gortari administration because of the conflict engendered with the finance department and new problems in the coordination of fiscal and monetary policy. For two administrations (Lopez Portillo's and de la Madrid's) the preliminary budget document was put together in that office; today this is done in the finance department. The proposed budget then is discussed within the Presidency of the Republic (the executive offices of the president) by those closest to the chief executive. Once approved by the president, the budget document goes to congress for formal discussion and action. What is new, of course, is a more independent congress, which questions budget items and imposes some of its own priorities. The outcome has been accommodation between the two institutions. But the process does not stop there. Today, as in the past, because the official document consistently underestimates governmental expenditures, supplementary funds and reserves are set aside by the executive and allocated on the basis of individual program requests and needs as the budget year proceeds. Such procedures have several benefits. They permit the office of the president and the finance department to maintain greater control over actual expenditures, and they permit greater flexibility in funding programs according to actual needs. A problem that consistently emerges in poor countries is difficulty in forecasting governmental expenditures accurately. Two problems arise: the lack of sufficient information on which to base forecasts, and economic uncertainty because of difficulties in predicting public revenues and/or estimating expenditures in an inflationary context. Generally speaking, the whole postwar period in Latin America has been characterized by inflationary pressures. Mexico was less susceptible to acute inflation during its era of sustained economic growth, but during the 1980s it, too, suffered from acute inflation, which peaked at 157 percent in 1987 before it was brought under control in the Salinas administration (during which it ran around 12 percent). In such a context, where major economic adjustments have had to be made, budgetary flexibility along these lines becomes absolutely essential and remains in place.

These budgetary procedures and the problems that they are designed to address point to a government bureaucracy that functions differently from that of the United States. As in many other countries, although there are the usual governmental services provided by administrative agencies, what is particularly characteristic of Mexican bureaucracy is the government's central role in creating the conditions for economic growth and developing social policies to respond to and anticipate mass needs. Despite a private sector that is much stronger than in the past, commitment to economic development continues to require active intervention by the state. Salinas's commitment to privatization and the extent to which the Mexican government has engaged in reducing the size of the public sector should not, however, lead one to conclude that Mexico embarked on a radically new set of policies during that era or afterwards in the administrations of Zedillo and Fox. There have been significant economic reforms, and despite opposition from the left, principally the PRD, Mexico has continued to support the North American Free Trade Agreement. In short, the centrality of the Mexican state in determining economic and social policy has not been altered in the least and continues to provide continuity in government.

This active role over the years in developing basic industries and expanding manufacturing has led to the emergence of a host of governmental agencies, state-owned banks and financial institutions, and public enterprises, past and present. In explaining this pattern of development it is important to add that state action in these areas has not taken place to the exclusion of domestic private capital or foreign private investment; instead, it is handled on a cooperative basis. Since the Salinas administration, government economic policy has actively promoted strengthening the domestic private sector and creating conditions that will attract foreign private capital. In Mexico a major outcome of the revolution was economic nationalism and determination to see that the nation's economy would never again become dominated by foreign interests to the extent that it was during the *porfiriato* (the years preceding the revolution, when Porfirio Diaz was Mexico's dictator). Since 1940, the Mexican government has continued to maintain a policy designed to attract foreign investment, but in a context in which the Mexican state regulates, controls, and directs where such investment will take place. And, it should be added, this sustained policy of providing guarantees and opportunities for the foreign investor has attracted a great deal of U.S. capital over the years. Especially active and successful in creating opportunities and developing a business climate attractive to the investor,

domestic or foreign, as well as beneficial to the government's objective of producing real economic growth, has been the institution known as *Nacional
Financiera.*

As a consequence, Mexico today has a very large and diverse public sector in
which economic agencies and organizations constitute a major component. For
purposes of illustration, a listing of the government's major financial institutions, in addition to *Nacional Financiera,* will suffice: the Bank of Mexico, the
National Agricultural Credit Bank, the National Urban Mortgage and Public
Works Bank, the National Ejidal Credit Bank, National Warehouses, the
National Foreign Trade Bank, the National Workers and Industrial
Development Bank, and the National Bank for Cooperative Development. In
addition to those financial organizations, one should add a host of public enterprises involved directly in productive activities. Although the Salinas administration privatized many of these enterprises, organizations such as PEMEX
(which has a monopoly on the exploration and production of oil) and CONA-
SUPO (which is responsible for subsidizing basic food commodities and maintaining a national system of stores where these goods are sold at below-market
prices) remain under state control.

As in the United States, public bureaucracy in Mexico is not limited to agencies of the federal government. Complementing the federal bureaucracy are
numerous state and local government organizations. Although Mexico was for
many years a unitary republic in effect, and not a federal system when it came
to questions of political power, even at the high point of presidential power
under PRI auspices federalism did function in the administrative sphere. In that
regard, an important component of the Mexican economic and political transition, which began with the Salinas administration, has been strengthening
federalism as enshrined in the constitution and decentralization policies. This
evolution has been continuous, and its consequence today is a functioning federal system.

Thus, like the United States, Mexico today has a two-tiered administrative
and political system (federal and state), within which each state government has
a separate system of municipal organizations. Even though the states historically have been starved for funds, and many have become dependencies of the
federal government, where there is a vital regional autonomy one finds substantial amounts of program autonomy and administrative action through
autonomous state and local organizations.

Consequently, in every state one finds a parallel set of state bureaucratic
organizations replicating federal entities, as in the United States, and now state
legislatures and courts that have been empowered through the process of
decentralization. Four in particular stand out as significant in the functioning
of Mexican government: state departments of education, which have responsibility for primary education; state roads and public works departments, which
must maintain all public roads outside the federal highway system, as well as
all public buildings not included in the patrimony of the national government;
state finance departments, charged with responsibility for collecting those

taxes that belong exclusively to state government; and state departments for public security (state *direcciones de gobernacón,* which parallel the federal agency responsible for public security at the national level and which have oversight authority over local governments and jurisdiction over questions of local conflict).

As Mexican government has increased in complexity and bottlenecks have developed because of the difficulty of breaking the old pattern of the concentration of decision making and financial resources in Mexico City, there has been increased reliance on state governments to attend to state needs. But even before this became the practice in the larger and more important states, state government has long constituted a distinct policy arena in Mexico, one whose significance has frequently been overlooked because of the emphasis on the concentration of power at the center. During the 1920s and the 1930s regional *caciques* (political bosses) dominated state governorships, and this pattern continued in many states until the 1970s and 1980s. As the national government grew in size and complexity and the economy developed, important changes also took place in state government. Paralleling developments in the Mexican presidency, the offices of state governors likewise have grown in size and importance. Today regional alliances center on the individuals occupying those offices and provide crucial linkages between center and periphery in a variety of roles: as political brokers for the states they represent, as government officials responsible for the maintenance of law and order, as representatives of the national government within the periphery, and as leaders of state PRI organizations. Although these roles have changed as a consequence of opposition parties' capturing control of various states in the federation, governors nevertheless continue as important public officials and serve as focal points in subnational politics and as spokesmen for regional interests at variance with those of the federal government. One of the strengths of the move to decentralize, coupled with the rise of viable opposition parties, has been the revitalization of state and local government.

Once again, in examining the evolution of Mexican politics and administration, what stands out in the first years of the twenty-first century is the way in which federalism has been strengthened. Until the Lopez Portillo administration (1976–1982), the primacy of politics in state government meant that coordinated administrative action on a territorial basis was the exception rather than the rule. By the late 1970s, however, politics-as-usual was no longer sufficient to meet the country's developmental needs. In response to the need for greater coordination and control of economic and social policy at the subnational level, *técnicos* in the office of the president undertook reforms designed to increase the administrative responsibilities of state governors; they shifted to the state governors' jurisdiction responsibility for coordinating, on a territorial basis, the actions of various administrative agencies. To give meaning to these endeavors, grants-in-aid were introduced through which funds could be transferred to state governments from the federal government, and the governors could be given primary responsibility for coordinating such activities.

Accordingly, two new programs were introduced: *Convenios Unicos de Coordinacón* (CUC, Program-Specific Coordination Agreements) and *Programas de Inversiones Públicas para el Desarrollo Rural* (PIDER, Public Investment Programs for Rural Development). Whereas the latter programs were designed to pull together public agencies with overlapping activities affecting rural communities and to stimulate integrated rural development schemes, the former were more concerned with public works and programs involving physical construction. Complementing these activities was the creation of state committees chaired by the governors, known as *Comités Promotores del Desarrollo Socio-Económico* (COPRODE, State Action Committees for Socioeconomic Development).

These specific programs have long since come to an end, but these developments and practices once again illustrate why it is important to examine carefully the internal processes of government and politics under way in terms of continual changes and adjustments in formal and informal patterns of power, rather than focus on the failures and problems in Mexican governance. When Mexican governmental institutions are viewed from this perspective, it becomes clear that one of the great changes in Mexico has been the emergence of strengthened federalism. As a consequence, Mexico today has two distinct tiers or levels of government, with separately elected and separately appointed public officials. At the same time, there is far more reliance on the federal government in Mexico than in the United States. Nevertheless, where there is a coincidence between political demarcations and regional centers of economic and political power, one can point to the existence of a vital set of intergovernmental relationships. Such is the case with the economic and political cores of the state of Nuevo León and the city of Monterrey, as well as with Jalisco and its city of Guadalajara. Perhaps even more appropriate examples would be economically poorer states where regional ties and identifications are very strong: the states of Guanajuato and Michoacán where, in addition to their state capitals, there are networks of medium-sized cities that are viable economic entities in their own right. Equally important would be states on the periphery, such as Oaxaca and Yucatán.

For all the changes that have been going on in Mexico in state and local executive institutions, governors and mayors (*presidentes municipals*) remain the most important, and legislatures and courts are of much less significance. In this regard it should be noted that, whereas the Mexican congress is bicameral, state legislatures are unicameral. Also, given the preeminence of executive-centered institutions, administrative courts and state-controlled arbitration commissions have jurisdiction over cases that involve governmental action. Generally speaking, however, the judicial system remains the weakest and the area most in need of reform and revitalization.

Although historically they have been marginal to the political process, local governments are equally in evidence in federal and state constitutions. In principle strong legal status is given to local government, to provisions for free and autonomous municipalities. But local governments have few functions other than to administer the day-to-day affairs of the community. Replicating patterns at state and national levels, mayors are the most important local officials. Their major role is to serve as political brokers for their communities in extracting external resources from extracommunity political and administrative organs. Prevailing practice provides for a *síndico,* who is designated to look after local financial affairs and substitutes for the mayor in his absence; a *secretario,* who looks after legal affairs and attends to routine administrative activities; and several *vereadores* (council members), who generally divide among themselves responsibility for overseeing the municipality's various administrative offices.

The System in Action

Despite commitment to economic and political reforms, the rise of competitive, party politics, and the strengthening of federalism, Mexico has found it very difficult to break with its past. It continues to have enormous disparities in income. Yet, its national ideology, identified with the revolution, contributes to popular support for initiatives designed to ameliorate social conditions for urban and rural inhabitants. For many years, the PRI's identification with the rhetoric and symbolism of the revolution and its identification with Mexican nationalism gave it the essential margin of public support that enabled it to survive as the largest party, despite corruption and officials who amassed personal fortunes during their tenure in public office. All in all, while one can speculate about alternative scenarios leading to regime breakdown and the mounting of alternative governments, the experience with the Fox administration has shown that, despite the PRI's loss of the presidency in 2000 and its warring factions, it remains a vital force in national politics. The nation's economic and social problems are immense, yet within the present setting one can always discover a certain degree of realism, understanding that there are no short-term and easy solutions available and no real and viable alternatives to the priority that continues to be given to economic and political reforms. In short, so well institutionalized has the present regime become that, for all Mexico's current difficulties, accommodation among the three major parties, continuity in the midst of moderate reforms, and a reorientation of economic and social policy seem the most likely courses for the future.

BRAZIL

Whereas many Americans have a decided point of view in discussing Mexico, Brazil is largely an unknown quantity, not least because its peoples speak Portuguese, not Spanish. In South America, a continent larger than North America, more people speak Portuguese (182 million) than Spanish. Institutionally today, Brazil, the United States, and Mexico share in common that they are federal republics with presidential forms of government, based on separation of powers among the executive, congress, and the judiciary and a division of powers between national and subnational governments. Although all three make a distinction between federal and state governments, Brazil has gone the farthest in writing into its basic law, the constitution of 1988, three distinct levels of governance, each autonomous and self-governing in its own sphere of competence. Brazil has functioned under three-tiered federalism since its constitution of 1891, but its return to democratic rule in the mid-1980s, after twenty years of centralized, authoritarian rule by military-dominated governments, has brought a determination to make federalism work as a way to ensure greater governmental responsiveness to the will of the people by bringing state and local government into direct contact with the public.

Constitutional Development

What is distinctive about Brazilian governance is the primacy since colonial times of the concept of free and self-governing municipalities. Never subjected to effective central control from Lisbon, population centers established along the coast of South America became the nucleus of urban development in the Portuguese New World, and distinctive regional governments developed around them. Although the Portuguese crown did eventually assert its authority over these quasi-independent "capitancies" (*capitanias*), it was not until the Portuguese court (with the assistance of the British navy) abandoned Lisbon in 1808, rather than submit to French rule during the Napoleonic invasion of the Iberian peninsula, and relocated itself in Rio de Janeiro that centralized rule emerged in Brazil. From 1807 to 1822 Rio de Janeiro was the seat of the Portuguese empire, and in the process of creating institutions of central governance Brazil for the first time came to be governed as a single unit. As a consequence, when Brazil became independent in 1822, it faced none of the internal dissension present in Spanish America, and it emerged on the map as a single state rather than split up into a series of independent republics, as was the case with Spain's colonies in the Americas.

In 1889 Brazil ceased to function as a unitary constitutional monarchy, and its constitution of 1891, patterned after the U.S. Constitution, established a presidential federal republic. In 1930, following economic crisis engendered by the 1929 Great Depression, Brazil moved away from its governance as a decentralized, rural-based federal republic in the direction of an increasingly centralized form of rule under the leadership of Getulio Vargas. Under the constitution of 1937 it became an authoritarian regime, designated as an *Estado Novo*, replicating the shift to the right in Italy and Portugal. With the Allied victory in 1945 and the abandonment of right-wing military and civilian rule by major segments of the military and the civilian leadership, the Vargas government was replaced and a democratic regime established. The constitution of 1946 reaffirmed Brazil's commitment to representative government determined by regularly held elections, within the parameters of a presidential federal republic, but with a far stronger and more effective federal government than had been the case from 1889 until 1930.

In 1965 a military coup overthrew what had became an increasingly leftist, populist government under President João Golart. For the next twenty years Brazil was governed by a succession of military presidents chosen in controlled, indirect elections, until the opponents of authoritarian rule gained the upper hand and negotiated a return to democratic rule. The basic charter since has been the constitution of 1988, a hybrid document reaffirming the country's commitment to a presidential federal republic, but with enhanced revenues set aside for state and local governments to ensure their viability and effectiveness. This document differs from the U.S. Constitution in its incorporation of social policy commitments taken from continental European experience and its strong affirmation of individual rights and liberties, which are at the core of the document rather than embodied in amendments. Whereas the Mexican constitution of 1917, in its implementation, has always been weak in its ability to establish a strong and independent judiciary, the Brazilian constitution sets forth clear-cut parameters for the rule of law at the federal, state, and local levels. A civil law system patterned after Continental jurisprudence also permits the use of judicial precedents taken from U.S. constitutional experience in defining the powers of the federal government and how intergovernmental relations will function if there is conflict among federal, state, and local authorities. Unlike the Mexican constitution, the Brazilian constitution also makes provision for bicameralism at the state as well as the national level.

Social Forces

The most important point to be made about social forces in Brazil is the close linkage between social protest against authoritarian rule and the increasing intensity of opposition to authoritarianism in the early 1970s, which mobilized virtually all sectors of Brazilian society, urban and rural. This movement culminated in a negotiated transition back to representative democracy and was followed by popular consultations regarding the form of democratic rule and the selection of representatives for a constituent assembly. Whereas the constitution of 1946 was the consequence of the mobilization of civilian and military middle-sector leadership in urban society, the protest movements throughout the 1970s and into the 1980s involved all sectors of Brazilian society in the repudiation of authoritarian rule.

During the era of protest hundreds, if not thousands, of social and political action groups organized themselves at the grassroots level throughout the country. There were essentially three strands in this massive and spontaneous organization of civil society: human rights protests in urban areas against repressive authoritarian rule and violations of individual rights and liberties; the rural movement on behalf of the landless, at the state level, in a coalition of popular and church-based organizations; and massive protests (once the military agreed to disengage from power on the condition of indirect election of the president and military amnesties) demanding direct elections immediately (*as direitas já*). Issues such as the right to vote, basic human rights, social justice, and land redistribution galvanized people throughout the country.

A plebiscite on popular preferences for the form of democratic rule—constitutional monarchy, presidentialism, or parliamentarism—resulted in an overwhelming majority for a presidential system of government. Once it and the constituent assembly were in place, people joined a multitude of citizen-based initiatives advocating women's rights, health care, disability legislation, land distribution, environmental protection, the rights of indigenous peoples, direct government at the local level, and participatory budgeting in local governments. Social protest lessened in time, but what has remained a fact of social life is a mobilized public who want to vote, desire social policies improving the human condition, demand governmental attention to basic human necessities for all, and call for honesty and direct involvement of citizens in government.

Interest Groups

By the late 1990s, with the waning of popular movements on behalf of democratic initiatives and basic human rights, those groups that survived did so by becoming more formal organizations in civil society. In this regard, foreign support from a host of foundations and foreign government technical assistance played a crucial role. The difficult moments have come since, as financial support from abroad has declined and interest groups advocating about social issues have had to find financial resources and volunteers from within. Even though this has not been an easy transition, Brazil has entered the twenty-first century with solid and diverse interest group representation. In consequence, today Brazil has become a mass-based democracy, in which support for authoritarian solutions to national problems, on the right or the left, has virtually disappeared. This can best be seen in the 2005 corruption scandal, which has weakened the presidency of Luis Inácio "Lula" da Silva (2002–2006). This is the first instance in national history when a candidate of the left has been able to take power by popular mandate and constitute a viable center-left government. Even though the president's authority has been damaged, there have been no serious calls for his impeachment, as occurred with Fernando Collor de Mello, nor have there been popular protests or a destabilization of financial markets.

Every sector of Brazilian society has its advocates, ranging from labor unions to human rights activists to environmental groups, as well as defenders of Indian rights, probusiness organizations, and military and police associations, not to mention firefighters' and other groups, such as civic associations working at the local level. Likewise, for the first time, there is also burgeoning interest in philanthropy and a realization among the well-to-do of the benefits to be gained for themselves in supporting social causes.

Political Parties

Since the 1940s Brazil has had a fluid multiparty system without much continuity from one regime to another. The First Republic (1891–1930) was largely a decentralized single-party regime of state-based Republican Parties that vied for control of the presidency. In those years, two states dominated the selection of the president of the republic: São Paulo and Minas Gerais, in what became known as "politics of coffee and milk," in reference to the concentration of coffee-producing interests in the state of São Paulo and dairy farming and cattle in Minas Gerais. This form of political engagement was largely centered around the mobilization of political clienteles by elite groups, which recruited rural workers to vote for their candidates.

After 1946, with the economic growth of Brazil and the shift of population from rural to urban areas, this political pattern expanded to newly mobilized voters, again organized in clientele groups but drawn from more diverse and numerous followings in urban areas. Two of the three major parties in this era were political organizations created by the leader Getulio Vargas—the Social Democratic Party (*Partido Social Democrático*, PSD) and the Brazilian Labor Party (PTB). The other was an anti-Vargas, pro-liberal democracy alliance, the National Democratic Union (*União Democrática Nacional*, UDN). This form of mass mobilization became known as "populism" (*populismo*) and was closely tied to a new form of clientele politics, largely created by Getulio Vargas. Vargas, once he realized that the right-wing nationalist politics of the 1930s could no longer work after the Allied victory in World War II, arrived at a more democratic formula based on his personal appeal to middle-sector and working-class groups in urban areas. Vargas committed suicide in 1954, as his ability to govern as an elected president based on popular appeals and support collapsed. But his style of national politics became institutionalized until the military intervened in 1964 to halt the shift leftward of popular, mass-based organizations under the leadership of João Goulart. Goulart was vice president, elected by his PTB constituency, and later president of the country.

After a twenty years of military rule, with an interlude of attempted official imposition of a two-party system (the progovernment ARENA, or *Aliança Renovadora Nacional*, and the official opposition MDB, or *Movimento Democrático Brasileiro*), a new multiparty system with an expanded mass basis emerged in the Brazilian transition to democratic rule. In this realignment of Brazilian politics, with dozens of smaller political organizations entering and exiting the political arena, four political forces have become the major players: the center-left Workers' Party (*Partido dos Trabalhadores*, PT); the centrist Brazilian Social Democratic Party (*Partido da Social Democracia Brasileira*, PSDB), the party of former president Fernando Henrique Cardoso, who preceded Lula in power; the Party of the Brazilian Democratic Movement (*Partido do Movimento Democrático Brasileiro*, or PMDB), a successor to the MDB; and the center-right Liberal Front Party (*Partido da Frente Liberal*, or PFL). Since the rise of the PT to national prominence in the late 1970s and the 1980s, this multiparty system has been become much more expansive and programmatic in character, although populist political organizations still abound and there are residues of the earlier party organizations that dominated in the 1950s and early 1960s, for example, the survival in much reduced form of the PTB.

Governmental Institutions

Brazil's democratization, prior to undertaking economic restructuring, has had an impact on its institutions and produced an outcome different from Mexico's. In Mexico, where leaders opted to undertake economic reforms first, before opening up politics, that policy choice had a great deal to do with the continued primacy of the presidency, dependency on presidential leadership, and single-party rule under the PRI. The consequence has been that when Vicente Fox opted not to take a firm stand in establishing an alternative party government and sought accommodation with the PRI leadership in congress instead, he severely limited his capacity to initiate further reforms and to fulfill his electoral promises to reconstitute government. In Brazil the outcome was much more turbulence in politics and uncontrolled inflation during the 1980s and early 1990s, as the governments in power failed to tackle pressing economic needs effectively. But once Fernando Henrique Cardoso took power, first as finance minister in the Itamar Franco government (1993–1994), where he developed a successful plan to bring inflation under control, and later as a two-term president (1994–2002) engaged in political and economic institutional reform, all this changed. The consequence of this dynamic has been a strengthened federal system in which competitive politics could function and sufficient political space could allow a bargaining style of politics to take precedence.

Today no single individual or group dominates politics at all three levels of government. While Cardoso was bargaining and compromising with leaders in congress, individual states and municipal governments could pursue their own agendas. Some of their initiatives led to innovative reforms in public management, such as participatory budget reforms in the city of Pôrto Alegre, in Brazil's southernmost state, Rio Grande do Sul. Others pursued traditional, clientelistic politics, as was the case in the northeastern state of Bahia and its capital, Salvador, under António Carlos Magalhães, who dominated state and local politics. A system of government has been institutionalized in which the separation of powers between president and congress has led to a political style in which bargaining and compromise predominate in pursuing major political and economic reforms at the national level. It has created and sustained sufficient autonomy at the state and local levels for political forces that span the political spectrum to regroup and engage in regional and local politics. While the political culture of Brazil and the organization of civil society are very different than in the United States, these developments have many more parallels with the way presidential federalism has evolved in the United States than with Mexico. To use the language of intergovernmental relations, Brazil's is what is known as an "overlapping-authority model" of federalism, which works well in large national states such as the United States and Brazil by creating multiple arenas in which social and economic policy issues can be confronted and political competition can take place without moving immediately to confrontation and crisis. Yet when serious national challenges arise—such as the unparalleled natural disaster in Louisiana and Mississippi, in the United States, and a corruption scandal reaching from the presidency into congress in Brazil, in 2005—such patterns of governance make it difficult for the government to provide a coordinated response quickly and effectively, cutting across multiple layers of jurisdiction and competing interests.

None of this is meant to idealize governmental institutions in Brazil, however. There are many serious problems, not the least of which are institutional corruption and lack of progress in overcoming enormous income disparities. But considering the distance traveled over the last decade in taming acute inflation and economic turbulence and making the transition from authoritarian to democratic rule, much has been accomplished without approaching system breakdown such as occurred in the mid-1960s.

The System in Action

Compared with the past, Brazil's great accomplishments in government and politics have been that as the country has entered the twenty-first century, its governmental institutions and socioeconomic policies have stabilized. It has arrived at a framework, as a federal republic, in which order and progress (the two ideals emblazoned on the Brazilian flag) have been secured to the extent that competitive elections have become the accepted way for determining government leadership, regardless of major differences between left and right. It has established the use of the majority principle to resolve tensions between executives and legislatures and determine outcomes in public policy.

Suggestions for Additional Reading

Mexico

Bailey, John J. *Governing Mexico: The Statecraft of Crisis Management.* New York: St. Martin's Press, 1988.

Camp, Roderic A. I. *Generals in the Palacio: The Military in Modern Mexico.* New York: Oxford University Press, 1992.

_____. *Politics in Mexico.* New York: Oxford University Press, 1993.

Crandall, Russell, Guadalupe Paz, and Riordan Roett, eds. *Mexico's Democracy at Work: Political and Economic Dynamics.* Boulder: Lynne Rienner, 2004.

Dominguez, Jorge I., and Chappell H. Lawson. *Mexico's Pivotal Democratic Election: Candidates, Voters, and the Presidential Campaign of 2000.* Stanford: Stanford University Press, 2005.

Fagen, Richard, and William S. Touhy. *Politics and Privilege in a Mexican Community.* Stanford: Stanford University Press, 1972.

Newell-Garcia, Roberto, and Luis Rubio. *Mexico's Dilemma: The Political Origins of Economic Crisis.* Boulder: Westview Press, 1984.

Rubio, Luis, and Susan Kaufman Purcell, eds. *Mexico under Fox.* Boulder: Lynne Rienner, 2004.

Smith, Peter H. *Labyrinths of Power: Political Recruitment in Twentieth-Century Mexico.* Princeton: Princeton University Press, 1979.

Tulchin, Joseph, and Andrew D. Selee, eds. *Mexico's Politics and Society in Transition.* Boulder: Lynne Rienner, 2003.

Ward, Peter M., and Victoria E. Rodriguez. *New Federalism and State Government in Mexico: "Bringing the States Back In."* Austin: U.S.-Mexico Policy Studies Monograph Series No. 10, LBJ School of Public Affairs, University of Texas at Austin, 1999.

Brazil

Baiocchi, Gianpaolo. *Militants and Citizens: The Politics of Participatory Democracy in Porto Alegre.* Stanford: Stanford University Press, 2005.

Graham, Lawrence S., and Robert H. Wilson, eds. *The Political Economy of Brazil: Public Policies in an Era of Transition.* Austin: University of Texas Press, 1990.

Hagopian, Frances. *Traditional Politics and Regime Change in Brazil.* New York: Cambridge University Press, 1996.

Keck, Margaret E. *The Workers' Party and Democratization in Brazil.* New Haven: Yale University Press, 1992.

Kingstone, Peter R., and Timothy Power. *Democratic Brazil: Actors, Institutions and Processes.* Pittsburgh: University of Pittsburgh Press, 2000.

Stepan, Alfred, ed. *Democratizing Brazil: Problems of Transition and Consolidation.* New York: Oxford University Press, 1989.

Weyland, Kurt. *The Politics of Market Reform in Fragile Democracies: Argentina, Brazil, Peru, and Venezuela.* Princeton: Princeton University Press, 2002.

Wilson, Robert, Peter Ward, Peter Spink, and Victoria Rodriguez, et al. *Decentralization and the Federalist Subnational State.* Notre Dame: University of Notre Dame Press, forthcoming.

Web-Based Materials

Elections of the World—Brazil, www.electionworld.org/brazil.htm

Elections of the World—Mexico, www.electionworld.org/mexico.htm

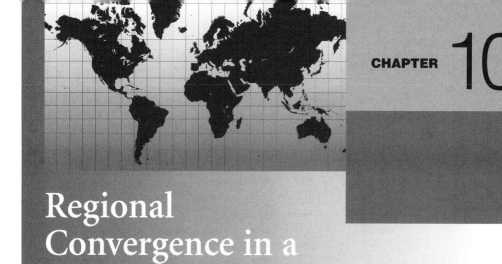

CHAPTER 10

Regional Convergence in a Diverse World

The first three country chapters of this book surveyed political systems in the United States and Western Europe. These North American and Western European polities were among the first to undergo the political and economic changes associated with the Renaissance, the Enlightenment, and the Industrial Revolution. From feudalism through monarchy and mercantilism emerged a number of national societies whose political systems came to be called "democratic" and whose economic systems came to be known as "capitalist." Widespread political beliefs in each of them came to emphasize some version of "popular sovereignty" or "rule by the people," and of national independence or "self-determination." Their governments included elected civilian chief executives and/or legislatures, and their customs and laws provided some measure of civil rights and liberties. Their economies were based on private (individual or corporate) ownership of land, businesses, and factories and on beliefs about markets and competition as mechanisms for setting wages and prices and as arbiters of economic success or failure. The changes that brought these politico-economic systems into being were accompanied by a great deal of civil strife, violence, and international warfare.

THE NEW REGIONALISM

The most significant change in this Atlantic world is the rise of the European Union (EU), now a union of twenty-five countries. They are now more integrated in their collective action than at any point in the past, despite all the problems encountered in defining the nature of this new union—whether it be a new form of federalism in the making, a confederation of states, or an economic association with supranational governing institutions designed to make the regional market work and resolve concomitant problems. Chapters 3 and 4 make it very clear to the reader what these complex institutional arrangements mean in surveying politics within Great Britain, France, and Germany and the way in which, overlaying their actions as autonomous political systems, there is a higher level of governance reflected in a complex set of supranational governmental institutions. While the initial rejection of the proposed EU constitution in plebiscites in France and the Netherlands in 2005 has placed ratification of that document on hold, as with the British constitution there exists a clear-cut set of arrangements, accords, and institutions that define the union and its evolving structures. Although one must be careful in choosing terms to explain this union, and always keep in mind that the "federalism" label is frequently avoided by Europeans themselves, it is clearly a new form of association that places this entity on equal footing with the United States in its global economic and political clout.

So dynamic has this new union become that it has rapidly expanded to embrace countries of Eastern and Central Europe that for more than a generation were assigned to the Soviet sphere of influence and which, when the Soviet Union collapsed in 1989, moved quickly to associate themselves with the new forms of governance in Western Europe. In contrast to those countries, as discussed in chapter 5, are the outlying areas defined in chapter 6, for the purposes of this book, as Russia (revamped as the Russian Federation), which is still a major actor internationally; the Ukraine, as the case study selected from the successor states of the old Soviet Union in Europe as opposed to Asia; and the Balkans. Some of these states, most notably Bulgaria and Romania, will eventually move into closer association with the EU, but the others, most notably the Russian Federation, will probably remain external actors bordering an expanded and more dynamic Europe, suspicious of its intents but desirous of participating in its benefits.

The core of this association is a common market in which there is now not only free movement of goods and services, but also free movement of its peoples, and which has policymaking structures—executive, legislative, judicial, and economic—that transcend and override the actions of its member states.

As we have seen in chapter 7, regional dynamics are even more fluid and complex in Asia. In the previous edition of this book, we focused on a single country: Japan. A latecomer to the industrial world that previously was confined to the United States, Canada, and Western Europe, Japan is a nation that succeeded in dramatically transforming itself after World War II into both an industrial power and a political democracy. Today, as a consequence, Japan is very much part of the industrial world and has become the first nonwestern nation successfully to make the transition to a fully developed market economy and a consolidated democracy. But surveying the politics of this region in the twenty-first century reveals that it is the People's Republic of China that is most important today in terms of global politics and shifts under way in world regions. One must include in that the areas adjacent to the PRC with Chinese populations—Hong Kong, under a special self-governing arrangement now that British sovereignty over this highly developed economic enclave on the Chinese mainland has ended, and Taiwan, as an independent state. With the world's largest population, China, now that a dynamic economic transition is under way, is emerging as by far the most important actor in the region. China's enormous size and population, a single market within a national state, put it into the same league as the European Union and the United States, whose transborder economies are rapidly expanding and becoming continental in nature.

The new regionalisms under way in the Western Hemisphere are being built around national states jealous of retaining their sovereignty. The supranational structures being built there have little in common with the development of common markets, even though Brazil and its South American partners aspire to just such an arrangement. The new North American market in the making is accordingly a free trade agreement, with a complex set of regulations built around protocols establishing which goods and services can move freely across the region, based on country of origin. The first trade agreement in North America was the U.S.-Canadian free trade agreement, which recognized the economic convergence already under way in the complementarities present in U.S. and Canadian industries and commercialized agriculture. During the first Clinton administration, a broader agreement was reached among the United States, Canada, and Mexico establishing a free trade area known as the North American Free Trade Agreement, NAFTA. To this has now been added a U.S. initiative called the Central American Free Trade Agreement, CAFTA, which was approved by the U.S. Congress in mid-2005. Once again, this agreement recognizes the economic dislocations that are already in place in Central America as a consequence of the free flow of goods and services among Mexico, the U.S., and Canada, and it establishes a series of protocols giving firms and industries in the region equal access to an expanded market that now extends from Canada through the United States to Mexico and from Mexico into Central America.

While discussions continue about a larger "Free Trade Association of the Americas," more likely at this writing is the emergence of two distinct trading blocs in the Americas: a North American one eventually including the Caribbean, and a South American one under a common market agreement called "Mercosur," or "Mercosul," depending on whether one uses its Spanish or Portuguese designation—the *Mercado Común de América del Sur* (or *do Sul*). Like the original Coal and Steel Community created in Europe in the 1940s and later expanded into the European Economic Community, this agreement establishes a set of supranational institutions, housed for the most part in Montevideo, Uruguay. Its original signatories were Brazil, Argentina, and Uruguay, to which were added Paraguay and later, under associate member status, Bolivia and Chile. Although the agreement begins with lofty aspirations, the economic disparities between Brazil and Argentina have been such that the actual scope of goods and services accorded free movement is extremely limited. Nevertheless, Brazil has continued to advocate this agreement as the most appropriate vehicle for a wider association through which the South American countries can more effectively offset U.S. influence in their area of the world. At this moment Venezuela and Peru have signed formal accords bringing them under the Mercosur umbrella, and negotiations with Ecuador and Colombia continue. Brazil's economy is the driver in South America because, as with the United States in North America, it has the largest and most diverse national market. Just as Mexico has experienced severe economic dislocations in joining NAFTA but reaped major benefits in expanded trade, so too Argentina continues in a "love/hate" relation with the Brazilians. Neither country wants to break the agreement, but there are enormous conflicts between the two over specifics. Argentina finds itself more and more dominated by Brazilian firms but also benefiting from its oil and gas resources' finding ample markets in Brazil. Likewise, the oil and gas reserves of Bolivia have been enormously important for the São Paulo area in central Brazil. It is hoped that new agreements with Venezuela will facilitate greater commerce between it and Brazil and that Brazilian products will gain easier access to Venezuelan markets, while Venezuelan oil and gas meet the demands of northeastern and northern Brazil. For central and interior Brazil, Ecuador and Colombia bring additional supplies of oil and gas to the table, although at the moment guerrilla activity in the Amazon, especially on the frontier with Colombia, is creating enormous difficulties.

These developments, coupled with the near-disappearance of the communist world (a "second world" as opposed to the "first world" of industrial nations, except for outlying cases such as mainland China, North Korea, and Cuba), bring us to what was previously called the "third world," a term many scholars preferred in place of the dichotomization of the world into "developed" and "underdeveloped" countries. None of these categories really match current world patterns outside Europe, North America, Australia and New Zealand, and South America. An enormous range of countries and world regions is embraced in the category of developing, nonwestern countries struggling with great poverty, natural disasters, debilitating disease, and poor economic performance requiring attention.

Many of these countries think of themselves as "new nations." Mainly erstwhile colonies of first world nations, and located in the Middle East, Africa, and Asia, this third category also includes older national states, primarily in Latin America, that likewise have not found any easy road out of their conditions of underdevelopment (namely, Haiti, Bolivia, and Nicaragua). Although they vary considerably in size, resources, culture, and historical background, these countries embody a "third wave" of modernization initiatives, especially in their aspirations and efforts to develop economically and to provide their peoples with better conditions of life. Consequently they represent yet another set of concerns in world politics. During the cold war between the Western and

Soviet-bloc countries, third world countries continued to interject concerns and interests of a very different nature from those found in the United States and the Soviet Union, but they also found in the competition between the two blocs ample opportunities for leveraging external assistance. Today, although the transitions going on in the successor states of the former Soviet Union and East Europe continue to reflect a distinct body of concerns, North-South tensions persist unabated.

While "third world" terminology really is no longer appropriate, given the collapse of the second world, these "developing countries" continue to seek their own routes to attain the levels of living and economic productivity identified with the industrial world. Although the developing countries possess raw materials and natural resources, some of which are needed by the industries of the more developed world, the industrial countries continue to be the only sources of the capital and technology they so desperately need for their development. In addition, the industrial countries remain interested in existing and potential markets for both capital investment and manufactured goods in the developing countries. Moreover, because the developing countries often found in the competition between the first and second worlds a way to minimize their external dependency, today their quandary is how to emulate the development of the industrial countries without falling into new forms of dependency on them.

The labels of this older, three-part classification were always far from satisfactory. Portugal, for example, nominally a first world nation because of its economy, imperialist history, and more recent democratic government, is poorer than the rest of Western Europe and much in need of further economic development. Incorporation into the European Union has provided no easy solution to its economic and social needs. The People's Republic of China, the Democratic People's Republic of Korea, and the Socialist Republic of Vietnam are likewise very different; their diverse ruling parties, official ideologies, and international alliances really no longer fit into the categorization of belonging to the second world. Yet, although they are experimenting with various market reforms, they continue to stand alone as countries ruled by Communist Parties. Further complicating these images of the international community is the fact that the metropolitan regions of a number of the Latin American, Middle Eastern, and Asian countries are comparable in many ways to first world urban areas. Japan, in particular, calls attention to the limitations of all these attempts at classification. As noted earlier, it is today an integral part of the first world in that its political history has been noncommunist; it possesses a consolidated democracy; and its high level of economic development has become the envy of the older industrial countries. Yet in its long history as an independent country and in its culture, it differs considerably from Western nations.

Moreover, while within each of these three different groups of countries there is recognition of important shared interests in international relations, none of them—and least of all the developing countries in Asia, Africa, the Middle East, and Latin America—acts as a unit in relation to the other two.

True, the NATO alliance links many of the Western nations. Also, during the heyday of the Soviet Union, the Warsaw Pact included most of the East European communist nations. And more than one hundred developing-country government leaders met periodically in conferences of "nonaligned" nations. But NATO does not include Austria, Finland, Ireland, Sweden, and Switzerland, in Western Europe, while it does include Turkey in the Middle East and today recognizes the "Europeanization" of modern Turkey and Turkey's desire to be incorporated in the EU as a legitimate aspiration despite reservations within Western Europe. Furthermore, France has long placed significant limitations on its participation in this Western alliance, and within the EU, it continues to express reservations about readily admitting Turkey into that Union. In addition, the NATO system is in the midst of redefinition since the collapse of the Soviet Union and the abolition of the Warsaw Pact, and there are serious questions as to its viability in the new world of the twenty-first century. Yet even before the enormous changes in these various alliances that followed the dissolution of the Soviet Union, the communist world was split by differences between the USSR and Yugoslavia, on the one hand, and the USSR and the People's Republic of China, on the other. Under Tito, Yugoslavia was one of the leaders of the nonaligned nations, only to find that once the cold war came to an end, and without an heir to Tito (who died in 1980), it too became subject to dissolution. Likewise, the developing countries defy any easy categorization. During the cold war, some, such as South Korea and Panama, Cuba and North Korea, clearly aligned themselves with the United States or the USSR. Others, although ostensibly nonaligned (notably India), have incorporated social democratic norms into their political systems. Still others reject labels associated with the cold war era and have proclaimed their own, third way, arguing that such choices are necessary to avoid the excesses and defects identified with the earlier competition between the communist and noncommunist countries.

Why should we be concerned with these ill-defined categories in general and the various designations used for the developing countries? They come to the attention of most of us, at least momentarily, when the news media report natural or other disasters in them; when they experience abrupt (to us) changes in leadership; and when crises, often violent, erupt in their governments and politics. In recognizing the presence of so many such countries—well over a hundred—how can we hope to make sense of the fleeting news images of military takeovers, assassinations, urban riots, terrorist acts, and guerrilla warfare? Surely we cannot be expected, even as informed and conscientious citizens, to know enough of individual countries to understand the causes and meanings of the religious fighting in India, the continued tensions between Iraq and Iran, the assassination of Anwar Sadat in Egypt, or conflicts in the Balkans and the Transcaucasus (in the former Soviet Union).

Besides, there are so many baffling differences in culture; in political, economic, and social systems; and in what we each consider to be relevant to our own concerns. Small wonder, then, that many people—even educated people—

tend to treat most such events and the news reporting them as peripheral, as not important enough to warrant sustained attention, much less serious study.

Sometimes, however, dramatic events, such as the capture and holding for more than a year of U.S. diplomatic hostages in Iran, or U.S. military involvement in Kuwait and in Iraq, not only grip our attention but also can have a direct and keenly felt impact on our daily lives and our political processes. It is no exaggeration to say that prior ignorance aggravates the importance of such episodes in faraway lands—ignorance not only on the part of the vast public but also on the part of many of those at the highest levels of both the government and the military. Lack of adequate knowledge and the resulting inappropriate assumptions in analyzing events and trends outside our experience have led to tragic chains of miscalculations and policy decisions. The events that were termed "Irangate" and those that led to an escalation of the bitter civil war in Bosnia are classic examples of woeful ignorance in high places. Better knowledge and understanding can help control more effectively the circumstances that produce such events and minimize their regional and worldwide impact.

There are additional reasons for trying to learn more about the politics and governments in the developing countries. Three-fourths of the world's population is Asian, African, or Latin American. Their population growth rates are well above those in Europe, North America, and other industrialized parts of the world. Large proportions of the world's supply of various natural resources essential to the survival of industrial societies come from this third set of countries, those we designate here as "developing" in the absence of a more appropriate term. Petroleum is one of which we have become acutely conscious. But there are others, such as bauxite and aluminum, chromium, cobalt, and zinc.

To the extent that we ignore what is happening in the developing countries, to the extent that we screen out these nations and people from our attention, we contribute to conditions in which our government (and other important representatives of the industrial countries, such as large multinational corporations) can more easily make the kinds of mistakes that increase the tensions, hostilities, and restiveness already apparent in relations among the three sets of countries—the industrial countries, the postcommunist regimes in the successor states of the USSR and in East Europe, and the developing countries. Such ignorance can have calamitous consequences.

Just as important in the long run, although less obvious, is one essential kind of knowledge that we can acquire by directing our attention to the developing world. Rapid political change, interacting with economic and social change, is under way there. Cultural as well as geographic distance makes it possible for us to observe the complexities of such change much more objectively than we can in our own society. The more we understand political change in the varying conditions of the developing countries, the better we can understand it at home, since the common denominator everywhere is the human species, with all its potentials and its limitations. The knowledge we gain through comparison can be crucial to realizing our hope of bringing politics and government within the range of our aspirations for our own society.

We cannot go into more detail or depth about individual countries here. But we can try to specify some of the salient general considerations that can provide a context and framework for understanding the political systems of many developing countries. With this in mind, it should at least be possible to ask the most relevant questions when, for whatever reason, we want to be able to interpret political events in the developing world when they are reported in the mass media.

All these concerns were present in the decision to expand this new edition to embrace the Muslim world (chapter 8) and to clarify by example the complexities we encounter in examining the developing countries. The author of chapter 8, George Joffé, argued from the beginning that we ought not define that world as essentially Middle Eastern, but rather should approach it through its human geography defined in cultural and religious terms by Islam, cutting across North Africa, into the Middle East, and from there into South Asia, where Indonesia has the largest population in a single national state who have embraced Islam.

GREAT VARIETY—COMMON ECONOMIC PROBLEMS

Given their geographic distribution around the world and their individual histories, it is hardly surprising that there is extraordinary variety among the developing countries. They range in population from a few tens of thousands (Dominica, Seychelles) to hundreds of millions (India). Ethnic groups speaking all the major languages and between 2,500 and 5,000 other languages (depending on how "language" is defined) can be found, usually several and sometimes many per country. All imaginable races and racial mixtures, all the major religions, and many more religions than most of us have even heard of, some based on combinations of elements of others, some ancient and some new, flourish in profusion. Differing languages, racial characteristics, and religious identifications are often related in complex ways to class, caste, and social status and are often important factors in political conflict. But some examples of relatively harmonious coexistence among such diverse groups can be found, as new and old nationalisms seek some form of political unity and recognition.

Other aspects of cultural variety among the developing countries are also important for understanding their politics. In some there is a long and rich heritage of sophisticated artistic expression, including literature, music, sculpture, and architecture. Much of this, just as in the history of Western art, expresses or is inspired by religious themes. In others, art mainly takes the form of handicrafts, body decoration, storytelling, and folk music and dance. In both instances, some political activists and leaders find a wealth of symbols to draw on to mobilize popular sentiments for political purposes. This may be related to movements of awakening national consciousness or in opposition to foreign (Western) technology and lifestyles, which are depicted as threats to traditional values, or both. In India, Mahatma Gandhi chose the spinning wheel to symbolize both his opposition to foreign colonial rule and his desire to resist the erosion of village institutions by industrial technology. At the same time, he and his followers promoted far-reaching social reforms in the name of justice, such as the abolition of caste oppression of "untouchables."

Some traditional cultures emphasize a division of labor in which women do the agricultural work as well as the housework, in addition to bearing and raising children. Men are responsible for hunting, animal husbandry, fishing, village or tribal politics and religious ritual, and fighting to defend the village or tribe or to acquire booty, including wives. In other cultures both men and women share the agricultural and other heavy work and divide other tasks and activities according to different patterns. Values associated with some cultural patterns—such as handicraft production and trade, as well as agriculture—are more receptive to technological change than are others rooted in different cultures. These factors are of obvious relevance to governmental programs of economic development, which are under way almost universally in the developing world.

Among all the kaleidoscopic diversity within and between these countries, we can nevertheless point out a few similarities that are crucial for any approach to understanding their politics. A fundamental problem that conditions much of life in developing countries is poverty. To envisage entire societies as poor may not be easy for those who have never lived in such a society or who have never experienced real poverty. Yet we must try, for poverty and its consequences pervade so much of the life of most developing countries that, unless we can begin to comprehend it, we will find it next to impossible to see their governments and politics clearly.

Imagine, first, that your chances are small to live much beyond the age of forty or fifty. Imagine that you have had no more than three or four years of schooling—or none at all. This you may not see as a deprivation, for the same is true for all your family and friends. And perhaps, given the life ahead of you, you may not even be able to conceive of any use for formal education; certainly it will not make you rich, for everyone knows that the few who have any wealth got it because they were lucky enough to be born into families that already had it. What would your life be like if you had never read a book? Imagine also that your mother or father is very ill and that there is no medicine, no doctor, no hospital. While the illness lasts, you and your brothers and sisters may have to reduce the amount of your already insufficient food to contribute to the nourishment of the sick parent, and you will have to do his or her work in addition to your own. Imagine that one or two of your brothers or sisters died as infants—and that such is the normal experience in all the families you know. Imagine having had to work in the fields since the age of six. Imagine not being able to think about doing much else for the rest of your life.

These examples are but an effort to gain a few glimpses into the lives of the great majority of the people in most developing countries. They are intended to give human meaning to otherwise cold statistics such as the following: A quarter of the world's population lives in economically developed countries where they enjoy the fruit of more than three-quarters of the world's total output. Nearly half of the human race lives in poorly developed countries, where they must try to survive with only 5 percent of the goods produced. Furthermore, this huge chasm is widening. Per capita income in the United States grew (in constant 1980 dollars) from $7,000 in 1955 to $11,500 in 1980. During that same period it grew in India from $170 to $260. By 1990 the income gap in these two countries was even greater: $21,790 in the United States to $350 in India (in 1990 dollars).

World poverty is even worse than per capita income figures suggest. Per capita income is calculated simply by dividing a country's income by its population; it tells us nothing about the distribution of income within the country. Several developing countries—chiefly oil producers—have high per capita income figures ($20,140 for the United Arab Emirates, compared with $22,240 in the United States in 1991 dollars), but national riches have done little to improve the quality of life for the bulk of the population. Typically in developing countries there is a small elite of wealthy or privileged people. Its size in relation to the total population, although it is always very small, varies; but the homes, automobiles, clothing, clubs, and banks and the restaurants and other retail businesses they support stand in stark contrast to the masses of the poor in the cities. The contrast is all the greater with rural peasants, who typically make up the largest proportion of the total population. In the cities, one can also see middle-class people. Many are civil servants—functionaries of the government. Others work in or own small shops or are professional people: lawyers, doctors, engineers, and so on. But such middle classes as exist are proportionally much smaller than the comparable classes in the United States, Canada, or Western Europe.

The poverty of much of the world's people is worsened by growing indebtedness in the developing countries. Many less-developed countries are unable to sell enough products to other countries to pay for the goods that they must import to survive. They must borrow from developed countries—in many cases, large American, European, or Japanese banks—to pay for these imports. The huge budget deficit of the American government produced extraordinarily high interest rates during the 1980s. Many (about 40 percent) of the loans to developing nations carry variable, rather than fixed, rates of interests. Thus when interest rates rise in the United States or Germany they greatly increase debts already larger than many of these countries can ever hope to pay off. The interest payments alone on Argentina's foreign debt two decades ago were 70 percent of all that it earned in a year by the sale of exports, and they remain around 50 percent for both Mexico and Brazil. None of these countries, as we enter the twenty-first century, has been able to escape from these problems of indebtedness. A mere increase of 1 percent in the U.S. interest rate adds well over $4 billion to the debt of developing countries. As a consequence, developing countries have run up a total debt of over $800 billion, and a large number of them continue to lag behind in the payments on their loans.

Most of the big debtor countries are in Latin America, and much of their debt is owed to U.S. banks. Although much has been done to restructure this debt, and Argentina and Mexico have embarked on ambitious privatization programs to redress the imbalances, Brazil remains the world's largest debtor nation, owing approximately $116 billion (1993), and public sector debt continues to climb in Africa. Thus, for all the progress made in some countries in market reforms, there is always the danger that an Argentina or an Ecuador will not be able to meet its payments. Default on their loans would provoke a major crisis for U.S. and European banks. Even apart from such an event, the economic implications are serious for the United States and other industrial countries. For excessive debt burdens—private or public—can impose further restrictions on world trade and constrain export markets.

Fluctuations in interest rates in the major industrial countries also introduce distortions into world trade and affect individual national currencies. Not so many years ago, the U.S. dollar was strong; then it became weak vis-á-vis the Japanese yen and the German mark. Then it recovered. And then, with the coming of the euro, the enormous costs of the war in Iraq, and a spiraling negative U.S. trade balance, the dollar has been subjected to enormous fluctuations and concern about its viability in international exchange markets. When its currency is strong, it creates opportunities for citizens of a country when they travel abroad or wish to acquire luxury items. But it greatly increases the cost of that country's products that developing countries need to buy, adding to their debt and their difficulties in obtaining necessary goods and services. It also has an impact on the industrial countries themselves, for as export markets decline, companies are forced to cut back their production and lay off workers, thus creating unemployment and recession in the domestic economy.

During the 1980s and into the twenty-first century, as economic relations among countries grew in complexity, we all became much more vulnerable to external conditions over which we had less and less direct control. Whereas historically the U.S. domestic economy was relatively independent of the world economy, and it was easier to see direct correlations between actions of the U.S. government and what occurred at home and abroad, new forms of global interdependency and the development of a world economy have constrained the ability of the U.S. government to make major adjustments alone. An example is the ending of high interest rates in the United States and the shift from a strong to a weak dollar, back to a strong dollar, and then again to a weak dollar. Although the weak dollar has had the effect of making American goods and services cheaper abroad and hence more desirable in some countries, it has not automatically produced the hoped-for stimulus. Partly this situation is a consequence of the emergence of three very different economic centers—one in North America, dominated largely by the United States; another in Asia, centered in Japan; and a third in an expanded Europe now functioning as a single unit economically through the European Union. Thus, whereas the reduction in the debt burdens of many of the Latin American economies, coupled with privatization initiatives and economic restructuring, stimulated Western

Hemisphere trade, the competitiveness of the Japanese economy made Japan an even stronger world economic center, and changes in the U.S.-Japanese trade imbalance have been minimal. Today concern about Japan has been replaced by concern about mainland China, as it has become a major economic actor provoking all sorts of dislocations in the United States and the European Union. This shift is reflected in chapter 7, where the focus is on the People's Republic of China, instead of an in-depth case study of Japan as in previous editions. Independent of these developments, after a decade of economic productivity and expansion by the European Union, the high cost of incorporating East Germany into a reunited German Federal Republic, coupled with an inability to compete with the Japanese automobile industry or Chinese textiles, has constrained economic growth in Europe. That in turn has had an impact on the United States, further complicating an already troubled relationship.

As a consequence, older images of a world divided between industrial nations, such as the United States, that dominate trade and finance, and a much larger number of developing countries dependent on them for trade, finance, and assistance, no longer have the same explanatory power. The Latin American scene illuminates what has been occurring on a worldwide basis, that is, notable differences among countries in their response to the development of a world economy and increased global interdependency. Whereas Chile, Mexico, and Argentina have experienced dramatic turnarounds in comparison with past economic difficulties, offsetting their accomplishments are cases such as Bolivia, Ecuador, and Peru, where inflation, indebtedness, and poor economic growth rates continue to constitute major constraints.

At the same time, enormous shifts have been occurring in U.S. trade patterns. For example, in 1980, for the first time, U.S. trade with twenty-one Asian Pacific basin countries surpassed U.S. trade with Europe. And by 1983 U.S. trade with the Pacific rim was a quarter larger than it was with Europe. Even more incredible, much of what the United States sells to these Asian countries is farm products and natural resources, and most of what it imports is manufactured products. In other words, trade patterns between the United States and these Asian states reflect a very different set of economic relationships from those between the United States and its Western Hemisphere trading partners, raising the question of who is dependent on whom.

Nothing illustrates better than changing patterns in debt and trade how interrelated the world economy has become. The United States simply cannot isolate itself behind a barrier of tariffs, quotas, and other constraints on international trade and hope for economic health. Much of the world's poverty is located outside U.S. boundaries, but Americans can ignore it only at their peril. Having indicated the economic problems common to much of the developing world and why and how they have become American concerns, we turn to consideration of the political problems of the developing world to see how these further complicate efforts to deal with economic weaknesses. (Other factors, such as religious, tribal, and ethnic loyalties, also have an impact on economics and politics at home and abroad.)

COMMON THIRD WORLD
POLITICAL PROBLEMS

In looking for general explanations of patterns of politics in developing countries, we need to go beyond the immediate historical causes, such as the interrelated events that resulted from the overthrow of the shah of Iran and the replacement of his government by one dominated by Islamic religious leaders. To understand such events, we must interpret them through ideas about trends and causes that are applicable to other instances of political change. To the extent that our general explanations are applicable to more than one instance, we can save much time and effort in understanding each individual case. We often do this anyway, consciously or not; for example, we project our beliefs about human nature, or morality and immorality, into our explanations. The analyst's task is to find concepts that can be used without allowing personal preferences to prejudge the means and outcomes under consideration.

Here we use the concepts "traditional society" and "modernization" to organize our explanations. In doing so we must avoid the implication that one concept is good and the other is therefore bad. This is difficult, for we do assume that modern society (of which the United States is an example) is more consistent than traditional society in such things as science, industrial technology, and rational bases of law, which we consider good. We need to keep in mind that change related to these has been, and still is, accompanied by violent conflict, exploitation, and misery and that incorporating modern ideas and ways into society by no means guarantees an end to such scourges.

The economies of traditional societies tend to be poor and predominantly agricultural. The bulk of the population is rural, typically living in many small villages. There is little mobility, social or geographic. Families tend to be large, and family obligations (such as caring for the aged and ill, defending family honor, and treating relatives more favorably than others) are stressed. Very few people are literate, and those few are often priests or officials—members of a privileged class. Infant mortality is high, and life spans are generally short. Custom, tradition, and ritual govern most aspects of life.

Towns and cities may exist as centers of religious worship, government, and trade. But their size is limited by the agricultural production of surrounding areas, or of other areas with which trade is carried on, for urban centers depend on the availability of an agricultural surplus for their survival. A tiny minority of relatively wealthy landowning families often constitute a ruling class, access to which is closed to most of the population. Trade, commerce, and military conquest may permit growth of cities to considerable size, and in some the arts may flourish.

Government maintains the social order in relative internal peace by supporting the prevalent religion, often leading the performance of important rituals; by settling disputes; by punishing transgressors; and by maintaining armed forces. It sometimes constructs temples, monuments, roads, dikes, canals, and other kinds of what we would call "public works." For all these things, as well as to provide a privileged and comfortable if not luxurious way of life for rulers and officials, it collects taxes or tribute. When needed, it drafts labor for construction work and manpower for military service. Often religious, economic, and political beliefs and institutions are blended and combined, or at least are not clearly separated.

Such societies may eventually support civilizations, as in ancient Egypt or Babylonia, or that of the Olmecs in what is now Mexico. Classical Greece and Rome are examples closer to us in culture as sources of Western civilization. But most of us are aware mainly of the lives and achievements of the elite of such civilizations, rather than of the much more numerous rural populations supporting the elite. Traditional society need not be restricted to earlier civilizations. More generally, the concept can, with allowance for variations of degree, be usefully applied to most preindustrial societies, including those whose basic organization is tribal.

The beliefs common in traditional society tend to foster acceptance of the status quo. To identify a problem is, for many people in modern societies, to set in motion a search for its causes. There is an almost automatic assumption that there must be one or more causes that explain the situation we define as a problem. Once found, the causes may turn out to be (or can be made) susceptible to human intervention. By dealing with the causes, we can hope to eliminate, reduce, or otherwise change the problem to make it more tolerable. At least we may discover a way of getting around the problem or avoiding contact with it. This applies as much to economic and social problems as to those of the natural, physical world. All this is but common sense, we would say, if asked.

It was not always so in what are today modern societies. And it is not always merely "common sense" in many other societies today. For the overwhelmingly greater part of human existence, traditional views of life explained as being ordained by nature or divine power many kinds of events and conditions that we regard as avoidable, changeable, or fixable by human actions. Conservative, traditional beliefs counseled resignation to natural disasters, such as devastating storms, floods, droughts, and earthquakes. The social order, no matter how grotesquely unjust, harmful, or inefficient, was also a part of nature, divinely sanctioned, or both. The path of wisdom was therefore to accept these things. If we look about, we can see surviving influences and remnants of such beliefs in contemporary society. Many, for example, conceive of economic competition in a capitalist system of private ownership—quite apart from its virtues of technological innovation and productivity—as somehow more natural than other economic systems. Such a view overlooks the human-made changes and innovations that created property law, market systems, the legal invention of the corporation, and the like.

What we call "modernization" began with technological innovations in Western Europe only a few centuries ago, in association with the Renaissance, the Enlightenment, and the Industrial Revolution. Mining, manufacturing, construction, travel, and trade began to transform societies, as economic production and productivity increased far beyond the limits imposed by traditional technologies. Such changes rested on, and went hand in hand with, the increase of scientific knowledge. Much of the old order was swept away, often to the accompaniment of wars and revolutions. What remained of it had to adapt and accommodate itself to new and continually changing patterns of living and thinking.

We can single out three components of this fateful transformation: Ancient beliefs and attitudes gave way to new ways of viewing the world, nature, and the role and destiny of humankind. A new psychology began to spread in England and on the Continent. Many things, it was learned, could be brought under human control and rearranged to a much greater degree than traditional beliefs had conceived. A better life on earth could be achieved by knowledge and action. If traditional culture included such ideas, they were relegated to the realms of magic and the supernatural.

A second component of modernization is the physical or material. Application of new knowledge, which gradually was organized into the sciences, led to more and more complex and powerful technologies. Machines increased economic production. Disease control lowered mortality rates and prolonged life. Construction and travel were revolutionized. New sources of energy and new methods of converting it to human uses vastly increased human control of the natural environment—and the potential for human freedom. New material standards and styles of living became possible. These had the effect of greatly increasing the range of choices open to individuals and societies. This led to the third component: the social and political. New forms of human organization became possible. Among them were huge factories, far-flung business firms, cities of millions of people, and governments of vast complexity and power. New forms of social control as well as new forces of social disruption appeared. Both greater democratization of government and greater concentration of governmental power were made possible.

While these changes in Western thought, technology, and society were under way, their consequences began to be projected around the globe. European exploration, trade, religious missions, and military and political expeditions established and expanded colonial empires. A few Western nation-states extended their influence, control, and exploitation to traditional societies on distant continents. But inevitably the revolutionary ideas and technologies of the imperial powers sowed the seeds of destruction, not only of non-Western, traditional societies but of the colonial empires themselves.

Nevertheless—and here we can begin to understand some of the problems of the developing countries today—the various processes of modernization do not proceed at the same rate and certainly not in harmonious pattern. They produce dislocations, disorganization, and conflict in all aspects of political, economic, and social life. These processes have themselves contributed powerfully to the extent of human poverty and misery. Modern medicine and public health technologies are a leading example. They have brought many diseases under control and have reduced infant mortality. They also result in more people, living longer lives, who make even greater demands on already overburdened economies.

Also, modern means of transportation and communication have disseminated ideas and images from the more modernized societies to the less-modernized part of the world. This has fed and intensified the aspirations and expectations of hundreds of millions of people, whose traditional institutions are increasingly unable to satisfy their needs and hopes. The spread of images of modern life was begun well before the economic, technological, and political means were available that might allow the realization of such aspirations. As aspirations for a better life are reduced by population growth to a basic struggle for mere survival, and as traditional beliefs and order-maintaining social structures are weakened, little imagination is needed to foresee mounting political pressures and problems. Thus we can see that it is not poverty as such that causes the political problems of the present world, but poverty in conditions of weakened traditional beliefs and structures, that is, of weakened mechanisms of social control, where awareness of possibilities of a better life is widespread.

Let us look more closely at four clusters of political problems confronting many developing countries: ambivalence and frustration related to modernization, internal cleavages based on subnational loyalties, political instability, and prominence of the military in politics. As traditional beliefs about the bases of legitimate government, such as divinely sanctioned hereditary monarchy, have eroded, more modern beliefs, such as the primacy of the consent and representation of the governed, have not been widely accepted beyond the educated few. In many countries, elites with Western-style educations reveal ambivalent attitudes, seeking to conserve valued elements and aspects of traditional culture while adopting much of modern knowledge, technology, and ways of living. In some instances, such as Pakistan and Saudi Arabia, many of the educated few seek a viable way of retaining and strengthening the religious basis of government authority. This may be accompanied by both resentment of the West and reluctance to give up positions of influence and privilege as economic and social change spreads through society. Or some of the elite may share the frustration and sense of injustice of the less-advantaged at their inability to break the grip of poverty on the country. Whatever the individual reaction to the experience of socialization by two different cultures, traditional and Western, problems of self-identity and ambivalence toward goals often prove difficult to handle. Their effects generate behavior that may be difficult for observers who have not had such experience to understand. It is in some ways analogous to the experience of racial minorities in a society such as the United States, except that in the developing world it is the favored elites who have experienced this "double socialization."

Another constellation of problems aggravated by modernization processes in many developing countries has to do with cleavages based on ethnic, regional, and class differences. Ambivalence among elites is one manifestation of this kind of cleavage, in which socioeconomic class differences are reinforced by a foreign-style language, the lack of which may effectively bar many from channels of upward social mobility, such as governmental employment, at levels other than the lowest and most menial and which has often caused suspicions about the true loyalties of members of the elite. But on a larger scale, loyalties to groups such as tribes or to those speaking different languages, particularly when such groups are identified with particular regions, may result in extremely difficult problems of integration and assimilation into a nation-state.

For the "new" nations, especially in Africa, boundaries are a legacy of colonialism, drawn by colonial powers. Such boundaries were often the result of conflict and treaties among colonial powers; thus they sometimes grouped traditionally hostile people within a colony, while splitting previously unified people and their lands on both sides of an artificial line. Postindependence political leaders have had to bring diverse people to accept a common and newly created national identity, so that a government of all can acquire enough legitimacy to function. This has never been easy, and in some instances brutal civil wars have been fought, as in Nigeria. Such situations have provided regional leverage for foreign involvement, as in Zaire (the Congo) just after independence. Given its many different languages and internal ethnic antagonisms, which erupt into violence not infrequently, one of India's principal accomplishments has been sheer survival without breaking into pieces along ethnic lines. Even more important is India's status today as the world's most populous democracy. It is significant that the common language of governmental administration has continued to be English. The imposition of the official language, Hindi, is still resisted in non-Hindi-speaking states.

Given the presence to some degree of divisive factors such as these, many developing countries lack sufficiently widespread acceptance of basic rules to govern political conflict. Political leaders often cannot assume that their opponents will refrain from violence, and they therefore are ready to use it themselves. Significantly, this has become true of older developing nations as well as newer ones, as the unsettling forces of modernization have spread. Latin American politics, perhaps more clearly than African, is often riven by conflicts along socioeconomic class lines, as in Argentina, Brazil, Bolivia, Chile, Nicaragua, and El Salvador in recent years. In such conflicts the military forces of the government are often the decisive factor. Nicaragua is a recent exception, as was Cuba over two decades ago. In these two the government's armies were not able to resist guerrilla forces.

A major part of the explanation in Cuba and Nicaragua was corruption and repression on the part of the government and the military, which destroyed the government's legitimacy in the eyes of much of the population, especially rural peasants, as well as many middle- and lower-class urban people. On the other hand, a frequently invoked justification for military forces' turning on their civilian masters, overthrowing the government, and setting up a military dictatorship is corruption and incompetence on the part of civilian government.

To summarize, we can often find a few important explanatory factors underlying seemingly unpredictable political conflict and change in developing countries. One of them is poverty, which is often more acute and more politically explosive as a consequence of partial modernization of traditional societies and reaction to U.S. and European economic, cultural, and political influences. Such partial modernization has weakened or undermined traditional institutions and values and has disseminated images of and aspirations for a better life to millions. But the means for realizing such aims are insufficient or absent. Elites, partly modernized, are ambivalent about the modernization process, not only because they are socialized into both Western and domestic culture, but also because the changes under way may threaten their privileged positions. Internal cleavages hinder the development of national consciousness in many countries. Without sufficiently institutionalized rules for the nonviolent resolution of political conflict, military forces are often involved in the maintenance of order by repression of rebellions. The outcome is often military dictatorship, civilian authoritarian rule, or in the Muslim world fundamentalist governments that seek to isolate their societies from foreign influences.

POLITICAL INSTITUTIONS AND PROCESSES

In relatively stable political systems it is possible to identify fairly well defined institutions of government. Through the activities of individuals who hold office, legitimate and authoritative decisions are made or ratified—laws, decrees, and so forth—which establish government policies and spell out rules that affect the people subject to that government. Specific governmental institutions are authorized to enforce or carry out the decisions made. Other political processes—involving individuals, parties, interest groups, and nongovernmental institutions—go on in relation to government decision-making processes, seeking to influence them. The general reason for seeking such influence is that the outcomes of governmental decisions affect the distribution of burdens and benefits throughout society: who pays how much in taxes; whose activities are regulated and in what ways; who receives what services, subsidies, authorizations, and exemptions, and so on. Although the threat of coercion by police or military forces is never absent in enforcement of such decisions, rules, and policies, it is normally used only to maintain public order and to apprehend and punish criminals.

The organization, processes, and functions of these governmental institutions can be examined with the assumption that one is dealing with matters directly relevant to the question of how that society is governed. This is so even if one discovers that other individuals, groups, institutions, or classes or people, not a part of the formal government and contrary to official doctrine and public symbolism, exercise great influence, even to the point of controlling the decisions the government makes.

In many developing countries, however, the performance of governmental institutions is not as clear-cut as that. In some, change may be occurring so rapidly, or may have occurred so recently, that both participants and observers may be uncertain as to who is doing what, or who is supposed to be doing what. Some government organizations may be at a standstill, doing little or nothing, or they may be engaging in activities other than those one would expect from their titles or their place in the structure. Other organizations and activities may exist only on paper. Officials may be giving attention and deference to persons or organizations whose place and role in the political process are far from obvious, even if detectable. In short, image and reality may be not only unclear but also inconsistent with each other, or they may be related in such complex or indirect ways that even participants may be uncertain about some of them.

The consequences of this is that formal government structures, often designed according to models taken from the industrial countries, may not be the best place to start looking for evidence as to how developing countries are governed. One may find offices such as president or prime minister or organizations labeled "legislature," "senate," "assembly," or "high court of justice." But until we discover just what the officials in these offices and organizations do, and with what consequences, it is not safe to assume that the functions associated with such names in the governments of modernized countries are those actually carried out.

This is not to suggest that in the industrial countries there is an exact one-to-one fit between the formal structure and image of government and the actual structure of power and influence. Inevitably discrepancies exist. For example, it is commonly recognized in the U.S. government that the Executive Office of the President exerts much more influence over lawmaking than a reading of the Constitution might suggest. But the office itself and its relations with Congress and the courts are sufficiently institutionalized that a fairly elaborate and intricate set of understandings and expectations exists for any incumbent. This is often not the case in offices of the chief executive of the government in developing countries.

Here we need to be more specific about the concept of "institution" and the process of "institutionalization." When we say that certain organized activities are institutionalized, we mean that they have become habitual and normal and that they endure because they are valued by participants and others affected by or related to them in beneficial ways. A criminal justice system composed of police, courts, and jails becomes institutionalized because both the people employed by them and the public at large value them. This support is enough to outweigh the lack of support by those who are punished by the system. Similarly, other organizations set up to perform governmental functions by exercising legitimate power ("authority") can become infused with value and can endure as long as they are so valued. To say that an institution is valued means more than saying that it is wanted or desired. It means that those valuing it share some degree of consensus that it should or ought to exist, as a matter of what is right or proper.

Three further points must be noted about institutions. It takes time for a structure of activities to be institutionalized to the degree that it will be supported and maintained beyond the time that particular individuals who happen to be popular occupy positions and perform roles in them. Second, to endure, institutions have to change to adapt to changes in their environment. At the same time, and third, they do not merely react passively to such changes. They usually seem, and are able, to influence or control significant parts of their environment so as to ensure their survival.

From these comments we can gain some understanding of why some governmental organizations in developing countries seem not to be doing what one would expect, or why they seem to lack permanence and strength. Let us take the example of a body set up as a legislature. Leaders of many newly independent nations came to power, over the last forty-five years or so, promising to set up democratic governments. Many tried this by drafting and promulgating written constitutions modeled on those of more modernized countries of the industrial world. To be democratic, it was assumed, a government should have, among other things, an elected legislature. Thus the new constitution provided for one. But two problems had to be faced. One was that many in the population had little or no understanding of elections or legislative bodies. Their conception of government may have been limited to experience with colonial officials or to traditional chieftains, or kings often supported (and manipulated) by colonial officials. This problem was not fatal; it was possible for the new government to mount a campaign of public information and propaganda and to have its supporters get large numbers of the population to turn out to vote.

The other problem was more serious. Before and at the time of independence, there may have been other contenders—rivals—for leadership. Some or all of them might be regarded by leaders currently in control not merely as rivals but as traitors to the national cause. Could one actually risk being defeated in an election by such people? Of course not. They could not even be allowed on the ballot. If, for whatever reason, they could not be excluded, there were other ways to ensure that one's opponents would not win. (Along with other modern ideas, political leaders in developing countries have also learned something of the fine art of rigging elections.)

The trouble with such methods of electing legislative bodies was that people—even uneducated peasants—were not so ignorant as to fail to see through the charade. If they did not see through it immediately, the rivals and their supporters made every effort to ensure that their eyes were opened. Thus the legislative body eventually elected did not stand much chance of becoming a working, effective institution. Even supporters of the leaders who organized such elections were hardly unaware of how they had won, and so they could not give unadulterated respect to this new symbol of democracy. Most of the time they adjusted to the reality that their legislative activity had to occur within limits acceptable to those wielding effective executive powers—often those assuming the title of president, sometimes military leaders. Meanwhile, the opponents, seeing their path to legitimate power blocked in such a way, were sometimes persuaded that their only chance was to foment revolt aimed at overturning the new government. Such is not a very good start for a government whose leaders may have been sincere in their desire to institute democracy.

Not all new nations, or older nations undergoing modernization, followed paths such as that just outlined. India, Colombia, Costa Rica, and South Africa are examples of countries that have made major advances in the institutionalization of elected governments and democratic politics. They have also experienced crises and setbacks, however, as well as severe economic problems. Typically in developing countries, often even in the more successful ones, the role of an elected legislative body is primarily symbolic. Its presence may express an aspiration for popular representation in lawmaking and in checking possible excesses of executive power. Additionally, and often primarily, a docile and compliant legislature is useful as a means of legitimating decisions made by chief executives, regardless of their intentions with regard to the eventual democratization of the political system.

The importance and power of chief executives in governments around the world reveal that such prominence is not uniquely a developing-country phenomenon. What is more characteristic of developing-country politics is that such powerful political leaders come into office by military coups, and many leave office the same way. Some of the reasons for and circumstances surrounding such military intervention have already been suggested. Here we need to inquire into variations in this pattern.

First, however, we should note that there are about a dozen hereditary monarchies or royalist governments in the developing world, in which the military are influential but subordinate to the rulers. They include such nations as Jordan, Saudi Arabia, Morocco, and Nepal. In Thailand the monarchy has been retained, but the military control the government. Such governments, generally conservative, seek to keep the disruptive forces of modernization under control through authoritarian government, some adaptation, and guidance of economic development so as to preserve the existing socioeconomic structure.

In another half-dozen or so developing countries, ranging from Mongolia, North Korea, and Vietnam in Asia, through Angola in Africa, Libya in North Africa, and South Yemen in the Middle East, to Cuba in the Western Hemisphere, Marxist regimes led or closely supported by military forces took power after coups or guerrilla wars. Leaders of most of these governments sought to organize single parties to mobilize and control popular support. Before the collapse of the Soviet Union and its satellite regimes in Eastern Europe, those governments also relied on military and economic aid from the USSR and governments allied with it. Even at the high point of that support, however, military forces proved to be more important than the official parties, and the model of state socialism failed to resolve their historical problems of underdevelopment. This was especially true in Africa. Like the successor states to the Soviet Union and the new governments in Eastern Europe, this group of countries is in the midst of significant economic and political transition, with some of them—such as Mozambique—having advanced so far in the process of economic restructuring and opening up the country politically that the Marxist label no longer applies. Others—notably Cuba—are desperately attempting to preserve state socialism.

In other parts of the developing world—ranging from Pakistan, Sri Lanka and Indonesia in Asia, through Iran and Yemen in the Middle East, to Somalia, Sudan, and Zaire in Africa—equally important transitions are under way. In some, the military plays a significant if not a dominant role; in others, the struggle between fundamentalist Muslim clerics and reformist sectors favoring liberalization continues to dominate local politics; in others bitter civil wars have broken out. Again, individual country cases vary greatly, especially in how they have handled economic policy. South Korea and Taiwan, for example, have behind them impressive economic records and today have become democratic societies. In contrast, Peru and Bolivia—despite very different experiences with economic restructuring—remain very poor but have in place democratic or quasi-democratic governments. In all of these, disillusionment with military intervention in politics is high, but in none of them can one say that the consolidation of democratic rules is a given.

South American experience is of particular interest here. During the 1960s and 1970s the military seized power throughout the region. In the Southern Cone of South America the breakdown of democratic regimes took place in a setting where constitutional government—with reasonably fair and competitive elections and effective civilian chief executives and legislative bodies—seemed to be well along toward institutionalization, although each of the countries faced severe economic difficulties. Notable among these were Brazil, Chile, and Uruguay. In Brazil and Chile, elections had produced governments and policies that, to conservative and not so democratically disposed officers with the support of major segments of the upper and middle classes, appeared dangerously radical and leftist. Specifically, the position and interests of landowning, business, and financial elites were threatened. The military officers seized power in coups and instituted purges that included uncharacteristically brutal torture of suspected leftist opponents. Many suspected opponents were killed or simply disappeared.

In Uruguay, the military intervened in a situation of economic deterioration aggravated by the inability of the civilian government to suppress an urban guerrilla movement. This was a country that for decades had been proud both of its relatively high living standards—ones that placed it in the upper tier of the developing world, in the category the World Bank calls the "upper-middle-income countries"—and of its accomplishments as a stable democracy that approximated the welfare states of northern Europe. The country's severe economic difficulties, coupled with a stalemated democracy in which the political leadership was unable to respond to deteriorating economic and social conditions, ultimately brought the military into politics. The military replaced the president, established a repressive authoritarian regime, and stamped out the guerrillas and terrorists. Eventually the military proved no more able to resolve the country's difficulties, and by 1984 Uruguay had begun a transition back to democracy.

Although the authoritarianism of the 1970s was superseded by the movement back to democratic regimes in the 1980s, these South American cases underline the fragility of democratic institutions. In many areas of the world, modernization has created expectations and demands that threaten the interests of well-entrenched economic elites, and which in any event are difficult to satisfy through democratic processes. This creates a painful dilemma for those who see the undeniable need for fundamental economic and social change in the interest of social justice, but who are dedicated to orderly and legal processes for effecting change. The actions of military governments in these circumstances contribute to intensified hatreds that, in the absence of significant improvement in the socioeconomic conditions of the large majority in such countries, portend even more violence in the future. Even though democracy is now on the upswing throughout South America, the unanswered question in the new preference for market economies and democratic governance is whether these countries will be any more successful than in the past in transcending the cycle of periodic economic and political crises and the subsequent breakdown of democratic institutions. The case in point at present is Venezuela, under the leadership of Hugo Chavez, a populist leader who has taken power with the support of the country's poor majority. In the process of consolidating his rule, he has destroyed what was one of the most stable political democracies in the region. Yet we should not forget that had the ruling political parties, *Acción Democrática* and COPEI, done a better job of creating a regime attentive to the needs of all Venezuelans, Chavez would never have gained the support he has today from those long excluded from the benefits of that country's oil wealth.

Although military rule is currently out of fashion, the involvement of military men in politics from the 1960s into the 1980s, the continued engagement of military and guerrilla groups in politics in some of the African countries, and the powerful role of the military in Pakistan and Sri Lanka call attention to the need to be aware that the person who appears to be the most powerful individual in the political system is often significantly dependent on others in his entourage. In some instances, for example, the military governments in Argentina (1976-1983) and Greece (1967-1974), these were councils of officers, whether or not such arrangements were formalized. Moreover, the formal title of president does not provide immunity from removal by a fellow officer or a group of them. Such has occurred as a consequence both of policy disagreements and of the ambition of other officers. Politicizing the upper levels of the armed forces can greatly weaken the discipline of military command. To the degree that an army has become professionalized, generals often discover that the aptitudes, skills, and knowledge required for a successful military career are not the same as those required for successful political leadership. Leaders of guerrilla forces, in contrast, are more likely to understand political leadership and can more easily function as leaders of governments. Nevertheless, nothing guarantees that either kind of leader will have much understanding of the complexities of economic policy. For that they often have to turn to people in the one set of structures that are likely to be fairly well institutionalized in developing countries—the civilian bureaucracies.

The bureaucracies, or administrative components of government, are employers of a fairly large proportion of the professional and technically trained people in many developing countries. Whether the product of colonial administration or of long-standing independent government, these agencies are indispensable instruments for the exercise of governmental authority. If the decisions and policies of political leaders are to be carried out, if the programs launched are to have any effect, it is the administrators who will do it.

Political leaders learn that their commands alone are not sufficient to ensure that these things will be done. They also find that they are dependent on administrators for much of the information they need for governing. Such information may be in the form of reports on the status and effects of programs. It may be in the form of technical knowledge required to plan and design such programs in the first place. The political leaders also discover that their orders and instructions are subject to much interpretation and reinterpretation as they pass downward and outward through the bureaucratic hierarchy. For all these reasons, it is often difficult for government leaders to accomplish what they intend. The administrative structure, in appearance nothing more than a tool for doing the government's work, is in reality a baffling network of power, resistant to change and often full of obstacles to action.

Whether political leaders seek to stimulate modernization or to channel it in desired directions, they often discover that the attitudes, knowledge, and skills required are scarce in the bureaucracy. Officials experienced in collecting revenues, issuing licenses and permits, drafting regulations, and keeping voluminous files of records may find it impossible to think of innovative ways of instituting and managing development programs. They may lack initiative or be unwilling to take responsibility for decision making when situations require flexibility and quick decisions.

Such shortcomings as these are frequently compounded by long-standing practices of petty bribery and the exchange of favors among administrative officials as means of getting things done. Employment by and advancement in administrative agencies may depend on complex networks of patronage and nepotism. On a larger scale, the complexity of regulations and procedures makes it possible for some administrators, who understand them from years of experience, to delay or block action, to conceal the embezzlement of funds, or to engage in smuggling of contraband materials. In other words, corruption of various degrees of magnitude may be embedded in the bureaucracy. Some political leaders may wish to profit from it themselves. Others may close their eyes to it, realizing that serious efforts to root it out will drain time and energies needed for trying to bring about desired or mandated results in governmental action.

Paradoxically, conditions such as these—and they are not unusual—present problems that are the opposite of those discussed previously with reference to modernization. Bureaucracies often suffer from an excess of institutionalization. This is often linked to traditional cultural patterns and other elements of society, such as the family. Thus bureaucracies cannot be easily reoriented, nor can they be purged and repopulated with new officials because there are not enough such new people with the necessary skills and experience.

Courts of law in developing countries also are often vulnerable to the political changes related to modernization. One reason is that, as organized structures, they are smaller than the complex of bureaucratic institutions. More important, the locus of judicial decision making is more visible. A judge, or a small panel of judges, presides at trials and renders decisions or hears appeals from lower courts and renders decisions. Judges may delay, but eventually they must decide. Thus, when political struggles break the molds of institutionalized government and become matters of sheer power and coercion, the very survival of judges and judicial institutions usually requires a keen awareness on their part of the goals and wishes of those wielding the greatest power. This can result in judicial decisions ranging from a general bias in favor of the dominant leaders and their supporters, up to the outright politicization of courts. In the latter event, harassment and persecution of the regime's opponents and dissidents can be given an aura of judicial legitimacy. (The politicization of courts of law is not, however, an invention of the developing world. Models in the industrial world can be found as well in Europe in Nazi Germany and Fascist Italy or in the former Soviet Union. It is now standard practice for revolutionary regimes, once in control of government, to set up "revolutionary tribunals" to convict and often execute captured leaders and followers of the overthrown regime.)

The emphasis thus far given to some of the consequences of modernization should not be allowed to imply that political turmoil is constant in the developing world. Between crises, changes of leaders, and outbreaks of civil disorder, individual countries may experience years of relative calm. During such periods, patterns of politics and governmental action proceed normally—but "normal" is of course shaped by the kinds of factors we have been discussing and by memories of the kinds of events mentioned. Depending on time and place, political discussions often have a semiconspiratorial air, with words chosen carefully and many indirect allusions. Or if a foreigner joins the group, the subject may be quickly changed. Media commentary is typically supportive of the regime, for the mass media often operate under government supervision. Tourists passing through a country may get a few insights into the workings of the political system, but if the regime is authoritarian, they usually see little evidence of it.

Political parties will exist if not prohibited, and to varying degrees they will go about their work of trying to mobilize and extend their support. If there is but one party, the official one, its posters carrying pictures, symbols, and slogans are much in evidence. Many of its activities may be carried out by government employees, and the distinction between party and government may be blurred. If there are several competing parties they are often small, with relatively little formal organization and few full-time workers. Some may be little more than loose networks of friends and relatives, inactive except at times of elections.

The country's political elite is small, and most of its members know one another personally. It includes, in addition to the top officials of the regime, high-level bureaucrats and military officers; members of wealthy business and landowning families (unless the regime happens to be Marxist) partly in, but not of, the elite; resident foreign businesspeople; and such cultural and intellectual figures as editors, artists, and prominent professors. There may be leaders of important interest groups, such as importers and exporters; producers of and dealers in raw materials and export crops; or students. But interest groups are not as numerous as in more economically developed and modernized countries, and the number of distinct interests is relatively small. In the capital city, much of the social life may revolve around the embassies of foreign governments, which give frequent receptions and formal dinners.

Despite its relatively small size, the elite is not a homogeneous group of people with identical political views. A frequent difference is that between pronationalist and proforeign groups. In time of crisis their division can become bitter. Another line often distinguishes those with modern scientific, technical, and professional education from those with more traditional educations, such as law or the liberal arts.

Usually the critical nature of political, economic, and social problems facing the country is not much in evidence in the daily lives and the official assemblies and ceremonies or social gatherings of the elite. It is politics and business as usual—until the next crisis begins to build or the next outbreak of open struggle or public disorder. It may be tomorrow. Or it may be next year.

FUTURES IN THE DEVELOPING WORLD

The changes of modernization in the industrial world have had several centuries to transform traditional societies into predominantly modern ones. Even so, these transformations produced revolutions, civil wars, wars of independence, and great international wars, not to mention hardships forced on the rural and urban poor. Developing-country political systems are having to undergo the transition—or its beginning phases—in a much briefer period. The destabilizing and exploitative effects of early modernization create revolutionary situations in which both indigenous rebels and foreign powers can seek to shape the direction of political change.

This problem of acceleration is intensified by three ominous trends. The first is rapid population growth, which exceeds many societies' ability to increase food production. The prospect is for more famines and epidemics as population pressure on resources increases. These have already begun in the poorest countries in Africa.

Second, the entire globe's natural resources, needed to sustain the world's high-technology societies, are being depleted at dizzying rates. International struggles for access to and control of such resources by the industrial powers are likely to intensify. The Persian Gulf crisis may be repeated in other regions, with reference to other natural resources. Weaker developing countries may well become increasingly dependent clients and pawns of the major world powers.

Third, the voracious consumption of resources is producing changes, some of them irreversible, in the earth's land surface and water, including the depletion of agricultural topsoil, the destruction of oxygen-producing foliage, the increased need for poisonous herbicides and insecticides, and the need for increasingly expensive (in energy conversion terms) fertilizers. Groundwater levels are being lowered in industrialized regions; acid rain has become a cause of international dispute; and rivers, lakes, and even oceans are showing serious consequences of continuing industrial pollution. In the earth's atmosphere, long-term temperature changes may already be under way as a result of smoke with chemical and particulate pollution, and solar radiation may become more dangerous because of such things as damage to ozone.

All of this leads to a pessimistic prognosis, particularly for the developing countries. Many of them will never catch up economically with the present industrialized countries. Some may once again come under the political and/or military control of rival industrial nations. The industrial countries cannot assume that they will emerge unscathed, for none can escape the consequences of resource depletion and environmental damage.

Science and technology have helped us into this dangerous impasse; we have little else to use to find a way out. But for ingenuity to be fruitful, we will have to develop greater wisdom in managing our collective affairs than has been apparent in the past. We will have to cope with the vast, degrading, and dangerous disparities between the rich and the poor nations. The benefits of modern life will have to be shared more equitably. And both rich and poor nations will have to learn to do much better in conserving the remaining natural resources. All this is likely to call for more sacrifice and greater changes in lifestyle on the part of the rich and resource-consuming nations on behalf of the poor.

Coping with world problems also is likely to require many people to rethink their moral priorities. Birthrates in developing countries continue at high levels, contributing a major share of the world's population growth —growth that rapidly is outrunning technology's ability to expand and distribute the food production required for the survival of much of the world's population. Humanity took a million years to grow to a population of one billion. The next billion increase took not much more than a century—120 years. A third billion was added in only few years, and a fourth in just fifteen years. In the last three decades of the twentieth century the world's population increased by more than the total number of people alive throughout the world in 1900. A billion of this increased population of the past fifty years has come in nations with per capita incomes of less than $400.

Finally, our many political systems and the people selected to operate them must transcend the dangerous conflicts of power and ideology in today's world. To be aware of common problems and to try to find the commonalities among contending ideologies may seem—given the millennia of conflict among humanity—merely pious utopianism. Failure to achieve this, however, seems likely to be calamitous. For modernization has forced not only the developing world but all of us into a race with time. And the process by which we seek to reconcile our differences and solve our problems is nothing other than politics. Thus, the study of politics, so as to make the process more effective and equitable, is essential for our survival. When we add to the list of problems the increased probability of pandemics, greater extremes in weather patterns from global warming, the recourse to terrorism, and the growing capability of small numbers to people to destroy civilian lives in the thousands, we see that these are no longer the problems of other societies. They are ours, too.

Suggestions for Additional Reading

Bailey, John, ed. *U.S.-Mexican Economic Integration: NAFTA and the Grassroots.* Austin: U.S.-Mexican Policy Report No. 11, Lyndon B. Johnson School of Public Affairs, University of Texas at Austin, 2001.

Boone, Catherine. *Political Topographies of the African State: Territorial Authority and Institutional Choice.* New York: Cambridge University Press, 2003.

DePalma, Anthony. *Here: A Biography of the New North American Continent.* New York: Public Affairs, Perseus, 2001.

Diamond, Larry, Juan Linz, and Seymour Martin Lipset, eds. *Democracy in Developing Countries.* 4 vols. Boulder: Lynne Rienner, 1988.

Graham, Lawrence S. "Modernization, Political." In *International Encyclopedia of Social and Behavior Sciences,* Nelson W. Polsby, Political Science ed. Oxford, UK: Elsevier Science Ltd., 2001.

Grindle, Merilee S., ed. *Politics and Policy Implementation in the Third World.* Princeton: Princeton University Press, 1980.

Huntington, Samuel P. *The Third Wave: Democratization in the Late Twentieth Century.* Norman: University of Oklahoma Press, 1993.

Kohli, Atul, ed. *The State and Development in the Third World.* Princeton: Princeton University Press, 1986.

Migdal, Joel S. *Strong Societies and Weak States: State-Society Relations and State Capabilities in the Third World.* Princeton: Princeton University Press, 1988.

Nelson, Joan M., ed. *Economic Crisis and Policy Choice: The Politics of Adjustment in the Third World.* Princeton: Princeton University Press, 1990.

O'Donnell, Guillermo, Philippe C. Schmitter, and Laurence Whitehead, eds. *Transitions from Authoritarian Rule.* Baltimore: Johns Hopkins University Press, 1986.

Przeworski, Adam. *Democracy and the Market: Political and Economic Reforms in Eastern Europe and Latin America.* New York: Cambridge University Press, 1991.

Reid, T. R. *The United States of Europe: The New Superpower and the End of American Supremacy.* New York: Penguin, 2004.

Roett, Riordan, ed. *Mercosur: Regional Integration, World Markets.* Boulder: Lynne Rienner, 1999.

United Nations Development Programme. *Human Development Report, 2003: Millennium Development Goals: A Compact among Nations to End Poverty.* New York: Oxford University Press, 2003.

World Bank. *World Development Report 2004: Making Services Work for Poor People.* New York: Oxford University Press, 2003.

Notes

Chapter 2: The United States

1. Studs Terkel, *Race: How Blacks and Whites Think and Feel about the American Obsession* (New York: Free Press, 1991).

2. Census Bureau, *Money Income in the United States: 2000,* Table A2: Share of Aggregate Income Received by Each Fifth and Top 5 Percent of Households: 1967–2000. Percentages in text are approximate due to rounding. The Census Bureau Web site is the entry to much useful data (www.census.gov).

3. *Business Week* and *The Wall Street Journal* publish annual reviews of compensation for U.S. corporate officers. In the United States the salary ratio of corporation chief executive officers (CEOs) to workers skyrocketed from an already high forty-two to one in 1980, to over four hundred to one in 2000. Compared to corporate compensation in other nations, U.S. CEOs garner approximately twice the average annual compensation of British and German CEOs, the next two most highly paid. On public acceptance of business privilege, see Charles E. Lindblom, *Politics and Markets* (New York: Basic Books, 1977), chap. 13.

4. See American Religion Data Archive (www.thearda.com). The data are as of 2000.

5. Estimates of disenfranchisement figures for former felons are made by the Sentencing Project, a nonprofit research and advocacy group, and the NAACP. See Eric Lichtblau, "Confusing Rules Deny Vote to Ex-Felons, Study Says," *New York Times,* February 20, 2005, sec. 1, p. 15, and Spencer Overton, "Stealing Liberty: How Politicians Manipulate the Electorate," *The Crisis* 112, no. 1 (January/February 2005): 15–18.

6. A "loophole" refers to a law's silence that permits something its sponsors likely would limit. Sometimes, however, loopholes are intended by a bill's sponsors, or are reluctantly provided as a way for sponsors to gain support or votes from congressional colleagues when a bill is voted on. *Soft money* is the term for money raised by parties and PACs for such activities as voter registration, get-out-the-vote drives (GOTV), and issue advocacy advertising. By contrast, *hard money* is for direct election campaign expenditures.

7. For contribution information on PACs, consult the FEC Web site (www.fec.gov). For 527 groups, consult the Web sites of the Internal Revenue Service (www.irs.

gov/charities/political) and the Center for Responsive Politics (www.
opensecrets.org/index.asp).

8. See Paul Light, *The True Size of Government* (Washington, D.C.: Brookings
   Institution Press, 1999). The size of the private contractor workforce is an estimate.
9. Seymour Martin Lipset, *The First New Nation* (Garden City, N.Y.:
   Doubleday/Anchor Books, 1963).
10. Louis Hartz, *The Liberal Tradition in America* (New York: Harcourt, Brace and
    World, 1955). Hartz provides the explanation for the absence of socialist and
    organic conservative traditions in America.

Chapter 5: Transitional Politics in Central Europe

1. Examples of election complexities illustrated in Marina Ottaway, *Democracy
   Challenged: The Rise of Semi-Authoritarianism* (Washington, D.C.: Carnegie
   Endowment for International Peace, 2003).
2. Thom Shanker, "Aftereffects: Rebuilding; Lessons for Iraq Seen in Balkan
   Aftermath," *New York Times,* May 22, 2003, late edition.

Chapter 8: Politics in the Muslim World

1. The term *jihad* is actually far more complex than this definition suggests, reflecting
   both internal self-discipline to achieve the Islamic ideal and, in a subsidiary context,
   communal defense both active and passive.
2. The term *imam,* a religious leader, the leader of the Islamic community, is used
   interchangeably with the term *khalifa.*
3. These two terms characterize Moroccan history and even find their echoes today.
   The *bilad al-makhzan* meant the "land of government"; *makhzan* was the term by
   which direct sultanic government was described in Morocco. The *bilad as-siba* was
   the "natural land"—that region outside the confines of legitimate government
   where the sultan's normative prestige alone gave him authority, if not power.
4. The term "tribe" in the Middle East and North Africa is loaded with implications
   and differentiated meanings. Normatively defined as the largest kin-structured
   entity capable of spontaneous political organization, it is, in reality, often no more
   than a centrally imposed administrative structure that used the vocabulary of kin
   interrelationships to legitimate itself. Subsequently, tradition and myth might give
   substance to such interrelationships without providing them with historical meaning. In other words, the existences of tribes can be as much evidence of central
   authority as of—as is conventionally suggested—its lack.
5. The *Mojahedin-e Khalq* emerged from the collapse of the *Tudeh,* Iran's Communist
   Party, after the end of the Second World War. Many of its militants, after a brief
   encounter with Mohammed Mossadegh's Freedom Movement, moved into the
   Mojahedin when it was created in the 1960s. It adopted an Islamic-Marxist agenda,
   of the kind to be popularized by Ali Shariati, one of the most important ideologues
   of the Islamic revolution

   The second movement, the *Fedayin-e Khalq,* was an unabashedly secular and
   Marxist-Leninist movement, which had no truck with religious legitimization. It
   also rejected the *Tudeh* party's slavish subjugation to the Soviet Union. It saw the
   world through the national-liberationalist eyes of the 1960s, in which the struggle
   against bourgeois repression was intimately linked with the struggle against

neoimperialism. Thus, for its militants, there was always a close link between the domestic repression of the shah and the role of the United States in Iran and the wider world.

The *Pasdaran* were to be used to eliminate both groups after the end of the Bani Sadr presidency in mid-1981. The *Fedayin*, after a major split in its ranks, has since declined into obscurity. The *Mojahedin*, however, moved into exile and re-created itself as an exile guerrilla movement, supported by the Iranian exile community and, eventually, the Saddam Hussain regime in Iraq. From its bases around Sulaymaniyya in Iraqi Kurdistan, it continued to attack into Iran until March 2003 when, in the brief war between the Saddam Hussain regime and the United States, it remained neutral and then had to negotiate its own future with victorious American forces.

6. Recently additional security services have begun to emerge, which now form the clandestine parallel institutions. The most prominent are the *Hefazat-e Etelaat-e Sepah Pasdaran* (the Intelligence Services of the Revolutionary Guards) or the *Hefazat-e Etelaat-e Ghovey-e Ghazai-e* (the Intelligence Services of the Judiciary). Since the 1990s the various organs of the Iran security system have begun to acquire their own intelligence services and prisons, which lie outside the formal security structure and are unregulated. They, together with the *baseej* and the *ansar-e hizbollah,* form the *nahad-emovazi,* the "parallel institutions" that are today responsible for much of the real repression in Iran. The parallel institutions are completely unaccountable.

Index

Note: *t* with page number indicates a table.

Access, for public input
  Central and Eastern Europe, 173
  Russia, 192–193
  Southeastern Europe, 207–208
  United States, 20–21, 25
Acción Democrática, Venezuela, 315
Acquis communautaire, EU, 138
Adamkus, Valdas, 176
Adams, Gerry, 119
Adams, John Quincy, 23
Adams (John) administration, U.S., 25
Adarand Constructors v. Pena (U.S., 1995),
  54
Administrative law, 50
Adversarial judicial systems, 50, 74
Affirmative action, 15, 109
Africa. *See also* Developing countries
  indebtedness, 303
  internal cleavages, 309
  sub-Saharan, 5–6
Agents, U.S. Representatives as, 43–44
Agricultural economies, 305
Agricultural-industrial cleavage, 101, 102.
    See also Developing countries
Agricultural interests, Mexico, 276
Agricultural organizations, lobbying by, 110
Agriculture, U.S. Department of, 47
Ahmadinejad, Mahmoud, 253
Albania. *See also* Southeastern Europe
  postcommunist political system in, 148,
    148*t*
Alemán, Miguel, 271

Ali, *rashidun* caliph, 239
Alianza por Cambio (Mexico), 278
Alianza por México, 278
Alliance of Liberals and Democrats for Europe,
  125
Alliance Party, Northern Ireland, 119
al Odah v. United States (2004), 52
Alsace-Lorraine, German-French disputes over,
  82
Alternative Labor and Social Justice Party,
  Germany, 123, 124
Amendment process, for U.S. Constitution, 9,
  12–13
American dream, 16
American exceptionalism, 266
American Revolution (1776), 2, 77, 101
Amicus curiae briefs, U.S., 21, 53
Amsterdam Treaty (1997), 89, 93
Anglicanism, 102
Ansar-i Hizbollah, Iran, 255–257
Antifederalists, U.S., 9, 23
Anti-Semitism. *See also* Judaism
  in Europe, 102, 108
Antitax movement, U.S., 27
Appropriations Committee, of U.S. House, 41
ARENA (*Aliança Renovadora Nacional*), Brazil,
  289
Aristotle, 3
Articles of Confederation, U.S., 8–9
Asia. *See also* Southeast Asia
  countries comprising, 213–214
  economic center in, 303–304
  political systems, 5
Association of Southeast Asian States
    (ASEAN), 214

Aubry, Martine, 120
Authoritarian regimes. *See also* Centralization
of authority
government purpose and functions under, 2
Ávila Camacho, Manuel, 271

Backbenchers, House of Commons, U.K., 73,
133
Baker v. Carr (U.S., 1962), 52
Balcerowicz, Leszek, 176
Balfour Declaration (1917), 242
Balkan countries, 201–202. *See also*
Southeastern Europe
European Union and, 181, 294
Ballots, U.S., citizen access and, 25, 27
Barroso, Jose Manuel Durao, 92
Basic Law of the Federal Republic of Germany,
83, 86, 95
Basque people, 82, 101
Bayrou, François, 121
Beliefs
modernization and, 307
political systems and, 3
in traditional societies, 306
Berezovsky, Boris, 187, 192
Berisha, Sali, 209
Berlin Wall, fall of, 62, 83
Bhutan, regional affiliations in, 214
Bicameral legislature(s), 71–74, 80–81, 267,
269, 287
Bill of rights, 10, 13, 68
Bipartisan Campaign Reform Act (BCRA, U.S.,
2002), 28
Bismarck, Otto von, 82, 103
Blair, Tony, 75, 115, 118, 142
Bonyad Moztazafin (Destitutes Foundation),
Iran, 254
Bonyad Shaheed (Martyrs Foundation), Iran,
254
Born-again democrats, 175, 176–177, 193–194,
209. *See also* Leadership
Bosnia. *See also* Southeastern Europe;
Yugoslavia
legislative-executive relations in, 160
western ignorance about, 299
Brazil, 285–286
constitutional development, 286–287
governmental institutions, 290–291
indebtedness, 303
interest groups, 288
military influence on modernization, 314
political parties, 289–290
social forces, 287–288
system in action, 291

Brazilian Labor Party (PTB), 289, 290
British National Party, 119
Brittany, France, separatist movements in, 82,
101
Brown, Gordon, 118
Brzezinski, Zbigniew, 176
Buckley v. Valeo (U.S., 1976), 28
Buckovski, Vlado, 209
Budget Impoundment and Control Act (U.S.,
1974), 37, 38
Bulgaria. *See* Southeastern Europe
Bundesrat, German, 84, 85, 86
Bundestag, German, 83, 84, 85, 86
Bureaucracy/bureaucracies, 45. *See also* Federal
bureaucracy, U.S.
developing countries, 315–317
Europe, 67
France, 80
Germany, 84–85
Mexico, 279, 280–284
United Kingdom, 71, 133
Burnham, Walter Dean, 278
Bush, George H. W., 30
Bush, George W.
election of 2000 and, 30, 31–32
EU foreign policy and, 143
judicial appointments, 55
public opinion polls and, 35–36
social security reform and, 29
Bush v. Gore (U.S., 2000), 31, 54
Business and commercial groups, lobbying in
Europe by, 110, 111

Cabinet(s). *See also* Council of Ministers,
France; Ministers
British, 70, 133
European countries, 67
European Union, 91
French, 80, 134
German, 85, 135
Iran, 251
U.S., 36–37
Calles, Plutarco Elías, 271
Cambodia, government of, 215
Cameron, David, 117, 137
Campaigning in U.S., 27–30, 44
CANACINTRA (*Confederación Nacional de
Industrias de Transformación*), Mexico,
275–276
Canada
divisiveness in Quebec, 2
U.S. and, 264, 295
Candidate-centered campaigns. *See also*
Leadership

Russia, 190–192
Ukraine, 197
United States, 27, 28–30
Capitalism
  Mexican constitution and, 268
  Russian expectations for, 183–184, 187
Cárdenas, Lázaro, 271, 275
Cárdenas Solórzano, Cuauhtémoc, 277, 278
Cardoso, Fernando Henrique, 289, 290
Case law, definition of, 50
Catholic Democratic Unionist Party, Northern
    Ireland, 119
CCI (independent peasant confederation),
    Mexico, 275
Census Bureau, U.S., 14
Center-periphery cleavage, 101
Central American Free Trade Agreement
    (CAFTA), 295
Central and Eastern Europe, 62–63
  analytical framework, 149–150
  communism in, 104
  comparisons in, 151
  economic architecture, 162, 164–166, 166t
  economies of, 100
  European Union and, 294
  German speakers in, 101
  leadership cadre, 175–178, 177t
  political and social dynamics, 166–167
    access for public input, 173
    civil society, 173–174
    elite accountability, 170–171
    forward- *versus* backward-facing, 167–168
    legitimacy, 169–170
    resource needs, 168–169
  political machinery
    centralization, 160–161
    constitution(s), 155–158
    law and politics, 161–162, 163t
    legislative-executive relations, 159–160
  political systems, 4–5
    under communism, 150–151
  prognosis, 178–179
  transitional systems, 147–148, 148t
  value systems, 152–154
Central Intelligence Agency, U.S., 37
Centralization of authority
  Central and Eastern Europe, 160–161
  European countries, 67
  Indonesia, 260
  Mexico, 279
  under Portuguese in Brazil, 286
  Russia, 191–192
  Ukraine, 197
  United Kingdom, 68

Chavez, Hugo, 315
Checks and balances, 11, 232. *See also*
    Separation of powers
Chekhov, Anton, 182
Chen Shui-bian, 232
Chiang Ching-kuo, 231, 232
Chiang Kai-shek, 231
Chief legislators, U.S. presidents as, 33–34
Chile, military influence on modernization of,
    314
China, People's Republic of
  classification of, 297
  Confucian values, 219–222
  East Asian influence, 218–219
  government, 216, 217, 222
  political system, 222–231
    constitution, 228–229
    limits of party-state control, 229–231
    political party structure, 225–227
    the state, 227–228
  regionalism and, 295
  as world economic center, 304
China, Republic of, 221–222, 223. *See also*
    Taiwan
Chinese People's Political Consultative
    Conference (CPPCC), 227
Chirac, Jacques, 79, 120, 121, 129, 134
Christian Democratic Union (CDU),
    Germany, 83, 121–123, 130, 137
Christianity, Europe and, 62
Christian Social Union, Bavaria, 122–123, 130
Citizenship
  after American and French Revolutions, 101
  Central and Eastern European constitutions
    on, 158
  in postcommunist states, 155–156
Civic Forum (Czechoslovakia), 154
Civil Aeronautics Board, U.S., 47
Civil cases, U.S. judiciary and, 50
Civil Rights Amendments, U.S., 13
Civil service. *See* Bureaucracy/bureaucracies
Civil society. *See also* Social dynamics; Welfare
    programs
  Brazil, 290
  Central and Eastern Europe, 173–174
  Europe, 107–109
  Japan, 234–235
  organization of, 6
  People's Republic of China, 229–231
  Southeastern Europe, 208
  Taiwan, 233
Civil war(s), 2, 309
Class politics, in Europe, 104–105, 128
Class system, United States, 15–16

Clientele relationships, U.S. federal bureaucracy and, 47
Clinton, Bill, 29, 30, 35, 38, 55
Clouthier, Manuel, 277
CNC (*Confederación Nacional Campesina*), Mexico, 273–274, 275
CNOP (*Confederación Nacional de Organizaciones Populares*), Mexico, 274
Coalition governments
  East Asia, 215
  Germany, 83–84
  United Kingdom, 72
Coalition of Islamic Associations, Iran, 252
Co-decision procedure, EU, 91, 93–94
Code law, inquisitional judicial systems
  EU law and, 94
  France, 74
  Germany, 86
Cohabitation, of political executive in France, 79, 137
Collective responsibility, of U.K. cabinet ministers, 70, 71
Collor de Mello, Fernando, 288
Comités Promotores del Desarrollo Socio Económico (COPRODE), Mexico, 284
Commission on the Voting System, U.K., 127
Committee of Permanent Representatives (EU, COREPER), 90, 91, 92
Committees
  Congress, U.S., 40, 41
  House of Commons, U.K., 73
Common Agricultural Policy (CAP, Europe), 88, 100, 102, 111
Common Cause, 19
Common law
  acquis communautaire, of EU, 138
  EU law and, 94
  judiciary in United Kingdom and, 74
  judiciary in United States and, 49
Common Market (Europe), 88
Communism. *See also* Communist Party; Marx, Karl; Socialism
  Central and Eastern Europe, 104, 150–151
  European influences on Islamic states and, 243
  fall of, 147
    EU expansion and, 88
    Europe and, 62
  France, 120
  government purpose and functions under, 2
  Marxist, owner-worker cleavage and, 103
  near disappearance of, 296
  taxation under, 189
Communist Manifesto, The (Marx), 103

Communist Party
  Chinese, 221–222, 225–227, 229–231
  Indonesia, 258, 259, 260
  Iran, 252
  Mexico, 277
  Russian, 190, 191
Comparative politics, 1–6
  Central and Eastern Europe, 151
  developing countries, 299–300, 305, 319–320
  Europe, 61–62
  Southeastern Europe, 210–211
CONACO (*Confederación de Cámaras de Comercio de México*), 275–276
CONCAMIN (*Confederación de Cámaras de Industrias*), Mexico, 275–276
Confucius
  East Asian political systems and, 216–217
  value systems in China and, 219–222
  value systems in Japan and, 235
Congress, U.S., 39
  constituent districts, gerrymanders, and safe seats, 42–43
  federal bureaucracy and, 48
  institutionalization, 44–45
  legislative powers, 39–40
  organization of, 40–42
  presidential relations with, 37–38
  representatives as agents or trustees, 43–44
  twentieth century presidential government and, 34
Congressional Government (Wilson), 37
Connecticut Plan, for U.S. Constitution, 9
Consensus decision making, in EU, 141
Conservative Party, U.K., 116–117, 132
Constituencies, for Central and Eastern European elections, 171
Constitution(s), 6
  Bosnia, 209–210
  Brazil, 286–287
  Britain, 67–77
  Central and Eastern Europe, 155–158, 157*t*
  for developing countries, institutionalization and, 312
  Europe, 66–67
    Southeastern, 204–205
  European Union, 87–96
  France, 77–82
  Germany, 82–87
  Indonesia, 259
  Iran, 250–253
  Islamic states, 241–242
  Japan, 234
  of Medina, 238
  Mexico, 267–270

Morocco, 247, 248
People's Republic of China, 228–229
Russia, 156–157, 186
Taiwan, 232–233
Ukraine, 196
United States
    amendment of, 12–13
    basic principles, 9–11
    Bill of Rights, 13
    writing of, 8–9
Constitutional Council, France, 81
Constitutional democracy, United States, 10
Constitutional government
    Iranian security system and, 254
    United Kingdom, 67–68
Constitutionalism
    European influences on Islamic states and,
        243
    French, Iranian system of governance and,
        250
    Morocco, 249
    United States, 10
Constitutionality, U.S. Supreme Court pre-
        sumption of, 53–54
Constitutional law, definition of, 50
Constitutional supremacy, United States, 10, 11
Consumer Product Safety Commission, U.S.,
        47
Convenios Unicos de Coordinación (CUC),
        Mexico, 284
COPARMEX (employers' organization),
        Mexico, 276
COPEI (political party), Venezuela, 315
Copenhagen criteria (EU, 1993), 88–89
Corporatist interest groups, 110
Corruption
    Brazil, 288
    definitions of, in developing countries, 316
    economic, Moroccan récuperation and, 248
    Iran, 257
    PRI, Mexico, 277
    in Russia, 187, 188
Corsica, France, separatist movements in, 82,
        101
Council of Expediency, Iran, 252–253
Council of Guardians, Iran, 251, 252
Council of Ministers
    European Union, 89, 90–91, 92, 93–94
    France, 79
    lobbying of, 110
    policy processes, 138–139
    political recruitment, 135
Council of State, France, 80
Cresson, Edith, 136

Criminal cases, U.S. judiciary and, 50
Crisis management, by U.S. presidents, 34–36
Croatia. *See also* Southeastern Europe
    constitution of, 158
CROM (*Confederación Regional Obrera
        Mexicana*), 274–275
Crvenkovski, Branko, 209
CTM (*Confederación Nacional de
        Trabajadores*), Mexico, 274, 275
Cultural values
    controversies in U.S. over, 13, 17
    emerging markets of Central and Eastern
        Europe and, 165
    in Mexico, 270
    technological changes and, 301
Culture(s)
    diversity in developing countries of, 300–301
    United States, 14–15
Czech Republic
    constitution of, 156
    legislative-executive relations in, 160
    postcommunist political system, 148, 148*t*

Dar al-harb, definition of, 238
Dar al-islam, definition of, 238
Darul Islam movement, Indonesia, 259
da Silva, Luis Inácio "Lula," 288
Davis v. Bandemer (U.S., 1986), 43
Dayton Accords (1995), 204
Debré, Michel, 78
Decentralization. *See also* Basic Law of the
        Federal Republic of Germany;
        Devolution
    in Europe, 95
    in France, 75
Declaration of Independence, U.S., 8
Declaration of the Rights of Man and of the
        Citizens (France, 1789), 77
Defense, U.S. Department of, 36, 47
De Gaulle, Charles
    early EU activities, 88
    EU intergovernmentalism and, 142
    as Euroskeptic, 140
    Gaullist party and, 120
    leadership at start of Fifth Republic by, 78
    resignation, 130
de la Madrid, Miguel
    austerity policies, 275
    budget forecasting under, 280–281
    as centrist candidate, 271
    fiscal and constitutional reforms under, 267
    Lopez Portillo's nationalization of private
        banks and, 268, 272
Delegates, U.S. Representatives as, 43–44

Delors, Jacques, 140, 142
Democracy/democracies
  Brazil, 286
  East Asia, 215, 216
  emerging, 208–209
  EU membership and, 88–89
  Europe, 62, 104
  European Union's deficit in, 93
  Indonesia, 260–261
  Japan, 234–235
  Latin America, 263
  liberal, 62, 67, 83
  participatory political processes and,
    237–238
  purpose and functions, 2
  Russian expectations for, 183–184
  Taiwan, 232–233
  United Kingdom, 68, 128
  United States, 10, 27
  U.S. federal bureaucracy and, 48–49
  Western, 4
Democratic corporatism, 110
Democratic Forum (Hungary), 154
Democratic National Committee (DNC, U.S.),
  22
Democratic Party, U.S., 23, 24, 25, 29
Democratic Progressive Party, Taiwan, 232
Democratic Republican Party, U.S., 23
Deng Xiaoping, 223, 227
Destitutes Foundation, Iran, 254
Developing countries, 5, 297. *See also* Third
    world countries; Traditional societies
  civilian bureaucracies, 315–317
  common economic problems, 300–304
  common political problems, 305–310
  indebtedness, 302–303
  industrial nations *versus,* 304
  internal cleavages, 308–309
  judiciary, 317
  military influence, 313–315
  modernization frustrations, 308, 312–313
  political institutions and processes,
    310–318
  population growth, natural resources of,
    and political change in, 299
  poverty, 301–302
  prognosis, 318–320
De Villepin, Dominique, 79, 121
Devolution. *See also* Decentralization
  local governments of United Kingdom and,
    75–77
Diaz, Porfirio, 267, 281
Diaz Ordaz, Gustavo, 271
Dictatorships, in East Asia, 217

Direct action, by U.S. interest groups, 21
Direct democracy reforms, United States, 27
Direct election plan, for U.S. presidential elec-
    tions, 30–31
Dismissal powers, of U.S. president, 12
Dispute resolution, U.S. judiciary and, 50
Districts, electoral
  Europe, single-member systems, 125,
    128–129, 130, 131
  U.S. Congress and, 42
  U.S. gerrymandering, 25, 42–43
  U.S. presidential elections and, 30
  U.S. Supreme Court on reapportionment of,
    52
Divided government
  Mexico, 279–280
  United States, 7–8, 29
Djindjic, Zoran, 209
Doors and windows. *See* Access
Doveme Khordad movement, Iran, 251
Drug trafficking, along U.S.-Mexican border,
    265, 276
Dual court system, in U.S., 50–51
Dual executive, France, 78
Dual federalism principle, 53
Dual government, Iran, 251
Dual sovereignty, United States, 10
Dutch colonialism. *See* Netherlands

East Asia. *See also* Asia; Southeast Asia
  countries comprising, 213–214
  political diversity in, 214–218
Echeverría, Luis, 271
Ecole Nationale d'Administration, 134
Economic architecture
  Central and Eastern Europe
    emerging markets, 164–166, 166t
    size considerations, 162, 164
  Mexico, 280–283
  Russia, 186–188
  Southeastern Europe, 205–206
  Ukraine, 197–198
Economic disparities. *See also* Poverty
  between developed and developing coun-
    tries, 301–302
  Mexico, 266, 267, 271, 285
  People's Republic of China, 224–225
Economic interest groups, 18–19
(The) Economist, 90
Education
  by interest groups, 19–20
  and value consensus in Central and Eastern
    Europe, 152–153
Education, U.S. Department of, 48

Education Amendments, Title IX (U.S., 1972), 48
Egypt, European government model and, 241
Eisenhower, Dwight, 34
Elastic clause, in U.S. Constitution, 12
Election systems
  Bosnia, 209–210
  Central and Eastern European, 171–173
  developing countries, 312, 317
  early, in Germany, 84
  Europe, 125–132, 126t
  European Union, 131–132
  France, 128–130
  Germany, 130–131
  Mexico, 267
  Morocco, 249
  Russia, 189–192
  Southeastern Europe, 207
  Ukraine, 199–200
  United Kingdom, 126–128
  United States, 25, 26–32
Electoral College, U.S., 30–32, 40
Electoral Count Act (U.S., 1887), 31, 54
Electoral Fairness Project , U.S., 30, 31–32
Elites. *See also* Leadership
  accountability of, 6
    Central and Eastern Europe, 169–170,
      172–173
    Russia, 192
    Southeastern Europe, 207
  ancient civilizations, 306
  developing countries, 308, 310, 317–318
  Mexico, 266, 267, 271
  socialization and political recruitment of,
    136
Elizabeth II, Queen of England, 69
Emerging markets
  Central and Eastern Europe, 164–166, 166t
  Ukraine, 198
Emerging republics or democracies, 208–209
England
  relationship to United Kingdom, 68
  state-church cleavage in, 102
Environmental Protection Agency, U.S., 47
Equal protection under Fourteenth
    Amendment (U.S.), 52
Estonia, constitution of, 158
Etalaat (Iranian security force), 254, 256
Ethnic cleansing, 168, 185
Ethnic groups. *See also* Southeastern Europe
  developing countries, 300
  Europe, 100–101
  Indonesia, 257, 260–261
  Iran, 257

People's Republic of China, 227
  Russia, 184–185
  United States, 14–15, 17
Ethnicity, nationalism *versus,* 184–185
Euro, 92, 93
Euroenthusiasts, 140
Europe. *See also* Central and Eastern Europe;
    European Union; France; Germany,
    Federal Republic of; Southeastern
    Europe; United Kingdom
  colonial influences on Islamic states, 241–243
  pressure on Morocco to reform, 246–247
  Southern, Islamic political tradition in, 240
  Western
    civil society and social movements,
      107–109
    constitutions and, 66–67
    electoral systems and elections, 125–132
    interest groups, 109–113
    international organizations and, 65–66
    media, 113–115
    policy processes, 137–139
    political culture, 105–107
    political recruitment, 132–137
    population and economies of, 63, 64t, 65
    postcommunist political systems, 148t
    socioeconomic setting, 99–105
    study of comparative politics in, 61–62
European Central Bank
  as EU organization, 90, 91, 92–93
  Germany and, 142–143
  political recruitment, 135
European Charter of Human Rights, 90
European Coal and Steel Community (ECSC),
    87–88, 295
European Commission
  as EU organization, 89, 90, 91–92
  European Parliament and, 93
  policy processes, 138, 139
  political recruitment, 136
European Convention on Human Rights,
    74–75
European Council
  as EU organization, 90, 91, 92
  policy processes, 138
  political recruitment, 135
European Court of Justice
  as EU organization, 87, 90, 91, 94
  policy processes, 139
  political recruitment, 135
European Court on Human Rights, 75
European Economic Area (EEA), 89
European Economic Community (EEC), 88,
    295

European Monetary Union, 142. *See also* Euro

European Parliament
as EU organization, 89, 90, 92, 93–94
party systems, 124–125
policy processes, 138–139
political parties in, 115–116
political recruitment, 135
voting in elections for, 131

European People's Party–European Democrats, 125

European Union (EU), 62
basic data on members of, 66*t*
Central and Eastern European countries and, 63, 152, 154, 178
constitution, 79, 87–90
constitutional prospects for, 94–95
development and governance theories, 139–140
domestic and foreign policies of members and, 141–143
as economic center, 303–304
elections, 131–132
Euro-Mediterranean Partnership, 247
institutions of, 90–94
lobbying of, 110–111
as new form of association, 293–294
news media and, 115
party systems, 124–125
policy processes, 138–139
political culture, 106–107
political recruitment, 135–136
political views of, 140–141
population and economy of, 64*t*, 65
postcommunist political systems, 148*t*
recent elections, 126*t*
religious groups' influence on, 113
United Kingdom and, 65

Euroskeptics, 140

Executive and executive power. *See also* Federal bureaucracy, U.S.; Political executive; President/presidency
Central and Eastern European transitional systems, 159–160
developing countries, 313–315
European countries, 67
European Union, 91–92
France, 80
Iran, 251
United Kingdom, 69
U.S. Constitution on, 32–33

Executive Office of the President (EOP, U.S.), 36

Ex post facto laws, under U.S. Constitution, 10

Family Research Council (U.S.), 19

Fascism, 62, 104, 243

Faubius, Laurent, 120

FDN (*Frente Democrática Liberal*), 277

Fedayin-i Khalq, Iran, 252

Federal bureaucracy, U.S., 45. *See also* Bureaucracy/bureaucracies
democracy and, 48–49
structure and functions, 45–48

Federal Bureau of Investigation (FBI, U.S.), 37

Federal Election Campaign Act (FECA, U.S., 1971), 20, 27–28

Federal Election Commission (FEC, U.S.), 28

Federalism
administrative, in Germany, 84
Brazil, 285–286, 290–291
Central and Eastern European constitutions on, 158
communist political systems, 155
Germany, 86–87
Mexico, 267, 269, 282–284
U.S., 10, 32

Federalist Papers, The, 18, 37, 43, 53, 106

Federalists, U.S., 9, 23

Federal Reserve Board, U.S., 47, 48

Federal Trade Commission, U.S., 48

Feingold, Russ, 28

Felons, convicted, voting rights in U.S. for, 26

Filibuster(s), in U.S. Senate, 41

First World War, 103–104, 242

Fischer, Joschka, 123

527 organizations, U.S., 28

Flemish people, Belgium, 2

Foreign policy, European Union and, 143

Forward- *versus* backward-facing viewpoints
in Central and Eastern Europe, 167–168
in Southeastern Europe, 203

Fox Quesada, Vicente, 267, 269–270, 278, 279

France, 65. *See also* French Revolution
bureaucracy, 80
colonial influences on Islamic states, 242, 245–246
communism in, 104
constitution, 77–82
decentralization, 75
as dominant EU decision maker, 141
electoral system, 128–130
European monarchies and, 101
European Union and, 90, 96, 142
Euroskeptics in, 140
immigrants and civil society in, 108–109
judiciary, 81
legislature, 80–81
media in, 114

pluralist interest groups in, 110
policy processes, 137–138
political culture, 4, 106
political executive, 78–79
political parties and party systems, 119–121
political recruitment, 133–135, 136, 137
population and economy of, 64t
recent elections, 126t
religious groups in, 112, 113
single-member district elections in, 125
trade unions in, 111
Franco, Itamar, 290
Free Democrats, Germany, 83, 123, 130
Freedom Movement, Iran, 252
Free Trade Association of the Americas, 295
French Revolution, 77, 78, 101, 102
Frontbenchers, House of Commons, U.K., 73

Gaidar, Yegor, 187, 198
Gandhi, Mahatma, 301
Gaullists, France, 120–121, 129
Gays and lesbians, United States, 17
Gender discrimination, Title IX of Education
    Amendments (U.S., 1972) on, 48
George V, King of England, 101
Geremek, Bronislaw, 176
Gerhardt, Wolfgang, 123
German speakers, in Central and Eastern
    Europe, 101
Germany, Federal Republic of, 65
    bureaucracy, 84–85
    constitution, 82–87
    corporatist interest groups in, 110
    as dominant EU decision maker, 141
    electoral system, 130–131
    as Euroenthusiast, 140
    European monarchies and, 101
    European Union and, 90, 96, 142–143
    federalism, 86–87
    gradualist socialism in, 104
    immigrants and civil society in, 108–109
    judiciary, 86
    legislature, 85
    media in, 114
    policy processes, 137–138
    political culture, 4, 106
    political executive, 83–84
    political parties and party systems, 121–124
    political recruitment, 135, 136
    population and economy of, 64t
    postindustrial economy of, 100
    proportional representation in, 125–126
    recent elections, 126t
    religious groups in, 112–113

state-church cleavage in, 101–102
    trade unions in, 111
Gerry, Elbridge, 42
Gerrymandering, 25, 42–43
Gini Index of Inequality, 64t
Giscard d'Estaing, Valéry, 121
Globalization, Keynesianism and, 104
Gomillion v. Lightfoot (U.S., 1960), 42
Good Friday Agreement (1998), 76, 119
Gorbachev, Mikhail, 150, 151, 154, 194
Gore, Al, 30, 31
Gotovina, Ante, 209
Goulart, João, 287, 289
Government. *See also* Political machinery
    extractive and distributive functions of, 189
    Mexican *versus* U.S. assumptions about, 268
    purpose and functions of, 2
Government-in-waiting, Germany, 84
Gradualist socialism, 104
Grassroots organizations, U.S., 19–20, 22
Gratz v. Bollinger (U.S., 2003), 15
"Great Compromise," for U.S. Constitution, 9
Great Depression, political parties in U.S. and,
    24
Great Leap Forward (China), 222
Great Proletariat Cultural Revolution (China),
    222–223
Greece. *See* Southeastern Europe
Green Party
    France, 120
    Germany
        coalition governments and, 83, 123
        elections and, 130
        rise of, 105
        SPD and, 122
        women candidates, 136
    Mexico, 278
    United Kingdom, 119
    U.S., 23
Group of 8 (G-8), 66, 79
Grutter v. Bollinger (U.S., 2003), 15
Gysi, Gregor, 124
Gyurcsány, Ferenc, 152

Habeas corpus, under U.S. Constitution, 10
Hamdi v. Rumsfeld (U.S., 2004), 52
Hamilton, Alexander, 53
Harrington, James, 8
Hartz, Louis, 56
Hassan II, King of Morocco, 246, 249
Havel, Vaclav, 172
Hayek, Friedrich, 238
Hayes, Rutherford B., 31
Henry VIII, King of England, 102

Her Majesty's Loyal Opposition, House of
Commons, U.K., 73
Hitler, Adolf, 82, 86, 87, 131
Hizb al-Adala wa'l-Tanmiya, Morocco, 249
Hizbollahi, Iran, 254, 255–257
Hobbes, Thomas, 103
Hollande, François, 120
Homeland Security, U.S. Department of, 36–37
Hong Kong, 216, 295
House of Commons, U.K.
collective responsibility and, 70
elections to, 68–69, 126–127
organization of, 72–73
political recruitment, 132, 133, 136
powers and composition of, 71–72
House of Lords, U.K.
Appellate Committee of, 75
political recruitment, 132, 133
powers and composition of, 71–72, 73–74
prime minister candidates from, 70
House of Representatives, U.S., 24, 40–42. *See
also* Congress, U.S.
Hu Jintao, 226, 227
Hukumat-i Islami (Islamic government), Iran,
250–253
Human Rights Act, United Kingdom, 75
Hume, John, 119
Hungary
constitution of, 158
Democratic Forum, 154
Democratic Youth Alliance Initiative, 174
legislative-executive relations in, 160
postcommunist political system, 148, 148*t*
value consensus in, 152–153
Husayn, Shi'a caliph, 239
Hybrid government, France, 78
Hybrid interest groups, 19
Hylton, v. United States (1796), 53

Immigration, into U.S., 14–15, 265
Impeachment, United States, 37, 38
Implied powers clause, U.S. Constitution, 12,
39
Imported leaders, in transitional Central and
Eastern Europe, 176, 177
Incumbents, in U.S. Congress, 44–45
India
British colonial rule in, 242
coverage of, 5–6
Gandhi and traditional culture in, 301
internal cleavages, 309
Islamic political tradition in, 240
Individual responsibility, of U.K. cabinet min-
isters, 70

Indonesia
European colonial influences on, 241, 242
governance in, 257–258
"guided democracy" in, 260–261
nationalism and Islam in, 258–259
Industrial nations
developing countries *versus,* 304
formal *versus* informal structures in, 311
Industrial revolution, 65, 101, 102
Inherent powers, (George) Washington's use
of, 33
Institutionalization. *See also* Political machinery
civilian bureaucracies of developing countries, 316–317
institutions *versus,* 311–312
INS v. Chadha (U.S., 1983), 38, 52
Interest groups, 6. *See also* Political machinery
amicus curiae briefs before Supreme Court
by, 53
Brazil, 288
democratic government and, 18
developing countries, 318
Europe, 109–113
Mexico, 273–276
politically stable systems, 310
significance of, 21
tactics, 19–21
types, 18–19
United States, 17–21
Interests, U.S. federal bureaucracy and promotion of, 46–47
Internal cleavages, in developing countries,
308–309
International Court of Justice (Hague), 207,
209
International Monetary Fund (IMF), 65–66,
152, 198, 272–273
Internet, 113–115, 152, 230
Interstate Commerce Commission, U.S., 47, 48
IRA (Irish Republican Army), 76–77
Iran
Constitutional Revolution (1906), 242
dual government system and jurisconsult
power, 250–253
hizbollahi and reform in, 255–257
supreme leader, 253–255
Irangate, 299
Ireland, Republic of, 63, 76. *See also* Northern
Ireland
Iron triangles, U.S., 20–21, 47
Irredentist (border) problems, 101
Islam, 102, 257. *See also* Muhammad, Prophet
of Islam

Islamic Revolutionary Courts, Iran, 255
Islamic Revolutionary Guard Corps, Iran, 253
Islamic states
  definition of, 300
  governance examples, 243–244
    Indonesia, 257–261
    Iran, 250–257
    Morocco, 244–250
  military influence, 314
  modernization and, 308, 310
  traditional governance principles, 238–243
    colonial experience, 241–243
    traditional institutions and political culture, 238–241
Israel, creation of, Islamic states and, 242
Issue voting, in U.S., 29–30
Italy
  colonial influences on Islamic states, 242
  as Euroenthusiast, 140
Izetbegovic, Alija, 172, 209

Jackson, Andrew, 23, 33
Jafaʿari school of jurisprudence, 251
Jakarta Charter (Indonesia, 1945), 259
Japan
  Confucian values in, 220
  government of, 216, 217
  Indonesian nationalists and, 258–259
  political system, 233–235
  regionalism and, 294–295
  as world economic center, 303–304
Jefferson, Thomas, 33
Jeffersonian Republicans, 23, 25
Jiang Jieshi, 231. *See also* Chiang Kai-shek
Jiang Jungguo, 231. *See also* Chiang Ching-kuo
Jiang Zemin, 227
Jihad, definition of, 238
Joffé, George, 300
Johnson, Lyndon B., 34
Jospin, Lionel, 120
Judaism. *See also* Anti-Semitism
  Europe and, 62
Judicial activism, by U.S. Supreme Court, 53–54
Judicial Appointments Commission, U.K., 75
Judicial review
  European Court of Justice, 94, 95
  France, 81
  Germany, 86
  post-WWII Europe, 95
  United Kingdom, 74
  United States, 49, 53–55
Judicial self-restraint, by U.S. Supreme Court, 54

Judiciary. *See also* Legal framework; Supreme Court
  Brazil, 287
  developing countries, 317
  Europe, 67
  European Union, 91
  France, 81
  Germany, 86
  Iran, 254–255
  Mexico, 269, 284
  Taiwan, 232
  United Kingdom, 74–75
  United States
    appointments to, 55
    common law, judicial review and, 49
    independence of, 11
    interpretation of U.S. Constitution by, 12
    organization and functions, 49–51
    statutory interpretation by, 53–55
    Supreme Court jurisdiction and criteria for review, 51–53
Judiciary Act (U.S., 1789), 50, 53
Juppé, Alan, 129
Jurisconsult power, in Iran, 250–253
Jus sanguinis, 101
Justice and Development Party, Morocco, 249

Karbashi, Ghollamhossein, 257
Kargozaran-i Sazandagi, Iran, 251
Kennedy, John F., 34, 35
Kerry, John, 30
Keynes, John Maynard, 104
Khalifa, of Islamic states, 239
Khalifa movement, South Asia, 242
Khamane'i, Ali, Ayatollah of Iran, 252, 253, 255
Khasbulatov, Ruslan, 190
Khatami, Mohamed, 251, 252, 253, 255, 256
Khodorkovsky, Mikhail, 192
Khomeini, Ayatollah, 250, 252, 256
Kim Il-Song, 215
Kim Jong-il, 215
Kohl, Helmut, 84, 131
Koizumi, Junichrio, 234
Korea, Democratic People's Republic of
  classification of, 297
  government of, 215, 217, 218
Korea, Republic of
  Confucian values in, 220
  government of, 215, 217, 218
  military influence, 314
Kosovo. *See* Southeastern Europe
Kostunica, Vojislav, 209
Kravchuk, Leonid, 196, 199
Kuchma, Leonid, 195, 196, 197, 199–200

Kuomintang (KMT), 231
Kutla political parties, Morocco, 247
Kwasniewski, Aleksander, 152

Labastida Ochoa, Francisco, 278
Labor unions. *See* Trade unions
Labour Party, U.K., 116, 117–119
  class politics and, 105
  devolution and local government under, 75–76
  elections and, 127, 128
  House of Lords reform and, 74
  political recruitment, 132, 137
Lafontaine, Oskar, 124
Länder, German. *See also* Bundesrat, German
  cabinets, 85
  elections of 2005 in, 84, 87
  federalism and, 86–87
Lang, Jack, 120
Language, Central and Eastern European constitutions on, 158
Latin America, 263–264. *See also* Brazil; Mexico
  global economy and, 304
  indebtedness, 303
  military influence on modernization, 314–315
  violent internal cleavages, 309
Latvia, constitution of, 158
Lawmaking
  France, 74–75
  Germany, 85
  House of Commons, U.K., 73
  U.S. Congress, 41–42
Leadership, 3–4
  under Communism, 151
  developing countries
    civilian bureaucracies and, 316
    elites and, 317–318
    institutionalization and, 312
    military and, 313–315
  Mexico, 271
  People's Republic of China, 223–224
  Russia, 193–194
  Southeastern Europe, 208–210
  sultanate in Morocco, 244–245
  supreme leader of Iran, 253–255
  transitional Central European political systems, 149, 150, 175–178, 177*t*
  Ukraine, 200–201
Lee Hsien Loong, 215
Lee Kuan Yew, 215
Lee Teng-hui, 232

Legal framework. *See also* Judiciary; Supreme Court
  Central and Eastern Europe, 161–162, 163*t*
  European influences on Islamic states and, 243
  Morocco, 249
Legalist tradition, in China, 220
Legislative veto, 37, 38
Legislature(s). *See also* Congress, U.S.
  in developing countries, institutionalization of, 312–313
  Europe, 67
  European Union, 91
  executive relations with
    Central and Eastern Europe, 159–160
    Ukraine, 197
  France, 80–81
  Germany, 85
  Iran, 251, 252
  Japan, 234
  Mexican states, 284
  Mexico, 267, 269, 278–279, 280
  Morocco, 247
  People's Republic of China, 227–228
  Russia, 190, 191
  Taiwan, 233
  United Kingdom, 71–74
  U.S. employees of, 46
Legitimacy
  Central and Eastern European transitional systems, 169–170
  Southeastern Europe, 206
Lenin, Vladimir, and political philosophy of, 103, 216–217, 225–226
Le Pen, Jean-Marie, 121, 129
Liberal democracy, 62, 67, 83
Liberal Democratic Party
  Japan, 216, 234
  Russia, ultranationalism and, 185, 190, 191
  United Kingdom, 118, 127, 132
Liberal intergovernmentalism (state-centered) theory, of European Union, 139
Liberalism, Europe and, 62
Limited government, United States, 10
Lincoln, Abraham, 33
Litigation, by U.S. interest groups, 21
Litmus tests, for U.S. judicial appointments, 55
Lobbying, by U.S. interest groups, 20
Local governments, Mexico, 282, 284–285
Locke, John, 8
Lombardo Toledano, Vicente, 275, 278
Lopez Mateos, Adolfo, 271
Lopez Portillo, José, 268, 271, 272, 280, 283
Louisiana Purchase, 33

Lukashenko, Alexander, 172
Lutheranism, 102

Maastricht Treaty (1992), 89, 92, 95
Macao, government of, 216
MacArthur, Douglas, 34
Macedonia. *See* Southeastern Europe
Machiavelli, Niccolò, 8
Madero, Francisco, 267
Madison, James, 18, 38, 106
Magalhães, António Carlos, 290
Majles-e Khebregan (Iranian Assembly of
    Experts), 253–254
Majlis-e Shora (Iranian consultative body),
    251–252
Majma-e Tashkhis-e Maslehat-e Nazan, Iran,
    252–253
Major, John, 117
Makhzan, Morocco. See Monarchy/monar-
    chies, Morocco
Manufacturing
    disincentives, in Russia, 187
    expansion, in Mexico, 281
Mao Zedong, 215, 217, 222–223, 231
Marbury v. Madison (U.S., 1803), 12, 49, 52,
    53
Marchuk, Yevhen, 199
Marovic, Svetozar, 209
Marshall, John, 12, 49, 53
Martyrs Foundation, Iran, 254
Marx, Karl
    on owner-worker cleavage, 103
    philosophy of
        East Asian political systems and, 216–217
        Mexican constitution and, 268
Massachusetts v. Laird (U.S., 1970), 52
Mass media communications. *See* Media
McCain, John, 28
McCain-Feingold Act (BCRA, U.S., 2002), 28
McCulloch v. Maryland (U.S., 1819), 12, 51
McGuinness, Martin, 119
MDB (*Movimento Democrático Brasileiro*), 289
Media. *See also* Press; Television
    Europe, 113–115
    Morocco, 249
    on stability in developing countries, 317
    United States, 35–36
Medicare (U.S.), 14
Mercado Común de América del Sur (or do Sul),
    295–296
Merkel, Angela, 123, 136
Mesic, Stipe, 209
Mexican Association of Insurance Institutions,
    276

Mexican Bankers Association, 276
Mexican Council of Businessmen, 276
Mexican Revolution (1910), 267, 270
Mexican United Socialist Party (PSUM),
    277
Mexico
    constitutional development, 267–270
    economic crisis of 1980s, 265–266, 272, 274
    governmental institutions, 278–285
    interest groups, 273–276
    political parties, 276–278
    shared border with U.S., 263–264, 269
    social forces, 270–273
    system in action, 285
    United States and, 264–266
Middle East. *See also* Iran; Islamic states;
    Morocco
    political systems, 5
Miksic, Boris, 176
Military
    Brazil, 287, 289
    developing countries and, 308, 309, 310,
        313–315
    East Asian governments and, 215
    Indonesian, 260
    Iranian, 254
    Mexican, 266–267, 276
Milosevic, Slobodan, 172, 200, 208, 209
Ministers. *See also* Cabinet(s); Council of
    Ministers; Prime minister(s)
    German selection of, 84
Minorities. *See also* Race, United States
    Central and Eastern European constitutions
        on, 158
    Iran, 251
Mitterand, François, 79, 82, 120
Modernization, 305
    developing countries and, 307–308, 310
    development of, 306–307
Mojahedin-e Khalq, Iran, 252
Moldova, constitution of, 158
Monarchy/monarchies
    East Asia, 215
    Europe, 67
    Japan, 216, 233
    Morocco, 244–246, 247–248, 249–250
    subordinate military influences in, 313
    United Kingdom, 69–70
Mongolia
    government of, 215
    regional affiliations, 214
Monnet, Jean, 87, 142
Montenegro. *See* Southeastern Europe
Montesquieu, Charles Louis de Secondat, 8

Morocco
  European colonial influences on, 242,
    245–246
  Islamic political tradition and, 241
  political stability, 248–250
  reform and institutionalization, 246–248
  the sultanate, 244–245
Morones, Luis, 275
Mossadegh, Mohammed, 252
Mu'awiya, caliph in Damascus, 239
Mu'talafat, Iran, 251
Mu'talafe, Iran, 251, 252
Mughals, 240–241
Muhammad, Prophet of Islam, 238, 239, 244,
  253
Muhammad Ali, Egyptian ruler, 241
Muhammad al-Mahdi, lesser and greater
  occultations and, 240
Muhammadiyah, Indonesia, 258
Muhammad VI, heir to Moroccan throne, 249
Multilevel governance theory, of European
  Union, 139, 140
Muslim countries. *See* Islamic states
Myanmar (Burma), government of, 215

NAACP, 19, 21
Nader, Ralph, 23
Napoleon Bonaparte, 78, 87, 241
Napoleonic Code, 74
Napoleon III, 78
National Abortion Rights Action League
  (U.S.), 19
National Assembly, France, 78, 79, 80–81
  elections to, 128–129, 130
National boundaries, 4
National Democratic Union (UDN, Brazil),
  289
National Front party, France, 108, 121
Nationalism
  Central and Eastern Europe, 167–168
  economic, in Mexico, 281
  Europe, 62
  Indonesia, 260–261
  Islam in Indonesia and, 258–259
  Mexican constitution and, 267
  nations *versus*, 184–185
  political culture and, 107
  Southeastern Europe, 202–203
Nationalist Party of China (KMT), 231
Nationalist problems, 101
Nationalization, of U.S. Bill of Rights, 13
National Labor Relations Board, U.S., 48
National Organization for Women (U.S.), 19
National Right to Life Committee (U.S.), 19

National Security Administration (U.S.), 37
National Security Council (U.S.), 36
National System of Fiscal Coordination
  (SNCF, Mexico), 267
Nation-state(s)
  allegiance to, 2
  French Revolution and, 77
  Latin America and, 263
Natural resources, technological changes and
  devastation of, 319–320
Nazi Party, Germany, 121
Necessary and proper clause, in U.S.
  Constitution, 12, 39
Neocorporatism, 110
Neofunctionalist theory, of European Union,
  139
Neo-Nazi National Democrats, Germany, 124
Nepal
  government of, 215
  regional affiliations, 214
Netherlands
  colonial influences on Islamic states, 242
  as colonial power, 61
  EU constitution ratification in, 90
  Sukarno's Partai Nasional Indonesia and,
    258–259
Neustadt, Richard, 33
New Jersey Plan, for U.S. Constitution, 9
New Left Party, Germany, 123
New Public Management (U.K., NPM), Next
  Steps Initiative, 71
Nice Treaty (2000), 89
Nixon, Richard, 38
No-confidence votes
  constructive, by German Bundestag, 84
  France, 81
  United Kingdom, 72
Nonaligned nations, 298
North America. *See also specific countries*
  economic center in, 303–304
North American Free Trade Agreement
  (NAFTA), 264, 281, 295, 296
North Atlantic Treaty Organization (NATO),
  63, 65, 298
Northeast Asia, countries comprising,
  213–214
Northern Ireland, 63. *See also* Ireland, Republic
  of
  divisive situation in, 2
  local government of, 75, 76–77
  nationalist movement in, 101, 102
  political culture, 106
  political parties, 118, 119, 127
  relationship to United Kingdom, 68

Office of Management and Budget (OMB, U.S.), 36
Office of Personnel Management, U.S., 46
Official Secrets Act (U.K., 1906), 71
Oligarchs
  Russia, 186, 187
  Ukraine, 196
Orange Revolution (Ukraine), 154, 195, 199
Orban, Viktor, 152, 172
Organized crime
  Russia, 188
  Southeastern Europe, 205
Originalist doctrine of judicial self-restraint, by U.S. Supreme Court, 54
Ottomans, 240–241, 242
Owner-worker cleavage, 101, 102–103

Paisley, Ian, 119
PAN (*Partido de Acción Nacional*), Mexico, 267, 277, 278
Panic, Milan, 176
Pantja Sila principles, Sukarno's, 259, 260
Parliament. *See also* European Parliament
  United Kingdom, 70, 132–133
Parliamentary governments, 4
  democracy and, 62
  East Asia, 215
  PRC as, 227–228
  presidential governments *versus*, 7–8
Parliamentary sovereignty, 68
PARM (*Partido Auténtico de la Revolución Mejicana*), 277, 278
Partai Nasional Indonesia, 258
Participatory political processes
  democracy and, 237–238
  European influences on Islamic states and, 243
  Morocco, 249
Partisan politics, U.S., interest groups and, 20
Party discipline, in U.S. Congress, 40
Party identification, U.S., 29
Party of Democratic Socialism, Germany, 123, 124
Party of European Socialists, European Union, 125
Party of God, Iran, 256
Party systems
  British, 116–119
  definition of, 116
  European, 115–125
  European Union, 124–125
  France, 119–121
  Germany, 121–124
Patriotism, political culture and, 107, 167–168

PCM (*Partido Comunista Mexicano*), 277
Perot, Ross, 23, 30
Perquisites of office (perks), for U.S. Congress, 44, 45
Persuasion, U.S. presidential power and, 33
PFL (*Partido da Frente Liberal*), Brazil, 289
Philippines, government of, 215
Plaid Cymru (PC), Wales, 118
Pluralist interest groups, 110, 273–276
PMDB (*Partido do Movimento Democrático Brasileiro*), 289
PMT (*Partido Mexicano de los Trabajadores*), 277
Poland
  constitution of, 158
  legislative-executive relations in, 160
  postcommunist political system, 148, 148*t*
  Solidarnosc, 154
  value consensus in, 152
Political action committees (PACS, U.S.), 20, 28, 44–45
Political actors, 3. *See also* Elites; Leadership
Political culture(s). *See also* Value systems
  Brazil, 290
  Europe, 105–107
  France, 77–78
  modernization and changes in, 307–308
  Western democracies, 4
Political executive. *See also* Executive and executive power
  European Union, 90–91
  France, 78–79
  Germany, 83–84
  United Kingdom, 70–71
Political gerrymandering, U.S., 43
Political instability, developing countries and, 308, 309, 310, 318
Political machinery, 3–4. *See also* Constitution(s)
  Brazil, 290–291
  Central and Eastern European transitional systems, 149–150
    architects of, 159
    centralization, 160–161
    constitution(s), 155–158
    legislative-executive relations, 159–160
  developing countries, 310–318
  elements of, 158–159
  Japan, 233–235
  Mexico, 278–285
  Morocco, 246–248
  People's Republic of China, 222–231
  Southeastern Europe, 204–205
  Taiwan, 231–233

Political parties, 6. *See also* Political machinery
  Brazil, 289–290
  British, 116–119
  definition of, 116
  developing countries, 317
  European, 115–125
  French, 119–121
  German, 121–124
  Indonesia, 258
  Iran, 251–252
  Mexico, 266–267, 276–278
  Morocco, 247, 249
  People's Republic of China, 225–227
  politically stable systems, 310
  Russian, 190–191
  Taiwanese, 232
  U.S., 21–25
    congressional, 40
    elections and representation by, 13
    factors sustaining two-party system,
      24–25
    organization, 22–23
    policy and ideological characteristics of, 24
    two-party system, 23–24
Political power, 2. *See also* Elites; Leadership
Political recruitment
  under Communism, 151
  Europe, 132–137
Political systems. *See also* Political machinery
  creation and evolution of, 3
  functions, 4
Pompidou, Georges, 121
Popular sovereignty, United States, 9
Population(s)
  Asia, Africa, and Latin America, 299
  China, 295
  developing countries, 308, 318, 319
  Islamic states, 300
  in poverty, 301–302, 305
  rural, supporting elites, 305
Pork barrel legislation, in U.S., 44, 45
Portugal
  as colonial power, 61
  economic needs of, 297
  government relocated to Brazil, 286
Post facto legislation, U.K., 74
Postmaterialism, social movement politics and,
  105
Poverty
  economic disparities and, 301–302
  effects on United States, 304
  imagining, 301
  indebtedness and, 302–303
  political problems and, 308, 310

PPS (*Partido Popular Socialista*), Mexico,
  277–278
PRD (*Partido de la Revolución Democrática*),
  Mexico, 277
Presidential government
  Brazil, 288
  Mexico and Latin America, 278
  United States, 4, 7, 30
Presidential Power and the Modern Presidents
  (Neustadt), 33
President/presidency. *See also* Executive and
  executive power
  European Union, 89–90, 92
  France, 67, 78
  Germany, 83
  Mexico, 269, 271, 278–280
  United States, 32–38
    Congressional relations and impeachment,
      37–38
    Constitutional vagueness, historical prece-
      dents and, 32–34
    crisis management and popular leadership
      under, 34–36
    federal bureaucracy and, 48–49
    institutional, 36–37
    twentieth century, 34
President *pro tempore,* U.S., 40
Press. *See also* Media
  Iranian bans on, 257
PRI (*Partido Revolucionario Institucional*),
  Mexico
  austerity measures during 1980s and, 272
  competition for, 277, 278
  end of hegemony of, 273
  hegemony of, 266, 279, 285
  as single official party, 276
Prime minister(s). *See also* Executive and exec-
  utive power
  Japan, 234
  Morocco, 247
  United Kingdom, 70, 72
*Programa de Inversiones Públicas para el
  Desarrollo Rural* (PIDER), Mexico, 284
Progressive era reforms, U.S., 27
Progressive Party, U.S., 30
Proportional election plan, for U.S. presiden-
  tial elections, 30–31
Proportional representation systems, 125–126
  European Union, 131
  Germany, 130
  Ukraine, 196–197
  women candidates and, 136–137
Protest(s), by U.S. interest groups, 21
Protestant Reformation, 101–102

Provisional Irish Republican Army (PIRA), 76
PSD. *See* Social Democratic Party
PSDB (*Partido da Social Democracia Brasileira*), 289
PST (*Partido Socialista Trabajador*), 277, 278
PT (*Partido dos Trabalhadores*), Brazil, 289–290
Public goods, U.S. federal bureaucracy and, 46
Public interest groups, United States, 19
Public opinion polling
    Central and Eastern Europe, 153
    on Congress, 44
    presidential government in U.S. and, 35–36
    on U.S. federal bureaucracy, 49
Public relations, by interest groups, 19–20
Putin, Vladimir
    consolidation of power by, 190–192
    leadership by, 193–194
    public consensus and, 182–183
    Russian constitution and, 186
    tax plan, 188
    value consensus in Russia and, 152

Qing dynasty, China, 221, 223
Qur'an. *See also* Shari'a
    law derived from, 238–239
Qualified majority voting, EU, 91, 139, 140
Question time, House of Commons, U.K., 73

Race. *See also* Minorities
    United States, 15
        gerrymandering and, 42–43
        voting rights and, 26
Radical Party, France, 120
Radio, in Europe, 114
Raffarin, Jean-Pierre, 79
Rafsanjani, Ali Akbar Hashemi, 251, 253, 256
Reagan, Ronald, 35
Recall elections, in U.S., 28
Rechstaat concept (state based on law), 86
Redistributive activities, of U.S. federal bureaucracy, 47–48
Red Sarekat Islam, Indonesia, 258
Referendum Party, U.K., 119
Referendums, voter
    France, 130
    Germany, 131
    Russia constitution, 157
    Switzerland, 237
    United Kingdom, 128
    United States, 28
Reform fatigue, Central and Eastern Europe, 164
Reform Party, U.S., 23

Regents of the University of California v. Bakke (U.S., 1978), 15
Regionalism
    Asia, 294–295
    dramatic events and, 299
    Europe, 293–294
    NATO, Warsaw Pact, and nonaligned countries, 298
    third-world countries and, 296–297
    Western Hemisphere, 5, 295–296
Regulatory activities, of U.S. federal bureaucracy, 47
Religion. *See also* Islamic states
    controversies in U.S. over, 13, 17
    in Europe after Protestant Reformation, 101
    in Mexico, 276
    in postcommunist Russia, 185
    in Southeastern Europe, 203
    state-church cleavage and, 101–102
    and value consensus in Central and Eastern Europe, 152
Religious groups
    influence in Europe by, 112–113
    lobbying in Europe by, 110
Representative democracy. *See* Democracy/democracies
Representativeness, 6. *See also* Democracy/democracies
    in Central and Eastern Europe, 172
Repressive policies, Morocco, 249
Republican government, United States, 7, 10
Republican National Committee (RNC, U.S.), 22
Republican Party, U.S., 24, 25, 29
Revolutionary tribunals, 317. *See also* Judiciary
Rexhepi, Bajram, 209
Rodina Party, Russia, 191
Romania. *See also* Southeastern Europe
    constitution of, 158
Rookie leaders, 175–176, 176, 193–194, 209. *See also* Leadership
Roosevelt, Franklin, 24, 35, 36
Roosevelt, Theodore, 30, 33
Roth, Claudia, 123
Rowhani, Hassan, 253
Rugova, Ibrahim, 209
Ruiz Cortinez, Adolfo, 271
Rule by law, in East Asia, 217
Rule of law
    Brazil, 287
    developing countries, 309
    participatory political processes and, 237–238
    Taiwan, 233

Rule of law *(cont.)*
  United Kingdom, representative democracy
    and, 68
  United States, 10
Rules Committee, of U.S. House, 41
Rural-urban balance
  developing countries, 305
  People's Republic of China, 224
Russia
  constitution of, 156–158, 186
  East Asia and, 214
  economic architecture, 186–188
  Europe and, 63
  European Union and, 181, 294
  internal empire of, 61
  leadership, 193–194
  legislative-executive relations in, 160
  Ottoman and Iranian territories and, 241
  political and social dynamics, 189–193
    access for public input, 192–193
    elections, 189–192
    elite accountability, 192
    postcommunist political system, 148, 148*t*
    prognosis, 194
    timeline, 182
    transitional politics in, 182–194
    value consensus in, 152, 182–185
    Yeltsin's *ad hoc* efforts in, 154
Rutskoi, Aleksander, 190
Rybkin, Ivan, 192

Sadat, Anwar, 298
Safavids, Islamic political tradition and,
  240–241
Salafiyya movement, 242–243
Salinas de Gortari, Carlos
  budget forecasting under, 280–281
  CNC relations with PRI under, 275
  corruption and electoral fraud under, 273
  economic reforms under, 268–269
  as PRI candidate, 277
  privatization under, 282
  structural adjustments under, 266, 271
Sarekat Islam, Indonesia, 258
Sarkozy, Nicolas, 121
Schmidt, Helmut, 84
Schröder, Gerhard, 84, 123
Schuman, Robert, 87, 142
Scotland
  local government of, 75–76
  political parties, 118–119, 127
  relationship to United Kingdom, 68
  separatist movements in, 101
  state-church cleavage in, 102

Semipresidential government
  France, 78
  Taiwan, 233
Senate. *See also* Congress, U.S.; Legislature(s)
  France, 81
  United States, 40–42, 43, 55
Senior Executive Service, U.S., 46
Sepah (Iranian security force), 254, 256
Separation of powers
  Brazil, 285
  impeachment and, 38
  Mexico, 267, 269
  United Kingdom, 75
  United States, 11, 25, 52
Separatist movements/problems, 101
September 11, 2001, terrorist attacks, 56, 109
Serbia. *See* Southeastern Europe
Seventeenth Amendment, U.S. Constitution,
  43–44
Sex Discrimination (Electoral Candidates) Act
  (U.K., 2002), 137
Shadow cabinet, House of Commons, U.K., 73
Shariʿa
  Indonesian law and, 258, 259
  Iranian judiciary and, 255
  as Islamic law derived from Qurʾan, 238–239
  participatory political processes in Morocco
    and, 249
Shariati, Ali, 250
Shaw v. Reno (U.S., 1993), 54
Shelley v. Kraemer (U.S.), 51–52
Shiʿa Muslims, 239–241, 250, 257. *See also* Iran
Shora-e Nejahban, Iran, 251, 252
Singapore, government of, 215
Single European Act (1986)
  co-decision powers and, 93
  European Council legal status and, 92
  postindustrial economies and, 100
  qualified majority voting and, 91
  trade barriers in Europe and, 89
  United Kingdom signing of, 95
Single-issue interest groups, U.S., 19
Single-member district systems, 125, 128–129,
  130, 131
Sinn Fein, 76, 119
Slavery, United States, 15
Slovakia, constitution of, 158
Slovenia
  constitution of, 156
  legislative-executive relations in, 160
  postcommunist political system, 148, 148*t*
Social capital, political culture and, 107
Social democracy. *See also* Democracy/
  democracies

in Europe, 104
Social Democratic and Labour Party, Northern Ireland, 119
Social Democratic Party
  Brazil, 289
  Germany, 83, 105, 121–122, 130
  United Kingdom, 118, 136
Social dynamics. *See also* Civil society
  Brazil, 287–288
  Europe, 107–109
  Mexico, 270–273
  modernization and changes in, 307–308
  United States, 14–17
Socialism. *See also* Communism
  developing countries, 313
  France, 120
  owner-worker cleavage and rise of, 103–104
Social partnerships, 110
Social Security, U.S., 14
Socioeconomic settings in Europe
  class politics, 104–105
  human capital and, 99–100
  major cleavages, 101–103
  Marxist communism, 103–104
  postmaterialism, 105
  social democracy, 104
Soft money, in U.S. election campaigns, 28
Solicitor general, U.S., Supreme Court and, 53
Solidarnosc (Poland), 154
South America. *See* Latin America
South Asia. *See also* Asia
  Khalifa movement of, 242
Southeast Asia. *See also* Asia
  Confucian values, 219–222
  countries comprising, 213–214
  Islamic states, 240
  political diversity, 214–218
  political systems
    Japan, 233–235
    People's Republic of China, 222–231
    Taiwan, 231–233
  PRC influence, 218–219
Southeastern Europe, 201–202. *See also* Europe
  economic architecture, 205–206
  leadership, 208–210
  political and social dynamics, 206–208
  political architecture, 204–205
  prognosis, 210
  value consensus, 202–203
Sovereignty. *See* Dual sovereignty;
    Parliamentary sovereignty; Popular sovereignty; State sovereignty
Soviet Union, 103. *See also* Communism
  breakup of, 2

economic and military successes, 104
Spain, colonial influences on Islamic states, 242
SPD. *See* Social Democratic Party
Speaker
  House of Commons, U.K., 72
  House of Lords, U.K., 75
  House of Representatives, U.S., 40
Staff, of U.S. Congress, 41–42
Stare decisis principle, 50, 74
State-church cleavage, 101–102
State governments, Mexico, 282–284
State sovereignty
  Central and Eastern European constitutions on, 158
  Europe and, 62, 63, 93–94
  European influences on Islamic states and, 243
  Iran, 251
  Islamic states, 239
  participatory political processes and, 237–238
  U.K. role in EU and, 142
  United States, 9
Status and class, United States, 16
Statutory law, definition of, 50
Stoiber, Edmund, 123
Strauss-Kahn, Dominique, 120
Strict constructionism, by U.S. judiciary, 54
Strict scrutiny standard, by U.S. Supreme Court, 54
Subgovernments, U.S., 20–21, 47
Suharto, 260
Sukarno, 258–259, 260
Sunni Muslims, 239–241, 257
Sun Yat-sen, 233
Supreme Court. *See also* Judiciary
  United Kingdom, 75
  United States
    criteria for case on appeal, 52
    criteria for litigants, 51–52
    enforcement criteria, 52–53
    judicial review and, 49
    jurisdiction, 51–52
Supreme leader, Iran, 253–255, 256
Supreme National Security Council, Iran, 253

Tafwih (delegation of Islamic political control), 240
Taiwan. *See also* China, Republic of
  Confucian values, 220
  government, 216
  military influence, 314
  political system, 231–233

Taiwan *(cont.)*
regional affiliations, 214
regionalism and, 295
Takings clause, U.S. private property and, 13
Taney, Roger B., 53
Tawhid, definition of, 238
Taxes/taxation
Central and Eastern European transitional
systems, 168–169
under communism, 189
progressive *versus* regressive, 47–48
Russia, 187, 188
traditional societies, 306
Ukraine, 197–198
Technological changes
cultural values and, 301
modernization and, 307
natural resources and, 319–320
Television. *See also* Media
Europe, 113–115
Ukrainian elections of 2004 and, 200
and value consensus in Central and Eastern
Europe, 152
Terkel, Studs, 15
Thailand, government of, 215
Thatcher, Margaret, 71, 117, 136, 140, 142
Third (political) parties, in U.S., 23, 30–31
Third world countries. *See also* Developing
countries; Traditional societies
modernization in, 296–297
population growth, natural resources of, and
political change in, 299
"Three-fifths compromise," for U.S.
Constitution, 9
Tilden, Samuel J., 31
Times Higher Education Supplement (2004),
153
Tito, Josip Broz, 298
Tocqueville, Alexis de, 238
Torture, in Morocco, 249
Totalitarian regimes, in East Asia, 215
Trade unions
Britain, 111–112
lobbying in Europe by, 110, 111
Mexico, 274–275
owner-worker cleavage and, 103
Traditional societies. *See also* Developing
countries; Third world countries
economies and government of, 305–306
Trajkovski, Boris, 209
Transparency
Central and Eastern European transitional
systems, 170
Southeastern Europe, 207

Treasury Department, U.S., 47
Treaty of Rome (1957), 88, 89, 91
Treaty of Westphalia (1648), 63, 90, 94
Trimble, David, 119
Tripartism, 110
Truman, Harry, 24, 34
Trustees
elected officials in Central and Eastern
Europe as, 171, 172
U.S. Representatives as, 43–44
Tudeh (Communist) Party, Iran, 252
Tudjman, Franjo, 172, 208, 209
Tunisia
European colonial rule in, 242
European government model and, 241–242
Turkey
creation of, 242
Europe and, 63
Morocco and, 244
Tyminski, Stan, 176

Ukraine
constitution of, 158
economic architecture, 197–198
European Union and, 181, 294
legislative-executive relations in, 160
political and social dynamics
elections, 199–200
leadership, 200–201
political architecture, 196–197
postcommunist political system, 148, 148*t*
prognosis, 201
timeline, 196
transitional politics in, 194–201
value consensus, 154, 195
Ulster Unionist Party, Northern Ireland, 119
Ultranationalism, in Russia, 185, 190
Ultra vires principle, 74
Unicity, in Islamic states, 238–239
Union for French Democracy, 129
Union of French Democrats, 120
Unions. *See* Trade unions
Union-state, United Kingdom as, 75
Unitary systems, 155
United Kingdom
bureaucracy, 71
as colonial power, 61
constitution, 67–77
devolution and local government, 75–77
electoral system, 126–128
European Economic Community and, 88
European monarchies and, 101
European Union and, 90, 95, 96, 142
German occupation by, 83

gradualist socialism, 104
immigrants and civil society in, 108–109
judiciary, 74–75
legislature, 71–74
as maritime power, 63, 65
media, 114
the monarchy, 69–70
pluralist interest groups, 110
policy processes, 137–138
political culture, 4, 106
political executive, 70–71
political parties and party system, 116–119
political recruitment, 132–133
postindustrial economy of, 100
proportional representation and, 127
recent elections, 126*t*
religious groups, 112
single-member district elections, 125,
126–127
trade unions, 111–112
United Kingdom Independence Party, 119
United Nations
European countries and, 65
leadership in Bosnia by, 210
United States. *See also* North American Free
Trade Agreement
Canadian free trade agreement with, 295
Congress, 39–45
Constitution, 8–13
elections, 26–32
European unity and Marshall Plan aid by, 87
federal bureaucracy, 45–49
German occupation by, 83
indebtedness of poor countries and, 303
interest groups, 17–21
invention and reinvention of, 55–56
judiciary, 49–55
Mexican-American War and, 264–265
political culture, 4
political parties, 21–25
population and economy of, 64*t*
the presidency, 32–38
as presidential government, 7–8
pressure on Morocco to reform, 246–247
social dynamics, 14–17
trade patterns, shifts in, 304
United States v. Nixon (1974), 52
United We Stand, America party, 23
Urban League, 19
Uruguay, military influence on modernization
of, 314
ʿUthman, *rashidun* caliph, 239

Value systems, 3–4

Confucian, in PRC, 219–222
institutionalization and, 311–312
postcommunist Russia, 182–185
Southeastern Europe, 202–203
transitional Central European political sys-
tems, 149, 152–154
Ukraine, 195
Western democracies, 4
Vargas, Getulio, 286, 289
Venezuela, modernization in, 314
Veritas (party), U.K., 119
Vichy government, France, 78
Vietnam, Socialist Republic of, 297
Virginia Plan, for U.S. Constitution, 9
Voter initiatives. *See* Referendums, voter
Voters
campaigning in U.S. and, 29–30
class system in U.S. and, 16
U.S. eligibility and rights for, 26
Voting. *See also* Districts, electoral
class-based, in U.K., 128
in European Union elections, 91, 131
for European working class, 104–105
in France, 129–130
in Germany, 131
Voting rates (turnout)
Central and Eastern European elections, 171
Europe, 107
United States, 22, 27
Voting Rights Act (U.S., 1965), 42
Voting Rights Act (U.S., 1982), 54

Wales
local government of, 75–76
political parties, 118, 127
relationship to United Kingdom, 68
separatist movements in, 101
state-church cleavage in, 102
Walesa, Lech, 172
War Crimes Tribunal, 209
War Powers Resolution (U.S., 1973), 34, 37–38
Warsaw Pact, 298
Washington, George, 33
Washington (George) administration, U.S., 25
Ways and Means Committee, of U.S. House, 41
Weber, Max, 45, 84
Weimar Republic, 82, 83, 130
Welfare and commerce clause, U.S. environ-
mental regulation and, 13
Welfare programs. *See also* Civil society
Europe, 104
United States, 15
Wen Jiabao, 228
Western values and influences, Europe and, 62

Westerwelle, Guido, 123
Westphalia, Treaty of, 63, 90, 94
Whig Party, U.S., 23, 24, 25
White House Office or Staff, U.S., 36
Wifaq political parties, Morocco, 247
Wilhelm I, King of Prussia, 82
Wilhelm II, Kaiser of Germany, 101
Wilson, Woodrow, 37, 39
Wolfowitz, Paul, 173, 207
Women, 26, 109, 136–137, 227
World Bank, 65, 152, 198, 314
World Economic Forum, 161–162, 163*t*, 164
World Trade Organization, 66
World War I, 103–104, 242
Writ of *amparo*, Mexico, 268

Yanukovych, Viktor, 200
Yazid, caliph in Damascus, 239
Yeltsin, Boris
  Duma election of 1993 and, 190

leadership efforts, 154
nationalism in Russia and, 185
public skepticism of economic architecture
  and, 187
Russian constitution and, 156–157,
  186
Yes, Minister (British TV series), 71
Yugoslavia. *See also* Bosnia; Southeastern
  Europe
dissolution of, 2, 62–63
nationalism and breakup of, 168
nonaligned nations and, 298
timeline, 204
U.S. view of dissolution of, 203
Yushenko, Victor, 196, 197, 198, 199–200,
  201

Zedillo, Ernesto, 267, 278, 281
Zhirinovsky, Vladimir, 185, 190